THE STRUGGLE FOR SOCIAL JUSTICE IN BRITISH COLUMBIA

Helena Gutteridge was a socialist and feminist whose vision helped to shape social reform legislation in British Columbia in the first decades of the twentieth century. She also became one of the first women to hold high public office there when she was elected to Vancouver City Council in 1937.

As was typical for women of her class and time, Helena did not keep personal records, nor did organizational records exist to any extent. Irene Howard made it her task, over a period of years, to search out and assemble details of Helena's life and career, and to interview old comrades who knew Helena and the turbulent times in which she lived. The result is a lively biography, shot through with humour and pathos, that pays homage to Helena Gutteridge and to many of the people who have been inspired by a cause and who have taught us about the politics of caring.

IRENE HOWARD writes about the social history of Vancouver and has contributed articles to many journals and collections, among them *Vancouver Past*. She is the author of a book about the early Swedish community in Vancouver and of the local bestseller, *Bowen Island, 1872-1972*.

IRENE HOWARD

The Struggle for Social
Justice in British Columbia
Helena Gutteridge,
the Unknown Reformer

UBC Press / Vancouver

ISBN 0-7748-0425-4

Canadian Cataloguing in Publication Data

Howard, Irene.
The struggle for social justice in British Columbia

Includes bibliographical references and index.
ISBN 0-7748-0425-4

1. Gutteridge, Helena, 1879-1960.   2. Feminists
– British Columbia – Biography.   3. Women socialists
– British Columbia – Biography.   4. Trade-unions
– British Columbia – Officials and employees – Biography.
5. Women in politics – British Columbia – Biography.
I. Title.

HQ1455.G88H69 1992   305.42'092   C92-091625-2

This book has been published with the help of a grant from the
Social Sciences Federation of Canada, using funds provided by
the Social Sciences and Humanities Research Council of Canada. This
book has also been financially assisted by the Boag Foundation Ltd.,
and by the Province of British Columbia through the
British Columbia Heritage Trust and the BC Lottery Fund.

UBC Press
University of British Columbia
6344 Memorial Rd
Vancouver, BC V6T 1Z2
(604) 822-3259
Fax: (604) 822-6083

To Stephen, Louise, Katherine, and Nicholas
and
in memory of Ed Nelson
who worked for a better world

Politics is the science which teaches the people of a country to care for each other.
  – William Lyon Mackenzie, 'To the People of Dundee and Aberdeen'

◆ ◆ ◆

If we act only for ourselves, to neglect the study of history is not prudent: if we are entrusted with the care of others, it is not just.
                                            – Dr. Samuel Johnson, *Rasselas*

◆ ◆ ◆

How do we seize the past? How do we seize the foreign past? We read, we learn, we ask, we remember, we are humble; and then a casual detail shifts everything.
                                            – Julian Barnes, *Flaubert's Parrot*

Contents

Illustrations

Abbreviations

AFL	American Federation of Labor
AMMC	Angus MacInnis Memorial Collection, UBCL
BCSC	British Columbia Security Commission
BC *Fed.*	*British Columbia Federationist*
BCARS	British Columbia Archives and Records Service
BCPEL	British Columbia Political Equality League
BCWSL	British Columbia Woman's Suffrage League
BP	Frank Buck Papers, UBCL
CAR	*Canadian Annual Review*
CCF	Co-operative Commonwealth Federation
CSA	Canadian Suffrage Association
CVA	City of Vancouver Archives
CVR	*Chelsea Vestry Reports*, Chelsea Library, London, England
CW	*The Commonwealth*
DHA	Dominion Housing Act
DLB	*Dictionary of Labour Biography*
DNA	Vancouver *Daily News-Advertiser*
FAD	Federal Archives Division, NAC
HCD	*House of Commons Debates*
IWW	International Workers of the World
LCM	Langley Centennial Museum
LCW	Local Council of Women
LSR	League for Social Reconstruction
LWIU	Lumber Workers' Industrial Unit
NAC	National Archives of Canada
NCWC	National Council of Women of Canada
NHA	National Housing Act
NIC	National Industrial Conference
NPA	Non-Partisan Association

NUWSS   National Union of Women's Suffrage Societies
OBU   One Big Union
PEL   Political Equality League
POLSD   *Post Office London Street Directory*
PPEL   Pioneer Political Equality League
PRO   Public Records Office, London, England
RMP   Richard McBride Papers, BCARS
SBC   *Statutes of British Columbia*
SC   *Statutes of Canada*
SFC   Suffragette Fellowship Collection, Museum of London
SPC   Socialist Party of Canada
TPC   Town Planning Commission
UBCL   University of British Columbia Library, Special Collections
Van. Dir. *Henderson's Greater Vancouver and New Westminster Directory*
VLCW   Vancouver Local Council of Women
VTLC   Vancouver Trades and Labor Council
WBP   William Bowser Papers, BCARS
WCTU   Woman's Christian Temperance Union
WEL   Women's Employment League
WFL   Women's Freedom League
WILPF   Women's International League for Peace and Freedom
WSPU   Women's Social and Political Union

Preface

On 16 November 1982, I made my first research journey to uncover the past of Helena Gutteridge. I knew she had spent ten years as a poultry farmer in the Fraser Valley. I knew the farm was near the village of Mount Lehman: in the Vancouver Public Library's Northwest Room I had found her married name in the British Columbia Directory for 1922. But of those years I knew nothing more. However, if I could obtain the legal description of her property, I could apply to the New Westminster Land Title Office to discover its precise location. And so on this very rainy day, I drove east on the Trans-Canada Highway to Clearbrook Town Centre, sixty kilometres from Vancouver.

The tax office was in Matsqui Municipal Hall, and there I spoke with Treasurer Bruce McIntyre. Old tax records? Yes, I was welcome to search them, but 1922? Not in this building. He found a bunch of keys and we went outside and across a large open space – where one knew cows must have grazed not too long ago – to a two-storey stucco-and-brick building, the old Municipal Hall. He opened a steel door and let me into a windowless, musty-smelling room filled with shelves of old record books, one of two storage rooms lined with reinforced concrete and called 'the vaults.' We looked for the 1922 Assessment and Collectors' Rolls; they were missing, but we found those for 1926 and 1930 in a pile on the floor. He pulled them out, heavy binders, two feet wide, and left me there in the vault behind the steel door to search the pages for Helena's name. I soon found it, recorded in the careful, deliberate handwriting of some municipal clerk in the days of pen-nibs and inkwells, and copied the legal description on a note card: 'Pt. of S.E. quarter (SW) Sec. 12, Tshp 14, Map 282, 3.07.' Helena owned 3.07 acres, assessed at $122.80. Taxes for 1926 were $2.46. She had been in arrears for 1925 but had discharged them with a payment of $5.15.

Mr. McIntyre also offered me the name of a local history buff, Douglas Taylor. I found a telephone booth and dialled his number. He was immediately interested and suggested that I visit his mother, who had known Helena. Within the hour I was having tea in her Mount Lehman living room and she was telling me that when she played the piano in a Mount Lehman dance band during the twenties, Helena played the mandolin. Afterwards, we drove the short distance to Burgess Road and stood for a few minutes in the rain, surveying the farmhouse now on the site of Helena's property and half expecting Helena herself to open the door, on her way to feed the chickens.

Thus began my research into the life of Helena Gutteridge, and so the research would continue – archivists and librarians producing directories, files of clippings, and boxes of private papers, though never any belonging to Helena; government officials and civil servants making records available; individuals sharing their memories, giving me leads to other informants. I engaged research agents in England who, with the slimmest of clues, discovered the names of Helena's brothers and sisters in General Registers and Parish Registers. I went to England twice and Scotland once. I explored the narrow, little London street where Helena was born, and found the very house number, though not the house, long since demolished. I visited her school: Headmaster Riley showed me around and served me tea and digestive biscuits in the staff room, where I sat beside a little boy who was recovering from a nosebleed and was in need of comfort. I spent days in the British Library Reading Room and would have liked to move my bed in there and stay forever in that peaceful, well-ordered place. I located one of Helena's nephews and a niece, and they received me kindly and told me about grandmother and grandfather Gutteridge, though they had no direct knowledge of Helena.

The discovery that brought me right into the family came about almost by accident. I guessed from what I knew of Helena's father, Charles Gutteridge, that he had worked for Vigers Brothers, Timber Merchants. I did not find this firm listed in the National Register of Archives catalogue, but I did find listed records of T. Vigers and Co., Funeral Directors, in the archives of Victoria Library, London. Thinking that timber merchants might very well also be makers of coffins, I took the Piccadilly and Circle lines to Victoria Station and found Victoria Library, where an archivist kindly selected some account books at random from the Vigers collection, then as yet uncatalogued. I began to search methodically through the chronologically disordered pages, but could find no immediate connection between the timber merchants and the funeral furnishers, though I soon learned that the price of a workhouse funeral was three pounds, including a coffin for nine shillings, whereas a funeral for a Countess cost twenty-two pounds. From correspondence with the

Bailiff of the Royal Parks Office in London, who had searched Brompton Cemetery Records for me, I knew that Helena's baby brother
Charles had been buried on 17 April 1886. I thought I might find some
record of the funeral in the Cash Book. I opened it at random and my
eye fell immediately on the name 'Gutteridge.' Beside it was an invoice
number and amount billed for 15 April – three pounds – and a cash
receipt number and amount paid for 19 April – three pounds. That was
all, but I felt immediately that I was in the presence of Sophia Gutteridge
and her husband Charles, the mother and father who had suffered the
death of their infant son.

   Yet none of my research brought me close to Helena herself. I found
no letters or diaries, nothing that revealed her innermost feelings. And
I thought about her mandolin. I could imagine Helena having fun; she
had arranged many, many whist-drive-and-dance parties in her younger
days. But I would never have thought of her strumming a mandolin, not
Alderman Gutteridge, preoccupied with feeding the hungry and finding shelter for the homeless. Moreover, any life history is so full of possibilities as to defy random speculation. The mandolin reminded me to
avoid uninformed guesses and to give due notice to the reader whenever I ventured to speculate on the basis of incomplete evidence. In the
absence of personal papers, I could not write a subjective life of Helena,
but I was satisfied that I could, nevertheless, write a biography faithful
to her spirit. Helena's whole life was political, and I have written a political biography. She would not, I am sure, have approved of any other
kind, for she was not a self-confessing person.

   A great many people have helped me in my task, not least the many
librarians and archivists who applied their expertise to my research problems. I wish to acknowledge with thanks the assistance of the staff of
Chelsea Library in London, England, whose research started me on my
discovery of Helena's Chelsea. At the National Archives of Canada, the
staff of the Federal Archives Division were consistently helpful whether
I applied for help by phone, by mail, or in person. At the University of
British Columbia Library, Anne Yandle and her staff in Special Collections were a steady support, as were the knowledgeable people at
Interlibrary Loans and Suzanne Cates and assistants in Government
Records and Microforms, where I spent so much time reading microfilm.
The librarians at the Vancouver Public Library helped me fill gaps in
many a paragraph by patiently answering queries on any and every sub-
ject. Sue Baptie and staff at the City of Vancouver Archives guided me
through Finding Aids to boxes of documents, as did the people at the
British Columbia Archives and Records Service. Kate Abbott of Pacific
Press Information Service also gave courteous assistance.

Interviews, letters of inquiry, and telephone conversations yielded much important material, without which I could scarcely have written this biography. I am grateful to the many people who responded so courteously to my requests for information and I acknowledge them individually in the bibliography. If I have missed some people, I wish them to know that I do indeed value their help and thank them for it. I wish especially to thank Thomas Charles Edward Gutteridge and Lilian Lambert Delchar for welcoming me into their homes and sharing their memories with me, and John Delchar for answering my letters on his mother's behalf.

Friends, relatives, and colleagues have also generously assisted in the research and writing, and I offer grateful thanks to the following: David Nelson for medical information; Elspeth Gardner for legal opinions and many hours of legal research; Roderick Barman for interpreting military data and for suggesting the main title; Diana Sonderhoff for suggesting the subtitle. David Hayley and Jeannette Leitch for insights into the history of forest management; Frederick N. Nelson for leading me through the forests of Marxist ideology; Constance Roberts Wilcox for research in the University of Toronto Thomas Fisher Rare Book Room; Jean Barman for spending a morning of a London holiday at Chelsea Library; Philip Thomas for spending a morning of his holiday at the General Register Office at St. Catherine's House; Gillian Weiss for allowing me access to her research material; Jill Wade for offering me her dissertation-in-progress to read; Stephen Howard for giving me my first computer instruction and generally relieving my computer angst; Linda Hale for archival assistance; Viva Flood for scanning the *Nelson Daily News*; Frank Flood for the use of his automobile on my research junket to Slocan; Emil Bjarnason for emergency computer back-up service; Viviane McClelland, Frances Zlotnick, and Anne Yandle for helping me prepare the final manuscript; Jean Mallinson for believing in me and in Helena, and for years of sympathetic listening and much astute and sensitive editorial advice; Barbara Beach for being companion and driver on my pilgrimage to Hampshire to discover the birthplace of Helena's father, and for staying with me to the end of the manuscript road; Esther Birney, another sustaining Muse, for nurture and nourishment.

Jean Barman, Gordon Elliott, and Keith Ralston read the manuscript at various stages and helped me find historical direction and organization; they also made editorial comments and asked perceptive questions. Others read the manuscript in part, bringing to it their special expertise and knowledge: Emil Bjarnason, Robert Macdonald, Jean Mallinson, Jill Wade, and Elizabeth Walker. I thank them all for their interest in my manuscript and for their valuable help. I wish also to thank the anonymous readers who put aside their unmarked student essays and their own research and writing to read my five hundred pages of manuscript and pass rigorous but kindly judgment on it.

Despite the help of so many people, I have doubtless made errors of fact and interpretation, and I take full responsibility for these.

A teacher of English does not become a freelance writer of biography and local history on her own, and I have been fortunate in my apprenticeship to have had the benefit of some of the best editorial and academic minds in the history business. Robert J. Macdonald, an exemplary scholar setting high standards for himself and others, has taught me much about writing history and has been a friendly, unseen presence looking over my shoulder, checking any wayward venture into pseudo-history. Jean Barman, generous with her time and with her extensive knowledge of British Columbia history, cheerfully urged me and the manuscript along and instructed me in the ways of editors and publishers. Gordon Elliott, respected dean of local historians, has been for twenty years my wise counsellor and editorial adviser in matters historical; by his interest in my work and his rigorous criticism he has made me a better writer. I wish to thank these three for standing by me so faithfully and guiding me in my historical writing.

I wish to thank the Canada Council and the Boag Foundation for their financial assistance and for the moral support and encouragement that such assistance lends to the writer.

I wish to thank the London House for Overseas Graduates for providing an ambience that made it possible to work productively in a strange city, only an underground journey on the Piccadilly and Circle lines from Sloane Square in Chelsea, where Helena Gutteridge was born.

'On staff' at different stages of the project and performing most competently were research assistants Linda Bain and Eilleen Steele, and computer consultant Dan Hunter, ever cheerful and helpful at the other end of the phone.

Finally, I acknowledge with thanks the professional advice and assistance of executive editor, Jean Wilson, and the capable services of the staff of UBC Press, who have worked their own changes on this protean manuscript and transformed it finally into a book about Helena Gutteridge.

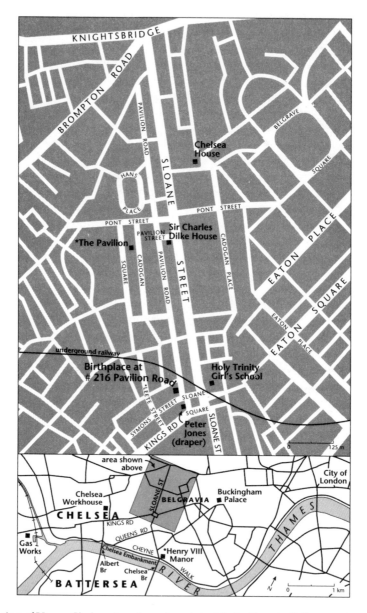

Section of Upper Chelsea, London, 1895. Asterisks indicate buildings not in existence at that time and Leete Street under development. (Base information from *Philip's New Plan of London*, George Philip and Son, London [1895]; thematic details from *Philip's* and from 'Map of Chelsea to accompany *Blunt's Historical Handbook*,' in Reginald Blunt, *An Illustrated Handbook to the Parish of Chelsea* [London: Lamley and Co. 1900])

CHAPTER ONE

The Chelsea Childhood of Nell Gutteridge

What's bred in the bone ...
– English proverb

24 March 1937. On that day Helena Rose Gutteridge became the first woman ever elected to Vancouver City Council. She won in a by-election, and listening to her speak during her campaign, the voters knew that she must have won many other audiences in other campaigns. Indeed she had, in England and Canada, on London street corners, in a Vancouver union hall, even, on one occasion, in the Senate Chamber in Ottawa. But not many understood that this plain, fifty-eight-year-old woman in her navy-blue round-brimmed hat was a standard bearer and that she had been carrying her banner for thirty years, marching for women's rights, for workers' rights. And now she was Alderman Gutteridge.

In 1911, when at the age of thirty-two she arrived in Vancouver from London, England, a militant suffragist, a tailor looking for work in her trade, women did not even have the vote, not in Britain or in Canada; much less did they qualify to become aldermen. By law women were forbidden to vote, forbidden to hold public office, except perhaps on school boards in certain localities. No woman had ever debated a government bill from the floor of a provincial legislature or gone to Ottawa to represent her fellow citizens as a Member of Parliament. In any case, 'nice' women did not engage in such activities. They stayed in the background, helpful to and supportive of the men who looked after the affairs of government. But Helena was never a nice woman: she was a feminist and a socialist. Fresh from the Hyde Park soap box and the inspired militancy of the Pankhursts, she plunged into the suffragist movement in British Columbia, taking it out of middle class parlours and into trade union halls and working class areas. She organized Vancouver's working women, educating them not only in their right to the franchise but also in their right to a living wage. At the same time, she reached out to middle class reform-minded women, lending them, if they only knew, certain trade union principles and tactics to better achieve their ends. Helena's life is the story of women and reform in British Columbia, crammed with political incident and dynamically linked with the stories of other women who dared to demand their rights as citizens and to assume the responsibilities of citizenship.

For fifty years Helena championed women's rights and the cause of labour. When she died in 1960, woman suffrage had been long established. The minimum wage was a fact of everyday life, as were workers' compensation, union recognition, and collective bargaining – all urged on governments over the years by a new socialist party, the Co-operative Commonwealth Federation, later the New Democratic Party. Even the concept of social housing had taken root and Vancouver's first low-rental housing units had been built. Helena Gutteridge had been a vital part of it all, her life's work our legacy. We are her inheritors.

Helena's father was Charles Henry Gutteridge, a blacksmith by trade. Born in 1854 in the Hampshire village of Micheldever, he might have taken his place at his father's forge, but he was a restless young man and according to his granddaughter, Lilian Lambert Delchar, ran away twice to join the army, his father buying him out both times. As a child Lilian often visited her grandparents when they lived in Peckham on London's South Bank, and she remembered both of them vividly.[1] Eventually he left Micheldever for good and looked for work in London, part of a widespread migration of country folk to the city. He was a big man, nearly six feet tall and very broad. In 1876 he married a labourer's daughter, Sophia Richardson. They settled briefly in the Wandsworth area of Battersea, at 23 Aegis Grove, on the same street as the local blacksmith, an indication that Charles found work in his trade. Here in 1877 their first child, Emily, was born. On the marriage certificate and on Emily's birth certificate Charles gave his occupation as blacksmith.[2]

Sophia, Helena's mother, was born in Marylebone in 1858, in the Regent Park area of northwest London, the daughter of James Richardson, 'ground labourer,' and widow Matilda Coward, née Landsell. As Matilda had signed the birth certificate with her mark, so did Sophia, 'spinster,' eighteen years old, sign her marriage certificate. She did not give her occupation but may very well have been in domestic service for three or four years before her marriage. She was tall and had the rather broad face and high forehead that found their likeness in both her older daughters. Over a twenty-five-year period she bore Charles seven children.

The Gutteridge family did not remain long in Battersea, for Charles found work as a labourer across the river in Chelsea. Massive development was going on there as the decaying old mansions of Upper

Chelsea fell to the onslaught of the wreckers and excavation and construction of all kinds transformed the landscape. An underground station at Sloane Square had just been opened to serve the new commuter population living in suburban Chelsea and working in the city. The main landowner and developer was the Fifth Earl of Cadogan, who had just rebuilt the family mansion at Cadogan Place, near Sloane Square. His development schemes created much new employment, but they also dislocated the lives of thousands of workers and their families in Chelsea, among them the Gutteridge family.

In 1879 one of those venerable old mansions, the Pavilion, was being torn down to make way for Cadogan Square, which would fill in all the grounds of the Pavilion from Pont Street to Cadogan Terrace with substantial red brick houses, with individual stables behind each. The dwellings would be arranged about a rectangle of grass, trees, and shrubs to form the customary residential square. Around this time Charles and Sophia rented either house or lodgings at 216 Pavilion Road, a short distance from the site of the demolition, and on 8 April 1879 Sophia gave birth to their second child, Helen Rose. They called her Nell.[3]

Pavilion Road is just next to Sloane Street, nowadays providing a back lane for fashionable boutiques and professional offices and for gentrified coach houses, neatly painted but giving no outward sign of the lives of the inhabitants, with garages, equally discreet, equally well-painted, replacing the stables of an earlier era. Today a car dealership occupies most of the block where the Gutteridges used to live, and 216 is a ground-floor flat, its white-painted door opening directly on Pavilion Road. Above 216 are other flats, among whose tenants is a woman whose psychic powers make her prescient of the arrival of visitors, including researchers tracing the lives of tenants long dead. On the same side of Pavilion Road and just across the street is the Holy Trinity Church of England Infants' School, in the preceding century only for the children of ordinary folk like the Gutteridges. At the other end of their block and opposite Sloane Square is Peter Jones Department Store, built in the 1880s but very modern and fronting on King's Road, the heart of Upper Chelsea.

Redevelopment of this part of Chelsea began soon after the Second World War. In the 1960s penniless artists who had found cheap quarters in decaying old houses had to move out to make way for developers. Meanwhile, one 'tatty unfurnished upstairs flat' in a 'small mews house on Pavilion Road' received new tenants when Peter Wright and other M.I.5 spycatchers set up headquarters for investigating a senior agent suspected of being a mole.[4] Little old shops of earlier decades were demolished and replaced with coffee houses vibrating to the beat of rock-

and-roll and boutiques like Mary Quant's Bazaar, which introduced the world to the mini-skirt.[5] By the 1980s, the Chelsea set had been replaced in turn by nihilistic 'punk' kids sporting, with insouciant defiance, purple or orange hair and tattoos and nose-rings, to the amazement of tourists. Directly east of Pavilion Road, east of Sloane Street and within a few minutes' walk, Belgravia is still Belgravia and Eaton Place is still a very good address, even without butlers and footmen. Now, however, the posh residential terraces must share their neighbourhood with foreign embassies and the Belgravia Sheraton. The Cadogan estate office is near the corner of Pont Street and Sloane.

The Cadogan estate had already gone through an earlier development in the last decades of the eighteenth century when architect Henry Holland leased eighty-nine acres on the east side of Chelsea from Charles, Second Baron of Cadogan, and created a residential suburb called Hans Town for members of the aristocracy and well-to-do businessmen or professionals who could afford to own a home in secluded Chelsea, then still largely a rural area, a pleasant little village on the Thames surrounded by green fields and market gardens. Holland's own grand mansion, Sloane Place, built largely of timber with Ionic columns sanded to look like stone, dominated the whole area west of present-day Sloane Street, also part of his grand design, though still on the drawing board. He laid out other streets too, among them New Road, later Pavilion Road, providing access to Sloane Place. Built in 1780, it came to be called the Pavilion because Holland was said to have built its south colonnade as a model, though never used as such, for the Brighton Pavilion. The gardens of Holland's Pavilion, created by his father-in-law, the famous Capability Brown, extended south all the way to King's Road. They comprised some twenty acres designed to emulate Nature, with manufactured lake and deer park and obligatory 'Gothic' ruin – a turreted priory camouflaging an ice house – all set in a picturesque landscape of lawns and trees and ornamental shrubbery.[6]

By 1870, a hundred years later, all this had fallen into decay and New Road, renamed Pavilion Road though no longer recognizable as a public thoroughfare, was a back lane, a series of mews with stables and coach houses and dung-pits where tradespeople made deliveries and servants washed their masters' carriages.[7] By the time Nell was born in 1879, the neighbourhood was beginning to be renewed, but for the next two decades it would be in a state of radical transformation. Of Pavilion Road, a contemporary researcher and social historian, Charles Booth, reported thus: 'Most of these people are of a decent, comfortable class. The poorer houses are being demolished and mansions erected on the site. A good many coachmen and servants reside here, and a fair number of lodging-house keepers.'[8]

The house at 216 Pavilion Road was indeed demolished, not by private developers but by the Metropolitan Board of Works for Chelsea Fire Station. Thereupon the Gutteridges moved to nearby 4 Pavilion Place, where lived four other labourers, a saddler, a grocer, a charwoman, a laundress, a general servant, and a builder. Charles Gutteridge in the meantime obtained employment as a porter carrying lumber for a timber merchant. Lilian Delchar recalled that her grandfather worked for Vigers, presumably Vigers Brothers, Timber Merchants located on Pavilion Road, but could not say just when he started with them. In any case, the firm was listed in 1885 at an unnumbered property between 216 and 220 Pavilion Road. The Gutteridge family lived in Chelsea for some twenty years, moving to a different street every two or three years, always one step ahead of the developers.[9]

The redevelopment of Chelsea in these decades created a serious shortage of housing. The question of the expropriation of houses on the Cadogan estate came up in the House of Commons in 1886 when one of the members expressed great concern that ten thousand working class families would be evicted 'in order to erect upon their site blocks of palatial residences.' The Secretary of State for the Home Department objected: the new residences were not palatial and only fourteen hundred houses would be affected. He assured the House that Lord Cadogan fully accepted his social responsibilities in this regard: 'Lord Cadogan has insisted on industrial dwellings being provided sufficient to accommodate eight hundred persons' and also agreed 'to do more than any Standing Order would require.' The ratepayers of Chelsea held a public meeting on Chelsea Common, passed resolutions opposing Lord Cadogan's development schemes, and sent a delegation to present them to the Vestry, at that time the local governing body. But the Vestry had already given its support to Lord Cadogan.[10]

By the time Nell was four years old, her father was a 'foreman of works,' as he described himself in 1883 on the birth certificate of his first son, Thomas Henry. As a builder's foreman, Charles Gutteridge was employed in the reconstruction of the demolished areas. Like thousands of workers he was continually moving his family to escape the wreckers, but at least he always managed to find decent quarters, judging by the descriptions of neighbourhoods in the Charles Booth survey. Moving house was just as stressful then as now, especially for a pregnant woman with small children, and during these moves Sophia was either pregnant or had an infant to nurse and diapers to wash while she was packing the family crockery.

Fortunately for her, the family was well established at 4 Pavilion Place when Thomas was born in November 1883. Then that property was needed for an electric power station, electric lighting just then becoming established in Chelsea. Between 1883 and 1886 the Gutteridges moved back to Pavilion Road, farther north this time to number 4, where, according to Charles Booth, the householders in one part were quite well-to-do; the other part was 'thickly populated by artisans and labourers.' It was a hard time for the Gutteridges, especially for Sophia. She gave birth to baby Charles in February 1886 at 4 Pavilion Road, and only a few weeks later had to cope once again with moving. They found a place further south at 214, presumably in the same building as Holy Trinity Upper Chelsea Parish Hall and still very close to Vigers Brothers.[11]

Of course, nine-year-old Emily and seven-year-old Nell could now help with household chores and mind little Thomas. Such small mercies were to no avail, however, against the scourge of illness. On 14 April the infant Charles, just two months old, died – 'pertussis apnoea,' says the death certificate, or whooping cough. Within the next two years the family moved again, this time to Leete Street; the fifth child, William James, arrived around this time, in March 1888. Just east of Pavilion Road, this was a street of shopkeepers – tailor, bootmaker, and greengrocer; fishmonger, pawnbroker, and dairyman. The Gutteridges lived above the hairdresser's shop at number 11, but it was already time for them to move on. According to the *Chelsea Vestry Report* of 1886-87, the Earl of Cadogan's plans for making Leete Street part of Cadogan Gardens had been approved and demolition had already begun that past autumn, around Michaelmas. About another stage of the Cadogan development on nearby Lower Sloane Street a contemporary magazine, *The Builder*, commented: 'So great a change has been made here that no one who visited the district four or five years ago would know it. Narrow streets of squalid houses have given place to wide avenues of mansions.'[12]

Because of the transforming of Leete Street, the Gutteridges had to move yet again. Their next recorded address is a few blocks east of Chelsea in Pimlico, where, on Graham Street in 1895, Sophia gave birth to her sixth child, Daisy. By this time Charles was no longer a builder's foreman for Vigers. On Daisy's birth certificate he gave his occupation as 'timber merchant's porter.' Probably Vigers had kept him in their employ. Emily at eighteen years and Nell at sixteen had left home to earn their own keep, making room for the younger children.

Eventually the Gutteridges moved back to Chelsea, but this time to the southern part, on the waterfront near Chelsea Creek, the West London Railway nearby and the Imperial Gas Works on the other side of the tracks. Vigers Brothers moved to Tetcott Road and Charles found living quarters there too. Here, at 35A Tetcott Road in 1901, Sophia's last child, Lily Sophia, was born. Of this area Charles Booth recorded that the western half was newly built, partly on the site of the Cremorne Pleasure Gardens, and that eight-roomed houses were occupied by 'decent mechanics, police, shop assistants, clerks and labourers.' Now foreman at Vigers Brothers' Timber Yard, Charles with Sophia were among the 'decent' tenants of Tetcott Road, with Hetzler the confectioner and Mrs. Esther Podger, laundress, for neighbours.[13]

Moving house was among Nell's formative childhood experiences, the recurring theme in her family history a sense of impermanence and dislocation. But there is another strand in Gutteridge family history woven from the sustaining traditions of country life. The Gutteridges were blacksmiths, originating in Oxford County, in the parish of Caversham. Charles's father, George, son of John Gutheridge, blacksmith, went to live in Micheldever as a young man and worked at the forge. In 1854 he married Martha Bye, dressmaker, daughter of John Bye, carpenter. She died when Charles Henry, their only son, was just four years old.[14]

The census returns reveal the continuing family history. By 1861 George Gutheridge is himself the village blacksmith, with eighteen-year-old John Gutheridge (his brother?) as the forge helper. George has remarried and Charles Henry has a mother again. Louisa is her name, a young woman from the village.

In the 1871 census returns, neither Charles Henry, then seventeen, nor young John are listed as members of George and Louisa's household or as living in Micheldever. Nor does it appear that Louisa bore George any children, at least not any who lived. She is busy enough just the same, because their helper at the forge, one Thomas Goodfew, is also their lodger. Moreover, George and Louisa have opened a beer shop in their cottage. They call it the Half-Moon. A twelve-year-old niece from Southampton lives with them, providing another pair of hands for Louisa. In the census returns for 1851 to 1871, the name is still Gutheridge. And thus the birth of Charles Gutteridge was registered in 1854, though the Hampshire directory for 1878 lists the beer shop proprietor and blacksmith as 'Gutteridge.'

The village of Micheldever is eleven kilometres northeast of Winchester, near the south coast of England. At Sutton Scotney on the A34, a narrow asphalt road winds eastward a kilometre or two between high, grassy banks that gradually open to a view of broad green fields with little copses of oak and elm and lines of trees in windbreaks. The River Dever follows along, a pleasant, shallow stream completing the pastoral scene. The village consists of church, school, grocery store, butchershop, pub, and, of course, the blacksmith shop or forge. The houses are timber and thatch. The Church of St. Mary the Virgin is an accretion of structures from earlier centuries, the oldest dating from 1380.[15]

For Micheldever is old, and Nell's father grew up in a village embracing centuries of tradition. Financier Sir Francis Baring bought the

Micheldever estate in 1801 from the Eighth Duke of Bedford. At that time, the village smith 'had a large cottage, timber and thatch, hovel and pigsty, with a good blacksmith's shop in good repair.' Mary Neal also had a blacksmith's shop of timber and tile. Before Sir Francis and the Duke of Bedford, the line of possession of Micheldever land goes back to those ardent royalists, the Wriothesleys, among whom was Rachel, Lady Russell, a woman of great spirit who refused to be dispossessed of land and privilege after the execution of her husband for conspiring against Charles II. It goes back to the time of Henry VIII and the dissolution of the monasteries, when an earlier Wriothesley purchased Hyde Abbey and its lands, and when, at the surrender of the Abbey, 'a cottage called the Forge was occupied by Thomas Wickham and Peter Leffe.' It goes back to the Domesday Book, when the estate was called Miceldeuvre, property of St. Peter's Abbey at Winchester. Even before William the Conqueror, Miceldeuvre was King Alfred's own property, and before him the Romans were in possession and had built a road from Winchester and a villa in Micheldever Wood. The very hedgerows are old, inviting archaeologists to make botanical studies to calculate their age in hundreds of years. The Gutteridge family at the Micheldever forge was carrying on in the ancient traditions of an English village where people still spoke of the principal landowner as Lord of the Manor and remembered when the feudal common was enclosed in 1842.[16]

Blacksmiths have lived in the forge cottage next to the shop ever since 1569, according to Micheldever blacksmith Harry Symes, now retired, who still lives there with his wife. With its thatched roof and the familiar dark brown supporting timbers on the white outside walls, it looks just as the English village cottage should. Inside, the axe marks on the hand-hewn oak beams are clearly visible and the doorways are inconveniently low. A tour of the cottage further reveals a sliding window that used to open onto the public room, now the family living room, and that was, in George Gutteridge's time, the Half-Moon pass-through for serving beer. The blacksmith shop, with its arched rafters fashioned from ships' beams, is even older and still has its three forges, each with a big round iron-pot bellows. Here Nell's father learned his trade, pumping the long wooden handle of the bellows with one hand, with the other, hammering out the horseshoe.[17]

But Charles turned his back on Micheldever and went to try his luck in London. Micheldever was, conveniently, a station on the through line from Southampton to Nine Elms in London's Battersea district, where he started married life as a blacksmith. In his later years he returned to Hampshire to live in the town of Petersfield, not far from his boyhood home.

Helena never spoke of her father and mother, at least not to friends of her later life. She said only that when she left home she never saw them again and completely lost touch with her family. Fortunately, besides niece Lilian Delchar, nephew Thomas Edward Charles Gutteridge also vividly remembers Charles and Sophia Gutteridge, their grandfather and grandmother, and both recall Gutteridge family life as they knew it.[18]

Grey-haired and bespectacled, with a broad forehead, Thomas Gutteridge bears a striking resemblance to his Aunt Helena. In his comfortable little Kensington apartment, surrounded by photographs of his grandchildren and his collection of country and western records, he recalls the pleasures of his country boyhood. His mother had died when he was quite young, and when his father remarried, little Thomas was sent to live with his grandparents and their young daughter Lily in their big red brick house in Petersfield, where Charles Gutteridge was employed as a night-watchman.

Thomas Gutteridge knew London too, for he was born just west of Chelsea in industrialized Fulham, and one of his first memories is the smell of chocolate and coffee from the Cadbury plant. He left school to join the merchant navy and, like his father and grandfather, had been a wage worker all his life – ship's stoker, buyer of materials for a court dressmaker, tar paver, night-watchman, electro-plater, hot-tin-dipper. He had several times suffered grievous injury on the job, and during hard times had scrambled for work, always managing somehow to feed and house his family.

Then country memories rush in as he remembers the big garden at the back of the red brick house in Petersfield and the strange animal that lived there: 'It was a pig, a black and white spotted pig, and when I first saw it I can remember as clear as anything that I ran, because I didn't know what it was, and it was grunting, you know.' For the city boy life in the country with his grandparents was secure and happy. It was ample and free, the Hampshire downs beautiful. Great stores of food filled the red-tiled larder: home-cured bacon and hams hanging from the ceiling, and big earthenware jars of lard and salt pork in brine; a huge black pot of nuts from the hedgerows and barrels of apples from their own trees. He went birds' nesting in the hills and 'scrumping' for apples in farmers' orchards. Then home to a supper of grandmother's good rabbit pie.

In the grandson's nostalgia can be read the grandfather's own desire to escape the harsh city and recapture the more benevolent and more wholesome conditions of his Micheldever boyhood, however far from reality his memories might be. Helena would attempt her own idyllic version of Micheldever when, like her father, she retired in mid-life to the Fraser Valley and became a poultry farmer. Stories about Micheldever figured in family legend. And Micheldever was, after all, no more than an hour's journey from London on the Southampton train.

The grandson remembers Charles Gutteridge as a man getting on in years: 'He had a full set of beard and moustache, white, and his hair was white and his eyes were blue. Yes, yes, a very big man.' He used to play football and hide-and-seek with his grandson. Helena's niece, Lilian Delchar, thought he looked like King Edward. To her young eyes he was 'smashing,' which meant he always behaved like a gentleman. 'He wouldn't have any nonsense. Everything had got to be all just right. He wouldn't hear us quarrel ... he used to stop us.' She liked his speech too, which retained its broad, Hampshire accent. According to her mother, Emily Lambert, he went to the same school as the young son of Lord Northcott, Lord of the Manor; that is, the village school. A photograph taken at Petersfield shows a tall, clean-shaven old man in a peaked cap and black cravat, wide-lapelled dark jacket hanging loosely from shoulders that are still broad. Little Thomas is standing in front of him. The occasion could be the day Thomas started going to school, for he is wearing the schoolboy's regulation short pants, sharply creased, with knee socks, woolen waistcoat and jacket. His hair is carefully parted and neatly combed. The grandfather's hands hold the boy's shoulders protectively, big workman's hands. 'He was a grand man,' mused Thomas Gutteridge. Evidently both Thomas and Lilian remembered their grandfather as he must have appeared in photographs taken during his younger days, imposing in beard and moustache and looking like King Edward, not like an aging night-watchman.

In a late photograph, Sophia Gutteridge looks out at the world with serious, steady eyes which, like Helena's in younger days, seem to be full of sad knowledge. There is also quite a resemblance between mother and daughter as they appeared in later years, especially in the facial expression. Lilian Delchar remembers her grandmother as being quite stout and 'haughty' in manner: 'Very ladylike, shall I say that?' Thomas remembers that his grandmother used to read the Bible to him. However, as a young woman, she did not know how to write: she made her mark on the birth certificates for both Emily and Helen Rose. Yet at some time in her life she must have learned, because Lily's birth certificate bears her signature. 'She used to cook lots of lovely things,' he further recalls, thinking of the pickles and preserves that filled the larder. Sophia belonged to the Church of England, although she did not often go to church. She heard her grandson's prayers at bedtime, sitting on the edge of the bed while he went through his 'God bless,' finishing with 'Our Father.' She nursed him when he was ill and he remembers particularly her loving care when he had scarlet fever.

But Grandmother Gutteridge could be very strict, demanding that Thomas be unflinching under trial and summon up courage he did not know he had to cast out fear. He remembers that he used to be afraid of thunderstorms. Once when thunder was crashing around the house and garden and lightning flashing in the window, she put a chair in front of the window and sat there. 'And she got ahold of me and pulled me around, and said, "Now, watch it." And when it was finished she said, "There, see? That didn't hurt, did it?" And from that time onwards I was never afraid of thunderstorms.' As a housekeeper she was almost obsessively clean. Lilian Delchar recalls that when her grandmother used the little black coal shovel, she always gave it a bit of a polish before she put it away again.

Charles had that same streak of rigorous self-discipline. Thomas remembers that his grandfather 'was very fanatical as regards cleanliness, inwardly and outwardly. He used to have epsom salts every morning, regular as clockwork. He used to make up a big bottle of it.' He bathed frequently, kept beard and moustache trimmed, waistcoat and trousers brushed, boots cleaned and shined. He was orderly in his habits too. 'Everything had to be put in its place. Grandmother was the same. If you used something, you had to put it back exactly where you found it.' Helena had the same kind of self-discipline, the same instinct for neatness and order. Her 1940s friend and landlady, Hilda Kristiansen, recalls that in Helena's little housekeeping room nothing was ever out of place. Dishes never piled up. Helena would use a plate and cup, then wash them and put them back in their place.

Although Thomas Gutteridge and Lilian Delchar remember the Gutteridges as they were in later years, none of their memories suggest that the grandparents were ever anything but sober, industrious people. Charles Gutteridge was not a drinker: sometimes he sent his grandson to the off-licence for a jug of beer but 'he'd never go out drinking.' Sophia thriftily made pickles and preserves and jam from the raspberries, gooseberries, and currants in the garden. Her grandson particularly savours in memory the lovely brawn she made, thick with meat and jelly, from cheap cuttings of bullock at the butcher shop.

Not all the Gutteridges were as sober and austerely self-disciplined as Charles and Sophia. Thomas recalls one relative, a bargee who helped with the loading and unloading of barges on the Thames. She was a little woman with a fair complexion and strikingly dark hair, and 'she wore a black straw boater, I can see that.' She sometimes became quite drunk, and would be picked up by the police and, according to practice, hoisted onto one of their push barrows and trundled to the police station, where she was fined for being drunk and disorderly.

Although the peaceful, gentle life of the country with its settled ways is a sustaining family memory, the Gutteridges belong more with the coal wharves and barges of the Thames embankment, and even with the bargee, than with the age-old smith at his Micheldever forge or the pig at the end of that nostalgic Petersfield garden. For the Charles Gutteridge family were Londoners, shaped by the hardships of Victorian working class life, their history ephemeral, transitory. They were attuned to the rude energy of the city: to the street sounds of the muffin man ringing his bell, the milkman crying 'Milko' and the dustman clattering by with his cart, collecting 'dust,' as garbage was called; to the jostling crowds on the horse-drawn buses and the London underground. Moreover, they endured its discomforts. Nell grew up breathing London air filled with sulphurous smoke from coal fires, the stench from fish shops and from animal and human waste on the streets, and nauseating fumes from gas lights in poorly ventilated rooms. Dense, smoke-laden fogs rolled up from the river. Chelsea, her Chelsea, was bred in the bone – its streets and houses in their changing landscape, its people in all their daily commerce and manifold connections – and would never leave her, even accompanying her along a political path that eventually brought her to Canada.

Half a mile away from Pavilion Road was the Chelsea workhouse, where the Chelsea Guardians of the Poor doled out to paupers a meagre subsistence in return for untwisting old rope and picking out the hemp fibres to make oakum for caulking the seams of ships. Orphans looked to the Guardians of the Poor to choose their destiny for them – general servant, usually; sometimes emigration. ('That Ellen Hickey, an orphan child, being chargeable to the parish of Chelsea, and having consented to emigrate to Canada, the necessary steps be immediately taken to effect the emigration.') Poverty was still considered immoral, the unfortunate result of weakness of character. Social investigators like Beatrice and Sidney Webb and Charles Booth, however, were putting forward the idea that poverty was related to the economic workings of society and that the poor were not a separate breed of humanity. They also proposed another new notion – that if the health of the poor was attended to, their poverty would be diminished.[19]

Little is known of the daily lives of the Gutteridges, because 'the short and simple annals of the poor' yield scant information. Since the poor do not own property, their names do not appear in the rate books. Accumulating no wealth, they leave no wills describing their estates. That they were born, married, had children and died – this much is recorded.

But of that other Chelsea of the rich and powerful, or of the talented and famous, a freight of documents testifies to its lives and times. We know that Sir Thomas More built a 'commodious house' on the Thames; Erasmus has told us so. And that King Henry VIII used to sail up to Chelsea in the royal barge to visit in happier days before Sir Thomas was constrained to put God before King. On Cheyne Walk by the river the tourist guide will point to where Henry's Manor House used to stand and, nearby, the house where Thomas Carlyle, cossetted by his wife, Jane, wrote *The French Revolution*. Gossipy anecdote about the personal lives of the writers and artists who used to live along the Chelsea waterfront exists in abundance. That the poet Rossetti's white peacock found shelter under the sofa and died there; that Whistler's mother was the reason the painter's mistress moved out; that Oscar Wilde's dining room was done in shades of white and that Wilde was arrested on a charge of sodomy at the Cadogan Hotel on Sloane Street – all this gratifying detail is a matter of record.[20] But of the daily lives of working people we know very little, unless they were brought drunk and disorderly before a magistrate, or were robbed, or themselves stole their master's spoons, in which case an account would appear in some local newspaper. Of what they thought and felt we know even less: their whole energy went into maintaining physical subsistence. Working folk do not often write diaries and journals.

For all that, they are always a part of the life of their times, and the Gutteridges were a part of theirs. Thus Nell was fostered by Victorian values, Victorian currents of thought and feeling – religious earnestness and loss of faith, entrenched class feeling, new ideas in medical science, an evolving social order. Victorian social history, especially in certain aspects, is Gutteridge family history. Questions of overcrowding, the prevalence of disease, and lack of sanitation come right home to Pavilion Road and Leete Street.

In the spring of 1879, when Nell was born, sixty-four cases of smallpox had already been recorded in Chelsea between February and April, and during the year three occurred on Pavilion Road. An epidemic had raged for several years throughout England, and now, reviewing numbers for the preceding years, the Medical Officer of Health for Chelsea concluded that the epidemic was over. Child mortality in general was high: under five years, it actually reached 70.4 deaths per thousand in Chelsea in 1885, compared to the national rate of 65.7. Diarrhea killed 50 to 100 children a year, most of them under the age of five. Measles, scarlet fever, and whooping cough were other killers, summarily snuffing out small lives. In 1885 in Chelsea, 69 children under five died from whooping cough alone. One little slum schoolchild confided that he was saving his pennies 'to buy a coffin when I die.' 'Grandmother, Grandmother/Tell me the Truth/How many years am I/Going to live?' sang the children, and even as they sang and counted 'one, two, three, four ...,' knew they could be marked for death.[21]

The Gutteridges knew something about whooping cough, for little Charles, Sophia's fourth child, died from it at the age of two months on 14 April 1886. The account books for T. Vigers and Co., Funeral Directors (connection with Vigers Brothers on Pavilion Road unknown), show that the next day Charles Gutteridge paid three pounds for funeral expenses, which, though not itemized for baby Charles, usually included a carriage and pair and a coachman. A three-foot elm coffin cost nine shillings. On 17 April the family walked behind the funeral carriage to Brompton Cemetery, where the infant was buried in a common grave. The Gutteridges could not afford a plot of their own, but Baby Charles would have a proper funeral just the same. Nell had just passed her seventh birthday.[22]

The Gutteridge family also knew about tuberculosis. Lily, Nell's youngest sister, had tubercular meningitis, then a common disease among children – and usually fatal. Lily, however, recovered, only to die later from the disease, though indirectly. During the war, Charles and Sophia moved from Petersfield back to London and lived in a rented flat on the south bank in Peckham, where Charles had a job as night-watchman. Lily boldly took a wartime job as a telegraph messenger. One day on her rounds in the Denmark Hill area, she was assaulted, and in the struggle with her assailant must have suffered some injury to the brain for she died a few days later, from the shock, the family said. The death certificate, however, records tubercular meningitis as the cause, suggesting that the physical trauma had injured the protective scar tissue of the healed tubercular lesions, resulting in slow bleeding between the outer coverings of the brain, and ultimately in death. In three days she would have been fifteen years old.[23]

There was in England by the last half of the nineteenth century a rudimentary understanding of bacterial contagion, although the theory had not been universally accepted. Disinfectants, however, were in general use. If Helena had been asked in later years what smells she associated with her childhood, she would certainly have replied, 'carbolic acid.' Bottles of the disinfectant were free and liberally distributed at the Vestry Halls, where children were sent to ask for them. The smell of burning sulphur was also associated with her childhood: the fumes of sulphur dioxide were mistakenly believed to be a powerful disinfectant. The fumigation of all houses infected with contagious disease was thorough and rigorous, and the sanitary officer who carried it out was a familiar figure on Chelsea streets. Dr. Andrew Whyte Barclay, Medical Officer of Health for Chelsea, described how, after the patient was removed to the Small Pox Hospital, all bedding and clothing and even the bed were sent to the disinfecting stove. Then 'the room was closed, and a pan of burning sulphur placed on the floor, and after 24 hours exposure to the sulphurous gas, the paper was stripped, the paint washed, the ceiling and walls distempered, the staircase cleansed.'[24]

The Inspector of Nuisances was another familiar household visitor, one whom the Gutteridges in their many lodgings would have come to expect. Appointed by the Medical Officers of Health, the inspectors went door to door investigating complaints and reporting 'nuisances': overcrowding, nasty drains and privies, uncovered filthy water cisterns, toilets without water supply, dwellings in disrepair. Chelsea was fortunate in having the services of Dr. Barclay because he was an acknowledged expert on sanitary management and tentatively accepted the germ theory. 'Can it be,' he pondered, 'that specific fevers of the human race have each their own bacillus? ... May we hope in each of them [specific fevers] some day to inoculate a mild form of the disease which will preserve the individual from a more severe attack?'[25] He was assiduous in carrying out the health regulations of the Local Government Act of 1855. There were still backyard piggeries in Chelsea; he had them closed down. There were toilets without water supply; his inspectors went systematically from house to house to discover them and give orders to have water closets installed. At one house, the inspector called seventy-eight times. Dr. Barclay himself called twenty-four times, and gave evidence at police court three times.[26]

In the mandatory registration of lodging houses he was equally diligent, his inspectors going house to house, measuring the rooms to see if they were of the legally required three hundred cubic feet per person and entering the particulars in a register. Dr. Barclay then personally calculated the number of persons allowed in each room. Kitchens and sculleries were banned as sleeping rooms, and more than two adults of different sexes were forbidden to occupy the same bedroom. He found certain properties, among them some owned by the Earl of Cadogan, so dilapidated, so 'filthy,' dank, and ill-ventilated that he urged their demolition. Some members of the Vestry Board did indeed want the Earl of Cadogan to be notified, through his solicitors, that under the Artisans' and Labourers' Dwelling Act he must demolish his Charles Place properties. In the end they were voted down and the matter was shelved.[27] The Act was difficult to enforce because it made no provision for new housing; moreover, the owners were not compensated for the confiscation of condemned property. Helena was to discover the same difficulty with enforcing the law when, as Alderman Gutteridge, she sought to eradicate certain slum tenements in Vancouver.

Carbolic acid. Fumigation. The Inspector of Nuisances. The Sanitary Officer. Slum clearance. In Nell's Victorian Chelsea childhood, these were as familiar as the milkman or dustman clattering down the street, components of a cultural milieu that by the end of the century manifested the compassionate values of the welfare state. As early as 1874, the Royal College of Physicians, in which the Medical Health Officers were a vocal group, presented a petition to the prime minister condemning 'philanthropy' and 'laissez faire' and declaring private enterprise incapable of providing adequate low-rental housing. Growing concern over the shocking plight of the poor was further roused by the publication in 1883 of Congregationalist minister Andrew Mearns's pamphlet *The Bitter Cry of Outcast London* (first published anonymously), which made the now obvious connection between low wages and overcrowding: workers simply could not afford decent accommodation. Queen Victoria herself had read the pamphlet and had been moved to write to Prime Minister Gladstone about it. The housing question was by now a national issue. In the House of Commons, Tory leader Lord Salisbury put the problem of housing the poor in a new light, dealing with the economics of building houses instead of with remedies for bad sanitation. He urged a formal inquiry, and a Royal Commission on the Housing of the Working Classes was set up in 1884, chaired by radical Liberal reformer Sir Charles Dilke, Member of Parliament for Chelsea. On the larger political scene, the Fabian socialists led by Beatrice and Sidney Webb were investigating social and economic conditions in England and advocating state intervention to provide a decent standard of living, every person's right, according to the Fabians.[28]

In Victorian Chelsea, rich and poor lived in close proximity. A certain population of workers was necessary, after all, to service the business enterprises and domestic and social lives of the upper classes. Charles and Sophia Gutteridge had done well to come to Chelsea, for there was a difference between being poor in the pleasant milieu of London's West End and being poor in the East End, where whole areas were scorched by the filth and degradation of the slum. However, poverty in the West End, overshadowed by upper class affluence, could be ignored because it was less visible, though Chelsea did have some notorious slums. In fact, Oscar Wilde placed a Persian screen in front of his smoking room window to hide a particularly ugly street from view.[29]

In an anti-conscription speech in Vancouver in 1917, Helena spoke of how, as a child, she had observed the difference between the lives of the rich and the lives of the poor. When she asked the reason for this difference, she was told that 'it was the will of God.'[30] The clear implication was that God wanted Lord Cadogan to live in a splendid mansion and families like hers to live in rundown cottages and crowded flats.

Chelsea House was situated at the east end of the north terrace of Cadogan Place near Sloane Street. Rebuilt in 1874 when the Fifth Earl of Cadogan was Disraeli's undersecretary for war, its beauties were so ' "prodigious," so "astounding," that even thirty years later the mansion could only be described with breathless reverence as a place of "sumptuous magnificence and gold-gleaming splendour," "full of slumbrous peace too infinitely reposeful to be categorized".' The family was in residence during May, June, and July each year. They required a staff of thirty.[31]

In the block west of Cadogan Place, and still only a few blocks away from any one of the streets where the Gutteridges had managed to find housing, lived Sir Charles Dilke, honoured by trade unionists for his work in bringing about legislation limiting hours of work for shop assistants. Sir Charles was born at 76 Sloane Street, the family home for four decades. During the parliamentary session, he kept in shape by fencing with his friends on the paved terrace outside the dining room. 'The clash of the foils and shouts of laughter from Dilke himself were recalled many years later as being familiar sounds in the neighbouring gardens,' wrote one biographer.[32] After Dilke's marriage to Mrs. Emma Pattison in 1885, the house was also the centre for her activities in the Women's Protective and Provident League, later the Women's Trade Union League.[33]

Cadogan Place was a notch higher on the social scale than Sloane Street, which was closer to the shops and business houses carrying on trade – in other words, producing wealth rather than simply inheriting it. Earlier in the century, Charles Dickens, with his intimate knowledge of London streets and neighbourhoods, commented on the subtle class distinctions that separated one part of Chelsea from another. In his time Cadogan Place, with its terraces of fine houses on Sloane Street, was not on the same social footing as the even finer houses of Belgravia, just a few doors east. As Dickens observed in *Nicholas Nickleby*, Belgravia was not Chelsea, and the dividing line was Sloane Street:

> Cadogan Place is the one slight bond that joins two great extremes; it is the connecting link between the aristocratic pavements of Belgrave Square, and the barbarism of Chelsea. It is in Sloane Street, but not of it. The people of Cadogan Place look down upon Sloane Street, and think Brompton low. They affect fashion too, and wonder where the New Road is.[34]

The New Road, just west of Sloane Street and parallel to it, had been built by Holland to service his Hans Place development, where the gentility of the residents, wealthy businessmen and professionals, though beyond dispute was still not of the order of the social and economic elite of Belgravia. What Dickens called 'barbarism' referred to the deterioration of Lower Chelsea, where the mansions of the rich and famous had been pulled down or turned into factories, lodging houses, or houses to let, or perhaps to writers like the impecunious Leigh Hunt, who moved his family to Cheyne Row near the river 'from the noise and dirt of the New Road' in Upper Chelsea.[35]

Fifty years later, when the New Road was Pavilion Road and the Gutteridge family came to live there, Upper Chelsea would have been regarded as even more 'barbarous' according to the standards of Belgravia. For commerce had come to King's Road and its side streets. On Draycott Street, sanitary engineer Thomas Crapper was appointed Royal Plumber in the 1880s, having served a long apprenticeship in Chelsea supplying and servicing water closets and finally inventing one of his own – 'Crapper's Valveless Waste Preventer: Certain Flush with Easy Pull.' Peter Jones, the Welsh draper, had moved his shop to Sloane Square, employing 150 people by 1884 and expanding even more in the next decade, expropriating in the process ten more neighbouring houses. In Chelsea, rich and poor, merchant and aristocrat, well-placed and humble came into easy contact, and in so doing affirmed their place in the social hierarchy.[36]

In Nell's childhood, lessons of class were daily learned and relearned, not least in church. The Gutteridges were Anglican, and Holy Trinity on Sloane Street, that splendid new Church of England edifice largely financed by the Earl of Cadogan, offered all Anglicans, regardless of class, the beauty of the stained glass east window, where saints' robes in flaming reds and purples, rich blues and soft sepias, ambers and olive greens had been designed and executed by Sir Edward Burne-Jones and William Morris. Otherwise, rich and poor were segregated, pews being rented in those days. The poor occupied the free benches down the nave.[37]

Noblesse oblige required that the spiritual and physical needs of parish folk be looked after, and the ladies of the church, elegant and imposing in rustling satin, went house to house as parish visitors. On the Holy Trinity visiting roster, the Honourable M. Manners was assigned to the part of Leete Street where the Gutteridges lived in 1888. Her duty was to inquire after the health of the family, remind them to go to church and Sunday School, and supply them with improving Christian tracts. A minister's wife is recalled as not wanting to have her children read them. Such things were for the lower orders. So were the special Sunday School excursions up the Thames and the school children's holiday in the country.[38]

Helena always maintained throughout her public career a vivid awareness of the importance of class in political life. Interviewed in 1937 when she was elected to Vancouver City Council, she did not clearly present herself as the daughter of a labourer. The new socialist councillor provided no clues to her working class background except for identifying her English accent as 'cockney.' On the contrary, she deployed biographical details in a strategic way. She said, quite correctly, that she was born in London in Sloane Square, in 'one of those high houses that have since been torn down,' but without any reported mention of the circumstances surrounding this or other demolitions by which the family was affected.[39] In another election interview, she is reported to have been educated at 'fashionable' Holy Trinity Church School.[40] We do not know whether Helena or the reporter supplied the word 'fashionable,' but in any case, intentionally or unintentionally she gave the impression that she attended a rather exclusive girls' school. In fact, Holy Trinity Upper Chelsea Girls' and Infants' School was fashionable only to the extent that it was new and well endowed, opened in 1888 by the Church of England for working class children of the neighbourhood and certainly not attended by the daughters of gentlemen, who had their own private governesses. Nell was nine years old at the time. Before this, she probably attended the original Infants' School on Pavilion Road, which exists today as the Holy Trinity Church of England Infants' School. The new school was located on Upper George Street, now Sedding Street, only a block from Sloane Square underground station. This century-old building, accommodating as many as 250 children, today houses the co-educational Holy Trinity Junior School.

Church schools were classified as 'voluntary' schools. Nell might have attended instead a 'board' school administered by the London School Board. Regulated by the 1862 Revised Code of the Education Ministry, both had the same curriculum and both were funded by the 'payment by result' system: the government grant was based on the number of pupils who successfully passed their examinations. Parents paid a weekly fee according to ability to pay, though it was waived altogether for very poor families. Free elementary school education was not established until 1891, when twelve-year-old Nell was almost ready to leave school, and even then some board schools required payment.[41]

Children entered the infant class at age five. The legal school-leaving age for elementary school children who had passed their Fourth Standard, approximately Canadian Grade 8, was thirteen. Helena told Hilda Kristiansen that she left home when she was fourteen because her parents were going to give her brothers but not her an education, a reconstruction of events that accommodated a lifelong feminist stance but that was at variance with family and social circumstances. In Nell's day, free secondary schools did not exist; secondary education was a class privilege enjoyed by middle and upper class children. They attended either endowed schools or 'proprietary schools' run for profit. The boys trained to become members of the governing class, the girls to be wives and consorts. A girls' private school at 40 Sloane Street advertised itself as 'Middle Class Day Schools for Girls and Infants,' French, music, and drawing extra. Nell could not have qualified as a pupil because of her father's occupation – timber porter. The lower classes were restricted in their education by a system designed to make them literate enough to be useful workers. Like most working class parents, Charles and Sophia Gutteridge only wanted their children to 'pass their standards' and go out into the world to earn their livings. As it turned out, Nell was destined to be the only member of the family to get an education, and even hers was not extensive.[42]

The 1890 Board of Education requirements for passing Fourth Standard comprised arithmetic, reading, 'writing any passage of prose or poetry from dictation, with Spelling. More than three mistakes "fail" a child'; reciting from memory eighty lines of poetry; needlework for girls and drawing for boys; some geography, history, perhaps even elementary science, and a great deal of grammar. Holy Trinity Log Book for 1906, the earliest one available, confirms this curriculum, with the addition of scripture, cooking lessons, and sewing. ('The garments which are all marked have now been taken home by the children as the cupboards are still not free from mice.') Because of the 'payment by result' system, teachers crammed their pupils rigorously to get them through their Standards. Nell was accordingly crammed and Holy Trinity received the grant money due on her account. If she did not indeed leave home until she was fourteen, she may have gone on to Fifth Standard.[43]

Holy Trinity Girls' School confirmed in Nell a strong sense of class difference and a respect for the power of position and money, which would stand her in good stead years later in her political work. The day the school opened in 1888 brought a special sense of privilege to the children of the parish, Nell Gutteridge among them, who were the first to file into the new classrooms. The Bishop of Ripon had preached at a commemorative church service; then the rector had said a few words thanking the Earl of Cadogan for donating the land for the school, after which the Countess of Cadogan presided at the official opening. The classrooms were spacious, with high ceilings and large windows, a far cry from some of the wretched 'schools' of earlier decades, when children crowded into badly ventilated makeshift rooms without books or apparatus, sometimes even without seats. In the basement of the new school a large hall served as a gymnasium; the staircase from the infants' floor led to – oh, great delight! – a rooftop playground.[44]

For three memorable afternoons in the spring of 1889, classes were interrupted on account of the money-making bazaar held at the school to pay off the school debt and to buy an organ for the new church, then under construction. The bazaar was opened by the Duchess of Edinburgh, to whom Lord Cadogan expressed his 'sincere gratitude.' Among a small legion of aristocratic ladies tending the stalls, the Countess of Cadogan graciously took charge of cushions and rugs, the Dowager Countess of Shrewsbury sold painted glass screens, and a host of Honourables and Ladies performed in dramatic sketches followed by 'a series of performances in the "Café Chantant".'[45] During those three days, when affluent Belgravia flocked to the school to spend easily and frivolously, the ten-year-old daughter of a builder's foreman, lately timber porter, had ample opportunity to have impressed on her not just the difference between rich and poor but also the power of money and position to make more money. She was learning how useful the rich could be in the service of a cause.

Nell was not growing up in a cultural wilderness by any means. Holy Trinity Parish Hall, located at 214 Pavilion Road, just next door to where she was born, provided a lending library, lender's ticket one penny a month. When she was seven years old, her family even lived in the same building as the library. The Upper Chelsea Institute held weekly lectures there: 'A Month in America and Canada,' 'Modern Fiction,' 'How Shall We House our Poor?' On 4 December 1888 the topic was 'The Practical Politics of Socialism,' the speaker, Mr. G. Bernard Shaw of the Fabian Society. Moreover, the Dilke household at 76 Sloane Street was a centre of political activity. Sir Charles, as one of Gladstone's Radicals, proposed reforms such as the eight-hour day and provision of social services by the municipalities. He fought for legislation to protect workers from industrial disease, notably in the china and earthenware trades, where white lead was used, and also to improve conditions in tailoring, shirtmaking, and other 'sweated trades.'[46]

Three women at 76 Sloane Street were prototypes of the woman Nell was to become. The wife of Sir Charles Dilke, Lady Emily, was a scholar and critic specializing in the history of French art. However, she devoted the second half of her life to the trade union movement. As a leading member of the Women's Trade Union League, she travelled throughout England organizing new branches and delivering her passionate message that only by banding together in unions could working men and women improve their lot. 'The name of trade unionist,' she declared, 'which once was a name of shame, is the name of soldiers of labour, who are fighting to preserve to the nation all that is noble in human life.'[47]

Lady Dilke's niece and personal secretary, Gertrude Tuckwell, later secretary and then president of the league, lived with her at 76 Sloane Street for a while. She had been a schoolteacher in the poorer part of Chelsea and had campaigned to prevent lead poisoning in the potteries and 'phossy jaw' in the match factories, brought on by breathing in and ingesting phosphorus. As a proponent of women's trade unions and as one of the initiators of the National Anti-Sweating League, she became well known throughout England. May Abraham also lived at

76 Sloane Street during her time as Lady Dilke's personal secretary. When the 1891 Royal Commission on Labour was prodded by Lady Dilke to concern itself about women workers, May Abraham was appointed one of four 'Lady Assistant Commissioners.' In 1893 she became the first woman inspector of factories. She and Gertrude Tuckwell were good friends, sharing rooms in Chelsea for a few years. Inspired by Lady Dilke, both devoted most of their lives to service in the cause of women workers, especially in the sweated trades, organizing, doing investigative work, lecturing.[48]

The careers of these three women precede in a remarkably analogous way to Helena's own Canadian career in the labour movement. In Canada, Helena also organized women workers and devoted herself to the trade union movement. The available evidence does not indicate whether or not as a young girl she was aware of the ferment of ideas and organization continually brewing at 76 Sloane Street or of the struggle for workers' rights initiated behind its aristocratic doors. Yet for a working class girl growing up in that Chelsea neighbourhood, aware of class differences and asking questions about them, herself destined to be one of the exploited in tailoring workshops, the inspiration for taking part in the struggle was all around her. In any case, knowingly or unknowingly, she was to carry on in British Columbia the work of the three women at 76 Sloane Street, 'fighting,' in the words of Lady Dilke, 'to deliver the sacred city of the spirit from captivity to the heathenish conditions of modern industry.'[49]

There were other such women crusaders in the larger London scene at this time. Beatrice Potter, later Webb, disguising herself as a 'trouser hand' in an East End tailor's shop and living among the workers, gathered evidence for Charles Booth's study of the London poor, a venture that trained her rigorously for her future career as a social investigator in the cause of socialism.[50] Margaret Bondfield of the National Union of Shop Assistants, later Britain's first woman cabinet minister, worked incognito in a number of shops to provide first-hand evidence exposing living and working conditions in the shops. The 'Life in the Shop' articles in the *Daily Chronicle* of 1898, based on material she collected, were widely read, and the name of Margaret Bondfield was well known, especially among shop workers.[51] Helena, early in her career in Vancouver, would also do such investigative work when she applied at various work places in the guise of a woman looking for a job, in order to gather evidence to present to a Royal Commission on Labour.[52]

And then there was the controversial and charismatic Annie Besant, freethinker, birth control advocate, socialist, theosophist, equally compelling whether speaking to a Queen's Hall audience or to a crowd in Trafalgar Square. In her brief career in Fabian socialism she took up the cause of the girls at the Bryant and May match factory and led their strike in 1888 for better working conditions and higher wages. In 1890 she left Beatrice Potter, Sidney Webb, and George Bernard Shaw for Madame Blavatsky and the secret doctrine of theosophy. When Nell was in her twenties, Annie Besant of the Theosophical Society was a profound influence on her. Under her spell, Nell began to prepare herself for a life of service. But first she would leave home to earn her own living. She would begin to fulfil her aspirations and discover a sense of her own worth. Nell Gutteridge would become Helena.[53]

The Emergence of Helena

Duty is that which *is due* to Humanity.
– Helena Petrovna Blavatsky, *The Secret Doctrine*

Nell left home in 1893 when she was fourteen years old and became an anonymous worker in London. By her own frugal account, many years later, she worked for ten years in 'a London ladies' clothing department.' This does not mean that she was a clerk selling clothing.[1] Although department stores had for some years been selling ready-made clothing, especially for boys and men, sales of yard goods far exceeded those of women's clothes. It was not until around 1900 that partly ready-made gowns came on the market. At the beginning of the century the draper, besides selling fabrics, was still making up the customer's purchase into gowns, coats, suits, and undergarments in a fashion workroom attached to the shop. Given her early career as a tailor, it is more than likely that Nell learned her trade in such a workroom. We do not know the name of her employer.[2]

The apprentice or 'learner' in such a workroom began without pay, making the tea and running errands, sorting buttons and doing other odd jobs. Next, as an 'improver' she learned to sew, by hand and on the treadle machine. When she gained a little skill, she advanced to a table as one of several assistants working under a 'hand' at some special stage of the garment – skirt, bodice, sleeve, collar. Here she stayed, or if she was skilled and ambitious, moved on to become a hand herself, then finally a fitter or even a cutter, supervising the whole operation and dealing with the customer. The hours were long: in 1900 in the John Lewis establishment on Oxford Street, from eight in the morning until eight at night on weekdays, and until four in the afternoon on Saturdays. If garments had to be finished for a ball or country weekend, the work went on through the night until they were finished, with no overtime pay. Wages were very low. At one reputable shop the weekly wage for assistants in 1907 was only 44 pence a week, less than half a pound in today's new pence. Even as late as 1918 in London's West End, not in some East End sweat shop, wages for hands and assistants in one establishment ranged from 16 to 21 shillings a week. In slack seasons, a token wage of a few pence might be paid for a full day's work. Nell's apprenticeship and rise to the position of cutter, in the normal course of events would have followed this pattern of training, with similar hours and wages.[3]

Nell did not have to find a room somewhere in the indifferent city. The shop provided board and room on its premises as part of wages. This 'living-in' system accommodated some 400,000 to 450,000 British shop-workers, both men and women. Three to four people might be crowded into one bedroom, without any of the amenities of a home allowed, such as pictures on the wall, flowers, or other personal touches. One bathroom might serve as many as twenty people, if indeed there was a bathroom at all. Meals were coarse and monotonous, and evening tea, even at so humane a place as John Lewis of Oxford Street, was likely to be bread and butter, with jam or beef dripping as an occasional treat. The rules were strict: special permission had to be obtained to sleep off the premises; no visiting in other rooms was allowed; fines were levied for breakages or for transgression of the eleven o'clock curfew. Employees were not allowed to marry, for then they would want to sleep elsewhere. Some did marry and stay on, but kept their marriage a secret. The National Union of Shop Assistants vigorously opposed the living-in system but the employers just as vigorously defended it on the ostensible grounds that it preserved morality: young men and women could not be allowed the freedom of the streets at night on their own. In fact, the living-in system relieved the employer of the necessity of paying a decent wage and hindered the workers from meeting freely among themselves for their own advancement.[4]

Helena did not mention the name of the establishment she worked in, but the likeliest possibility is Peter Jones, the draper at the end of Pavilion Road, who by 1893 had enlarged his shop by acquiring another ten properties and increased his staff proportionately. Living-in conditions were more agreeable at Peter Jones than in most shops. The Welsh draper and his wife were considerate employers, providing good food and extras for employees in the hostel above the shop, such as billiard tables, a piano, and a library. The premises, recently built, had incandescent lighting and 'sanitary arrangements by Messrs. Crapper,' so it is possible that workers living-in at Peter Jones enjoyed these amenities in their quarters. The costume department, occupying two storeys, was fitted with walnut and ebony display cases, handsomely carved and pleasing to the rich customers from Cadogan Square and Belgravia. Regular deliveries of hats for the royal children were made to Buckingham Palace. Milliners at Peter Jones, and dressmakers and tailoresses too, could feel a certain pride in sewing for an aristocratic clientele.[5]

Peter Jones fell ill in 1903 and the business went into a decline. Coincidentally, this year marked the end of Nell's ten-year stint in the London ladies' clothing department, assuming that she entered that employment upon leaving school. The following year found her across the river in lodgings at 70 Tonsley Hill in Wandsworth, entering a new life. She was an attractive young woman, tall and well-formed. Once again, we do not know where she was employed, only that she was a tailor. This much can be inferred from her own testimony: when she sailed for Canada in 1911, she gave her occupation on the ship's manifest as 'cutter.'[6]

The cutter had the most responsible job in the trade, except perhaps that of fitter. She could have been promoted to the job of cutter during her ten years in the ladies' clothing department or, less likely because of her other activities after 1903, left a menial position there to learn her trade from journeymen tailors in London shops. If so, she would have been quite unusual in the tailoring trade because cutters were men. Investigating the tailoring trade in 1904, the Women's Industrial Council spoke of the 'importance and power' of cutters and fitters, earning six to seven pounds a week:

> To one of the investigators they were described in a moment of frankness as being 'the very deuce ... and you do not know them from the swells they fit.' One of these gentlemen will be practically the employer of a little outside staff of tailors, with each of whom he will deal separately, and who will receive their pay from him.[7]

However, the investigators found 'one instance ... which is probably not quite the only one existing, of a woman who has acquired the art of cutting and fitting skirts, receives high pay, and is much valued by her employers.' Helena might very well have been one of those cutters in a 'ladies' tailoring' establishment where the other women – tailoresses – were doing the 'button-holing, felling, finishing, and trimming.' Some tailoresses, however, rented workrooms of their own and employed helpers, so Helena, even more highly trained, possibly could have done the same.[8]

She was still in touch with her sister Emily Lambert, who was living in Fulham, preoccupied with starting her own family with Albert Lambert, a horse-bus driver and strong union man. Their first child was born in 1904, followed by Lilian in 1906. Soon after, Emily and Albert moved farther west in the city, to Acton, and farther away from Nell in Wandsworth. Emily had been a waitress in a teashop in Knightsbridge, and after her husband's death did casual work in a laundry. Lilian spent twelve years in domestic service and twenty-three years in the packing room of a baby food laboratory. Emily did not speak much about her family, never mentioned that Nell had emigrated, if indeed she knew. But what she did say, as recalled by her daughter Lilian, was eloquent.

Interviewed in her pleasant home in the London suburb of Upminster at the end of the District Line, Lilian Delchar proved to be completely unlike her Aunt Helena. The niece was a little woman with a mass of unruly grey hair and a mobile face expressing anxious concern, disarming by her total willingness to please. She too had attended a church school, but St. Mary's 'was not a posh place – just a normal, everyday-life schooling.' Unlike Helena, she was not the least assertive; she was rather the womanly woman who makes life possible for others. Indeed, from the age of ten, while still a schoolgirl, she had spent much of her life in this way, as domestic help, waitress in a pub, housewife. Even now in her eighties she was keeping house, shopping, and gardening for her son and adult grandsons. Like most women who have spent their lives in humble yet invaluable service to others, she has little sense of her own worth, looking rather with pride and respect at the portrait of her daughter-in-law, a headmistress in academic gown, for whom she had kept house until the young woman's early death. Yet Lilian Delchar is a woman of spirit. She spoke fluently and openly, and about Helena she was forthright and definite, without pretence.

Lilian had never heard from her mother that Helena emigrated to Canada. 'It's news to me,' she said, and added, 'We always knew her as Nell.'

'I remember three things my mother told me about Nell. She was a model. She was sitting in a bus one day, and somebody asked if they could paint her mouth, to be painted into another portrait; to use her mouth on a painting they were doing. And as far as I know they did.' And did Helena go on to do more modelling? Lilian Delchar is direct and unevasive. 'I couldn't tell you.'

Of all the biographical possibilities for the formative years of a future socialist, this one must be voted the least likely. Evidently socially significant connections in the young adulthood of Helena Gutteridge must wait a little longer. Nevertheless, Lilian's report serves to underline the rich cultural milieu of Chelsea. Even Emily, who made no claims to education or to political development, knew painter Augustus John to speak to: he was a familiar figure in Chelsea and he may have frequented the Knightsbridge teashop where she worked.

'Nell was very hoity-toity,' continued Lilian Delchar. 'My mother said she was very la-di-da. Shall I put it that way? She seemed to think she was a cut above my mother and her own mother.' Evidently Nell viewed herself as separate from her family and had aspirations for a better life than the one God had ordained for the other Gutteridges. She was a member of a craft elite, enjoying a sense of her own skill and power. 'Cutting successfully is the power to cut beautiful and symmetrical clothes and at the same time please the customer,' wrote one practitioner. To do this one had to study the customer and form a 'mental opinion' on which to base one's decision as to an appropriate style. Thus, Nell was accustomed to exercising her judgment, to feeling herself a person in her own right, not just a worker carrying out orders.[9]

The third and final revelation: 'My mother said she married into the Lonsdale [Lansdale?] family. But who it was I couldn't tell you. I know no more than that.' Now Nell's grandmother Matilda, Sophia's mother, was a Lansdell or Lansdale – the name appears on birth certificates in both spellings. It is quite possible that Nell made an early marriage with a distant relative on her mother's side. Moreover, by Lilian's account, she did not simply marry a man by a certain name; she married *into* his family. However, a search through the General Index of Marriages at London's General Register Office uncovers no such marriage, or indeed any marriage for Helen Rose Gutteridge, closing the door on further speculation. Nevertheless Lilian Delchar's recollections serve most usefully to emphasize that Nell Gutteridge had a private life that we know nothing of, one full of unknown, surprising realities.

When Helena was about twenty-four years old, her life took a direction that can be followed. She came under the influence of the teachings of Madame Blavatsky – Helena Petrovna Blavatsky, one of the founders of the Theosophical Society – and on 4 October 1904 joined the Society's Battersea Lodge.[10] In her application for membership she added an 'a' to her name, perhaps thus announcing, in the person of Helena, her new discipleship. The religious mysticism of theosophy was very appealing in post-Darwinian England, where the validity of Christian doctrine was questioned by many and new anchors were eagerly grasped by troubled seekers after truth, among them Helena Gutteridge. In 1888 the London Society for Psychical Research declared Madame Blavatsky's claims of psychic power fraudulent, but the new religion of theosophy flourished just the same. After Madame Blavatsky's death in 1891, the inspiring and controversial Annie Besant was hailed as its leader. She became international president of the Theosophical Society in 1907.[11]

Madame Blavatsky set forth her theosophical doctrine in *The Secret Doctrine*, published in 1888 and drawing eclectically from the eastern religions. She added her own supernatural trappings, such as the incorporeal yet somehow living mahatmas or holy men, ultimate sources of spiritual truth; spirits, not of the dead but of 'disembodied personalities' emitting 'astral reflections'; and other occult phenomena. After five years with the society, Helena was ready to give all this up, though she took from the society a concept of duty to others that would be a guiding precept for the rest of her life. The Church of England taught that God's grace could be received through acts of goodness, and Helena had doubtless learned in childhood to heed the words of Jesus in the Sermon on the Mount: 'Let your light so shine before men that they may see your good works.' The Anglican God, moreover, removes ultimate responsibility from the individual by offering redemption for sin through the self-sacrifice of Jesus Christ. Theosophy, on the other hand, takes from Buddhism and Hinduism the doctrine of Karma and thus gives no such absolution, for the universal law of Karma holds each individual responsible for his acts. It governs all humanity through succeeding reincarnations according to the accumulating and interrelated actions of all individuals. No one may escape responsibility because every action of every person affects the whole body of humanity. Karma, the wellspring of justice, exacts retribution, deals out reward and punishment. Prayer is to no avail, but each person acting for the betterment of the world can influence the workings of Karma and thus help alleviate human suffering.[12]

Helena's long career in social reform owes a great deal to the altruistic element in theosophy, which embraces all races, creeds, and classes of people. True, theosophy avoids politics, although Annie Besant herself did not, involving herself in later years in the turmoil of Indian nationalism. Just the same, she too believed that social reform can come only through the gradual transformation of human beings. Hence the belief in the progress of the spirit towards perfection and its ultimate emergence in Nirvana. On the other hand, theosophy recognizes that humanity is conditioned by social forces and that if the social milieu is changed, so too is human nature. 'Duty,' says Madame Blavatsky in *The Secret Doctrine*, 'is that which *is due* to Humanity, to our fellow men, neighbours, family, and especially that which we owe to all those who are poorer and more helpless than we are ourselves (her italics).' This was Helena's creed too, to which she held unswervingly, even after she had discarded the belief in the dire moral consequences in the next incarnation of failing in one's duty.[13]

Those who remember Helena are unanimous about one special aspect of her character: her strength of conviction. She was never afraid to speak her mind. Here again theosophy provided a stern commandment, for Madame Blavatsky counselled:

Never to do a thing by halves; *i.e.*, if he thinks it the right thing to do, let him do it openly and boldly, and if wrong, never touch it at all. It is the duty of a Theosophist to lighten his burden by thinking of the wise aphorism

of Epictetus, who says: 'Be not diverted from your duty *by any idle reflection the silly world may make upon you'* [her italics] ...[14]

In other words, stand up to the world, and don't flinch before thunder
and lightning. Helena's mother would have approved.

Helena never engaged in petty gossip about the private lives of her
friends or passed judgment on them, at least not in later life, according
to her friend and landlady Hilda Kristiansen. Once again, theosophy is
an influence, urging open and direct dealings with others, without
backbiting and slander.[15]

The Theosophical Society was a training ground for Helena. In
Canada, when she joined the new political movement of the 1930s
known as the Co-operative Commonwealth Federation, she already
knew the duties of a member, for they were essentially the same as those
enjoined on members of the society: to study the doctrines, to spread the
word, to circulate its books and pamphlets, to uphold the society
against attack, and to bear witness by the example of their own lives.[16]

Unfortunately for the practical reformer, Karmic law operates slowly:
one atones in the present life for the wrongdoings of an earlier incarnation without, however, knowing what those sins are. Karma works
on a vast cosmic scale over the centuries, during which erring human
beings in succeeding reincarnations are gradually ennobled, their gross
matter purified so that eventually humanity receives the benefits of this
purification.

During these years, Helena also belonged to another organization
steeped in ritual and symbolism – the Co-Freemasons.[17] Again, she was
under the influence of Annie Besant, who introduced Universal Co-
Freemasonry into Britain. The Masonic Order does not, of course,
admit women. However, in 1879 a dissident group had rebelled against
the Masonic Supreme Council of France, and in the course of its independent evolution came to admit women. Annie Besant was installed
in this first Co-Masonic Grand Lodge, and, becoming British representative on the Supreme Council, established in London in 1902 the first
British lodge, 'Human Duty, No. 6.' Thus Co-Freemasonry took root in
England, drawing early supporters from the Theosophical Society,
with which it had strong links.[18] We do not know when Helena joined
the Co-Masons or which of the two organizations she joined first. The
important point is that both put her on the road to self-improvement and
political consciousness.

The Co-Masons practised their own version of the sacred lore of
Freemasonry, though the male Order of Freemasons refused to recognize their existence. Like theosophy, Co-Masonry is egalitarian, its
declared purpose the welfare of all humanity. At their meetings mem-

bers approved candidates for Masonic degrees, learned about such Masonic traditions as the cornerstone and various knots and cords. They listened to talks on astrology and alchemy and held discussions on Freemasonry and the Ideals of the Coming Race. 'How can Masonry hasten the New Day?' they pondered. They believed that the women's movement was 'part of that great stirring of the whole world' and 'a partial manifestation of a larger life'; that 'the human race needs both sexes for its full expression, alike in the home, the world and the lodge.' Annie Besant was herself an acknowledged champion of women's rights, and other members were active suffragists. At the meeting of Human Duty Lodge on 4 April 1910, Sister Charlotte Despard, also a leading member of the National Union of Women's Suffrage Societies, opened the discussion on the child in the modern world. In July 1911 Sister Besant, of the thirty-third degree, attended the meeting of Human Duty, No. 6 and addressed the members. Whether or not Helena belonged to this particular lodge, during the years of her membership she would have heard Annie Besant speak at some lodge meeting.[19]

Theosophists and Co-Masons provided Helena's intellectual milieu during her twenties. Then in 1906 the Pankhursts came from Manchester, where they had organized the Women's Social and Political Union (WSPU), and set up their headquarters in London. In the suffragist campaign for the vote, the WSPU quickly became a powerful political force, and Helena joined with these militant suffragists in direct action. Since there were active suffragists among the Co-Masons, she could well have come to the suffragist movement through them. After all, Annie Besant herself, in full regalia, led a contingent of Co-Masons in the big suffragist procession of 1911 and was one of the main speakers at the Albert Hall rally that ended the day.[20] The feminist cause became an urgent matter for Helena and, although theosophy was not hostile to feminism, she resigned from the Theosophical Society on 7 April 1909.[21] She could not wait for Karma.

During these years of growing social awareness and intellectual development, Helena was one of the great crowds of working people flocking to the London Polytechnics, which in 1892-93 had been taken up by the London County Council. They were under the enthusiastic direction of Councillor Sidney Webb, who translated his Fabian belief in the necessity of education into this practical endeavour.[22] Helena attended the St. Marylebone branch of the Regent Street Polytechnic, where she chose to study Hygiene. In the 'Results of the Examinations in Science, 1905,' she is recorded as Helena R. Gutteridge, with a second class in Hygiene, stage two. Presumably the missing record book for 1904 recorded her passing stage one. In 1906 she failed stage three, but passed it the following year.[23] According to her own account many years later, she obtained her South Kensington Department of Education certificate for this course, and also for teaching and sanitary science.[24] No record was found to verify these certificates, but Regent Street Polytechnic was developing normal classes in educational methods at this time, so in 1907 and 1908 she could very well have been in teacher-training and in sanitary science classes there.

The Polytechnics also provided recreation and opportunities for social intercourse for young working men and women, 'separated in many cases,' observed the compassionate Sidney Webb, 'from their relations and condemned to lonely lodgings; and all of them inhabiting a great city which has outgrown the simple social intercourse of neigh-bourliness.'[25] The description surely applies to Helena in her Tonsley Hill lodgings, and it is therefore reassuring to know that among the recreational activities offered by the Regent Street Polytechnic was Mandolin and Guitar Band on Thursday evenings. Years later, when she had retired to her poultry farm in the Fraser Valley, Helena still had her mandolin, which neighbours remembered her playing.

What emerges from this jigsaw picture of Helena's education is the ambition of a young woman, not just to improve herself but to lend her energies towards improving social conditions. She could have elected to study bookkeeping and shorthand, or even elementary French or mathematics or history, with the aim of getting university credits. She decided instead to study sanitation, for a new profession had opened to women: they were now sought as sanitary inspectors, employed to work under the Medical Health Officers to implement health regulations. Their job was to inspect laundries, factories, and workshops where women were living-in; to investigate cases of tuberculosis and deaths of infants from diarrhea; to make home visits among the poor, teaching mothers the rudiments of hygiene and nutrition and explaining that boiled bread and sausage rolls are not a proper diet for infants.[26] The duties of the woman sanitary inspector echo the concerns of the working poor of Chelsea, of just such a family as the Gutteridges, of Nell herself when she was a child on Pavilion Road and Leete Street: the visits of the housing inspector, perhaps even on occasion Medical Health Officer Dr. Andrew Barclay himself; the funeral processions for neighbourhood children struck down by disease; the death of her own baby brother. And the reek of burning sulphur and carbolic acid scarring memory.

The new opportunities for women in the field of sanitation were the result of the work of the nineteenth-century British sanitary reformers who sought to educate a whole population with the idea of sanitation. Among the most influential of them was Edwin Chadwick, whose *Inquiry into the Sanitary Condition of the Labouring Population of Great Britain*

(1842) laid the basis for developing public health legislation in England. He made the now obvious connection between dirt and disease, and as Public Health Commissioner from 1848 to 1854 campaigned for state intervention to bring about sanitary reform.[27]

According to the prevailing theory of disease, putrefying waste, especially animal waste, generated 'effluvia,' which by corrupting the atmosphere caused disease or created favourable conditions for the spread of specific contagia. Intense smell was equated with the occurrence of disease. Thus the way to combat smallpox, cholera, typhoid, and other scourges was to eliminate the foul cesspools and defective sewers that polluted the soil and lakes and rivers; to eliminate also the filthy privies and other accumulations of human and animal excreta in the streets and yards, and the refuse from the slaughterhouses, fish markets, and barnyards that were so much a part of everyday life in Victorian England.[28]

With Edwin Chadwick sanitation became an obsession, and his mother is held responsible, because she had instilled in him by daily admonition the need for cleanliness. He did not believe in the new germ theory. Soap and water would eradicate disease – and properly engineered sewage systems and adequate supplies of clean water.[29] Although other sanitary reformers – Sir John Simon, Benjamin Ward Richardson, Neil Arnott, Southwood Smith – were not as fanatic as Chadwick, like him they distrusted the new science of bacteriology and were as dedicated as he to the sanitary conversion of the individual Briton as a means of preventing disease. Like an evangelical preacher, Richardson exhorted the British public to heed the call to personal hygienic redemption and warned against being misled by experiments in immunization:

> Let us cleanse our outward garments, our bodies, our food, our drink and keep them cleansed. Let us cleanse our minds, as well as our garments, and keep them clean ... Then all elaborate experiments for the prevention of disease will appear, as they are, mysterious additions to evil, which ought not to exist ...[30]

The sanitary reform movement was, observes social historian Anthony Wohl, 'a piety, a crusade of puritanical zeal against the sin of dirt.'[31] In light of this crusade, the daily purgative taken by Helena's father resounds with meaning, as does her mother's obsessive polishing of the coal shovel.

Considering the general omnipresence of dirt, foul smells, lice, fleas, and bedbugs in the houses and streets of the poor, there was ample scope for missionary work. The Ladies' Sanitary Association had been formed in mid-century to bring the message of personal and domestic hygiene to the working class. Between 1857 and 1881 the association distributed 1.5 million tracts on hygienic housekeeping, ventilation, the care of infants, the uses of soap and water. In addition, they brought the soap, if not the water – always in short supply and often carried in from a tap on the street – to the homes of the poor, and whitewash and disinfectant as well, with brooms and brushes on loan.[32]

Many Canadians, recalling family poverty in the 1930s, can still hear the proud, if tight-lipped, dictum of their mothers: 'At least we can be clean.' In Victorian England, it was scarcely possible for a labourer's daughter like Helena to grow up without being aware of the enormous labour a woman must expend to keep her dwelling and her family clean: carrying water from a tap in the courtyard or street, heating it on the stove, washing clothes in heavy, iron-hooped tubs. Taking a bath was no easy matter, as many will recall from their own Canadian childhood, when each member of the family bathed in turn in the metal tub in the middle of the kitchen floor, the water becoming progressively dirtier even though replenished for each bather from the big copper boiler or cauldron on the stove. But a great many working class people in Victorian England would not have had access to even these primitive facilities: they simply remained dirty and smelly, contemptuously referred to as 'the Great Unwashed.' The Association for the Establishment of Baths and Washhouses for the Labouring Poor was founded in 1846 in the face of the received wisdom that the poor *liked* being dirty, and by the 1860s many London parishes had bathhouses for working people, where they could take a bath in a tub or a shower and also use the laundry facilities. The building of bathhouses was encouraged by the Cleansing of Persons Act of 1897, and the new facilities, which often included disinfecting rooms for clothing, proved very popular among labourers. At St. Marylebone, two thousand people used the two baths in the first six months of their existence. Chelsea had no public baths, but when in 1884 the ladies of the parish petitioned the Vestry for 'properly equipped and furnished baths and wash houses,' they were refused.[33] Chelsea, however, was out of step in this matter, for the building of imposing municipal bathhouses had become a national priority. In Wandsworth, where Helena was living, the 'English Renaissance' bathhouse 'had a frontage of seventy-five feet and cost £20,000.' 'The sums spent on the municipal baths and the style of architecture and interior fittings,' observes Wohl, 'suggest that by the 1890s the concept of cleanliness for the masses had so permeated national consciousness that it was an ideal which called for appropriate municipal monuments.'[34]

The sanitary idea doubtless influenced Helena in her choice of studies and potential new career, for it had surrounded her in some way from childhood in the form of the public health movement. The very word 'sanitation' rang in her ears the way 'environment' rings in the ears of today's generation and half a century later, in 1941, would find an echo as she campaigned for re-election to city council:

> 'What a mess!' The voice of Helena Gutteridge, CCF aldermanic candidate was heavy with disgust as she stood on the city dump in False Creek flats Friday afternoon ...
>   'An incinerator is the obvious solution,' Miss Gutteridge said. 'But first we must take steps to clean up rat infestation here and the breeding places and find a way to dispose of garbage so the rats can't breed.'[35]

In 1907, however, she was sitting her final examination in Hygiene, writing about such things as the disadvantages of storage cisterns for water and precautions for preventing the spread of measles. With her second-class grade, she went on to take a course in Sanitary Science at the Royal Sanitary Institute. 'Give the substance of the London County Council Bye-Laws in reference to the construction of new water-closets,' demanded a typical examination paper. 'Define motion, velocity, force, matter and pressure.' The physical effects of breathing carbon monoxide, the hydraulicity of Portland cement, the toxicity of water in lead pipes – all were topics of study in a typical three-month course.[36] Unfortunately, no record has been found of her name as a successful candidate receiving a certificate.[37] Since she never claimed to have received one from the Sanitary Institute, in all likelihood she either did not finish the course or failed the examination. In any case, her intention is obvious – to enter the field of sanitation as either a teacher or a sanitary inspector.

In the event, she did neither. For by now she was working for a cause that soon totally absorbed her – the Cause, as suffragists called the woman's right to the franchise. And the rights of women would eventually lead her to a life's career in social reform and politics.

CHAPTER THREE

Fighting for the Cause

To thee old cause!
Thou peerless, passionate, good cause,
Thou stern, remorseless, sweet idea ...
　　　　　　－ Walt Whitman, 'To Thee Old Cause'

When we next catch a glimpse of Helena, she is standing on an Islington street corner in London with another suffragist, making a speech on votes for women. It is Saturday, 11 June 1910. The Women's Social and Political Union (WSPU) will be staging a massive procession to Albert Hall the following week, and in preparation has organized daily procession meetings such as the one Helena is addressing. Her name appears in 'London Meetings for the Forthcoming Week,' a regular feature of the WSPU newspaper, Votes for Women. Obviously, Helena has been recognized as leadership material. The speakers at these meetings go out in pairs to all parts of London, a well-known suffragist with a rank-and-file member. Helena will speak three times during the week, on one evening with Marie Brackenbury, who has already spent six weeks in Holloway prison for the Cause. The Brackenbury women – Marie, a landscape painter; her sister, Georgina, a portrait painter; and their mother, Hilda, born and raised in Quebec – are all militant suffragettes. Marie and Georgina had been among those descending on the House of Commons from a furniture van and arrested in an attempt to gain entrance. Speaking on a street corner with a Brackenbury was no small recognition of one's value as a member of the WSPU. More important, these women provided a powerful example of fearless devotion to belief.[1]

The WSPU offered instruction in public speaking to develop leaders. Classes were held in Georgina's studio in Campden Hill Square. Organizing in Chelsea and Fulham, and in Wandsworth where Helena was living for a time, Sylvia Pankhurst trained 'a band of young speakers' for the big Hyde Park demonstration of 1908. Helena may have been one of this band; certainly she had ample opportunity to develop her speaking skills and to work with Sylvia Pankhurst and other WSPU organizers on the big suffragist demonstrations that had become a feature of

London life. For several weeks in the summer of 1910, under the watch-ful and critical eye of her mentors, she received valuable training in pub-lic speaking and discovered the power of her own voice and person.[2]

Speaking at street corners required a good deal of wit and presence of mind. Gathering an audience was not easy. 'The audience had to be started by almost lassoing individuals – to a crowd of ten,' recalls Teresa Billington-Greig. 'Mrs. Drummond started it; it grew to twenty – Mrs. Pankhurst built it up; others followed until there were some hun-dreds listening and many sympathetic.'[3] A contemporary account by a WSPU militant dramatizes the experience of the fledgling speaker:

> 'People of London!' faltered the lady who had just stepped upon the sugar-box at the edge of the pavement.
> The people of London, who happened just then to be a very little girl car-rying a very large baby, stared in some astonishment. Another lady, who had been distributing handbills farther along the street, came back and prompted the speaker encouragingly.
> 'Go on; that's splendid!' she said with friendly warmth.
> The woman on the sugar-box, who had never stood on a sugar-box before, smiled wanly ...
> 'Why, it's these 'ere Suffragites!' suddenly yelled the people of London, shifting the baby on to the other arm ...

Hecklers grumble, shout, create confusion and altercation. A hostile man wants to know how a woman with a husband and six children can find time to vote. The little street-corner drama continues:

> 'How does a man find time to vote, if he has a wife and six children to sup-port?' she [the speaker] demanded; and the woman with the bundle nod-ded approvingly.
> 'Now she's talkin' sense, and I likes sense,' she remarked to her com-panion. 'I don't 'old with women bein' Prime Ministers, but I likes sense.'[4]

Helena was well-suited to speaking to this kind of audience. Work-ing class women were a minority in the WSPU, and even fewer were those who could give leadership. Although the WSPU depended in its early years on the support of the mill women of Manchester and environs, and indeed had been a passionate advocate for working women, when it moved to London it transferred its loyalties to educated middle and upper class women. When the WSPU divorced itself from the newly formed Independent Labour Party, even from the loyal and sympathetic Keir Hardie, and began to employ violence in confrontations with the ruling Liberals, it distanced itself from working class women as well.[5]

Years later, Christabel Pankhurst, the WSPU's strategist, recalled her motives: 'It was evident that the House of Commons, and even its Labour members, were more impressed by the demonstrations of the feminine bourgeoisie than of the female proletariat.'[6] Emmeline Pankhurst herself observed that the struggle for the vote was most effectively carried on by 'the fortunate ones,' by which she meant 'the women who have drawn prizes in the lucky bag of life.'[7]

The Central London Committee of the WSPU was dominated by a small clique consisting of Emmeline Pankhurst, Christabel Pankhurst, and Emmeline Pethick Lawrence. Frederick Pethick Lawrence, a wealthy man with labour and feminist sympathies, was also heavily involved in the work of the WSPU. (He and Emmeline Pethick had adopted the double name when they married.) He edited *Votes for Women*, defended militants in court, and himself suffered imprisonment and forced feeding. The three women adopted the policies and strategies of military command: they formulated policy, made decisions and issued instructions to the membership without their approval or consent, and demanded unquestioning obedience. Sylvia Pankhurst was not one of the clique because she did not agree with these undemocratic methods. In 1907 a little group led by socialists Charlotte Despard and Teresa Billington-Greig, disturbed by the 'trinitarian dictatorship' of the Pankhursts, broke away from the WSPU and formed the Women's Freedom League (WFL). Sylvia Pankhurst was not one of them. She continued to work with the WSPU.[8] Helena did not go over to the Women's Freedom League: on the evidence of the speakers' lists in *Votes for Women*, in 1910 she was with the Pankhursts in the WSPU. By her own account she took an active part in its militant demonstrations: 'I took the stump at Hyde Park corner, took part in hundreds of parades, got thrown out of numerous meetings, waved banners in the House of Commons, anything at all to attract attention to our cause.'[9]

Liberal Prime Minister Herbert Asquith was openly hostile to the enfranchisement of women. Unable to gain any concessions from the government, the WSPU adopted militant tactics. It campaigned in elections against the Liberals and harassed their speakers at public meetings. It convened 'Women's Parliaments' from which deputations would march to the House of Commons to seek an audience with the prime minister. These marches, or 'raids,' were made up of thirteen women, the number chosen so that the raiding party would exceed by one the number of citizens allowed by a law two centuries old to petition Parliament in a body.[10] Refused admission, the women would rush against police lines guarding the entrance and suffer physical assault and humiliation. Courting imprisonment, they returned again and again, provoking Members of Parliament, defying the police. Arrested and jailed, they went on hunger strikes and then were forcibly fed. Released from prison they returned to the attack, obdurate, insistent, angry. Some began to employ violence: Mary Leigh with Edith New smashed Asquith's windows at Number 10 Downing Street, and, sentenced to two months in prison, declared, '"It will be a bomb next time".'[11]

The banners that Helena waved carried the rallying cry 'Votes for Women.' *Which* women should get the vote had, however, by 1910 become a divisive question among suffragists of all persuasions. Originally, the aim of the WSPU was based on sex equality – to give the vote to women 'on the same terms as it is or may be given to men.' The National Union of Women's Suffrage Societies (NUWSS), headed by Millicent Fawcett, had adopted this formulation in 1897.[12] Implicit in it was the maintenance of a franchise tied to property qualifications, which in 1910 excluded more than half of the male population. Thus a suffragist could with a clear conscience campaign for votes for women without supporting adult suffrage. Indeed some women suffragists, including Millicent Fawcett, were opposed to universal suffrage.[13] The feminist seeking equal rights could, however, also adopt the 'same terms as men' formulation in the firm belief that as a matter of practical politics the vote had to be won in stages.[14]

As the WSPU became more and more entrammelled in political events, it narrowed its demands and accepted a proposal for a limited franchise as put forward by the Conciliation Bill of 1910, drafted by a committee of MPs supporting woman suffrage. This bill would enfranchise mainly single propertied women by awarding them the same rights as men under the Representation of the Peoples Act of 1884, which restricted the franchise to tax-paying householders and to 'occupiers' of business premises paying more than ten pounds a year in rent. Thus, only better-paid workers would qualify, those able to afford nearly four shillings a week in rent. Moreover, under the terms of the Conciliation Bill most married women would not qualify, for the same property could not confer the vote on both husband and wife. Lloyd George, an avowed suffragist, nevertheless opposed the bill, as did Winston Churchill and other suffragist Liberals, afraid that the enfranchisement of single propertied women would increase the Tory vote at a time when they were attempting to push reform legislation through the House. But the Women's Freedom League, the NUWSS, and other suffrage organizations, along with the WSPU, supported the bill. The Labour Party, meanwhile, despite the opposition of Keir Hardie, Sylvia Pankhurst's dear friend and loyal ally in the Cause, took its stand in favour of universal adult suffrage, fully aware of the class interests that would be served by a limited suffrage bill and dedicated to universal adult suffrage as the best and most efficient way of achieving sex equality.[15] This policy caused a break with the WSPU.

Whether or not Helena expected to be one of the women getting the vote under the provisions of the Conciliation Bill we cannot say, not knowing the rent she paid. Moreover, the complexity of British law on the franchise and registration of voters at that time forbids speculation and commands a judicious reticence. In any case, as Christabel Pankhurst herself declared, the vote was a symbol. It represented recognition of a woman's existence as a social and political being.

The Asquith government had just passed the Old Age Pension Act and was introducing other progressive social measures, such as universal free education and a sickness and unemployment benefits bill – the sort of legislation that a later Canadian Helena would spend her life fighting for. Lloyd George called his 1909 budget a 'war budget' because, as he said, 'it is for raising money to wage implacable warfare against poverty and squalidness.'[16] With only a slim parliamentary majority, he was vitally concerned with staying in power. Thus woman suffrage became a political gambit, for the government depended for support on the Irish Nationalists, who were anti-suffragist, and the Labour Party, who favoured universal adult suffrage. Meanwhile, the suffragettes, whatever their individual attitudes to social reform, were not to be diverted by the government's reform measures. They concentrated on one issue only, the Vote, and branded the Liberals and Lloyd George as traitors.[17]

Militant activities were suspended in the months when the Conciliation Bill was being considered. During this truce in the summer of 1910, several great suffrage processions were held in the full expectation of a successful outcome, and Helena was among those who participated. She remembered especially the procession of 18 June as the 'greatest parade of women ever organized anywhere,' when thousands of women 'marched from Thames Embankment to Albert Hall,' and she was one of the marchers.[18] The *Times* of London spoke of the 'spectacular beauty' of the procession, describing it as 'a scene to be witnessed in a sunny city of Southern Europe on the high festival of the beneficent patron saint ...'[19] Because full mourning for the death of Edward VII had ended the day before, the women were able to dress in their colours, in white gowns with purple and green regalia. Ten thousand women in seven contingents from many suffrage societies and occupational groups converged at the Thames Embankment and marched through the city. They carried armfuls of flowers and held aloft silken banners proclaiming 'freedom' and 'emancipation.' The WSPU led off with 'General' Flora Drummond in trooper's great coat and beaver hat mounted astride her horse. On either side rode her two aides-de-camp, in riding gowns and tall silk hats. Behind them walked Charlotte Marsh, the first hunger-striker to have been force-fed. Then came the Fife and Drum Band of the WSPU led by Drum Major Mary Leigh, playing the *Marseil-*

laise. The Prisoners' Pageant followed, led by Emmeline Pankhurst, Emmeline Pethick Lawrence, and Annie Kenney: 617 women who had suffered imprisonment for the Cause, in robes of white and carrying tall silver wands topped with 'the broad arrow of the prisons.' The WSPU contingents gathered in Albert Hall, where they passed a resolution calling on the government to pass the Conciliation Bill and pledged themselves 'regardless of personal cost or sacrifice to push forward the campaign for the emancipation of women until victory be won.'[20] To have been among the promoters of this demonstration was valuable political training for Helena, and marching in that splendid procession an unforgettable experience, her own self submerged in the great suffragist Will, but sharing in the exaltation of Womanhood.

The Conciliation Bill passed second reading by a large majority, even though Lloyd George, Winston Churchill, and other declared suffragist Liberals voted against it. But the House voted to refer the bill to a committee of the whole House, thus effectively dashing hopes of its passing into law.[21] However, the WSPU maintained its truce, hopeful that passage of the suffrage bill would be completed in the next session. They held a second mass demonstration on 23 July, again drawing in the other suffrage societies, rallying the crowds to forty platforms in Hyde Park. Again, the theme of martyrdom, with hunger-striker Charlotte Marsh, alone and on foot, leading the contingent of former prisoners, 'a slight fair woman whose name is engraven on the hearts of women as the doer of a golden deed.'[22] Again the martial theme: three horsewomen carrying lances led the parade, and WSPU marchers bore aloft their standards, emblazoned like those of Roman soldiers.

One of the horsewomen was Maud Joachim, university-educated and the niece of the famous violinist. She had already spent four and a half months in prison and had gone on a hunger strike at Dundee prison the year before. In the week before the demonstration, she was one of the speakers at the street-corner procession meetings, and Helena shared a platform with her at Islington. The next night, Helena was at St. John's Road with Mary Leigh. In the role of martyr for the Cause, Mrs. Leigh could not be excelled. Six times in prison, once serving seven months in a single year, she had three times gone on a hunger strike and had once been forcibly fed for six weeks. Helena's other co-speakers were equally militant: Rosamond Massy, daughter of a peeress and wife of a British colonel, was a hunger striker, first imprisoned in 1909. Ada Wright, like Sylvia Pankhurst, was concerned for the welfare of working women and had helped run a Working Girls Club in Soho. She had been jailed every year for the past three, and had been forcibly fed. Victor Duval, founder of the Men's Political Union for Women's Enfranchisement (MPUWE), would be imprisoned after a confrontation with Lloyd George, and forcibly fed as well. On Black Friday, 18 November 1910, he and his mother and three sisters would all go to prison.[23] In that week before the mass demonstration of 23 July, Helena was out on some street corner every night except Sunday addressing a crowd of Londoners in company with one or another prominent middle or upper class suffragist.

When Parliament met in November, Prime Minister Asquith made no provision to complete passage of the Conciliation Bill. The WSPU accordingly ended the truce and mounted a demonstration on 18 November, the day of the opening of Parliament. The Ninth Woman's Parliament, convened at Caxton Hall, sent out three hundred women in detachments of twelve to the House of Commons. Approaching the Strangers' Entrance to the House, the women attempted, as in other raids, to gain entrance. This time, however, the police delayed arrest to actually fight the women, grabbing and twisting their breasts, shoving their knees between the women's legs, and delivering other forms of sexual assault. They punched the women and struck them to the ground. Sylvia Pankhurst reported, 'I saw Ada Wright knocked down a dozen times in succession. A tall man with a silk hat fought to protect her as she lay on the ground, but a group of policemen thrust him away, seized her again, hurled her into the crowd and felled her again as she turned.'[24] At intervals of two or three minutes, a fresh detachment of women came forward and one by one were brutally set upon by the police, who even used the rowdies in a particularly hostile crowd to make the ordeal even more painful and humiliating for the suffragettes.

Helena was in one of these detachments, and in her fragmentary account of the demonstration in a newspaper interview some twenty-five years later, she does not mention being assaulted by the police. The battle lasted for six hours, and by the end of the day 115 women and 4 men had been arrested and charged. When they appeared in Bow Street Police Court next morning, however, most of them were discharged, Helena among them. As she explained, 'There was no room for us all in the jail.'[25]

Mrs. Pankhurst led another raid on Downing Street on 22 November; again a brutal fight took place, and this time 159 were arrested, including Mrs. Pankhurst. The following day, yet another raid – and more arrests.[26] The events of these three days gave Helena an experience of police brutality and civic disorder that she would never forget. More than twenty-five years later, during the demonstrations of the Relief Camp Workers and the post office sit-down strike in Vancouver, the events of Black Friday and the Battle of Downing Street provided a memory backdrop for the uprising of a very different class of people.

The following year a revised Conciliation Bill limiting the women's franchise to qualifying householders passed second reading in the

House, Lloyd George this time voting in favour of the measure. Sylvia Pankhurst commented disapprovingly: 'The Bill now applies only to women householders. The £10 occupiers (usually poor lodgers in unfurnished rooms) were thrown out as a sop to Liberal democratic ideas.'[27] She was referring to Lloyd George's insistence on an extended franchise that would enfranchise working men's wives as well as spinsters and widows. In the event, Lloyd George would announce that the bill had been 'torpedoed.' The effective destruction of the bill came with Asquith's announcement that a manhood suffrage bill would be introduced, capable of being amended to provide for the enfranchisement of women. The WSPU was convinced that such an amendment would never receive the full government support needed in the face of strong Conservative and Irish Nationalist opposition. Enraged over the political manoeuvring of Asquith and Lloyd George, it ended the truce and renewed its militancy, becoming ever fiercer in a new strategy of secret destruction of property that did not stop at arson.[28] 'The argument of the broken pane is the most valuable argument in modern politics,' Mrs. Pankhurst declared to her supporters, preparing them to take part in yet another vendetta of mass window smashing.[29]

The radical women suffragists from northern England had always disapproved of militancy as a tactic, as did the NUWSS, labelled 'constitutionalists.'[30] Sylvia Pankhurst herself disagreed with the new policy, believing that a mass franchise movement was the only force that could influence the government. She did not at first openly repudiate WSPU policy, but instead in 1912 began to organize a campaign to bring the suffrage movement to the working women of the East End. In 1913 she formed the East London Federation of the WSPU. It became a separate organization in 1914 – the East London Federation of the Suffragettes. Her vision was very different from that of her mother:

> I wanted to rouse these women of the submerged mass to be, not merely the argument of more fortunate people, but to be fighters on their own account, despising mere platitudes and catch-cries, revolting against the hideous conditions about them, and demanding for themselves and their families a full share of the benefits of civilization and progress.[31]

Helena pursued this vision of the awakened and politically conscious working class woman when she joined the woman suffrage movement in Vancouver.

For she had decided to emigrate. Evidently, she had not succeeded in changing her occupation.[32] Moreover, the WSPU was evolving in a way that denied democratic participation. Emmeline and Christabel Pankhurst, who had shared the direction of the WSPU with the Pethick

Lawrences, now summarily dismissed them and arrogated complete control to themselves. Christabel fled to Paris in 1912 to escape a police raid, and from there decided policy and directed the activities of the union. The new policy of violence was alienating many of its own members, who were beginning to have doubts about the integrity of the WSPU's position. Was it right to break the law by inciting violence and then claim the status of long-suffering martyr? Teresa Billington-Greig called this shifting position 'the double shuffle between revolution and injured innocence,' and was much troubled by it.[33] The time was opportune for those who wanted to escape such tactical problems or simply felt the urge to move on to new fields of action.

The suffrage movement was international in scope and the WSPU claimed to have suffrage groups in Canada. 'We are not a national association, but an Imperial one,' a member of a WSPU deputation told Canadian Prime Minister Robert Borden when he visited London. 'And these members in Canada have asked us to help them and to instruct them ... We have members who have emigrated there,' she concluded, more or less warning the prime minister that he must remedy the condition of women in Canada. British suffragists had taken on the enfranchisement of Canadian women as part of the burden of Empire, but were not always considered desirable immigrants. In 1913 the London office of the Canadian Pacific Railway Company on Cockspur Street boarded up its windows, presumably after they had been smashed by militants, and posted this sign, 'We are looking for settlers, not suffragettes.'[34] Helena by this time, was already safe and law-abiding in Canada. Many years later, as Alderman Gutteridge, she recalled that she emigrated with a group of suffragettes who intended to stay in Canada for four years and then return, an indication of missionary purpose.[35] She was thirty-two years old, and she had aspirations for advancement and an appetite for adventure.

On 8 September 1911, Helena sailed for Canada on the *Empress of Ireland*.[36] The morning was already quite warm when she boarded the boat train for Liverpool at Euston Station, for England was in the middle of an unusual heat wave, with temperatures reaching into the eighties by midday.[37] Late in the afternoon aboard the ship the call came: 'All for the shore! Any more for the shore?' The gangplank was drawn up and the great ocean liner of the Canadian Pacific Railway's fleet slid from the Mersey quayside, the Union Jack and the CPR's six-chequered red and white flag flying on the mastheads. Helena had embarked on her new life.

The crossing time was six days and the *Empress of Ireland* was a fast ship, capable of nineteen knots. She was beautifully, even luxuriously, outfitted, with a music room panelled with satin and tulipwood, upholstered in old rose taffeta, with a white-and-gold-walled dining saloon for first class passengers; the second class saloon was only somewhat less handsome. Even third class passengers enjoyed a spacious dining room for their bread and corned beef suppers, as well as a play area with sandbox for their children. The cholera-ridden steerage of the century before, testing the endurance and health of immigrants with sickness and every kind of privation, had passed into history.[38]

Helena, however, travelled second class and so would not be called an immigrant. That term was reserved for the third class passengers who were confined to the main deck and fo'c's'le head. On this particular voyage they numbered over nine hundred – Swedes and Norwegians en route to North and South Dakota and Minnesota, and ordinary working folk from Britain, ready to take whatever physical labour was offered them at Immigration Hall in Winnipeg. Helena's second class ticket placed her in a smaller number, 341 in all, with well-defined plans and destinations, including a large group of returning Canadians and another of British tourists. A good many of the women passengers were going out to Canada to be married or to join their husbands or other relatives. Among other women, teachers and governesses made up the highest number, followed by domestics, dressmakers, and nurses. A little party of French nuns was going to Quebec. Among the men, ministers and engineers were well represented, and sundry other trades and occupations, not excluding 'gentlemen.' A large party of touring Welsh singers was en route to the United States. On the purser's manifest, Helena gave her occupation as 'cutter'; she was one of four tailors above the main deck. She carried ten dollars in Canadian money. To the question asked of all passengers, 'Do you intend to permanently reside in Canada?' she answered, 'yes,' and was duly so recorded in the ship's manifest.[39] Her intention, apparently, was quite different.

The ship made good time despite the poor quality of coal she took on at Liverpool. But the great hulks of icebergs, the bleak, dark coast of Labrador, and the fog at Belle Isle off Newfoundland could not have been reassuring portents for a new life in Canada. Worse, as she was preparing to enter the Gulf of St. Lawrence, 190 kilometres northeast of Heath Point, Ile d'Anticosti, a strong southeast gale blew up with heavy rain and thunder and lightning.[40]

Three years later, on 29 May 1914, the ill-fated *Empress of Ireland* was rammed in a dense fog by the Norwegian collier *Storstad* near Rimouski at the mouth of the St. Lawrence and sank in fourteen minutes, taking with her 1,000 passengers and crew. However, in September 1911 the CPR *Empress* accomplished her voyage without mishap and landed safely at Rimouski for the usual customs inspection and medical examinations. Then the ship proceeded up the river to Quebec City, where the very landscape spoke of widening possibilities and breathed hope and promise. She arrived at Quebec on 14 September at eight in the evening, and the passengers disembarked the next morning. To the English travellers, the Canadian landscape was at once bolder, more daring than their own quiet countryside. True, the peaceful-looking little farms along the St. Lawrence seemed comfortingly familiar, but back home there was nothing like the glorious display of the sugar maples, crimson, gold, and scarlet against the sombre dark green background of the forest. When the train left the St. Lawrence and turned north and west along the Ottawa River and the shores of Lake Superior, they watched for the forest to end, but the terrain only became wilder – trees and still more trees, and rocks and lakes and still more lakes. Nobody really lived here, they reflected. But the train stopped just the same, every eight to sixteen kilometres. Eau Claire, that would be French, but fancy calling a town Hagar after one of Abraham's wives in the Bible. And Chelmsford, just a little clearing in the forest, nothing like Chelmsford at home; no big brick farmhouses here, with green fields and hedgerows. Kaministikwia, that would be Indian.[41] And so the reverie would continue, until finally the travellers became aware of a change as they emerged from the forests of northern Ontario into the open country of the West with its wide, grassy plains and rolling hills and fields of golden stubble. So those were grain elevators! 'Yes, ma'am,' the porter would reply, and point in a proprietary way at the Canada geese flying south in formation and at green-headed mallards startled into flight from prairie marshes as the train rushed by. The railway tracks stretched endlessly across the prairies, into the future it seemed, which turned out, eventually, to be the Rocky Mountains.

'Can we get through them?' the travellers wonder.[42] The answer, they discover, is yes, as the train ascends mountain walls and passes by roadways and tunnels devised by the imagination and labour of human mind and hand. Through Rogers Pass, from mountain heights themselves looking up at mountain pinnacles, the train descends to historic Craigellachie, where the travellers crowd to the windows to see where the rails from east and west had finally and triumphantly been joined. But there are still three hundred miles to go, through more and yet more mountain ranges until at last the train enters the canyon of the Fraser River. They had read about this river and seen pictures of its deep, black gorges in CPR booklets. They had read that the canyon was 'so deep and narrow in many places that the rays of the sun hardly enter it'; that high above its 'deep and ferocious waters' the railway was 'notched into the face of the cliffs.'[43] Impossible to imagine what the Fraser canyon would really be like when one's only river bank had been the Embankment of the Thames. For that matter, nothing they had read could have prepared them for this first experience of Canada: the exhilarating challenge of its vast distances, the majestic heights, the breadth and depth of its generous waters. When Helena stepped off the train at the Canadian Pacific Railway station in Vancouver, like her fellow travellers she was confirmed in her hopes and fears for the adventure that lay ahead by the land itself, and by the impossible journey across it, which nevertheless had been accomplished.

CHAPTER FOUR

Dealing with Tricky Dicky:
The Vote and Premier Mcbride

Habits of submission make both men and women servile-minded and every human being suffers in their highest nature by disregarding the sacredness of human liberties.
– Dr. Augustus Stowe-Gullen, 'Women as Citizens,' 1904

Helena arrived in Vancouver on 21 September 1911.[1] It was election day: the Liberal government under Sir Wilfrid Laurier was seeking to be returned on its policy of reciprocity, or free trade, with the United States. The following evening a huge crowd gathered outside the office of the Vancouver *Province* to learn the results as they came in by wireless from the East. When it was confirmed that Laurier and reciprocity had been defeated and Robert Borden's Conservatives elected, the crowd marched down the street behind a military band, all fear of annexation to the United States banished, the Union Jack borne proudly aloft at the head of the parade, deferentially accompanied by the Canadian Ensign. 'Rule Britannia, Britannia rules the waves,' they sang, and just as lustily, a Canadian patriotic song. Unfamiliar to newcomers, it still embraced the Empire with its refrain, 'God Save the King, and Heaven Bless the Maple Leaf Forever.' For these colonials, evidently, Britain was 'the mother country,' but strong national feeling and aspirations for independence stirred within them too. Homeward bound on the streetcars that night, these Canadians were vociferous, ebullient. 'It just shows Taft and his crowd on the other side that the people of Canada won't stand for any butting in,' said a man on the Robson car.[2] In this atmosphere of exuberant and sometimes pugnacious optimism, Helena began to establish a place for herself in Vancouver.

The Help Wanted Female columns in the newspapers were not, however, promising. Cutters were not in demand, nor even tailors or tailoresses, but as in London, domestic servants were. Vancouver's real estate boom was coming to an end and the city was beginning to slide into severe economic depression with high unemployment. However, Helena had a skill to offer, unlike those young immigrant women reported to be sitting in tears in their rooms at the YWCA, bewailing, with good reason, the long hours and poor wages of domestic service.[3]

Tears and despair were, in any case, not characteristic of Helena. Not finding work as a cutter, she went back to tailoring and was soon well established in the trade as a journeyman tailor, or 'jour.' We do not know where she first found work, but she must have worked as a tailor, not as a cutter, in order to qualify for membership in the Journeymen Tailors' Union of America, an international union affiliated with the American Federation of Labor (AFL). Cutters had their own organization. She joined the union in May 1913 and was soon vice president of local 178 and one of its delegates at the regular meetings of the Vancouver Trades and Labor Council (VTLC). Her photograph appeared in the union's journal, *The Tailor*, announcing her as a delegate to the 1914 BC Federation of Labour convention.[4] At this time she was living in downtown Vancouver, having moved from Bute Apartments on Pender Street to Egeria Rooms, 1153 Melville Street, a respectable address in the centre of the city.[5] The Labor Temple, the VTLC's fine new building, was nearby at 411 Dunsmuir Street, and over the next eight years it would be the locus of her political life.

When Helena first arrived in Vancouver, she immediately joined the Vancouver branch of the British Columbia Political Equality League (BCPEL). In September 1911 it was holding parlour meetings almost daily to acquaint women with their newly acquired civic voting rights and persuade them to register so that they could vote in the coming election. Under the provincial Municipalities Act, women property owners qualified equally with men to vote in municipal elections. Vancouver, however, had its own city charter independent of the Municipalities Act, and the charter reserved the civic franchise for propertied unmarried women and widows. However, the mayor himself was in favour of complete woman suffrage at all levels of government. Louis Denison (L.D.) Taylor headed a City Council that in 1910 unanimously approved giving married women with property the municipal franchise. Thus in 1911 the city charter was duly amended to accommodate the council decision.[6]

Helena also joined the Vancouver Local Council of Women. The National Council of Women of Canada (NCWC) was founded in 1893 under the tutelage of its first president, Lady Ishbel, whose husband, the Earl of Aberdeen, was then Governor General of Canada. Throughout Canada, the Local Councils, eclectically embracing women's groups of all kinds from needlework guilds to church auxiliaries, worked for social reform, especially in the interests of women and children. The National Council rather dragged its heels on the matter of woman suffrage: it did not espouse the claims of 'the New Woman' to individual human rights; nor did it have any intention of taking to the field in political combat. Nevertheless, the Victoria Local Council passed a resolution in favour of woman suffrage in 1908, the first to do so. Other councils soon ventured to do the same, and in 1910 the NCWC officially endorsed the cause.[7]

Property was still the main qualification for the franchise and in many parts of Canada women with property were entitled to vote in both municipal and school board elections, although not necessarily to hold office. Even here, married women were disqualified on the grounds that they would be influenced by their husbands, thus giving a married man two votes. Yet the rules could be changed by a seemingly quixotic sweep of the legislative pen. In British Columbia in 1906 the Municipal Elections Act was amended to give militia men the vote by expanding occupancy qualifications for householders to include people living in housekeeping rooms and boarding houses, and as a further condition requiring only payment of municipal taxes totalling two dollars. The amended Act thus inadvertently gave *unpropertied* women the municipal vote. The McBride government soon remedied this oversight: in 1908 it summarily took this privilege away from women by passing amending legislation restoring them to their former unenfranchised state. Moreover, no woman under any city charter or Municipal Act could run for alderman in civic elections: there would be no women allowed on municipal councils until the provincial franchise was won in 1917, although they could serve on school boards.[8] It was 1937 before a woman won a place on Vancouver's City Council, and that woman was Helena Gutteridge.

In the parliamentary arena, the fight for equal rights was similarly protracted, and the conservative opposition was stoutly championed by tradition and orthodoxy. Ever since the 1880s private members' bills had brought the question of the parliamentary franchise for women to the provincial legislatures. The support of suffragist MLAs (MPPs in Ontario) was never sufficient to overcome a deep and often irrational opposition to political rights for women among the majority of their colleagues. In 1893, opposing a woman suffrage bill in the Ontario legislature, John Dryden cited the Bible as the highest authority and declared, 'There is no word in it from beginning to end about woman suffrage.'[9] Two decades later, Ontario's Premier Whitney, opposing yet another private member's bill, held that in such matters a Divine Plan was evolving. 'We must not attempt to hurry it on,' he declared in 1911, implying that a quarter of a century was scarcely long enough for God to complete his political handiwork.[10] In British Columbia, eleven suffrage bills had been introduced by private members between 1884 and 1899; none had passed second reading. From British Columbia to the Maritimes, the response to these bills was usually amused, a little contemptuous, and patronizing to the point of insult. The *real* business of the legislature had to do with roads and railways, with local improvements and the regulation and financing of industry.[11]

During the first decade of the century, all across the country suffragists carried on the fight sporadically, regrouping and realigning themselves. By the time Helena arrived in Canada in 1911, they had succeeded in creating a national dialogue on woman suffrage, and she would soon discover that Canadians east and west were just as inventive as the British in finding reasons to oppose votes for women. Politics was too corrupt; women should not sully themselves with it. Women should inhabit as always 'that high pure atmosphere in which men have decreed for themselves that she shall live and move and have her being.'[12] Moreover, politics would cause dissension in the home if women became involved. Husband and family would be neglected. And anyway, women already exercised power indirectly, by 'womanly' persuasion, so they did not need the ballot. Henri Bourassa, the great Canadian nationalist and defender of French Canadian language rights, summed up the basic belief of anti-suffragists: participation in the affairs of government was incompatible with the role of wife and mother, which remained, *malgré tout,* the normal function of most women. He firmly quashed all female pretensions by citing in French the old English dictum: 'Le parlement peut tout faire sauf changer une femme en homme' (Parliament is capable of doing everything except to change a woman into a man).[13]

Prairie suffragist Nellie McClung scoffed at such arguments. 'Hardy perennials,' she called them, and energetically rooted them out. What male resistance boiled down to, she shrewdly observed, was the question of power. In her humorous yet incisive way, she summed up the male anti-suffrage stance with an anecdote from her childhood about a greedy old ox called Mike, who, full to bursting with water, put his two front feet over the water trough so that the other cattle should not be able to drink. Years later, petitioning for the franchise, Nellie listened while an MLA uttered an outright refusal to her suffrage delegation, and suddenly knew why his face, his whole bearing, seemed so familiar: 'And in my heart I cried out: "Mike – old friend Mike! Dead these many years! Your bones lie buried under the fertile soil of the Souris Valley, but your soul goes marching on! Mike, old friend, I see you again – both feet in the trough".'[14]

Despite such stubborn intransigence, interest in woman suffrage reawakened and by 1911 was gathering strength. Canadians had already welcomed suffragist lecturers from abroad – from Britain, Ethel Snowden of the non-militant National Union of Women's Suffrage Societies (NUWSS) and Emmeline Pankhurst, heading the militant Women's Social and Political Union (WSPU); from the United States, Susan Anthony, Julia Ward Howe, and Dr. Anna Howard Shaw. They came as missionaries: certainly the two British organizations had every intention of setting up branches in Canada. The Canadian Suffrage Association (CSA), centred in Toronto and led by Flora MacDonald Denison and Dr. Augusta Stowe-Gullen, was building on the pioneering work of Dr. Emily Howard Stowe and gaining credibility and stature with every petition and delegation to the Ontario premier. The Woman's Christian Temperance Union (WCTU), which a decade earlier had swung its support behind the suffrage movement, joined forces with the CSA. The International Council of Women, meeting in Toronto in 1909, heard Lady Aberdeen herself espouse woman suffrage, which, thus cloaked in respectability, was soon endorsed by the National Council and subsequently by Local Councils across the country. The Manitoba Grain Growers' Association declared its support of woman suffrage, and the weekly *Grain Growers' Guide* opened up its pages to suffrage news and debate. In Saskatchewan, the first Homemakers' Clubs were organized, introducing farm women to social and political issues, including woman suffrage, and teaching them how to make their voices heard as citizens. The women of British Columbia were spurred to fresh effort by the passage of woman's franchise legislation in the state of Washington in 1910.[15]

The Victoria Political Equality League was formed in 1910, and its first president was Maria Heathfield Grant, who had already been campaigning for the franchise for over twenty years in her work with the Victoria Woman's Christian Temperance Union. She was influenced in her commitment to the cause by American suffragist Susan Anthony, who gave a series of lectures in Victoria in 1871. A devout Methodist in the first half of her life, Maria Grant was a founding member of the Victoria WCTU, formed in 1883, and as supervisor of its Department of Petition, Legislation and Franchise, had many times in the last decades of the century spoken before audiences on the need for women to be given the vote so that they might use their influence to bring about 'the downfall of the strongholds of Satan' by banishing alcohol through prohibition. For Maria Grant, the 'power next to prayer' was the franchise.[16] In middle age she turned away from Methodism to embrace the secular philosophy of the Unity Church, based on the idea of positive thinking. Her new sense of self broadened her suffrage outlook: the franchise was more than just a way of achieving social reform; it was also a right due to women as citizens.

The Victoria PEL was composed largely of middle class women, in politics Conservative, Liberal, or non-political; in religion Protestant, except for Maria Grant. Her Baptist friend, Cecilia Spofford, also a temperance worker, was a leading member of the Victoria Local Council of Women, focusing on reform legislation for women and children. A young Englishwoman, Dorothy Davis, was another founding member of the Victoria PEL, having come out to British Columbia as a representative for the Colonial Intelligence League for Educated Women.[17] The women of the Victoria PEL discussed the current theoretical issues being advanced by the militant English feminists of the day. 'When are we going to fully realise that instead of being a condition imposed, motherhood should bear the royal insignia of freedom?' one PEL member asked in the course of her talk on 'Women as the Mothers of the Race.' 'Women must serve in the larger life of the world as well as in the home,' declared another at the same study club meeting.[18]

From 1912 to 1913 the Victoria PEL published its own monthly journal, edited by Maria Grant and Dorothy Davis. *The Champion* borrowed its cover from the Women's Freedom League journal, *The Vote*, but printed material from a number of English suffragist journals. It also reviewed literature of the English feminist movement, notably two pamphlets on the sexual exploitation of women: Frances Swiney's *The Responsibilities of Fatherhood* and Lady Sybil Smith's *Women and Evolution*. 'We heartily agree with her [Swiney],' wrote the reviewer, 'that "when man ceases to seek in woman only a body, the new life of the race will have begun".'[19]

The PEL displayed on occasion the purple, green, and white colours of the WSPU and may have thought of itself as affiliated with that organization. Certainly Emmeline Pethick Lawrence, visiting Vancouver Island in the fall of 1912 and being greeted at her hotel dinner table by the WSPU colours, referred the young woman responsible for this friendly reception to 'the W.S.P.U. organization in the nearest town.'[20]

On the other hand, Vancouver's suffrage organization had been sparked by a representative from the National Union of Women's Suffrage Societies, Mrs. Brignall. On 4 January 1911 she spoke to a large Vancouver crowd about the suffrage movement in England, pointing out the differences between the NUWSS, whose members, under the leadership of Millicent Garrett Fawcett, adhered to constitutional means of achieving their goal, and the WSPU, which was resorting to violence. Mrs. Brignall concluded by suggesting that Vancouver set up a local branch of the NUWSS. Her proposal had been turned into a formal resolution when 'someone suddenly remembered that there was no need to join the English union for ... Canada had a Women's Suffrage Union [the Canadian Suffrage Association] or society of her own.'[21]

In the event, Vancouver women formed their own Political Equality League at a founding meeting at the Theosophical Hall on 16 January 1911, under the guidance of Maria Grant. However, they listened to a paper on suffrage sent to them by Mrs. Brignall. In choosing a name for the society, they decided to avoid the word 'suffrage,' which, they thought, had gained a certain notoriety. They elected as president WCTU worker Florence Hall, wife of Methodist minister Reverend William Lashley Hall. Their reading assignment was John Stuart Mill's 'On the Subjection of Women.'[22]

In May a suffrage convention was held in Vancouver, with Mayor L.D. Taylor in the chair. In his opening remarks he gave all the credit for his own adherence to the suffrage cause to his mother, who had complained bitterly to her children of the injustice of being denied the vote. For had she not gone out to work to support her children? And had she not paid her property taxes like any male voter? Thus, with the sturdy blessing of 'L.D.,' a provincial body was formed with the intent of bringing women in rural areas under the suffragist banner. Maria Grant was elected president of the new British Columbia Political Equality League and Florence Hall provincial organizer, yielding her position as president of the Vancouver PEL to journalist and clubwoman Alice Ashworth Townley. Later in the year, Florence Hall spent some weeks organizing branches of the British Columbia PEL in the lower part of the province, between Kamloops and Mission. Dorothy Davis, the other paid organizer, spent three months travelling throughout the Okanagan and the Kootenays. At suffrage meetings throughout the province, from Revelstoke to Greenwood, from Penticton to Agassiz, resolutions were passed unanimously, calling on Premier Richard McBride to give the vote to women.[23]

Like the Victoria PEL, the Vancouver organization was much concerned with reform legislation for women and children. It drew much support from the Local Council of Women, in which Helena was an active member. The leaders of the Vancouver PEL were professional women who, like the new Maria Grant, held strong convictions on the vote as a human right: Mary McConkey, Mary Ellen Smith, and Susan Lane Clark, all former teachers; and journalists Alice Townley, Lily Laverock, and Helen Gregory MacGill, who would be Helena's colleague and also her adversary later in the suffrage campaign and in the minimum wage campaign to come. A founding member of the Vancouver Women's Press Club, she had earned her living as a journalist and had co-edited a suffragist newspaper while living for a time in the United States. As the first woman to earn a Bachelor of Music degree from the University of Toronto, she had had to suffer her exams being sent to England in 1886 to be read. When she attended postgraduate philosophy courses, her professors treated her with undisguised hostility. Helen MacGill had long ago acknowledged the claims of the Self and fought against many obstacles to fulfil them.[24]

For women in British Columbia, or in other provinces for that matter, gaining entry to the professions was not easy, and the law is a case in point. In 1911, around the time Helena arrived in Vancouver, Mabel French of New Westminster, who had successfully fought a legal battle in New Brunswick to become a member of the bar in that province, applied to practise law in British Columbia. Her application was opposed by the Law Society on the grounds that in British Columbia's Legal Professions Act the word 'person' did not apply to women.[25] The same obstacle had confronted her in New Brunswick, where she had successfully challenged the 'persons' ruling. It was nearly two decades before this social and legal anomaly, later challenged in the famous Persons Case by Judge Emily Murphy and her band of Alberta suffragists, was finally corrected, when the Privy Council ruled that the persons summoned by the Governor General of a colony to become senators could include women. Thus in 1929 women became persons under the British North America Act.[26] In the meantime, the constitutional obstacle confronting women like Mabel French had to be surmounted by special provincial legislation redefining persons to include women practising law. On 27 February 1912 the 'Act to Remove the Disability of Women so far as it Relates to the Study and Practice of the Law' was passed by the British Columbia legislature.[27] Mabel French was finally allowed to practise her profession. The privilege was not won without obdurate struggle, and the incident was an indication of the legal position of women in Canada.

At the beginning of the century, the legal position of women in British Columbia was pure ignominy. This was at least in part because the laws of the province were based on archaic English law deriving from the years when 'divers of Her Majesty's Subjects' had 'settled on certain wild and unoccupied Territories on the North-west Coast of *North America*, commonly known by the Designation of *New Caledonia.'*[28] When the mainland of British Columbia became a crown colony in 1858, Governor James Douglas ordained that its laws should be those that existed in England at the date of the proclamation of the colony, unless local circumstances made them inapplicable, and that these English laws would remain in force, 'subject to future legislation.' After the union of the mainland and Vancouver Island, this decree extended to the whole colony.[29] Thus, where the British Columbia legislature had subsequently passed no civil law, and the federal government had passed no criminal law, the people of the province were ruled by English (that is, British) law as it was in 1858, even though Britain might have moved on since then to more enlightened legislation.

As far as women and children were concerned, 'future legislation' did not occur, and the result was that women were legally helpless. A mother, explained an eighteenth-century commentator on English law, 'is entitled to no power, but only to reverence and respect.'[30] Helen MacGill made herself an expert on British Columbia law as it affected women and children, and published in 1913 a compendium of such laws, *Daughters, Wives and Mothers in British Columbia and Some Laws Regarding Them*.[31] Her little book revealed in bald legal terms the shocking subjection of women. They had no rights to custody and control of their children; these were vested in the husband and father, who, even if he deserted his family, maintained guardianship of the children with a claim on their earnings until the age of twenty-one and had, moreover, no financial responsibility towards them or their mother if she earned sufficient income. In the matter of property, the law was equally unjust. A husband could, if he chose, leave nothing in his will to his wife, but existing legislation provided for a mistress and an illegitimate family. He could even will away from the mother a child unborn at his death. A widow could claim no dower from out of any land sold during her husband's lifetime, and every other debt took priority over her dower. If a husband died intestate and there were no children, the estate was divided among the widow and the husband's relatives, no matter how distant. If such relatives did not exist, the widow shared the estate with the Crown. Moreover, a wife could not divorce her husband for adultery no matter how flagrantly promiscuous he was, but the husband could divorce his wife for a single act of adultery. Nor was the 'fallen wife' entitled to *see* her children; it was otherwise for the husband, who, with his vested rights in his children, could see them whenever he wished no matter what his sexual misdemeanours. Children obviously were in danger of faring badly under old English law, which continued in effect in the absence of much-needed amending provincial statutes. Surely it was wrong that a girl of twelve or a boy of fourteen could contract a legal marriage with the consent of the father or of the guardian appointed by him. Yet in the absence of British Columbia statute to the contrary, such marriages were permissible under obsolete English law.

British Columbia suffragists saw the franchise as a means of gaining more enlightened laws for women and children, and set themselves the task of overcoming the resistance of the McBride government to woman suffrage. Helen MacGill wrote:

> Whenever sufficient funds could be raised, delegations went to the Government at Victoria. They slept or talked six and seven in two bed staterooms. They took babies and children when they could not be left, and one lady brought her dog because there was no one at home to feed it. Mrs. Spofford and Mrs. Gordon Grant gathered up the women from Victoria and environs. They planned their speeches and drilled their speakers. The only occasion they ran over their allotted time was when they were induced to

let some gentlemen join them, and the women had no means of putting on the brakes.[32]

When in 1911 Premier Richard McBride agreed to be interviewed by one such delegation, he suggested that the women first send letters to members of the legislature setting forth their case. They did so, and Florence Hall and Lily Laverock, chosen to meet with him, watched from the gallery of the legislature while the MLAs opened their letters. Mrs. Hall reported that most read them carefully; a few read them and put them in the wastepaper basket; but one tore his letter into bits, dropped it on the floor and turned his back on the watching women.[33] The premier, always urbane and charming, listened to the delegates with apparent sympathy. He was 'Glad-hand Dick' to the populace, but they also said of him that 'no man was as wise as Dick McBride looked.' Now, serious and grave of mien, in his wisdom he refused these women petitioners the vote. The suffragists called him 'Tricky Dicky.'[34]

McBride and his colleagues represented a large constituency that resisted all argument for woman suffrage, no matter how rational. A *Province* editorial reflected their general stance – inconsistent, illogical, obtuse. The editorial, while approving of women ratepayers having the municipal vote, at the same time maintained that a woman taxpayer should not be entitled to the parliamentary vote, dismissing the women's demands as a mere whim: 'The cry raised here for woman suffrage is, of course, an echo of the hysterical scream which for the past two years has pierced the ears of the people of Great Britain.' In any case, the editorial continued, the majority of women did not want the vote, and as soon as British women ceased their 'clamour,' suffrage would cease to be an issue in Canada and people would no longer 'be disturbed in this outlying portion of the Empire.' It concluded with the solemn warning that the 'experiment' of extending the franchise to women 'may look harmless enough, but history teaches that changes lightly made have from a ripple of apparent harmlessness spread with far-reaching consequences.'[35] Richard McBride was beloved of the populace for bringing prosperity and confidence to the province in the form of new railway construction, new capital investment and better financial terms from Ottawa. In the election of March 1912, the voters swept him back into office with a huge majority and a few months later were confirmed in their collective choice by King George himself, who bestowed on him the title of Knight Commander of St. Michael and St. George. Unfortunately, this knighthood did not spur Sir Richard on to gallant redress of injustice in the form of better terms for women. In the fall of 1912, the BCPEL embarked on a campaign to overcome the intransigence of Sir Richard and the anti-suffrage MLAs. The plan was to present a petition to the legislature to satisfy the doubt, so often raised, that the women of British Columbia really did want the vote. 'Taxation without Representation is Tyranny,' the petition began, and went on to claim women's right and privilege, as citizens, to the franchise. Unfortunately, at the same time it struck at the rights of other disenfranchised minorities, urging an 'Immediate Increase in the British-born Electorate' to counteract the great number of non-British or 'foreign' immigrants 'endangering through the vote, the Ideals and Standards, political and social, which have made our Empire what it is today.' More than ten thousand women signed the petition.[36]

The Socialists in the legislature supported woman suffrage: James Hawthornthwaite introduced bills to extend the franchise to women in 1906 and 1909, neither of which passed second reading. Now in 1913 Socialist MLA John Place was going to introduce another such private member's bill, and this on 14 February, the very day the BCPEL deputation was to present its petition. Dorothy Davis wrote in some alarm to Sir Richard to assure him that the suffragists had not asked Mr. Place to introduce a franchise bill and to inform him that, wishing to have a government measure passed, they had requested Place to withhold his bill, which he had agreed to do. She further instructed the premier that the Socialists doubtless saw an opportunity to make political capital by supporting the suffragists, and warned him that his government would lose favour if it refused women the vote. She concluded coyly that they looked upon his choice of date for the meeting, Valentine's Day, as a happy omen.[37]

On that day, at five in the afternoon, seventy-two women from various parts of the province assembled at the Parliament Buildings and were ushered into the Executive Chamber, where they were met by the premier and members of the cabinet. As president of the BCPEL, Maria Grant spoke first, urging the legislators to remove 'the stigma of inferiority' from 'the Women of the Race.' Then she succinctly announced the reasons they wanted the vote. The first was to 'obtain recognition as human beings, with full and responsible citizenship.' After that they wanted the 'Woman's point of view ... represented in the affairs of the Nation.' And finally they wanted 'to safeguard the interests of Women and Children in Social and Industrial Life.' With passion and eloquence she ended her address by invoking Justice, Honour, and Liberty. Janet Kemp, convenor of the BCPEL legislative committee, then presented the petitions containing the ten thousand names. Claiming woman's birthright of full citizenship, she did not scruple to put the rights of others in jeopardy when she warned of the 'power to be placed in the hands of the thousands of aliens who will undoubtedly flock to our shores upon the opening of the Panama Canal,' a stock suffragist argument, its racism in those days tacitly approved. Dorothy Davis reiterated the claim for full citizenship and assured the premier that their organizations would not resort to militancy.[38]

But Valentine's Day meant nothing to Sir Richard and his cabinet when the sharing of male power was in question. A week later he gave his reply and it was 'no.' Extending the franchise to women was not 'in the public interest.'[39] However, they could still get an individual member to introduce a bill, he reminded them. The next day John Place did just that. His measure was, of course, defeated, 23 to 9. But woman suffrage was no longer a matter for tolerant amusement. The Honourable A.E. McPhillips, both feet in the trough, spoke for an hour in opposition to the bill. He 'yielded to no man in his love and regard for women'; however, he warned that they were a dangerous element in society, as the events of the French Revolution made clear. For, disgracefully, they had marched with the men through the streets and stood at the barricades. Those women were responsible for the increase in infidelity, for the growth of atheism and lawlessness; in short for the breakdown of the social order. 'All idea of morality and of propriety had been lost,' he declared.[40]

Early in 1913, the Vancouver PEL split off from the British Columbia parent body to form an independent group, the Pioneer Political Equality League (PPEL). We do not know whether they were more or less militant than the Victoria women, or whether they read the same kind of feminist pamphlets. The split may have had nothing to do with beliefs but rather with power. Over half the delegates at the BCPEL convention of 1912 were from Vancouver, and it is possible that the Vancouver members wanted to belong to an organization centred in Vancouver and with a Vancouver president.[41]

Helena was a member of the newly constituted PPEL and was soon recognized for her energy and commitment to the Cause. But she was not quite like the others in the nature of her commitment. Enthusiastic as she was, she soon became dissatisfied with the league for the way its activities excluded working women. Most of its proselytizing was done at afternoon parlour meetings, where a small group of middle class housewives would gather to hear a speaker and then have afternoon tea. Their husbands were professional and business men who provided their wives with homes to look after, likely with the help of a domestic servant. Unlike women wage workers such as waitresses, dressmakers, sales clerks, and laundry employees, these middle class women had afternoons free for club work.[42]

Helena was accustomed to quite another style of work in London, where she had gone to all parts of the city to speak on street corners, often in the evening. She resolved to attempt the same strategy in Vancouver, and scarcely more than a year after her arrival, took the initiative in setting up within the PPEL an Evening Work Committee, with headquarters in the Labor Temple in the heart of downtown Vancouver.[43] In so doing she made known her criticism of the way the league operated and of the prevailing philosophy of the members. They thought in social-work terms of helping the less fortunate through legislation or charity, working on their behalf but regarding such people as more or less passive recipients of reform. Helena, as a working class woman, believed that women wage workers should be educated to take matters into their own hands to obtain better economic conditions. In London in 1912, Sylvia Pankhurst, rejecting the political direction and authoritarian methods of her mother and sister, which largely ignored women wage workers, eloquently declared the need for organizing them, believing that 'the creation of a woman's movement in that great abyss of poverty would be a call and a rallying cry to the rise of similar movements in all parts of the country.'[44] It was no accident that Helena's position on educating and organizing working class women was essentially the same as Sylvia's. In her first year away from London, Helena would almost certainly have been in touch with her suffragette friends and would have heard reports of the East End campaign. Then, too, it is possible that she knew Sylvia personally as a co-worker in suffragist demonstrations, or at least was directly influenced by her during the London years. Helena's own dedication to the welfare of working women would thus have been reinforced by Sylvia's staunch example. All of the Pankhurst women, with their iron wills and capacity for steely self-denial, were a powerful and lasting influence on Helena. One of her prized possessions was a photograph of Sylvia, or of Mrs. Pankhurst, it is not known which; even in old age that photograph still hung on the wall of her Barclay Street housekeeping room.[45]

Helena decided that she must make the voice of labour heard in the suffrage debate, and in a front-page story in the *World*, announced her plans for organizing an Evening Work Committee within the PPEL. Since the McBride government had rejected the appeal of the BCPEL, the new committee would launch its own campaign and set itself the goal of raising five thousand dollars for the 'purpose of conducting an agitation.'[46] The Evening Work Committee was also going to start a 'votes for women propaganda paper,' *The Pioneer Woman*, which would deal with local events as well as the 'universal aspect' of the woman suffrage movement. It would contain articles on the 'political, industrial, and economic position of women,' on the education of children, on women's sports. There would also be a column for anti-suffragists.[47] *The Pioneer Woman* would be published fortnightly, the first issue announced for 27 March 1913 at five cents a copy. Helena envisioned a lively paper addressing the practical interests and needs of ordinary women, keeping them abreast of events in the woman suffrage movement and educating them in its theoretical aspects. The paper did come out as planned, but it was too ambitious and soon died.[48] No copies of *The Pioneer Woman* are extant, but it was far different, in conception at least, from *The Champion*, the monthly publication of the BCPEL, which modelled itself on English suffragist papers, narrowly dedicated to one subject, the vote.

Helena also attempted street-corner meetings. One such meeting in the Grandview neighbourhood in the eastern part of the city aroused the kind of noisy confrontation that brings to mind the WSPU procession meetings on London street corners. The speaker, who might well have been Helena, mounted the soap box platform, but could not make herself heard for the uproar created by a crowd of men and boys equipped with every kind of noisemaker, including tin cans and metal roofing. Dust rose in clouds as they jostled one another in the unpaved street. They pressed forward against the soap box, which wobbled so alarmingly that the speaker fell from it. The suffragettes then went to have ice cream in a nearby restaurant, where they discussed plans for future meetings.[49] Although the newspaper account does not specifically identify the suffrage group, referring only to the 'Grandview suffragettes,' they could only have belonged to members of Helena's Evening Work Committee from the Grandview branch of the PPEL, ready to break away with Helena and adopt more aggressive strategies. Not many suffragist clubwomen were willing to violate the proprieties and suffer possible humiliation by taking their message into the street.

At the annual meeting of the PPEL in May 1913, Helena was able to give a favourable report of the activities of its Evening Work Committee. Between January and May, they had held public meetings every Wednesday evening in the Labor Temple, with an average attendance of well over a hundred, and planned now to take these meetings to every part of the city. The report was enthusiastically received and Helena's evening work declared to be the most important in the league.[50] As a further expression of confidence, Helena was elected second vice president, next in the executive hierarchy to Mary McConkey, a doctor's wife, a member of the Vancouver University Women's Club, and an establishment Liberal and Presbyterian.[51] Helena could fairly consider that she had, politically speaking, arrived. For the rest of the summer she maintained this high profile as one of the league's principal speakers, sharing the platform on different occasions with Mary McConkey and Mary Ellen Smith, wife of former Liberal MP Ralph Smith, later elected to the British Columbia legislature.[52] But for all the success of her style of campaigning, Helena did not gain the social approval of league

members. She was too unconventional, too unorthodox in her attitudes and strategies. The other clubwomen were interested in the
plight of working women too, but Helena was herself a worker, the only
one among the leadership. Mary Ellen Smith was the daughter of a
British coal miner and had married a coal miner, but she had been a
schoolteacher and her husband, Ralph Smith, had long since ceased to
be a miner.[53] Even socialist Mary Norton, formerly a stenographer, did
not present herself as working class or socialist. Her husband operated
a small hand-logging business, and for his sake she wore her socialism
discreetly.[54]

Mary Norton recalled that Helena was 'frowned on a bit when she
started evening classes or sidewalk gatherings.' Of all the suffragists
Helena was the one with whom Mary was most in sympathy, 'even
though she [Helena] was Conservative.' Over half a century later, Mary
was still feeling guilty for once having been disloyal to her friend,
remembering a tea she had held for the PPEL. She would have liked to
invite Helena, but decided not to because she knew other members were
critical of her. 'I often wondered what kind of a friend she thought I was
but it was to befriend her that I thought she'd be happier not to [be
invited].' Later in the interview she again felt impelled to justify her disloyalty to Helena, who was her 'favourite': 'I thought they [members of
the PPEL] might show some of their disfavour for anybody who was holding night meetings or speaking on the street.'[55]

Helena may indeed have been politically a Conservative when she first
arrived in Vancouver. After all, Emmeline and Christabel Pankhurst,
although their declared policy was to pursue votes for women without
seeking the aid of any political party, nevertheless pinned their hopes
on the Conservatives. They were hostile to the British Labour Party's
Ramsay MacDonald, who viewed the militant suffragists as 'harri-
dans' likely to cost him votes. As for Asquith's Liberal government, the
Pankhursts accused them of outright betrayal.[56] If Mary Norton remembered correctly, Helena was not a socialist at first. 'We held our socialist meetings in that Labor Temple too,' Mary recalled, 'and she once said
to me, "Mrs. Norton, I wish those socialists would keep out of my
meeting." They wanted to talk socialism and all she wanted was suffragist ... I thought, well, until we get the socialist platform we're not
going to get very far with the suffrage.'[57]

Helena soon found she needed her own suffrage organization, so different were her aims and methods of work from those of the PPEL. At their
July meeting, the Evening Work Committee decided to break away and
form a separate organization, the BC Woman's Suffrage League. The
Mount Pleasant and Grandview branches of the PPEL came over to the
new league, encouraging Helena's hope of building a provincewide net-

work of suffrage groups. Tensions within the two main Political Equality Leagues produced other splits. Some Conservative women, shunning loud political confrontation, had already broken away to form the BC Equal Franchise Association, headed by Alice Townley. Helen MacGill, even though confrontational since her earliest years, elected to join them. Dorothy Davis in Victoria set up the Women's Freedom Union, the 'Go-Aheads,' proposing a limited franchise for women.[58] Recalling the proliferation of new suffragist groups, Helen MacGill quipped, 'Like other pests, they grew by segmentation.'[59] She acknowledged that the disagreements were always about strategy and method; the goal was never in question. After Helena's breakaway, the response of the women remaining loyal to the PPEL was to recommend that all suffrage societies in British Columbia unite their efforts by forming a central parliamentary committee.[60]

With Helena as president, the BC Woman's Suffrage League continued the regular Wednesday evening public meetings in the Labor Temple and, following the example of the WSPU, instituted 'at homes' there every Tuesday afternoon. The main thrust of the new organization was to ally itself with labour, and this without a moment's delay. Within a week Helena had written the Vancouver Trades and Labor Council to arrange for a suffrage deputation to request their participation in the suffrage campaign she had originally planned for the Evening Work Committee.[61] As a delegate from the Tailors' Industrial Union, formerly the Journeymen Tailors, she knew the VTLC as a constituency friendly to her cause; knew also that the BC Federation of Labour had endorsed woman suffrage in January 1912.[62] Thus Helena's suffrage work took on a new orientation, geared towards workers. In addition to her clubwoman colleagues, she was now meeting women in the Tailors' Union who understood the meaning of working class solidarity – women like Molly Dolk, on the executive committee of the union when Helena was elected president in 1914 and with whom she would have a long association in the coming years.[63] Solidarity meant, for one thing, not being a scab; that is, not crossing a picket line, and Helena could read in *The Tailor* what an American woman worker thought about that loathsome enemy, the scab:

'Scab!' There is no word in the English language so fraught with hatred as this one word ... Girls cry it with tears of rage in their eyes and every primitive instinct aroused ... Men cry it with all the unleashed passion of their natures urging them to wage cave warfare.

If you ask them just what is a 'scab,' you will always get an answer like this: 'a low-down fink who is taking our jobs!' 'A gutter bum that's scabbing on the job and sucking in with the boss.'[64]

The trade union milieu also advanced Helena's political education enormously and gave a new dimension to her suffrage work. She was working with men and women whose contending socialist ideologies generated a strong radical influence in the Canadian socialist movement. The revolutionary Socialist Party of Canada (SPC) dedicated itself to the Marxist education of the working class rather than to the struggle for reforms, mere 'palliatives,' it believed, serving only to keep moribund capitalism alive a little longer. The SPC held to a rigid 'impossiblism'; that is, the conviction that capitalism could not be reformed and that it was useless to try. According to William (Bill) Pritchard, editor of the SPC's *Western Clarion*, woman suffrage was just such a palliative, along with 'clean blankets for hoboes.'[65] On the futility of unions, an earlier editor of the *Western Clarion*, E.T. Kingsley, could only shake his head and fervently declare, 'When I find a great mass of workers asking a handful of masters for favours, I get right down on my marrow-bones and pray they won't get 'em.' Lawyer Wallis Lefeaux was similarly doctrinaire. Helena at first belonged also to the Socialist Party of Canada, but she could not have been with them for long because she was no impossiblist. To her woman suffrage was no palliative, but a source of power: the vote would advance the economic and social interests of women and allow them to rise in the world. Indeed, Helena's whole career demonstrates a belief in the value of reform legislation. Similarly, most members of the SPC, including J.W. Wilkinson, Jack Kavanagh, and Bill Pritchard, all Helena's colleagues over the years, managed to accommodate socialist theory alongside practical union work in the VTLC. Two of Helena's closest colleagues in the VTLC, J.H. McVety, president of the VTLC for most of the decade, and R. Parmeter (Parm) Pettipiece, editor of the *British Columbia Federationist*, had recently left the revolutionary SPC but were still Marxists, albeit with more moderate views.[66]

The Social Democratic Party, which under Ernest Burns split off from the SPC in 1907, was reform-oriented and took a less uncompromising though still Marxist approach to the strategies for bringing about the death of capitalism. Universal adult suffrage was one of the planks in its reform platform, but under the influence of women members it also supported the woman suffrage campaign.[67] Both parties sought to be the political voice of labour, and their leaders competed for control of the VTLC and the BC Federation of Labour, members switching socialist allegiances from time to time as their individual ideologies evolved. In the union movement Helena came to know and work with members of both parties, and through them learned about the doctrinal intricacies of rival socialisms.

The SPC preached 'scientific' socialism – the pure doctrine of Marx and Engels, according to which capitalism would disintegrate under the stress of its own profound malaise, and the enlightened workers, defending their rights and freedoms, would rise up and take over the means of production in a revolution that would bring about the dictatorship of the proletariat and the gradual withering away of the state. 'Scientific' socialists held in contempt the 'utopian' views of socialists who thought that the transition from capitalism to socialism could be achieved by evolution, not revolution. The scientifics had a word for this kind of thinking – 'bourgeois' – and scorned the Social Democrats as little better than 'bourgeois liberals.' Both groups regarded themselves as socialists. We can do no better than to award the term 'socialist' to all of Helena's friends and colleagues who so passionately invoked Marx and Engels on behalf of the workers, that they might one day take control of the means of production and create a classless society where 'all the springs of co-operative wealth flow more abundantly ...' Kingsley and Kavanagh, Pritchard and Pettipiece and McVety – they all looked to that day. For, as Karl Marx foretold, 'Only then can ... society inscribe on its banners: from each according to his ability, to each according to his needs!'[68]

Probably Helena switched to the Social Democratic Party, although no documentary evidence has turned up as yet to prove that she belonged to the SDP. Judging from her rhetoric in this decade and from her long work history with leading socialists in the VTLC, we may safely say, however, that she was, generically speaking, a socialist, and believed that she and her comrades had, as Marx and Engels promised, 'a world to win.'

Helena's new awareness of labour issues influenced her approach to suffrage work. She arranged with Parm Pettipiece to give her a weekly page on woman suffrage, for with the demise of her own fledgling newspaper she had no way of making the voice of her new organization heard. In her first column she announced the larger political and economic dimensions of her BC Woman's Suffrage League:

We propose to deal with not only Votes for Women in these columns, but all matters connected with the interests of Women, particularly with those things that affect the woman out in the labor market.

Economic necessity has forced women out into the industrial world, and being a woman, and politically helpless, she is the bottom dog, her interests are not considered, her point of view not represented.[69]

Helen MacGill, Mary Ellen Smith, and Florence Hall were also convinced that wages, hours, and conditions of work were key elements in the oppression of women. They were not as concerned as Helena, however, about raising the political awareness of the working woman or eliminating her exploitation. Helena wrote: 'The need of political power for the working woman is greater than that of any other class, and only when she is able to influence industrial legislation will she cease to be exploited and forced into starvation or shame.'[70]

In November and December 1913 she conducted her campaign to bring the unions on side. Premier McBride had stated that woman suffrage 'would not be in the public interest.' Very well; she would engage the help of a section of the public not yet heard from. Representatives from the BC Woman's Suffrage League (BCWSL) attended union meetings to obtain membership endorsement of a resolution to extend the franchise to women at the next session of the legislature.[71] The plasterers, the steam engineers, the pattern makers, the painters and decorators all gave their support. So did the longshoremen and the bricklayers, the masons and garment workers, the sheet metal workers and carpenters and joiners – sixteen unions in all.[72] The BCWSL also blitzed the downtown area with public meetings, seven in less than a month. The rival PPEL sent speakers, for Helena always reached out for the broadest possible support.

'The woman's movement and the labour movement are the expressions of a great revolutionary wave that is passing over the whole world,' declared the Suffrage League's [read Helena's] report on the campaign. Then, quoting a British Labour MP and representative of the British Miners' Federation, 'The woman and the worker stand side by side.'[73] Her declaration of solidarity was heartfelt: she had been one of the speakers at a protest rally held by the Miners' Liberation League in support of Vancouver Island coal miners imprisoned for their part in the year-long strike.[74] When Attorney General Bowser dispatched a thousand militiamen and regular troops to subdue the mutinous population of the coal towns, the fighting spirit of workers throughout British Columbia was roused. Feelings ran high and at least one suffragist agreed with Helena in identifying the miners' cause with their own. When socialists took over a public meeting sponsored by the Conservatives, drowned out the national anthem with 'We'll Keep the Red Flag Flying Here,' and demanded the release of the imprisoned miners, Mrs. E. Crossfield, a founding member of the Vancouver PEL, 'moved amid the turmoil distributing literature in the suffrage cause.'[75] In the fall of 1913, a mere two years after she arrived here, Helena was riding a wave of working class protest that made her, like the enterprising Mrs. Crossfield, find common cause with the miners' wives who sang so lustily, 'Hooray, hooray, we'll drive the scabs away.'[76]

On her suffrage page Helena offered differing political views of the woman question. The orthodox socialist view was expressed in a review of Helen Keller's *Out of the Dark*, an account of the blind woman's heroic efforts to discover socialism through her fingers and of her passionate belief in the coming of the future commonwealth when '"the gyves shall be struck from the wrists of Labor, and the pulse of production shall be strong with joy".' 'As might be expected,' the review concludes, 'she [Helen Keller] is a keen suffragist, but she feels that the social revolution must precede the full emancipation of women – as of men.'[77]

However, excerpts from a paper given by an unnamed feminist/ socialist to a meeting of the Social Democratic Party offered a provocative view of women's emancipation that was not according to Marx. Under the headline 'Women and Socialism,' the unsigned article began disarmingly enough:

> On being asked to speak on the relation to socialism of the feminist movement I was reminded of an Irishman named Patrick O'Brian who, on being asked if he was any relation to Mike O'Brien [sic], answered that he was a distant relation, he being his mother's first child while Mike was her thirteenth. Just so 'distantly' is the question of the women's emancipation related to the question of the emancipation of the working class.[78]

Then the writer changed direction: once socialism has been achieved and the workers lose their chains, will women also become free and equal citizens? Not at all, the writer remonstrated, for in addition to the class struggle, a sex struggle was being waged in which women were fighting to win financial independence. Contrary to the views of some socialists, a woman had to be free to earn her own living, for economic dependence on the husband was psychologically damaging for both, but especially for the woman: 'The chains that bind are the chains of thought, and so soon as one thinks in freedom, so soon may one unite with others to achieve the widest liberty.'[79]

Helena's socialist friends in the BC Woman's Suffrage League were a spirited, articulate group in their early thirties. Susan Lane Clark, president of the Mount Pleasant branch, had been an American suffragist, tutored by Susan Anthony herself. Born in San Francisco, a schoolteacher by profession, Susie, as she was called, immigrated to Canada in 1907 with her printer husband, James Allan Clark, bringing with her the same lifelong commitment to the suffrage movement that Helena brought from England. An outspoken woman who knew nothing about feminine charm, she did not tack with the wind but sailed straight ahead, daring the storm.[80] Just as outspoken was another American immigrant, Evelyn LeSueur. A well-educated woman with a knowledge of the law and a flair for language, she was one of four women in the newly created Woman's Division of the Vancouver Police Force in 1919. She is remembered in the city's police history for having stood up to the chief of police when he fired her for allegedly acting as a spy for women's organizations and for having unorthodox religious beliefs. She subsequently worked as a probation officer with the Family Court, presided over by Judge Helen MacGill.[81] Ontario journalist Bertha Merrill had been a member of the Socialist Party of Canada from around 1903 to 1907, and had worked for the *Western Clarion* when it was edited by Parm Pettipiece. She married SPC comrade Ernest Burns, and with him founded the Social Democratic Party of Canada in 1907. From the farming community of Dewdney, where they lived, she contributed a regular column of pithy comment, 'The Sauce Box,' to the Woman Suffrage Page. Bertha Burns died in June 1917 at the age of fifty-one.[82]

Helena worked with other friends in the BC Woman's Suffrage League who did not demonstrate socialist sympathies, educated women of assured social status. Lily Laverock, a McGill honours graduate, had given up philosophy for journalism and worked for the Vancouver *Daily News-Advertiser* before launching the first woman's paper in British Columbia in 1911. In line with its policy of furthering 'the common interests of the women of British Columbia,' *The Chronicle* offered such solid fare as 'Russian Women and Higher Education,' a lecture on radium with a photograph of Madame Curie at her laboratory bench, and an account of a woman climber's experience in the Himalayas.[83] The newspaper's society page, however, which included obligatory guest lists describing what each woman wore at the latest ball or wedding, ventured into no new journalistic territory. *The Chronicle* soon folded and Lily Laverock found a more immediate way of furthering the interests of British Columbia women: she left the Pioneer Political Equality League for Helena's suffrage league, joining its Mount Pleasant branch under the leadership of Susie Clark. Lily later became a concert impresario, the local manager for the International Concert Series.[84] She was one of Helena's oldest friends; in retirement they were still going to concerts together, Lily supplying the tickets.

Elizabeth Arnett came from an upper class English family, with brothers all engaged in some way in the civilizing mission of Empire. One of them had been deputy governor of West Africa, another was in the service of the Hudson's Bay Company. Elizabeth came to Vancouver to live around 1911, about the same time as Helena, and stayed until 1918. Without a thought for the family silver teapot and milk jug going back to the time of William IV, she left the Queen Anne family home in Great Bookham, Surrey, surrounded by domesticated oaks and elms, to live in the raw, new residential Vancouver suburb of Mount Pleasant, scarcely a clearing in the untamed forest.[85] She had belonged to the National Union of Women Suffragists in England, and in Vancouver, as secretary of the Mount Pleasant branch of the BC Woman's Suffrage League, continued to be an ardent worker for the franchise.[86] Well educated and well travelled, she brought with her all the assurance and sense of noblesse oblige that goes with privilege and inherited wealth.

At this time, Helena became friends with yet another educated, articulate woman – Ida Douglas-Fearn, a Scotswoman shipwrecked, one might say, on the rocky shores of love. She and her family were to influence profoundly the course of Helena's life. Born Elizabeth Ida Bramwell in 1858 in Perth, Scotland, she was the daughter of James Paton Bramwell, respected Scottish physician, chief consulting surgeon at the Perth Royal Infirmary, and an elder in the Free Church of Scotland.[87] Fun-loving Elizabeth Ida rebelled against her Presbyterian father, for 'he was always preaching and praying at us and reading sermons at us,' and he called her 'proud, naughty, imperious, self-willed, wicked Ida.'[88] She travelled to Germany, became a teacher of German, and eventually converted to Catholicism. One of her brothers, John Milne Bramwell, was the Yorkshire physician who astonished the medical world with his work in clinical hypnotism.[89] Following the medical example of her father and brother, Ida trained as a nurse, probably at Queen Victoria Hospital in Southampton, England.[90] Then during General Charles Gordon's campaign in the Egyptian Sudan, she was put in charge of the Grenadier Guards Hospital in London: Sister Bramwell, now Elizabeth, of Her Majesty's Nursing Staff, wearing the Queen's Uniform – a grey dress, white apron and cap, and bright red cape. Here she fell in love with one of her patients, a soldier of the Grenadier Guards, part of the expeditionary force that fought in the Sudan after the fall of Khartoum.[91] She had watched the Guards leave for the Sudan and had been moved to write a poem inveighing against war, grieving that any mother should bear a son, 'For this, that the burning Egyptian sands / Should drink his young blood like rain.'[92]

Samuel Fearn had been a farm labourer serving in the local militia, still living with his parents on their Derbyshire farm, when a visiting recruiting officer enlisted him in the Guards for a term of twelve years. At age twenty-three, five feet, seven inches tall and weighing 145 pounds, he was a little older than the average Guard, and a little shorter and stockier. He had a 'fresh complexion' and, standing guard at Windsor Castle in his scarlet coat and bearskin cap with white plume, cut a fine figure just the same. While stationed there he spent four days in hospital in December and Elizabeth may have met him at this time. Six weeks later he left for the Sudan. He spent nine months with the Third Battalion in Egypt and Cyprus, and then was invalided home to London. He had not been wounded in battle but seems to have succumbed to the rigours of soldiering under the hostile conditions of the Middle East, or, as Elizabeth wrote, 'in the burning breath / of a pestilential shore.' He spent most of the next nine months in hospital, suffering from a succession of ailments – mumps, tonsillitis, dyspepsia, diarrhea, and finally ulcers.

Samuel Fearn was declared unfit for further service and discharged on 15 June 1886 with an Egyptian medal, commended for 'very good and temperate conduct.'[93] The next day, in the chapel of St. Edward's Church in London, he and Elizabeth Ida Bramwell were married in a Catholic ceremony by special licence, for he was Church of England. She was twenty-eight years old; he was twenty-five.[94] Elizabeth immediately became pregnant, and she and Samuel went to live in Tutbury, a village in Staffordshire near her brother John and not far from the Fearn family in Derbyshire.[95] Soon after, with their infant son Alastair, they embarked for Canada, settling first in Victoria. They had two more children, Douglas and Leslie.[96] The marriage failed, for Elizabeth and Samuel were ill matched. He was 'quite illiterate' and no companion for the strong-minded Elizabeth with her sharp intellect and educated ways. He drank to excess. She suffered from severe depression, 'cerebral anemia' and 'neurasthenia,' she called it.[97] In 1892, after the death of her father, she went home to Scotland with her three children, and obtained a diploma in obstetrics in Edinburgh. While there, five-year-old Alastair died from diphtheria. 'O sunken freight of hope and love,' she inscribed on his tombstone.[98] Soon after her return to Victoria, Samuel and Ida, as she now called herself, separated, and with her two children she made her way by paddle steamer up the Fraser to Fort Langley.[99] She was pregnant, and her fourth child, Oliver, was born in Vancouver in 1893. She pre-empted land in Langley and became the local midwife, going off at all hours in her horse and trap to answer the call of women in labour.[100] Of her struggle for physical and emotional survival she wrote: 'And a dream comes to her ... Always she stands alone upon a rock, a little rock in the midst of a wide sea, and it raging. She will not be clinging, for there will be nothing to cling to, only the little flat rock, and she standing on it.'[101]

By the time Ida entered Helena's life, those years of homesteading were behind her, and at age fifty-five she was living with her grown children in New Westminster. She was gaining a reputation as a witty speaker, sharing the suffrage platform with Helena and Mary Norton.[102] She changed her surname to Douglas-Fearn, although the Bramwells, originally from the north of England, had no clan connection and her mother's family belonged to Clan Fraser.[103] We do not know why she chose to identify herself with Clan Douglas. She may have wished to distance herself from the Derbyshire Fearns and also from the Bramwells, who, she says in her memoir, had left her and her children 'disowned and friendless.'

Ida Douglas-Fearn had sent her daughter Leslie to school in England, under the care of Leslie's Uncle John, who had moved his medical practice to London's Wimpole Street.[104] Leslie came back a spirited, well-travelled young woman. She and Helena hit it off very well: Helena recalled in later years at a Parks Board meeting how she and Leslie had been scolded off the beach by the woman in charge of the bathhouse for wearing bathing suits in the latest style, skirtless and sleeveless, actually revealing the bare shoulder. This was in the days when a woman entered the water fully clothed in a swim suit with puffed sleeves, knee-length skirt, and long stockings. Leslie had brought the two new bathing suits back from France. 'Of course, I was slimmer then and cut quite a figure,' mused Helena, then Alderman Gutteridge, calling to mind her friendship with Leslie, her mother, and two brothers.[105] Douglas, the eldest, was a logger and farmer with land in Bradner in the Fraser Valley. Ollie, the youngest, was a tinsmith. He was James Purvis Oliver Fearn, Helena's future husband. Helena would become 'Aunt Billy' to Leslie's children.[106]

Suffragists sometimes attacked men in general for their stunted humanity and lack of compassion, none more vigorously than Ida Douglas-Fearn. When a Vancouver child allegedly died from adulterated milk, she seethed with anger: 'It is men who sell poisoned milk for babies, or artificial milk on which the Vancouver baby was starved to death.' It was men who allowed this 'systematic massacre of the innocents,' beside which even Herod's cruelty paled.[107] An accomplished speaker with a sharp wit, she could lay about her a rhetoric calculated to devastate any male upstart questioning the femininity of a suffragist:

> Coming home from a suffrage meeting the other night I met, in the car, the editor of one of our daily papers. He was gloating over some newspaper cuttings and he told me the subject was atrophied femininity. He seemed to taste those two words like a sweet morsel, but he was generous, he made me a present of them for future use. There is just as much atrophied masculinity in the world or perhaps more, and men are responsible for it all. It is due to the exploitation of motherhood. To the exhaustion of the mother by too frequent child-bearing ...

Citing Norwegian feminist Ellen Key on the amaternal woman, Ida goes on to explain that worn-out mothers produce sons who become 'degenerate' men, a 'greater menace to society than ... the amaternal woman ... who does not wish for motherhood ...' Then comes a cry surely wrenched from her own experience: 'How could she? Her father robbed her of the joy of motherhood by his exploitation of her mother, who, for nine long months, imprinted on the soul and body of her child her own weakness and despair, and reluctance, and loathing.'[108] These seem like self-con-

fessing words from a woman who cried out that 'once she had a husband and children, but love never – only her own love that gave, and
gave to those that took, and went on their way,' and suggest the hidden
female traumas of compliant, dutiful domestic sex that feminists like
Frances Swiney and Lady Sybil Smith, reviewed in *The Champion*,
courageously exposed.[109]

Helena, still unmarried at the age of thirty-four, if she reflected at all
on her mother's pregnancies, doubtless carried with her from the
crowded, little rooms in Chelsea feelings about sex in marriage. Certainly
she had no illusions about 'sacred' motherhood or the home as a haven
for the male breadwinner to return to. Indeed, when she wrote about
women 'carrying coals upstairs, scrubbing floors, or wringing out dirty
garments,' she might be recalling the life of her own mother on Chelsea's
Pavilion Road or Leete Street. As for women who went out to work, their
triple labours as wage earners, mothers, and house workers made
them physically unfit to bear children. The result, Helena said, was
bound to be a 'sickly degenerate race.'[110]

In the fall of 1913 Helena was selling through the BC Woman's Suffrage
League a pamphlet that inveighed against the 'illogical horror of prostitution and the legalized horror of subject wifehood': *The New Mothers
of a New World* by American suffragist Charlotte Perkins Gilman.[111] In
her Woman Suffrage Page, Helena dealt from time to time with the question of prostitution, exposing it as a business enterprise backed by
finance capital and operating through international vice rings. The
ballot, she insisted, was the means for women to achieve a decent
livelihood without having to resort to the sordid life of the street:

> If women will concentrate their energies on getting the vote, they will then
> be able to do as the women of Washington did – clean out the restricted dis-
> trict and lessen the supply of women to the vice trust, by passing a mini-
> mum wage act – that all the women workers may get a living wage.
>
> Read the 'New Mothers of a New World' by Charlotte Perkins Gilman,
> and see the relationship between lack of votes and vice ...[112]

The Gilman pamphlet, however, dealt at more length with the question
of 'subject wifehood' than with prostitution. Denouncing 'the cult of male
indulgence,' it exposed the real objections to granting women political,
economic, and social freedom: men were afraid of losing the service of
women as mothers and housekeepers, and, greatest danger of all, of losing that service 'which in itself constitutes the biological base of woman's
revolt – this exploitation of one sex for the pleasure of the other.' Charlotte Perkins Gilman further declared, or rather trumpeted, what most
women were too modest or too afraid to say: 'Virtue is not celibacy.

Virtue is that high physiological integrity which refuses to eat when it is not hungry – even to oblige!'[113] Helena herself did not expatiate on this idea in her writing on the Woman Suffrage Page. She was more concerned with the economic aspect of women's liberation, but did print Ida Douglas-Fearn's passionate indictment of male sexual domination, with its confession of 'weakness and despair, and reluctance, and loathing.' The women who followed Helena into the BC Woman's Suffrage League evidently did not balk at frank discussions of the psychology of sex, which, for more conventional suffragists, were scarcely appropriate for public discourse. That women too had sexual natures and experienced an autonomous sexuality was a discovery yet to be openly acknowledged, although judging from the columns of *The Champion* and the Woman Suffrage Page many women were familiar with the sexual philosophies of leading feminists.

Ida Douglas-Fearn was sometimes hard put to reconcile her feminist views with Catholic anti-feminism, which branded the woman suffragist as an affront to 'true womanhood' as idealized by the Blessed Virgin. When Father W.P. O'Boyle, in a sermon to the Children of Mary Sodality, prescribed as their role model Mary, 'submissive to St. Joseph, and devoted to her Son,' and denounced the political woman as 'a magpie, all plumage and chatter,' suffragists were indignant.[114] He dismissed woman suffrage as 'merely a secondary matter when compared with the rearing of children.' Yet Ida Douglas-Fearn felt compelled to come to his defence. After all, he had been her priest at St. Peter's in New Westminster before being moved to Holy Rosary Cathedral in Vancouver. 'Since when have Protestant politicians guided their lives by the advice of a Catholic priest to virgins of tender years?' she caustically inquired, and offered by way of apologia the Archbishop of Ireland, who looked to women 'to hold back the forces of rottenness and give decency and fair-mindedness a chance.' On suffrage, however, despite Father O'Boyle's opposition, she did not retreat a single step: 'Through all the turmoil,' she declared, 'Christabel's voice rings clear, "We will go on"!'[115]

The suffrage movement was gaining credibility and the Labor Temple suffrage meetings were attracting great crowds. They came to hear English militant Barbara Wylie urge Canadian women to 'shake off the shackles of convention.' They came to hear American suffragist Adelle Parker tell of reforms that followed upon the enfranchisement of women in the state of Washington.[116]

On 17 November 1913 they came to hear smooth-tongued Father O'Boyle urge anti-suffrage, anti-New Woman against Mary Ellen Smith. That night the audience 'occupied every seat, perched on windowsills and platform, stood in the aisles and overflowed into the hallways.' And Father O'Boyle proclaimed: 'Behold the New Woman clothed not in the sun but in the spotlight of publicity,' and urged women to stay in the home and be a power behind the scene by rearing Christian citizens and making better people out of their husbands. Mary Ellen Smith countered that it was time women were restored to history and given their rightful place: 'We hear of the Pilgrim Fathers, the Revolutionary Fathers, the Confederation Fathers, the Civic Fathers, but what about the women?' She accused governments of being 'afraid of the conscience of women,' and demanded the franchise that was being withheld from them out of fear. She flung back at her formidable opponent the rational and legitimate demands of women for a voice in making the laws that affected them and their children.[117]

Helena was at the meeting. When she heard Father O'Boyle lamenting that women in politics would lose their feminine helplessness as had women in industry, she knew that this was the issue to address on her next Woman Suffrage Page. Her column headline was 'The Reverenced Helplessness of Women,' a phrase she credited to a 'writer from the daily press.' 'Does the Reverend Father walk around Vancouver with his eyes closed?' she asked. 'Perhaps the Reverend Father will devise some means of keeping the bodies and souls of women together without food, and their bodies warm without clothes or shelter that they may remain feminine and charming.' Then, matter-of-fact and practical as always: 'We live in an age of hard facts, not an ideal dream land, we have to deal with conditions as they are and not as they should be.' She reminded her readers of the way industrialization had, in the last hundred years, moved women out of the home, immensely broadening their sphere and putting on them responsibility for the problems of the world: 'The child, the home and the women in the labor market is [sic] affected by legislation, the woman must then, if she is to do her duty to home and child, have a right to a voice in the making of such legislation.'[118] Ida Douglas-Fearn could scarcely disagree with Helena's argument, having herself struggled alone for her own survival and for the survival of her children.

The Catholic Church was an awkward impediment to the friendship of the two women, claiming Ida's loyalty and arousing Helena's opposition. Nevertheless, the two women continued to speak from the same platform. Ida contributed frequently to the Woman Suffrage Page and even represented the BC Woman's Suffrage League at a meeting of the National Council of Women Voters in Tacoma.[119]

What held Helena and Ida together was the bond of a feminist ideology according to which women constituted a superior breed of human being with a maternal fund of moral rectitude, strength of character, and compassion lacking in the male of the species. In England, the WSPU, the Women's Freedom League, and the NUWSS all embraced in some way this idea of the moral pre-eminence of women. Canadian suffragists took up the same refrain: 'True woman is broader and more unselfish than man in her sympathetic love for humanity as a whole,' wrote one member of the BC Woman's Suffrage League. 'In spite of the many obstacles placed in her way, woman, the mother of the race and early originator of inventions and industries, has evolved along higher human lines that man has not reached yet ...'[120]

This 'maternal feminism,' as it has been labelled by feminist scholars, now seems at once arrogant and naive, most women today conceding that they are, after all, only ordinary human beings, or would be if they were allowed their full due as responsible citizens. Yet in all fairness to those early suffragists, their perception of the superior female was a reasonable response to intolerable social and economic abuses largely created by men. 'Manufacturers vote against woman suffrage because they do not want women with votes behind factory inspection and child labor laws,' wrote Ida Douglas-Fearn.[121] It was women against manufacturers, against the 'liquor interests,' against the male legislators who preserved feudal marriage and property legislation. Women had to claim the power vested in them by Nature and exercise their rightful responsibility for the welfare of humanity. When South African writer Olive Schreiner declared in *Woman and Labour* (1911), 'the sound we hear behind us is that of all earth's women, bearing within them the entire race,' Canadian women responded and adopted the rhetoric. With her they cried, 'Give us labour and the training which fits for labour! We demand this, not for ourselves alone, but for the race.'[122]

In the fall of 1913, Helena took the initiative in forming a parliamentary committee to facilitate unified action among the various suffrage groups: the Pioneer Political Equality League, the North Shore Suffrage Society, the South Vancouver Political Equality League, the BC Equal Franchise Association, the BC Woman's Suffrage League, with its Mount Pleasant branch as a separate member.[123] The United Suffrage Societies, as the new organization was called, sent a twelve-woman deputation to Premier McBride in December 1913, led by Mary McConkey of the PPEL. Representing the BCWSL, Helena went to Victoria as a member of the deputation. The women told the premier that British Columbia was the only place on the Pacific Coast from the Mexican Gulf to the North Pole where women did not have the vote. Sir Richard averred that he would support woman suffrage if a referendum showed that the majority of women were also in favour. The deputation pointed out that men had never had to submit to a referendum; neither should women have to.

'Sir Richard,' Helena reported, 'slipped around this in the usual manner of politicians' and resorted to 'well-worn platitudes': 'The home would be neglected and women would no doubt sit in parliament when they had the vote, then form a woman's party and run the affairs of the country.'

'Oh, nonsense,' called out one of the women, expressing the impatience of the whole deputation.

'Sir Richard shows himself truly conservative,' concluded Helena, 'one must almost infer fossilized to keep at the same place in this progressive west with all the world advancing on this woman question ...'[124]

The United Suffrage Societies delegation retreated this time, because Sir Richard, self-styled 'the People's Choice,' chose not to heed the supplications of these representatives of the people. Helena and her suffrage friends could only bide their time and try again – with the next premier.

A week later, Helena wrote another angry column for the Woman Suffrage Page in response to McBride's evasive rejection. The stereotype of women as 'ministering angels' always incurred her caustic comment. That was how Sir Herbert Beerbohm Tree had some months earlier thought to praise women working in a London East End hospital, adding the admonition that the harp, not the trombone, was woman's instrument. Helena, with both feet planted firmly on earth, and looking resignedly, one imagines, to Sir Herbert's heaven, observed that alas! the work of mercy that so exalts women would one day disappear: 'It is the great hope of the women ... by the proper use of the ballot to do away with much of the philanthropic work, to replace charity with justice. In British Columbia, the only harp the women are going to know is to "harp" on suffrage until they get it.'[125]

On this defiant note, Helena brought her suffrage campaigning for 1913 to a close.

The Cause Victorious: September 1916

Oh! I always deserve the best treatment, because I never put up with any other ...

— Jane Austen, *Emma*

In 1914 Helena became more and more involved in the problems of working women – low wages, unemployment, poor working conditions – and for the next year her suffrage activities took second place to her work with the Women's Employment League. She stopped editing the Woman Suffrage Page at the end of February; Susie Clark took over in July and August, and after that the page was discontinued.

Helena had already in 1913 appeared before the Royal Commission on Labour Conditions in British Columbia, representing the Vancouver Local Council of Women (LCW). In the guise of a woman seeking employment, she had gone into factory workrooms and talked with women workers. At Lipsett's on Water Street, canvas-awning makers averaged $7 or $8 a week, as did glovemakers at Rowe Canvas, where the highest weekly wage actually reached $15. At Terminus Cigar Factory, the only woman employed could earn $13 a week on piece work if she worked very hard. At Ramsay's Biscuit Factory, Helena reported, she caused some amusement when she asked the women if they earned $12 a week, for in fact their wages were scarcely half that amount – from $5 to $8. They worked from 8:00 to 5:30, half an hour longer than the usual factory day, and until noon on Saturday, for a total of 51½ hours a week. For unskilled women workers, $12 represented quite a high wage. Another witness at the hearings testified that a few older female department store clerks were paid $10 to $12 for a 57-hour week that demanded 13 hours on Saturdays, little enough to feed and clothe oneself (bread was six cents a loaf, and a pair of cheap shoes cost $3.50). Sixteen-year-old girls, however, earned only $5 or $6 for the same work week, and found it even more difficult to make ends meet. Male clerks were paid $15 a week. The LCW brief to the commission, recommending a minimum wage for women, was based on Helena's findings.[1]

Suffrage organizations in British Columbia, May 1916

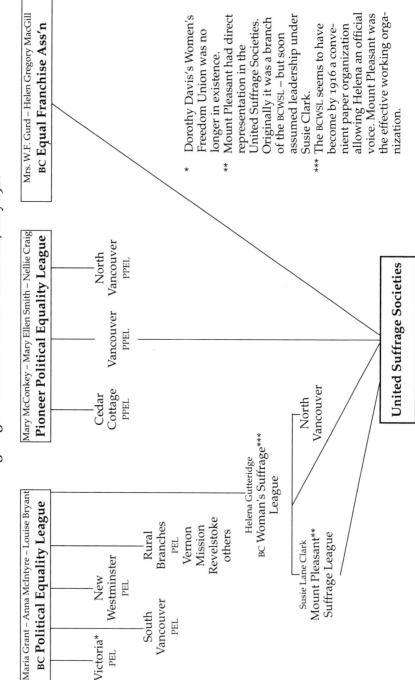

Maria Grant – Anna McIntyre – Louise Bryant
BC Political Equality League

Victoria*
PEL

South Vancouver
PEL

New Westminster
PEL

Rural Branches
PEL
Vernon
Mission
Revelstoke
others

Helena Gutteridge
BC Woman's Suffrage*
League

Mary McConkey – Mary Ellen Smith – Nellie Craig
Pioneer Political Equality League

Cedar Cottage
PPEL

Vancouver
PPEL

North Vancouver
PPEL

Mrs. W.F. Gurd – Helen Gregory MacGill
BC Equal Franchise Ass'n

Susie Lane Clark
Mount Pleasant**
Suffrage League

North Vancouver

United Suffrage Societies

*   Dorothy Davis's Women's Freedom Union was no longer in existence.

**   Mount Pleasant had direct representation in the United Suffrage Societies. Originally it was a branch of the BCWSL – but soon assumed leadership under Susie Clark.

*** The BCWSL seems to have become by 1916 a convenient paper organization allowing Helena an official voice. Mount Pleasant was the effective working organization.

The LCW also recommended to City Council the appointment of a 'woman sanitary inspector' to report on the working and living conditions of girls and women in stores and rooming houses. In some department stores, employees had nowhere to sit: they had to stand for the whole work day. Toilet facilities were sometimes inadequate, as were lighting and ventilation. Helena was probably the one who initiated the LCW recommendation, employing the English job title 'woman sanitary inspector.' City Council forthwith appointed a Lady Health Visitor to the staff of the Public Health Department, with duties that included, as for women sanitary inspectors in Helena's London, inspection of women workers for infectious diseases, especially tuberculosis, and 'infant protection' under a city health by-law.[2]

During the Royal Commission hearings, Helena met J.H. McVety of the Vancouver Trades and Labor Council. Evidently impressed by her performance, he suggested that she join the tailors' union. Closely involved with her union and with the VTLC, in 1913 she became the women's correspondent for the federal government's *Labour Gazette*, sending monthly reports on local conditions and events affecting working women, especially on unemployment.[3] She was wide-ranging in her reports and, being Helena, inevitably encroached on the territory of the other Vancouver correspondent, VTLC colleague J.W. Wilkinson, who reported unemployment as it affected men. Helena tended to think in terms of the whole picture: she could not talk about unemployed women without reference to the whole labour scene. A letter from the minister of labour brought her into line, eliciting a promise from her that she would henceforth 'deal only with female labor.'[4]

To gather information about women's employment, Helena spent three weeks in the summer of 1913 working in a fish cannery at nearby Steveston, on the Fraser River delta. She had heard that white women were replacing Chinese, but not being able to get the facts when she visited the cannery, asked for employment instead. At the bunkhouse – open to the street, no lock on the door, nine or ten women to a room – she discovered she should have brought her own blanket, like any migrant worker: 'My friends told me that I had become a "blanket stiff".' Her job was filling tins, or so one gathers from her report to her union comrades at the BC Federation of Labour convention in New Westminster early in 1914. The pay was '25 cents per hour and 3 cents per tray of 36 for filling tins, and I assure you, one had to work 18 hours to make any money at all.' (Does she mean that the worker could choose between hourly wages and piece work, or that there were two jobs, the first unspecified at 25 cents an hour and the second filling tins?)

Helena was speaking of her Steveston experience in connection with resolutions on the convention floor regarding working conditions for women. She observed that, although the work itself was 'perfectly clean and wholesome,' women should not be employed at the cannery 'under present conditions.' White men, she said, not Japanese, Chinese, or Hindus, were the problem. They hung around the cannery and brought liquor to 'quite young' girls, who, when work was slack, 'went round the town' with them. 'Not that I am a man-hater and think that girls should not go out with men,' but these men were not the type a father would like his daughter to go out with. She did not object to the girls working alongside the Japanese. 'I found the Japanese very nice indeed to work with; that is more than could be said of the behaviour of the white men there.'

Helena asked the manager, 'who, by the way, was drunk half the time,' why he had replaced Chinese workers with women, even though he claimed the Chinese were better at the job. He replied that because the Chinese had to be hired on contract, management paid only the contractor who supplied the labour; whereas if they hired white women, they had more control of their labour. She pointed out to the delegates that they had been 'complaining that the Orientals were used to displace the white man.' Here, she told them, was a case of white women, 'even lower' in the labour market, replacing Chinese. 'One of the things that organized labour should do,' she concluded, 'is to see that the standard of pay for the work of white women is more on the level of the white man. You can see how unfair the whole thing is.' The delegates applauded.[5] She did not suggest in this speech that the Chinese should also be paid white men's wages.

At the same convention, she framed a resolution for woman suffrage that spoke to the economic interests of working men as well as to those of working women, arguing that 'working women as an unenfranchised class are continually used to lower the wage standards of men,' and that employers unjustly 'use their political power to keep women from bettering their economic condition.' Referring again to Chinese and women workers as a supply of cheap labour, she pointed to Washington and California, where, she said, enfranchised women had been largely responsible for enlightened legislation giving financial assistance to widows and deserted wives, thus allowing them to stay at home and look after their children. The men listened and approved and again applauded. Parm Pettipiece said Miss Gutteridge had forgotten to credit the women of Washington State for also being 'largely responsible for securing the passing of the eight-hour law,' on which score alone he would be willing to give his own vote to his wife. Even Jack Kavanagh raised no objection and anticipated none from his fellow unionists, though remarking with impossiblist condescension that woman suffrage 'does not concern us very vitally.' The resolution for woman suffrage passed unanimously and the *Sun* commented that 'Miss Gutteridge played a leading part with a capital little speech.' At this convention Helena was also elected delegate to the Washington State Federation of Labor. When at the end of the year she spoke at the twenty-fifth anniversary celebration of the VTLC, urging women to organize, the *Sun* again approved of Helena Gutteridge – 'always bright and worth listening to.'[6]

Other women also had less time to campaign for the vote. War broke out in Europe in the summer of 1914, one nation after another joining the fray. When in August Britain declared war on Germany, the priorities of all Canadians underwent a radical readjustment and in Vancouver, for the next two years, for many women suffrage activities took second place to war work.

Helena took a stand against the war. Although no longer editing a suffrage page in the *British Columbia Federationist*, she still wrote for the newspaper and continued, war or no war, to advance the cause of women. Pointing to the profits accumulated by the armaments manufacturers, she blamed the war, not just on monopoly, but on male monopoly:

> If the present conditions are the best that male statescraft can accomplish, then surely the time has come for woman to take her place in the councils of the nations. That she may bring her experience, as a mother throughout the bygone ages, and her knowledge of the cost of human life into the governments of the world, as an antidote to the present false conception of man, that places property and possessions at a higher value than human welfare and life.[7]

That was in September 1914. With the war only a month old, she could still, with the most fervent feminists, allow motherhood its apotheosis. Yet the plight of unemployed women, which she knew intimately from her research for the *Labour Gazette*, made her rail against the system that she believed only crushed and trampled on motherhood. She did not call for revolution; that was not her way. But she left no doubt as to how she felt about motherhood, capitalism, and war:

> All these things give rise to a feeling of the need for a new and effective form of government, a government that will give the people an opportunity to develop the best in them, and not manufacture degenerates, criminals and weaklings; a system of government that will build nations of contented happy people, and war, with sacred motherhood called upon to supply the basic ammunition, will be held in abhorrence by all. Mothers will not then need to wonder if they must watch their babies starve.[8]

A year later, when women were being told that to campaign for suffrage in wartime was unpatriotic, she invoked equality and justice,
not motherhood:

> It seems as though man is inherently incapable of looking upon woman as
> a human being with desires, aspirations and understanding much like their
> own, and who are seeking equality, not special consideration on the one
> hand because they are women, or exploitation and all the drudgery of the
> world's work, just when it suits the male kind.[9]

She viewed with contempt the idealizing of women as international
peacemakers: 'Here we have the saviour of the race attitude ... What useful creatures women are and how we admire them.' One suspects that
she would not agree with those among today's radical feminists who,
in seeking the essential woman silenced by the patriarchy, are redis-
covering her as a superior moral being.[10]

In the spring of 1915, with a provincial election in the offing, Liberal
Party women formed the Greater Vancouver Liberal Women's Associ-
ation to campaign for the Liberals, with the understanding that their
party would adopt a woman suffrage plank in its platform.[11] The energies of some of the city's most effective suffragists were thus diffused.
Mary Ellen Smith was on the executive of the new association, as was
Helen MacGill, who, on the strength of the Liberals' promise, left the
Conservative Party and went over to the Liberals.[12] Mary McConkey also
became a Liberal Party worker. The year before, in Manitoba, Nellie
McClung and other suffragists had campaigned to help elect a Liberal
government in return for its supporting woman suffrage.[13] Helena was
sceptical about such alignments. She objected that the suffrage policy
of the British Columbia Liberals was so worded as to place all the
responsibility for enacting a franchise bill on the women: they would
have to demonstrate that a certain percentage of the women of the
province actually were in favour. Moreover, Helena warned, the shameful record of the Liberal government in Great Britain, which manipulated
the suffrage issue in the interests of political expediency, should make
all suffragists wary of trusting political promises. She remembered
only too well how Lloyd George had 'torpedoed' the Conciliation Bill.
She remembered that, on arrival in Vancouver, she had read with dismay reports of renewed militancy on the part of the WSPU; of how a hand-
picked squad of militants, armed with bags of stones and hammers, had
smashed windows of government offices and businesses, not excluding
those of the National Liberal Federation. Not that British Columbia
women were likely to be roused to such anger. Quite the opposite; the
suffrage movement here was too backward. If women did not have the

vote in Canada, she conceded, it was 'not due to the opposition of any party, or to the desire of men to dominate their women folk, but due to the lack of interest displayed by women themselves.'[14] Helena was quite dispirited over the suffrage movement in Vancouver, and now the Liberal Party had drawn away its best people.

Then something happened to reactivate the suffragists. On 15 December 1915, his government in crisis, Premier McBride resigned. On the same day, Helena, as secretary of the Central Committee of the United Suffrage Societies, wrote to the new premier, William John Bowser, asking for an interview with him as one of the five Vancouver MLAs. The deputation would also include representatives from other women's organizations and the VTLC.[15] He was no less opposed to woman suffrage than his predecessor, but by now political expediency urged him to deal in some way with the demands of the women.

William Bowser had in February assured the women when they collared him at the Hotel Vancouver as a private member that 'the members of the Government had always been set free to vote on such a [franchise] measure according to conviction, regardless of party affiliation.'[16] When on 21 March MLA John Place put forward his third woman suffrage bill, they fully expected the premier to honour this commitment by allowing Place's bill to go forward without impediment. Instead he asked Place to withdraw his bill in favour of the government's own proposed election bill for enfranchising soldiers, one that would allow an amendment giving women the franchise. A difficult condition was attached to this concession: the amendment would have to be approved by a special referendum.[17] When this was announced on 13 April, it snowed telegrams in Victoria as the United Suffrage Societies protested Bowser's proposed referendum. Helena sent off her own telegram, steely edged: 'The platform of the Women of BC is for a government bill to enfranchise women at this session of the legislature without either plebiscite or referendum.'[18] Place refused to withdraw his bill, and a heated debate ensued in the legislature.[19]

On 26 April suffrage representatives arrived in full force from all parts of the province to confront the premier. They came from Vancouver, Victoria, and the Lower Mainland; from Salmon Arm, Kelowna, Nelson, Vernon, Kamloops, Kaslo, and Rossland – some thirty women in all.[20] Privately, Billy Bowser didn't 'want skirts on the floor of the House,' and was known to have declared that 'women wouldn't get the franchise in his lifetime if he could help it.'[21] Before this deputation of women, he chose to evade the issue: his government had no mandate from the electorate to put women's franchise to a vote in the legislature.[22]

Helen MacGill voiced the indignant opposition of the women. It was not fair, she said, to submit the question to an electorate from which they, the interested party, were excluded. Moreover, like all Canadian women, they were fully engaged in war work, and the nation and the Empire could ill afford to be deprived of their energies at this critical time by an election issue that required their utmost participation. When Helena spoke she reiterated her stand that suffrage was a non-political question and should be kept free of election politics.[23] Bowser was adamant: he would go ahead with the referendum. The women, beaten again, retreated into their many organizations to reconsider strategy and tactics.

The British Columbia Political Equality League, of which Helena's BCWSL was a member, held an emergency convention on 15 May. For a whole afternoon the delegates went round and round and round the issue. They accused the government of employing subterfuge, of yielding to the powerful influence of the liquor interests, of using the franchise issue for political ends. Helena spoke strongly against the referendum and against political alignments. She was particularly severe with Harlan Brewster, the Liberal leader, accusing him of insincerity. She even made a veiled but ominous prediction that they might have to resort to direct action, for 'just as conditions in Canada made it absolutely unnecessary for Canadian women to resort to militancy, so conditions here now change the situation in that respect.'[24] Maria Grant declared that 'the home is her [woman's] first place,' and then eloquently redefined the home to mean 'the world where the children live,' the same world as a man's – the nation, the Empire.[25] In the end the discussion boiled down to this: a referendum of male voters was clearly unfair, but if women did not support it and work to influence the male voter, then they could lose the franchise by default. Another telegram appealing to Premier Bowser; another refusal – 'Regret very much that government cannot see its way clear to introduce legislation this session giving you the provincial franchise.'[26]

The next day, at the invitation of the British Columbia Political Equality League, two organizations that were not members of the league joined the conference despite their Liberal affiliations: the Pioneer Political Equality League, represented by Mary McConkey, and the BC Equal Franchise Association, represented by Helen MacGill and Mrs. C.B. Gurd. Helena summed up the proceedings to date for the newcomers, advising them to stand clear of political parties. After heated argument a vote was taken. The majority – those in organizations affiliated with the BCPEL – declared themselves willing to work for the referendum and set up a provincial referendum committee. But the two unaffiliated organizations voted against such action. And so a split occurred. It was not helped by Helena's attack on Brewster the day before, or by her blunt advice to avoid political alignments. She knew, of course, that Mary McConkey and Helen MacGill were both committed to the Liberal Party. Her remarks generated a good deal of ill feeling in a meeting already fraught with tension.[27]

On 17 May, John Place presented his private member's bill to extend the franchise to women. It was defeated 24 to 6, with only two Conservative MLAS breaking ranks to vote for the bill, but he kept the debate going for five days before Bowser finally called the vote. At their June convention the BC Women's Liberal Association took Helena to account, passing a formal resolution 'to call attention to Miss Gutteridge's misrepresentation of Mr. Brewster's letter.' 'We resent the unfounded and distorted statements that the Liberal party would not give suffrage if the referendum were defeated,' the resolution continued.[28] For the rest of the summer at least, Helena was persona non grata in the Liberal women's camp and did not speak on their platforms, although she spoke under Conservative auspices several times during the election campaign.

It does seem as though Helena, usually supremely rational, was moved by that profound anti-Liberal animus and spirit of mistrust she brought from England, rather than by any sober consideration of the exigencies of parliamentary democracy. Of course Harlan Brewster was right: the results of the referendum would have to be binding. Then, too, the British Columbia Liberals gained credibility from the Liberal government of Manitoba, which, under T.C. Norris, had fulfilled its election promise and brought in woman suffrage earlier in the year. However, Helena had some justification for her mistrust of the Manitoba Liberals, for initially Premier Norris's franchise bill excluded women from taking legislative office. Only because of the watchfulness of the Manitoba Political Equality League and its stern threat to expose this omission to the influential Grain Growers' Association, then meeting in convention, did the Norris government redraft the bill so that women would be able to sit in the legislature as well as cast their ballots.[29]

Because of the split, British Columbia women advanced in two contingents, the Women's Liberal Association and the Provincial Women's Suffrage Referendum Association. After these last five years in the field, petitioning, sending delegations, and buttonholing MLAS, holding public meetings, writing letters, and sending telegrams, the suffragists had become skilful political strategists, informed and cogent in their presentations. Helen MacGill remembered particularly 'Frances [sic] McConkey of the sweet face and soothing voice, Mary Ellen Smith, hearty and motherly and matronly, the chic and voluble Essie Brown, bluntspoken Helena Gutteridge and the sharp-featured and twangy Susie Lane Clark.'[30] Among other dedicated leaders were the efficient and hardworking Anna McIntyre, head of the South Vancouver Political Equality League; Nellie Craig, president of the Pioneer Political Equality League, succeeding Helena as secretary of the United Suffrage Societies (1916); and in Victoria, Maria Grant, Cecilia Spofford, and Alice Christie.

The Women's Liberal Association channelled their energies into getting Liberals elected, believing that they could get the vote more quickly and more easily in this way than by helping in the referendum, which they thought 'unfair and inexpedient' and 'not a true application of the principles of a referendum.'[31] They were not going to be innocently taken in by this 'ruse' offered by the Conservative government.[32]

The BC Political Equality League launched the Provincial Women's Suffrage Referendum Association on 1 June at a mass meeting in the Labor Temple, having sent out invitations to both men's and women's organizations throughout the province. The BCPEL also drew in the Pioneer Political Equality League and its branches, and other suffrage societies earlier opposed to working for the referendum, with the result that many Liberal women joined the campaign after all. Aiming at public credibility, the organizers invited a leading member of the establishment to chair the meeting – Sir Charles Hibbert Tupper, son of one of the Fathers of Confederation. A second meeting to elect an executive committee was scheduled for 19 June.[33]

But in the meantime an English visitor to the city diverted the attention of suffragists quite urgently to the war. Emmeline Pankhurst, no longer campaigning for votes for women, was on a North American recruiting mission for the war, having at the outbreak of hostilities undergone a sea change from suffragist to imperialist. The BCPEL had wanted to sponsor her, but in the competition that ensued to obtain her, the PPEL won that honour. On 8 June 1916 it held a public meeting for Mrs. Pankhurst at the Empress Theatre with gross receipts of $776, half of which was presented to her for war work. The rest, minus expenses, was given to the Greater Vancouver Recruiting League. She told her audience that she had from the first been in favour of compulsory service for both men and women. The PPEL also held a luncheon for her at the Hotel Vancouver, where Helen MacGill, Laura Jamieson, Mary McConkey, Mary Ellen Smith, and others among Helena's colleagues in the cause of women's rights sat at the table of honour. Mrs. Pankhurst observed that Canada, unlike England, had not put aside contentious issues for the duration of the war, and, without explicitly advising suffragists to discontinue their campaign, urged them to concentrate on the war effort. Suffragists, she said, were fighting for the same principles as the allied nations. 'It is not merely a question of maintaining the Empire or of the preservation of national independence. There are great spiritual issues at stake ... It must not be supposed that this is only a man's war, for it is also a woman's war. All that woman has been hoping for is in the balance.' At the Women's Canadian Club luncheon she again urged women to aid recruiting. Mary Ellen Smith chaired the meeting and Laura Jamieson moved a vote of thanks to 'this great woman who had been so misunderstood and misappreciated.'[34]

Emmeline Pankhurst's visit was an important event for Helena, and it could only have aroused in her conflicting thoughts and emotions. On the one hand, she valued her former association with the Women's Social and Political Union and felt a bond with Mrs. Pankhurst, under whose leadership she had first spoken out for the rights of women. Helena was moved to make some gesture to honour an old loyalty and placed a newspaper announcement inviting other former members of the WSPU now living 'at the coast' to join with her in 'arranging for a presentation' to Mrs. Pankhurst. We do not know if Helena and other former members did indeed meet and speak with her and present their gift, but the intention speaks for the bond she felt with the English suffragist leader.[35]

On the other hand, blaming the war on 'male monopoly,' Helena could not have been receptive to Mrs. Pankhurst's advice to women to urge men to enlist, though she was willing enough to make a humanitarian gesture for war prisoners. Later that year, when the Women's Canadian Club held a tag day for the Prisoner of War Fund, she stood on the street corner at Woodward's Store collecting money for it.[36] However, this did not mean that she had changed her mind about the war: a year later, when Prime Minister Borden announced his plans for compulsory military service, Helena supported the anti-conscription policy of the VTLC and the BC Federation of Labour: 'This is not a war of democracy against autocracy,' she declared at a public meeting to oppose conscription. 'It is simply a war of capital against capital, and Great Britain is fighting because she wishes to keep Germany from monopolizing the markets of the world.'[37] If Emmeline Pankhurst had heard this speech, she might have reacted as she did when, a few weeks before arriving in Vancouver, she heard of her daughter's anti-conscription activities in England: '"Strongly repudiate and condemn Sylvia's foolish and unpatriotic conduct".'[38]

Helena had little, if any, support in her opposition to the war from her suffragist friends. Elizabeth Arnett joined the Women's Volunteer Reserve; Susie Clark distributed 'Win the War' pledge cards and pamphlets for the National Service Department and served on the British Columbia section of the wartime Canada Food Board. Moreover, the women pacifists of the twenties were not yet on the scene: Lucy Woodsworth was teaching school and looking after her family in isolated Gibson's Landing on British Columbia's Howe Sound. Dorothy Steeves would not arrive in Vancouver from her native Holland until 1919. Laura Jamieson in 1917 was in Tranquille Sanatorium, ill with tuberculosis, and in any case before that apparently had not yet developed her pacifist philosophy, if her public support for Emmeline Pankhurst is any indication.[39]

Despite their show of support for Emmeline Pankhurst and despite their ongoing war work, Vancouver suffragists continued their 1916 campaign on Premier Bowser's franchise referendum. She had scarcely left the city before the various suffrage groups were in action again. At a meeting at the Khaki Home, Helena addressed the Soldiers' and Sailors' Mothers and Wives on 'the woman's suffrage movement and women's part in it at the present time,' and the South Vancouver Political Equality League actively recruited women for the referendum campaign committee.[40] For advancing the suffrage cause while Canadian soldiers were fighting and dying in France, Helena in no way had to suffer the stern disapprobation of such an organization as the Toronto Women's Patriotic League, which caused the Ontario Equal Franchise Campaign Committee to take umbrage at their public criticism and to insist that their suffrage work was patriotic. Nor did Mary Ellen Smith need to defend herself for continuing to urge support for the referendum. Even Sir Charles Hibbert Tupper, whose patriotism could not be impugned, was willing to resume his place in the chair for the Provincial Women's Suffrage Referendum Association at its 19 June meeting. William Bowser's referendum on the franchise had effectively rallied the British Columbia suffrage forces despite the war.[41]

At the 19 June meeting of the Provincial Women's Suffrage Referendum Association, Louise Bryan, a WCTU worker originally from Bruce County, Ontario, twenty-five years in the suffrage movement and honorary president of the BCPEL, was elected to the chair, with Anna McIntyre, secretary of the BCPEL, also secretary of the new organization. Prominent businessman Jonathan Rogers, head of the People's Prohibition Party, donated an office in his building; the Remington Typewriter Company supplied a typewriter; and chairs came from the Horse Show Building on Georgia Street, carted by Mainland Transfer. The campaign of the Referendum Association obviously had wide community support.[42]

Nor was it run just by women. Leon Ladner, well-known Vancouver lawyer, was elected vice chairman and served on the Joint Finance Board, presided over by I. Rubinowitz. Men headed two standing committees: J.Y. Adams, organization, and G.R. Cameron, voters' lists. They all volunteered for the speakers' list, as did H.H. Stevens, Conservative MP for Vancouver. And the Reverend Mr. Miller, Reeve Winram, Dr. Currie, and Councillor Grimmett. And Messrs. Cantelon, Holland, Lucas, Bridgeman, Hodgson, Pollock, McPharlane. Let not their names be forgotten in the roll call of suffrage workers.[43] However, the women did most of the work, and the Referendum Association was a useful vehicle for deploying their forces: Mrs. J.O. Perry, Catholic Liberal from the WCTU social council, was in charge of public meetings; from the PPEL, Jennie Smith, Methodist Liberal, wife of a real estate agent, headed the literature committee; Lily Laverock worked on publicity. Raising money was absolutely essential to the campaign, and on the Joint Finance Board the BC Woman's Suffrage League was heavily represented, including Mrs. Roy M. Taylor and Susie Clark, with Helena as secretary-treasurer. Because of the work of the BCPEL in the interior of the province, begun by Dorothy Davis and Florence Hall, the Referendum Association was able to set up referendum committees in twenty rural towns, from Summerland in the Okanagan to Murrayville in the Fraser Valley. In charge of the Rogers Building headquarters, coordinating the work, was Anna McIntyre, with Mrs. Roy Taylor from the Mount Pleasant Suffrage League as assistant secretary, handling office routine, organizing public meetings, mailing out thousands of pamphlets to soldiers in camps in England and Canada.[44]

Helena was off and running even before the provincial organization was formed. The plan of the BCPEL was to organize the whole city, ward by ward. One week before the 1 June mass meeting, she had already announced the plans of her BC Woman's Suffrage League for the organization of Ward VI, the Kitsilano area, and by the end of the week had the Ward VI committee in place. Susie Clark, Elizabeth Arnett, and other Mount Pleasant women set up a strong organization in Ward V, their own area. With the South Vancouver Political Equality League, they then formed in mid-June a coordinating body, the South Vancouver Central Woman's Suffrage Referendum Campaign Committee. That was a good start, but more direction, more push was needed: the six ward committees could not simply be left to their own devices. Helena and Susie set up the Vancouver City Central Woman's Suffrage Campaign Association and through it, with Susie as president and Helena as corresponding secretary, coordinated the whole city campaign. Every week the representatives of the ward committees met to report on the campaign and discuss strategy.[45]

Helena was not sectarian in her campaign tactics. In her single-minded way, she was willing to work with any group favouring suffrage. Before the referendum campaign started, she led a delegation of representatives, mostly Conservative, from five suffrage organizations to meet the central executive of the Conservative Party. On another occasion the USS sent a delegation to talk suffrage with the Young Conservatives Association. As a result, they had strong Conservative Party support, and even a Young Conservative, G.R. Cameron, serving on the City Central executive.[46] Helena and Susie did not neglect to approach

Premier Bowser for a donation; he politely complied with a cheque for twenty-five dollars.[47] Helena also worked closely with WCTU women, including Mrs. J.A. Gillespie, president of the WCTU District Union, Louise Bryan, and Jean Macken, a social service worker.

However, the constituency that Helena most counted on failed her in the end. The BC Federation of Labor officially supported woman suffrage and the Vancouver unions had cooperated with Helena in her 1913 campaign to win the workers to the suffrage cause, but now in wartime, with women replacing men in factories, the full economic implications of woman suffrage created doubt in the labour camp. Perhaps the women would not give back their wartime jobs to the returning men, and employers would be only too happy to use women as a source of cheap labour. A *British Columbia Federationist* editorial of 14 April 1916, just at the time the referendum was announced, predicted a 'war between the sexes over the possession of jobs.' The editorial was openly hostile, bitter, and insulting:

> The noisy advocates of 'votes for women' may rest assured that their pet hobby will go through with flying colors as soon as the war is ended. Industrially emancipated woman must needs be armed with political power in order to withstand such assaults as might be directed against her by those masculine workers who might feel exceeding sore because of her having invaded those industrial precincts previously held sacred to themselves. The master class will see that she gets the franchise. There is little doubt of that. And with her franchise she will become a bulwark of defense to everything that is conservative in political and industrial life ...[48]

This blinkered, narrow-minded piece was printed by Parm Pettipiece, *British Columbia Federationist* manager-editor, and he may very well have written it. If so, he had completely changed his mind about letting his wife use his vote, as he had so generously offered in 1914. Whoever the author, it was cruel testimony to the way labour really viewed women's rights and a real setback for suffragists, especially for Helena, who was herself a worker. Since July 1914 she had been secretary-treasurer of the VTLC and in January 1916 was elected general secretary.[49] She had also represented the VTLC on a suffrage deputation to the provincial government. Until this sudden about-face, she had reason to believe that she enjoyed the support of her male worker colleagues, especially since so many unions had supported her in her suffrage-labour campaign in 1913. A month before the election, slated for 14 September, the *British Columbia Federationist* returned to the attack in a front-page tirade that could only be taken as a signal for workers to turn thumbs down on woman suffrage. Claiming that after the war employers would hang on to their women workers because they provided cheap labour, the editorial painted a lugubrious picture of male social and economic displacement:

> The jobless men will start a ruction. The government will be able, with the vote of the women, to maintain their political power. Hence the 'heroes' will have to live on the memories of the battlefield, or accept employment at such work and wages as the employers see fit to give. The work of the trades union[s] for the past fifty years will have to [be] done over again.[50]

Unfortunately, no VTLC minute books exist for this particular part of 1916, and so Helena's response at the next regular meeting can only be conjectured. Knowing Helena's unyielding loyalty to her own sex and her complete dedication to the suffrage cause, one can safely say that for a labour colleague to characterize suffragist women as traitors to their class was extreme provocation. Significantly, she resigned as secretary of the VTLC soon after this editorial appeared.[51] As a public figure in the suffrage referendum campaign, she may have felt resignation from the VTLC executive to be the honourable course of action.

All that summer of 1916 the suffrage meetings proliferated, sometimes sweetened by a little entertainment in the hope that an attractive young woman reciting Kipling's 'If' or a baritone rendering 'Roses of Forgiveness' might make one more convert or gain one more worker for the Cause. Ward VI held a gala garden party, and Helena, Susie Clark, and Alderman R.H. Gale held forth on suffrage in the intervals between the pipers, the Scottish dancers, and the band of the Boys' Industrial School.[52] The Women's Liberal Association, meanwhile, went its own way, Mary McConkey and Helen MacGill not yielding in their opposition to the referendum but working for the Liberal Party, which they counted on to bring in woman suffrage. Association vice president Mary Ellen Smith, without loss of credibility, managed to work in both camps.[53]

The arguments of both groups were, however, much the same. The franchise was a human right. Moreover, women were uniquely endowed as mothers with the ability to lend a civilizing element to politics, and in social legislation particularly they would capably bear responsibility in the task of government. Another argument, as expressed by the Mount Pleasant Suffrage League, was openly racist, protesting the 'occupation of these shores by hordes of dark-skinned immigrants from the Far East,' a 'menace' that women, once enfranchised, could help to eradicate.[54] Many middle class women, however, employed Chinese servants and did not consider them a menace. Indeed, novelist Ethel Wilson, recreating the Malkin family servant in the character of the ill-mannered Yow, demonstrates a close relationship between Grandmother Anne Malkin, who thought him a good man and admitted him to family prayer, and Yow, 'who was too proud to say that he loved the Grandmother.'[55]

Suffragists also declared the injustice of naturalized 'foreigners' having the vote, while women of Anglo-Saxon origin who would uphold the 'Ideals and Standards, political and social' of the Empire were denied that privilege.[56] A clergyman election candidate in a 1916 suffrage speech even claimed that control of the state by men was 'the outcome of Teutonic civilization which Anglo-Saxons were outliving.'[57] In other words, votes for women would help society achieve its true Anglo-Saxon destiny. These racist arguments damaged the Cause not at all; on the contrary, they reassured the male establishment that in suffragist women it had an ally that would stand on guard beside it for a white, Christian, homogeneous Canada.[58]

Anti-Asian sentiment permeated all sections of society – workers, businessmen, clergy – in these decades, as the inflammatory exploits of the Asiatic Exclusion League in 1907 vividly testified, provoking riot and mayhem in Vancouver's Chinatown and 'Little Tokyo.' Moreover, anti-Asian sentiment was official: for decades, the federal government had levied on all Chinese immigrants an entry or 'head tax' of $100, raised to $500 under pressure from the provincial government; the immigration officers who in 1914 prevented a party of Sikh immigrants from disembarking from the *Komagata Maru* were obeying restrictions imposed by the federal government.[59] And 'white' meant British. In 1911 a school board member visiting the little Swedish-Canadian settlement of Silverdale turned to the teacher at the front of the class and in the full hearing of the children asked, 'Have you no white children in your school, only Swedes?'[60] Helena's own organization, the VTLC, from its very beginning had adopted anti-Asian policies on the grounds that Orientals and East Indians were unfair competition for white workers, a rationale that did not conceal a racist bias. Reporting to the Royal Commission on Labour, J.H. McVety had urged separate schools for Oriental children as they were 'a bad moral influence' on white children. Helena surely disagreed with her colleague on this score, for she was on record as saying that young cannery girls would suffer no harmful influence from Japanese co-workers and that she herself had found them 'very nice indeed.' Apparently, however, no matter how nice Japanese and Chinese were, when it came to jobs she believed they had to take their place in line – behind white workers. Still, in that xenophobic climate her friendly acceptance of Orientals was quite unusual and could have been highly suspect.[61]

In none of her reported suffrage speeches did Helena resort to the anti-foreigner argument, yet neither did she protest it. Nor did she press for the enfranchisement of Asian women, or men, for that matter: votes for women on the same terms as men was always her demand. Her contemporary, South African Olive Schreiner, represents the opposite, unpragmatic position. At first, in 1899, convinced that Africans were an inferior, undeveloped race, she stated the belief that '"dark man is the child the gods have given us in South Africa for our curse or our blessing".'[62] A decade later, however, now committed to racial equality, she championed women of colour. Resisting the plain reality of her country's colour bar, which nearly a century later still disenfranchises the black majority, she resigned from the Women's Enfranchisement League when it adopted the 'on-the-same-terms-as-men' demand, which excluded women of colour. Helena did not deal with suffrage on this level of first principles, but this does not mean that she was not a person of strong principle; only that, like a good tactician, she was willing to make judicious compromises to achieve her aims, compromises that would have offended more rigorously theoretical people like Olive Schreiner.

The referendum date, 14 September 1916, drew closer. Undeterred by the anti-feminist stance of her labour colleagues, as represented by the *British Columbia Federationist*, Helena, in what must have seemed a show of defiance, mounted the election platform with Premier Bowser himself. At the big opening meeting of the Conservative election campaign in the Empress Theatre on 1 September, a large and enthusiastic audience broke into cheers when the chairman announced that Helena Gutteridge would speak on woman suffrage.[63] She did not disappoint them. She reminded them that 'on September 14 they would exercise a right their forefathers had thought worth fighting and dying for.' Unfortunately, she said, British Columbia was the only black spot on the west coast of the North American continent: in every other state on the Pacific Coast women had the vote. But in this referendum, she continued, suffrage was divorced from party politics. 'It was purely a question of giving women the right to stand side by side with the men and have a voice in the way the country was run for the benefit of humanity in general.' She did not ask them to vote for woman suffrage because the women had 'come forward so gallantly during the present war,' but because the franchise was a human right and because 'women would be an uplifting power in the governing of the country.'[64] The meeting that night was for her the high point of the referendum campaign.

Just before election day she again sat on a platform with the premier, this time at his first appearance at one of the newly formed North Vancouver constituencies. She spoke briefly and concisely, tracing 'the evolution of women through the age of industrialism to the present day, when ... they stood side by side with men in all the varied walks of life.'[65]

On this occasion, the chairman confessed that he had been undecided, but having heard Helena Gutteridge speak, had made up his mind to vote for woman suffrage.

During the referendum campaign, there was no open opposition to the suffragists. All political parties were now giving their support, whether out of expediency or conviction. Commented the *World*:

> But they [suffragist speakers] are not even heckled; hence they and their well-wishers are apt to think the cause is won.
>
> It is just possible they may be too sanguine. There is an opposition to women securing the vote in this province even though it is an opposition that is little heard of.[66]

A letter to the editor of the *Daily News-Advertiser* was a case in point, expressing a deep-seated conviction that a woman with a vote was an aberration in the natural order. The writer was grave and patriarchal:

> I hope, on reflection, that the men of this country will realize that our women need protection against themselves. I think it is quite fair to assume that a good woman can exercise a more beneficent influence without the franchise than with it. I will conclude for the present with a quotation for the women's consideration ...
>   'Seek to be good, but aim not to be great.
>   A woman's noblest station is retreat,
>   Her fairest virtues fly from public sight,
>   Domestic worth that shuns too strong a light.'[67]

Retreat! For Helena Gutteridge the idea was so archaic as to be quite laughable – as it was also for Susie Clark, Mary Ellen Smith, Mary McConkey, Ida Douglas-Fearn, Florence Hall, Helen MacGill, Maria Grant, and all the other suffragists who knew their own potential and accepted their share of the work of the world. And yet on the eve of the referendum, despite a quarter-century of pleading and proselytizing, despite the last three months of vigorous campaigning, here was the same old argument for passivity and 'womanliness.' Sometimes it must have seemed to these women that the bulwarks of the old order were impregnable.

For the voters, suffrage was not even a main issue in the coming election; they were much more concerned with the question of prohibition, which was also being put to a referendum. The two issues were closely joined, of course, suffragists claiming that 'the liquor interests' were afraid of the power that voting women might wield against them. The People's Prohibition Party, headed by Board of Trade president Jonathan Rogers, waged a vigorous campaign, culminating on the eve of the election in a prohibition procession of the Committee of One Hundred led by the mayor and chief of police, with men, women, and children carrying banners, and businessmen in their automobiles bearing placards that shouted against drink.[68] In the event, the prohibitionists won their referendum and the BC Prohibition Act was brought into force the following year.[69]

On election day suffragists throughout the province participated in the only way they could: they acted as scrutineers, enjoying the novel experience of looking over the shoulders of male officials. In Susie Clark's Ward V, the twenty-two women on duty marched in impressive formation into the polling place, whereat the men cried out, 'Here come the ladies!' and 'standing gave them three cheers which rang through the building.'[70] In Vancouver, 130 women had been instructed in election procedure.[71] This lesson in practical citizenship must have seemed to them an initiation into a secret order whose rituals had hitherto been carefully guarded by men.

The voters of British Columbia approved the Bowser referendum, but not by an overwhelming majority. In Vancouver 63 per cent voted in favour; in Victoria, 59 per cent, indicating a strong, silent opposition to woman suffrage – stubborn, intransigent, and hostile to change. Indeed, in Vancouver's Ward III, an east side working class district north of Hastings Street, 61 per cent voted *against* the franchise. Vancouver City Central had not been successful in organizing this ward. By contrast, Wards V and VI, originally organized by Susie and Helena and developing into cohesive groups with great esprit de corps, returned over 70 per cent in favour.[72] The four months of hard campaigning, working through provincial, city, and ward organizations, had paid off. In rural areas, however, despite less intense campaigning, there was a more favourable response than in Vancouver, Victoria, and other urban centres.[73]

The Bowser Suffrage Act of 1916 could not be immediately proclaimed because the soldier vote had yet to be returned and counted. Thus in March 1917, when the new Liberal government took over, it could not implement the mandate given it by the suffrage referendum. Premier Harlan Brewster very quickly disposed of this dilemma: on 27 March, he repealed the Bowser Suffrage Act and also the relevant section of the 1916 Election Act. He then introduced a new bill giving women exactly the same provincial voting rights as men and the same privilege of being elected to the legislature.[74] Mr. Bowser, now speaking from the opposition side, declared himself in favour of the bill, in favour of extending the federal franchise to women – in short, in favour of women.[75]

On 5 April 1917 the bill was given third reading and royal assent. It

was a gala day: Mary McConkey, Helen MacGill, and other Liberal suffragists were given seats on the floor of the legislature in token of their
political support. They brought lilies and roses for the premier and the
attorney general.[76] The other suffragists, those who had worked to
win the referendum, were also present, but they looked down on the historic scene from the gallery: they could scarcely hope to be awarded special recognition by the Liberal Party. Although the three prairie provinces
had already accorded the vote to women, British Columbia women
would be the first in Canada to exercise their franchise. Running as an
independent in the January 1918 by-election, with no opposing Liberal
candidate, Mary Ellen Smith contested the seat in the legislature made
vacant by the death of her husband, and became British Columbia's first
woman MLA.[77]

Women still did not have the federal vote. True, the Dominion Franchise Act of 1898 stated that the qualifications for voting in federal elections were the same as for provincial elections, making no stipulations
as to sex. The federal voters' list was made up of all the provincial lists.
Thus, if British Columbia and Manitoba compiled their lists before the
next federal election, their new women voters would be on the federal
list too.[78] However, the possession of the provincial franchise did not
automatically confer on women the federal franchise. The Conservative
government was opposed to such a measure, and anti-suffrage Members of Parliament argued legal niceties to disqualify women from this
final prerogative of full Canadian citizenship. They were answered by
Sir Wilfrid Laurier and his Liberal opposition, who declared that any
legal problems could be solved quite simply by passing legislation
awarding the federal franchise to women.

Then Prime Minister Borden, after years of evasive temporizing,
suddenly made an about-face and announced himself in favour of
woman suffrage. His conversion had less to do with human rights
than with political strategy. His government's term of office expired in
October 1917, and he was preparing for the coming general election by
passing franchise legislation designed to help him win with a Union government that allied Conservative and Liberal pro-conscription forces.[79]

The War-time Elections Act of September 1917 first of all excluded
from the franchise, for the duration of the war, conscientious objectors
and foreign-born citizens from enemy countries, even those naturalized
in the last fifteen years. Thus Borden removed from the electorate voters potentially opposed to his war policy. Then it awarded the federal
franchise to women who had close relatives serving in the Canadian or
British armed forces at home or overseas.[80] Thus the names of thousands
of women, potential Conservative and Liberal pro-conscription supporters, were added to the voters' list. This was the part of the Act that

enraged suffragists. Borden's intention was clear, and it had nothing to do with granting the federal franchise to the women of Canada.[81]

Vancouver suffragists responded angrily to this ignominy. The United Suffrage Societies, Helena among the delegates, wired a protest to Sir Robert Borden and to the Liberal Opposition: 'Object to any extension of franchises to women except on same terms as to men. Demand federal franchise for women who are qualified as men are qualified.'[82] He wired back immediately that he would be sending a full explanation in the next mail.[83] Since soldiers could not campaign in the election, he was giving the vote to their nearest female relatives, who would otherwise be unable to vote. As voters, these women were only representing the interests at home of the men in the armed forces. If all women were given the vote, these men would not enjoy that special compensation earned by their service to King and country. As for the general enfranchisement of women, wartime security demanded caution: a whole population of foreign-born women, many of them German, had become British citizens through marriage.[84]

At Helena's prompting, the VTLC also wired Borden, objecting to the War-time Elections Act and urging the government to enfranchise women before proroguing Parliament. She told her fellow unionists that the Act was 'clearly a scheme designed for the return of the Borden government to power on its conscription schemes.' They received the same reply as the suffragists. 'Piffle!' snorted Helena contemptuously when the reply was read at the VTLC October meeting.[85] In this judgment she was in agreement with wide sections of the Canadian population, whose opinion was summed up by the Toronto *Mail and Empire*: 'There'd be no war-time election act if there were to be no war-time election.'[86] Meanwhile, Borden kept insisting that if he were re-elected, he would immediately introduce legislation extending the federal franchise to all Canadian women.[87]

The United Suffrage Societies telegram eventually reached the floor of the House of Commons, where New Brunswick Liberal MP William Pugsley read it aloud in a speech urging woman suffrage.[88] A few days later, H.H. Stevens, Conservative MP for Vancouver, who had actively supported the suffrage referendum campaign there, rose in his place and read a telegram from a Vancouver woman discrediting the USS as a body unrepresentative of patriotic British Columbia women: when the division was called, he voted in favour of the Act.[89] At this treachery, a delegation of fifteen indignant women from the USS confronted Stevens in his Vancouver office and hammered away at him for an hour and a half, reiterating that the USS, as a delegated body, officially represented four societies, which in turn represented a provincewide constituency of suffrage women opposed to this discriminatory legislation.

'Why did you not protest against it, and why did you vote in favour of it?' demanded Helena.[90]

The question was rhetorical. She knew as well as he that individual principle had to yield before party policy.

After his re-election, Borden kept his promise. He had exploited suffrage for his political ends; those achieved, he could afford the luxury of acting on principle. Speaking to the second reading of the Women's Franchise Bill, he declared that 'women are entitled to the franchise on their merits, and it is upon that basis that this Bill is presented to Parliament for its consideration.'[91] Despite eloquent opposition from Quebec MPs, whose deepest fears for the disintegration of the social order were attached to that female anomaly, a woman with the vote, the Women's Franchise Bill passed both House and Senate and received royal assent on 24 May 1918.[92] Women were now qualified to vote in federal elections and, with the passage of additional legislation in 1919, could run for office as Members of Parliament in the House of Commons. They could not yet be appointed to the Senate, however, not being persons under the British North America Act, as Emily Murphy discovered.

Helena had been a prime mover in the suffrage campaign: with her Evening Work Committee she had moved the campaign out of middle class parlours and into the community. She had taken the initiative in the formation of the United Suffrage Societies, which gave cohesion and solidarity to an otherwise fragmented movement. During the referendum campaign she had, with Susie Clark, organized Vancouver City Central to unite the scattered efforts of the ward referendum committees. She had helped to raise money on the Joint Finance Board, helped Anna McIntyre in the office, acted as scrutineer. She had been everywhere, organizing committees, chairing meetings, speaking from the public platform, an impassioned advocate for the Cause and recognized as one. She had brought to the suffrage campaign in British Columbia the organizing skills that she practised in her trade union work, and the worker's powerful article of faith – solidarity.

But the ubiquitous Miss Gutteridge was never fully accepted socially by the middle class women she worked with. She was, after all, a wage worker, a tailor. 'Seam, and gusset, and band,/Band, and gusset, and seam': Helena knew the 'Song of the Shirt' in her bones, and her very presence confronted others with its challenging accusation: 'It is not linen you're wearing out,/but human creatures' lives.'[93] They respected her, followed her lead more often than not, for they too were dedicated to social reform, but her union ways were foreign to them. She was a stranger from another galaxy, where a class struggle was being fought between strikers and scabs, workers and bosses, between *them* and *us*.

Also, many of the clubwomen were fervently imperialist; she was vocally anti-conscription, spoke of war profiteering, and used words like 'exploitation' and 'human slavery.'[94] Only among the women of the Mount Pleasant Suffrage League – Elizabeth Arnett, Susie Clark, Lily Laverock – did she find some degree of social acceptance. Mary Norton was right: Helena was 'frowned on a bit' by middle class clubwomen. She was excluded by 'Society.'

Society did have an opportunity to include her during Emmeline Pankhurst's 1916 visit. Here was an opportunity for the patriotic women of the Pioneer Political Equality League to underline the connection between British and Canadian suffragists, by bringing forward Helena and her little band of former WSPU militants, even though suffrage had yielded its place for the day to the war. Did they make their presentation to Mrs. Pankhurst as planned? Did they receive the gracious public recognition from her that loyalty to the Cause deserved? Newspaper reports of the luncheon make no mention of them. We do not know if Helena attended the luncheon. Certainly she was not at the head table, any more than were Susie Clark, Maria Grant, Anna McIntyre, and other suffragists persona non grata to the PPEL. However, Helena continued to reach out to middle class clubwomen on the question of the minimum wage, for example, for she knew how useful they could be if their undoubted clout could be turned to her purpose.[95]

Once the provincial vote was won in 1916, the exhilarating question of what women, true citizens at last, should do with the vote became an immediate practical problem. One group thought women should begin by learning about the political world they were entering. Two weeks after the referendum, they crowded into the Blue Room of the Hotel Vancouver to set up an 'educational organization to study political questions from a non-partisan point of view.'[96] However, the meeting soon became heatedly partisan, because a minority wanted to declare loyalties and challenge political foes in the battle for social reform.[97] Helena was among the organizers of this new Voters' Educational League, believing firmly that a non-partisan organization devoted to education was needed at this time. On an executive that was a roll call of Liberal and Conservative clubwomen, she found a place in the leadership hierarchy as head of the press committee, and ensured that the lecture topics included socialism and labour protection.[98]

Susie Clark was of a different mind. She thought women should use their new power to start reforming the world right away. After that first heated meeting to organize the Voters' Educational League, she withdrew, and with other women from the Mount Pleasant Suffrage League set up a rival organization. On 8 November 1916, at a mass meeting in the Knights of Pythias Hall in Mount Pleasant home territory, the

Wards V and VI suffrage referendum committees were transformed into the reform-oriented New Era League, with Susie Clark as president.[99] Helena was not on the executive, nor does her name appear in reports of its meetings.

'None of the new organizations seem to be making better progress than the New Era League,' the press reported six weeks later.[100] The reason was that it channelled the energy of women, exhilarated by their suffrage victory, into activities in which they felt themselves to be agents of change. They knew how to organize now, and planned to divide the city into districts as they had during the referendum campaign, in order to draw in women from all over the city. So they waded in and tackled issues, though not always with the careful research and study needed.[101] Equal pay for equal work, the drug problem, civic politics, the protection of children, international peace – all were at some time issues of vital concern, requiring an immediate resolution to be telegraphed to the mayor, the premier, the prime minister. However, the New Era League did very thorough work in connection with mothers' pensions, and, with the help of other women's groups, it succeeded in getting the Mothers' Pension Act through the legislature in 1920, under the vigorous sponsorship of their own women's advocate, MLA Mary Ellen Smith.[102] Helena and Molly Dolk, representing the VTLC, took an active part in the campaign, joining their efforts with those of Susie Clark and the New Era League and other women's organizations.[103]

By contrast, the Voters' Educational League, with a program on political philosophies and electoral and economic questions, focused on self-improvement through study and discussion.[104] Unfortunately, lectures on conservatism and socialism, on free trade and proportional representation could not, no matter how improving, sustain the original enthusiasm of the members. Helen MacGill recognized this when, at the close of the club's first year, she urged members to take up the question of the Married Woman's Property Act and other aspects of social reform legislation.[105] Such a change in program implied a more practical orientation, with less emphasis on the theoretical, but it was too late: war work was even more pressing now than the legal rights of women. The Voters' Educational League soon disbanded, and Helen MacGill took her expertise on laws for women and children to the New Era League, where she eventually became president.[106]

One would have thought the New Era League a natural place for Helena, its membership consisting of women from the Mount Pleasant Suffrage League and the BC Political Equality League with whom she had worked so closely during the suffrage referendum campaign.[107] They were all practical women like herself, dedicated to women's rights and convinced that they would indeed, with their hard-won franchise, now begin to usher in a new era. The New Era League continued into the thirties, and Helena would discover a useful role for it in the service of the unemployed. Just now she had other ideas. For although she believed that 'the reconstruction of society after the war, will rest upon an educated, awakened working class,' she was convinced that postwar reconstruction would also 'need the votes of an educated public opinion in a majority, of both men and women.'[108] In the Voters' Educational League she had an opportunity to be an agent in the educative process: she could help middle class women to become informed about politics. Always the proselytizer, she saw herself as a useful liberalizing influence, advancing the claims of labour, legitimizing socialism as a topic for study. She always had a sturdy sense of her own worth, which, if it did not break down class barriers, brought her the respect of others. When Helena spoke, people listened.

CHAPTER SIX

Hours and Wages

Yes, her hands may be hardened from labour,
And her dress may not be very fine.
But a heart in her bosom is beating,
Warm and true to her class and her kind.
That's the Rebel Girl, that's the Rebel Girl:
To the working class she's a precious pearl.
— Joe Hill, 'The Rebel Girl'

Until 1912 the west had been enjoying a period of prosperity, fuelled by a real estate boom and a spurt of construction generated by the rapid growth of a port city that was also the terminus for two transcontinental railways. In 1912 a recession set in, and not even the outbreak of war could halt the decline of the economy. A supplier of forest products and minerals, British Columbia could not be as quickly geared to war production as the eastern provinces, where manufacturing was already established as a major sector of the economy. The Dominion Trust Company and the Bank of Vancouver both failed; many small depositors lost their savings, betrayed by the unfulfilled promise of the Conservative government to guarantee trust funds. Jobless men and women flocked into Vancouver, increasing the number of unemployed to an estimated fifteen thousand in and around the city. Helena's union, however, warned all 'jours' to 'keep away from Vancouver as more than half the tailors in this city are idle.'[1] 'Up till this year,' reported *Labour Gazette* correspondent J.W. Wilkinson, 'it has been a most unusual thing to be accosted by a beggar on the street. Now it is very common to be asked for alms by men who obviously are not used to such a method of maintaining themselves.'[2]

The plight of women was even more serious, because Vancouver was a sawmill and railway city that, unlike Toronto and Winnipeg, did not have the manufacturing base in secondary industry to support a large female work force. Even in 1911, before the recession, the number of women employed in factory jobs in Vancouver was fewer than 10 per cent of the total manufacturing work force.[3] As the recession became worse, there were fewer and fewer jobs in the industries that traditionally employed women. In the summer of 1914, in response to a request from the editor of the *Labour Gazette* for statistics on unemployment among women, Helena replied that she could give him only approximate figures because the city had neither set up an employment bureau nor made any systematic effort to help increasing numbers of unemployed women to find work. In the absence of any such agency, the Municipal Crèche, 'Vancouver's youngest philanthropic institution' – a day nursery serving working mothers – was acting as an employment centre and was sending women out to do housework in people's homes while they left their children at the Crèche. Helena also collected statistics from other charitable organizations – the City Unemployment and Relief Association and the Employment Bureau of the Association of Idle or Unemployed, the Associated Charities – and from the YWCA, the Travellers' Aid, and the Victorian Order of Nurses. She had numbers at her fingertips. In May 1915 the Teachers' Relief Association gave 77 families with 185 children groceries, fuel, and children's boots to the amount of $506.93. Department stores were reducing staff, but Woolworth's had taken on 50 employees at their new store on Hastings Street. Some families who had kept two servants were economizing by letting their white maid go and keeping only the 'Chinaman' as general domestic. Steveston cannery was employing women brought out from a 'Scotch fishing village' instead of Chinese or 'Siwash Indians' to pack fish. Domestics receiving $25 per month before hard times struck Vancouver had left town rather than accept a reduced wage of $12.[4]

To Helena these statistics meant real people. If, as she reported for August 1914, 75 per cent of the city's tailoresses, dressmakers, and milliners were unemployed, she also knew that her fellow workers were scrimping and worrying about making ends meet, for she too had to manage somehow during slack seasons in the tailor trade. The Waitress and Lady Cooks' Union had their headquarters in the Labor Temple, as did the Home and Domestic Employees' Union, whose creed declaring the dignity of domestic labour was framed and hanging on the clubroom wall. Here Helena could meet with other women and trade stories about being laid off and about work on the job.

Whether or not Helena was one of the unemployed tailors we do not know, for only a few details can be gathered of her work history. From 1914 to 1916 she was secretary-treasurer of the VTLC, earning $15 per month. Then for eight months general secretary, earning the same stipend, which, however, was not enough to live on.[5] She must have been a working tailor as well; she was, after all, a delegate to the VTLC regular meetings from the Tailors' Industrial Union. Even though, as can be reasonably assumed, she had to earn a living during the day, she always seemed to be on hand for afternoon suffrage and unemployment meetings. Being a tailor, however, she did piece work and thus could have arranged her working hours to allow her to take part in suffrage and trade union activities in the afternoon as well as evening, counting on the extra income from the VTLC to make up any deficiency. The union paid sick benefits of $5 a week for ten weeks. She did not have the expense of paying a helper: local 178 enforced a strict rule against the 'aristocratic jour,' forbidding the employment of helpers. Around 1919, she was working for the firm of Perry and Dolk, Fred Perry, self-styled 'the Labor Temple Tailor,' evidently having gone into partnership.[6] If she worked for Fred Perry in 1914, when his union shop was in the Labor Temple, where she had her office, she could carry on her political and union work in the afternoons, fitting it in around her tailoring job or during the summer and fall slack seasons, when there was little work.

On either system tailors were poorly paid and worked long hours. Representing her union at one of the regular meetings of the VTLC, Helena reported that a piece-worker could, by very hard work, complete 3½ coats in a 9-hour day, in non-union shops receiving 50 cents a coat.[7] The daily wage would be only $1.75, amounting to less than $10 a week, even including earnings for Saturday morning. Presumably a union tailor would earn a little more. At Ladies Guarantee Tailors, she went on, the tailors were on strike for 60 cents an hour. They were also on strike at several other shops in the city. At Western Cloak and Suit, where women, in violation of the Factory Act, had to work a 54-hour week, the workers were on strike for an 8-hour day. Such shops were on the 'unfair' list for good union members who honoured demands for higher wages and the 8-hour day. Always strong on union solidarity, Helena was a leading member of the Label League, taking every occasion to urge workers to look for the union label and to buy locally manufactured garments.[8]

Most of the tailors in local 178 were still doing piece work, paid according to how much they produced. The union agreement stipulated the rates of pay, which varied according to the class of material used and the class of employer entering into the agreement. A silk dress or heavy whipcord trousers fetched a higher piece rate on the union scale than a flannel jacket or a seersucker cotton dress, and a high-class merchant tailor paid more than one in the cut-rate trade. Many tailors preferred piece work because wages were based on individual performance, as seemed only right and just. Tailors had traditionally accommodated the demands of the custom trade, working long hours during the summer and fall, when orders were plentiful, and scarcely at all when they were slack. The Journeymen Tailors' Union of America had been trying for some years to move to the weekly wage system with an eight-hour day, but because of the seasonal nature of the industry, attempts to regulate hours and abolish piece work proved difficult. The union secretary reported in 1914 that he knew of only two union shops in Vancouver on the weekly system with an eight-hour day, and these had been organized by local 178.[9]

The tailor's craft was being seriously threatened in these years by factory production, and one solution to this problem was to make common cause with the machine-operating garment workers. A great many journeymen tailors resisted the idea: 'How could *we* unite with such common people?' exclaimed one tailor in mock horror. He then seriously advised tailors to accept reality:

> We are fast following the steps taken by our predecessor, the once famous shoemaker and for the same reason: *'because the system of production has changed.'*
>
> People cannot afford the fifty dollar suit anymore; ready-made clothing is good enough for most people who are not jour tailors, and the more fastidious ones can indulge in a made-to-order suit from $15 up.[10]

In 1913, soon after Helena became a union member, the Journeymen Tailors' Union of America voted to unite all clothing workers in one organization, the Tailors' Industrial Union (TIU) of America, the better to protect the economic interests of the custom tailor. The VTLC supported the change, but Helena, a loyal advocate of craft unionism, opposed it.[11] She had served her apprenticeship, gone to the very top and beyond, leaving the trade to become a cutter: belonging to an industrial union challenged her sense of herself as a skilled worker set apart from 'basting pullers' and button sewers and common machine operators. As president of the TIU in 1914, she was one of the vocal opposition to the international membership, dubbed 'conservative and reactionary' by the radical industrial unionists for continuing to resist losing their craft identity in an industrial union.[12] In subsequent referendums conducted by international headquarters, her influence as president of local 178 was apparent: it voted unanimously against forming an Amalgamated Clothing Workers of America and for a return to the craft jurisdiction of the Journeymen Tailors. In the end, craft unionism won. In 1915 the tailors became Journeymen Tailors again and Samuel Gompers declared them restored to the AFL.

As president of local 178, Helena undertook an organizing drive to increase membership, and requested funds from the international office to carry out the work. Chinese tailors, perceived as serious competition in the early part of the decade at least, were not members of the union, and Helena, in line with the anti-Oriental policy of the VTLC, apparently took no initiative in this regard. Union membership did increase, but not among women as much as she had hoped. Unfortunately, lamented

Helena, Vancouver working women were not interested in trade unions: they were an apathetic lot.[13]

Her main organizing work in 1914 was among unemployed women. As secretary of the Local Council of Women committee on unemployment, she initiated a mass meeting of women in St. Andrew's Wesley Church, chaired by council president Mrs. J.K. Unsworth, a minister's wife. Helena, as one of the main speakers, declared that the unemployed women did not want charity; they wanted work. The purpose of the meeting was to discover how work might be found for them. The meeting decided to form a women's employment agency consisting of six members from the council and representatives from all the other women's organizations in Vancouver. Mayor T.S. Baxter cautiously offered the support of the city. The second contingent of volunteers now being trained for overseas would be needing 1,000 to 1,500 uniforms. If the federal government were to let that contract to Vancouver manufacturers, the city would see to it that their price was competitive with eastern prices. The Women's Employment League (WEL) was subsequently formed, with Mrs. Unsworth as president, and within ten days over three hundred women had registered for work. Helena, Mrs. Unsworth, and their committees were suddenly welfare workers, supplying destitute families with groceries and single women with meal tickets and accommodation in family homes, and scouting around to place as many as possible in jobs as domestics.[14]

In those first weeks of October, the unemployed women met every morning at the Labor Temple – stenographers, waitresses, store clerks; some strangers in the city with no one to turn to, others single with an unemployed father or ailing mother to support; women providing for children, their husbands out of work or, worse, simply having deserted them out of desperation at the impossibility of finding work. There was comfort in these meetings and a certain exhilaration in discovering that, talking and working with others, one might have some control over one's life after all. Certainly, it must have been bracing to hear Helena tear a strip off Premier Richard McBride, who, at a meeting to consider the effects of the war on the province's economy, had stoutly urged 'courage and confidence.'[15]

'Courage, indeed!' snorted Helena. 'The courage [shown] by many mothers who are striving to keep the bodies and souls of their children together and maintain the self-respect which shrinks from charity is enough to make angels weep.' Sir Richard had been apprehensive that, if women were given the vote, they might neglect their homes and children. 'Now is the time for Sir Richard to protect the homes and the children,' she observed drily. 'Give work to the fathers of families and the mothers will not have to neglect the home and children, when trying to get food for the family by doing washing, scrubbing, sewing, and for those who are, in theory, so very anxious to protect family life.'[16]

The WEL asked the provincial government for financial help, but received only $500, and that two and a half months after the women had launched a make-work scheme of their own. Repeated telegrams to Ottawa asking that soldiers' uniforms be made in Vancouver brought no response. In the fall of 1914, the league finally decided to start a toy-making cooperative, the toys to be ready for sale that Christmas. With this plan Helena and her committee approached Vancouver City Council with a request for $2,000 and obtained the money with no difficulty.[17]

But it was already the third week in October. They would have to work fast to organize their cooperative, house and feed the women, set up the workshop, train the workers, and produce a marketable commodity in time for a Christmas sale – a matter of only seven weeks.

They found a thirty-three-room building at 1027 Robson Street in downtown Vancouver, Carvell Hall, took a six-month lease, and energetically set about their task. This large room would be the workshop: by the end of the week they had installed the manufacturing equipment. Here would be the culinary department: counters, sink, stove, tables; and yes, Mrs. Hamilton Wood, culinary gold medallist from the Imperial Institute in London, England, would take charge. By 9 November sixty girls and women were making dolls and other toys at $3.50 per day, working three days a week to spread the work around.[18] Meanwhile, in the kitchen another crew chopped suet and citron, mixed batters, and put them on to steam and fill the rooms with the comforting aroma of Christmas pudding. The women also decided to take orders for dressmaking and other kinds of sewing, whereupon a captain of the Vancouver militia sent in an order for 1,200 'housewives' and 1,200 holdalls, and 12 garment workers began forthwith to cut and baste and stitch on their machines. Soon six more rooms had to be converted to workshops. Eventually, 150 women suffering varying degrees of poverty, family crisis, and physical and mental distress found work at the Carvell Hall Co-operative Settlement. Helena was familiar with the concept of the settlement house from England, where the cultural needs of the poorer city neighbourhoods were served by a resident staff of social workers. Carvell Hall was not a settlement house in this sense, the community working as a cooperative to provide employment and shelter.

The part of Carvell Hall not needed for workshops was made into a residence initially providing accommodation for some fifty women. Others found lodgings in private homes. The furnishing of the residence was undertaken by the United Suffrage Societies, who solicited donations and provided curtains and bedding. It was both home and workplace for these single women. They had their meals in the cafeteria, wages covering board and room, with a small amount left over for pocket money. They could invite friends to visit in pleasantly furnished sitting rooms. Helena and other WEL committee members were gratified to see these girls and women thus securely established, because one of the dangers confronting unemployed women was the last-ditch resort of turning to prostitution, or, as Helena phrased it in the euphemistic manner of the day, a 'terrible disaster from which they might never be rescued.'[19]

Help came from well-to-do people accustomed to accepting their charitable responsibilities towards the less fortunate. Members of the Vancouver elite held a French cabaret in aid of the WEL: the Rogerses, Jukeses, Dunsmuirses, Bell-Irvingses, and Van Rogganses sang 'Tipperary' and 'I'll Make a Man of Everyone of You' at the Avenue Theatre. The pupils of Madame Este Avery sang at a benefit recital. The San Francisco Fur Company on Granville Street donated a beautiful doll, put up for raffle as 'Lady Dorothy.' The Valcartier Chapter of the Daughters of the Empire held a musicale, 'the tea table ... centred by a huge bowl of red tulips and white narcissus resting on a mirror base ... bordered by blue tulle.'[20]

The toys went on sale three weeks before Christmas at the White Sewing Machine Company on Granville Street, where the cooperative had been given display space for their wares – the output of only three weeks of labour, and essentially unskilled labour at that. On that first Saturday they also set up eight stalls on Hastings and Granville Streets. Besides the traditional Mother Goose dolls and tinselled fairies and clowns and Punch and Judys, they offered a number of toys inspired by the war: Belgian milk carts drawn by dogs, military dolls representing France, Britain, and Russia of the Triple Entente; Scottish Highlanders in regimental kilts; Red Cross nurses, toy cannon, and even a wind-up toy setting in motion a wrestling match between King George V and the Kaiser. The anti-war Helena seems not to have been aware of the pro-war statement she and her colleagues were making by offering such toys for sale, or perhaps considered them harmless, even benevolent.

Just before Christmas they auctioned off the unsold goods, and when they added up their sales, including proceeds from sewing and Christmas cakes and puddings, the total came to $2,593.65. The plan was to invest most of this in a new enterprise in the new year. Neither Mrs. Unsworth nor Helena received any payment for their work.

Even though some fifteen hundred dollars' worth of stock and materials was still unsold, the toy factory was felt to be a big success, as was the whole Carvell Hall Co-operative Settlement scheme. The women who had been helped by the WEL – unemployed single women, destitute widows, and deserted wives – recognized Helena as the moving spirit, and showed their gratitude by presenting her with a gold watch, suitably inscribed.[21] Helena kept the watch to the end of her days, a daily testimony to her work during that urgent time when compassion and indignation demanded that every nerve be stretched to deal with immediate crisis.

In the new year, 1915, with the names of a thousand unemployed women on their register, the WEL bravely tried to set up another job-creation program. For unemployed men, City Council allotted funds for relief work, putting them to work on sewers, cemeteries, and streets, or providing them with piles of stones to break or logs to saw into cordwood. And, of course, there was always Stanley Park, where a thousand acres of rain forest needed to be cut back and tamed.[22] For unemployed women no such emergency programs were available.

The WEL, still staunchly believing that it could solve the unemployment problem by its own efforts, decided to set up an industrial department. The most obvious product was plain and fancy sewing. They went to city shops with sample items to take orders. They also opened up a delicatessen annex, directed by the worthy Mrs. Wood. It should have been possible for several dozen women to be employed making bread, cakes, and pressed meats and serving at the delicatessen counter, with several dozen more operating sewing machines or plying their embroidery needles. Here, after all, were enterprise and enormous energy and initiative. Disappointingly, Vancouver merchants did not, as the women hoped, eagerly greet them with large orders for embroidered pillow cases, and Vancouver homes did not abandon their bakers and butchers in the cause of needy women with floured loaves and jellied veal to sell. For, as a *Province* editorial made clear, women did not have to be unemployed: they could take jobs as domestics in return for board and room. Instead, they were stepping outside their allotted sphere, competing with men as clerks in offices and dry goods stores. 'But,' the editorial rumbled on, 'the trouble is with the inefficient girl who wants to have a good time and not work for it, or the girl who is willing to work but wants to do things her own way.'[23] If Vancouver merchants shared this attitude, little wonder they did not warm to the idea of women engaged in business for themselves.

The co-operative's industrial department faded away, but funds were set aside for a possible reopening. The six-month lease on Carvell Hall expired towards the end of March. In the four months of its operation, the Carvell Hall Co-operative Settlement had found employment for nearly 500 women. In February 1915, 700 women were still registered, women still looking for work. Meal tickets totalling $275 in value were given to such women, 'a veritable boon,' observed Helena, 'to women who were absolutely in need of food ...'[24] The WEL continued to exist as an employment bureau and relief agency for women. In November, Helena reported to the *Labour Gazette* that the WEL still had 350 unemployed women on its books but had decided not to undertake another Christmas job program. Single unemployed women would not be manufacturing toys that Christmas. Instead, any funds remaining in the treasury would be used to tide them over until they could find work. 'The Young Women's Christian Association,' she continued, 'will as usual during the winter months, provide free meals for women and girls in distress, also sleeping accomadation [*sic*] until such time as work can be found for them.' The dressmaking, tailoring, and garment industries were for the most part operating part time and, being seasonal trades, would be laying off their workers in January and February. Helena predicted that the worst was over; conditions were improving and 'although some distress is expected there is no doubt that help, if not employment will be forthcoming for those who are in need.'[25] Helena was a great one for the impersonal passive voice. What she meant was that she and Mrs. Unsworth and other members of the WEL would continue to listen to stories of hardship and do what they could to help. In this report, she does not mention Carvell Hall Co-operative Settlement; presumably the WEL had been forced to abandon it.

The closing of the workshop was a disappointment, but Helena understood that such projects would never solve the problem of unemployment in Vancouver or anywhere else. Certainly, if governments would not act, then women must act to help themselves. Yet the underlying causes of unemployment would remain as long as workers were exploited under capitalism. While the practical Helena was setting up the toy factory, the theoretical and socialist Helena was declaiming in the pages of the *British Columbia Federationist*:

> What is wrong with the system, that, at the first financial crisis, thousands of women and men are faced with starvation ...
> Surely the time has come for a radical change! A change whereby the bulk of the people – the workers – will really be represented by a system of government that will study the greatest good for the greatest number.[26]

The greatest number excluded Orientals, however. Her attitude was not surprising in a city with a history of anti-Asian feeling. In 1914 the BC Federation of Labor in convention passed a resolution demanding total exclusion of all Asians as a means of alleviating unemployment.[27] Oriental labourers, paid very low wages for longer hours, actually dominated the lumbering, fishing, and canning industries, the needle trades, and the laundry business.[28] Asians were commonly referred to as 'the yellow horde,' and the *British Columbia Federationist* had no scruples about printing racist slurs. Praising the food at the Carvell cooperative lunch counter, one of its writers exclaimed, 'No "chink hash ..." Good plain wholesome food cooked by white women ...'[29]

When Helena considered ways and means of putting unemployed women to work, she too seized upon the possibility of displacing the much-reviled Oriental worker. Early in 1915, when the industrial department of her Carvell cooperative was faltering, she appeared before the Board of Licence Commissioners at Vancouver City Hall to plead for Oriental hotel workers to be replaced by white women. 'I have no color prejudice,' she claimed, 'but I think in this case and in the interest of efficient white female labor in this city the board might put a white labor clause in the granting of hotel licenses, so that work being done by Chinese help to-day may be done by white women who are now out of employment.'[30]

For a woman with Helena's strong sense of justice and feeling of human kinship (as demonstrated when she worked alongside Japanese cannery workers), this is a surprising statement, even considering the basic assumptions of Canadian society at that time, which, refusing Orientals the vote, implicitly relegated them to the position of permanent foreigners. Totally preoccupied with the problems of women, she did not see that her preferential treatment of white women at the expense of the Chinese amounted to racial prejudice. White workers came before Chinese workers: that was her position. She understood full well that both were a supply of cheap labour, but she was essentially a unionist and adhered to unionist anti-Asian policy, as opposed to pure, unpragmatic socialist doctrine declaring the system the enemy, not the Chinese or Sikh worker. On this question she demonstrated a tenacity of mind that made her vulnerable to errors in judgment and led her to betray her decent, human feelings.[31]

The board later passed a motion recommending that hotels employ white women, and City Council financed alterations to the YWCA so that white women could be employed instead of 'Chinamen.'[32] In 1919, no longer preoccupied with jobs for white waitresses, she adopted the Socialist Party position of solidarity of all workers, white and Asian. Arguing for the minimum wage at the National Industrial Conference in Ottawa, she declared that 'Chinamen' would cease to be an economic threat if they, equally with all workers, regardless of race, were paid a living wage.[33]

As the war dragged on and more and more Vancouver men joined up, women began to take over their jobs. The idea that women might actually free men for active service was gaining credibility: 'Women allowed behind the dress goods departments of the big dry goods firms etc. would be of utmost value,' the Vancouver *World* boldly declared.[34] A

Women's Voluntary Reserve Corps had been formed, and one of its priorities was to register women who were willing to take men's jobs for the duration of the war, with the understanding that they would vacate these positions when the men returned. Even though the members of the Reserve Corps visited businessmen and solicited their cooperation, their efforts met with little success.[35] Neither were jobs immediately available in war work, because the war did not at once stimulate the economy and provide more jobs. In western Canada, women did not become employed as munitions workers until around 1917.[36]

Times got better, the Women's Employment League ceased to exist, but the problem of low wages and long hours still had to be tackled. Helena shifted focus, and in 1917 organized the Minimum Wage League to press the government to enact legislation that would 'ensure to the working woman a wage that is based upon the cost of living' and at the same time bring in the eight-hour day. 'Then,' Helena promised, 'will cease to exist the disgraceful affairs that prevailed at Christmas [1917], when one store manager paid the magnificent sum of ten cents per night to his employees who were working late for the Christmas trade.'[37] Helena engaged the active support of the Vancouver Trades and Labor Council. At the organizing meeting of 25 October, she had president J.H. McVety and secretary Victor Midgely on the platform with her to urge working women to organize. Twenty-five women immediately joined the new organization, among them Helena's future sister-in-law Leslie Fearn, who was on the committee to draft a constitution. Only self-supporting, wage-earning women were eligible to join the leagues but the twice-monthly meetings at the Labor Temple were open to everyone and attracted a diverse audience.[38]

The minimum wage movement to fix wages for workers, whether male or female, began in New Zealand and Australia in the 1890s, and the years before the First World War saw similar legislation enacted in Great Britain. In the United States, where freedom of contract was protected by the constitution, the wages of male workers could not be thus regulated. Women and children being exempt from such constitutional protection, minimum wage laws for them were enacted in ten American jurisdictions in 1912 and 1913. In British Columbia, the Local Councils of Women, the Women's Forum, the Political Equality League, and the University Women's Club all favoured such preferential wage legislation and could look to the example of California, Oregon, and Washington. However, the women had not gone beyond debating the issue and passing resolutions. Helena appealed to them to support the work of the Minimum Wage League and presented them with a plan for concerted action.[39] The University Women's Club was one of the societies that responded, with Helen MacGill taking the lead. Mary Ellen

Smith was another powerful ally, talking about minimum wage from the hustings during her election campaign. In her first speech to the legislature, she declared that she intended to press for 'legislation in the best interests of the women and children of the province.'[40]

Helena planned to take a deputation to the legislature requesting minimum wage legislation at the coming session in March. In February she set in motion the democratic machinery for accomplishing the plan – public meetings, invitations to other organizations, committee meetings to organize fundraising. She herself chaired a brisk meeting, keeping her eye on adjournment at ten o'clock. A masquerade ball, two hundred couples in the grand march, brought in a tidy sum for the league, and after that St. Patrick's Day happily provided the occasion for the obligatory whist drive and dance. Helena found time to serve on the ball committee.[41] Such affairs provided a full social calendar for women like Helena and her reformer friends.

With newly elected MLA Mary Ellen Smith speaking for the Minimum Wage League from the Labor Temple platform, the campaign could not fail to attract wide support. She spoke of the 'temptations' offered poorly paid girl workers and of the spread of tuberculosis among them because of malnutrition and overwork, and pledged herself to work for passage of minimum wage legislation.[42]

On the evening of 5 March 1918, Helena and her delegation took the night boat to Victoria. In the morning they consulted first with their own Mary Ellen, then made their proposals known to Attorney General J. deB. Farris. Helena's good friend, Leslie Fearn, was one of four delegates from the league. The Vancouver Local Council of Women, the New Era League, the Progressive Home Workers' League, the Women's Institutes of British Columbia, the Vancouver Retail Clerks' Association, and the BC Federation of Labour all sent representatives. In Victoria the delegates were joined by the Victoria Trades and Labor Council and the Retail Clerks' Association. Helena headed the delegation and, as first speaker, asked for a government measure, specifying in detail what it should contain: an industrial welfare commission with the deputy minister of labour as chairman and four women as members, one each from New Westminster and Victoria and two from Vancouver. Its task would be to investigate the cost of living and fix a minimum wage for an eight-hour day that would be a living wage; that is, adequate to keep a woman healthy and provide her with sufficient food, clothing, shelter, and recreation. Attorney General Farris assured the delegation that the government was favourably disposed to the proposed legislation and would indeed appoint a commission to administer the bill. He himself would have to introduce the bill, but would see to it that their woman MLA received due credit as its initiator.[43]

The bill was introduced on 22 March, and Mary Ellen Smith moved second reading four days later. In the debate, no MLAs spoke in opposition, and the Minimum Wage Bill for Women received royal assent on 23 April 1918, only six months from the beginning of the campaign Helena had started the previous autumn.[44] On 19 July the government appointed a Minimum Wage Board. To the women who took part in the campaign, who had been put off on similar missions again and again by an intransigent government, it must have seemed at first that the millennium had arrived. They did not obtain four women regional representatives on the board as they wished, but were pleased with the appointment of Helen Gregory MacGill, whose expertise on laws affecting women and children was much respected. Deputy Minister of Labour J.D. McNiven was chairman; the third member was Thomas Mathews, a member of the Vancouver School Board.

Most important, they had won the recognition that wages had to be based on the cost of living. The first task of the new three-member board was to send out questionnaires to women workers and their employers. The women were asked to give an itemized account of their yearly expenses: for rent and food, shoes and stockings, dresses and petticoats, corsets and coats; for doctor's bills and insurance as well as for newspapers and postage. The employers were simply asked to give the number of women over the age of eighteen in their employ and the weekly wage paid them. Women workers were divided into nine categories: mercantile (store clerks, checkers, mail-order workers, stock markers); laundry, cleaning and dyeing; public housekeeping (waitresses, housekeepers, cleaners, cooks, helpers, chambermaids, elevator operators); office occupations; manufacturing; personal service (manicuring, hairdressing, barbering, attendants at amusement places or garages and service stations, but not domestic servants); telephone and telegraph occupations; fishing; and the fruit and vegetable industries, excluding fruit pickers and farm labourers. The board would study the findings and make separate recommendations for each category.[45] Thus the women were no longer simply an anonymous supply of cheap labour. They were workers with special skills, individuals with specific needs that had to be supplied.

The board was charged with fixing a minimum wage for each category and also with fixing maximum hours and working conditions. In making its judgments, it was required to hold public hearings or 'conferences,' after which representatives for the employers and the employees with three members of the 'disinterested public' were to consider all the evidence presented and negotiate a wage 'adequate to supply the necessary cost of living.'[46] Employer and employee across the bargaining table from each other were like cat and canary sitting down together, since women wage workers, inexperienced at carrying on negotiations, scarcely wielded the necessary clout. As a result the wage arrived at was usually a compromise that fell short of a subsistence wage. Nevertheless, for the first time in their lives at least some unorganized women wage workers in British Columbia had a voice in determining what they should be paid. The board did not have to abide by the recommendations of these conferences, but in most cases it did.

The work of the Minimum Wage League was largely completed, but Helena did not want to leave the unskilled women workers unorganized, for they did not know how to fight for their own survival. She took on the task of organizing them by transforming the league into a union to work for better working conditions and wages. The Women's Industrial Union and Minimum Wage League accepted as members only those who did not belong to a recognized union – cannery workers, for example, whose work was seasonal. Helena was not a proponent of industrial unionism as advocated by the Industrial Workers of the World, which favoured a syndicalist or industrial form of organization for society. The radical socialists in the VTLC were talking industrial unionism. Helena herself was a strong craft unionist, but with the idea of industrial unionism so much in the air, in her practical way she thought of forming an umbrella group for unskilled women who went from job to job and had to submit to whatever hours, wages, and working conditions the bosses imposed. A women's union embracing a number of industries would, Helena reasoned, allow for concerted action and provide the solidarity needed for effective bargaining. The industries remaining to be unionized were relatively few, for the laundry workers had just organized their own union. The department store clerks could join the Retail Clerks' Association, though, as Helena observed, not many did, feeling themselves a cut above mere union workers.[47]

Helena's work in the summer and fall of 1918 was carried along on the wave of a labour movement growing in strength and confidence. The BC Federation of Labor had run candidates in the federal election of 1917, with Helena as campaign manager for her VTLC colleagues Victor Midgely and J.H. McVety. Her colleagues thought that she was 'probably the only woman in Canada to ever fill such a position.'[48] After the federation's convention in 1918, some delegates formed the Federated Labor Party. Helena was on the executive of this labour reform group, which, however, stated its Marxist intention to achieve 'collective ownership and democratic operation of the means of wealth production.' Thus oriented, the new party won over former SPC members Parm Pettipiece, J.H. McVety, J.H. Hawthornthwaite, and even that fiery revolutionary, E.T. Kingsley. Another, more radical group in the VTLC was impatient with parliamentary reform: socialist visionaries, they were inspired by the events of November 1917 and had hopes for the establishment of Canadian Soviets. Both factions aggressively demanded higher wages and better working conditions, and strikes were endemic throughout the province. Angry talk of a general strike was in the air, fuelled by the federal government's conscription bill and by its order-in-council on censorship, which made illegal the possession of socialist publications. The new War Labour Policy was equally galling because it gave lip service to collective bargaining and the right to organize while outlawing strikes and lockouts for the duration of the war. When the general strike did come in August, it was in response to the shooting of a labour leader, Albert 'Ginger' Goodwin, hiding out in the wilderness of Vancouver Island to evade the draft.

The BC Federation of Labor actively opposed conscription and Helena was one of the speakers in their campaign. From the platform of Vancouver's Avenue Theatre on Main Street one warm summer evening, she stated the labour-socialist view (and this was the speech that would have shocked Emmeline Pankhurst) that Britain was not fighting to preserve freedom but to maintain her share of world markets. 'Until they take over the whole question of food and wealth, and see that all receive their fair share of the products of the country, I will not believe their talk of democracy,' she declared. She did not mince words: 'They talk of gallant little Belgium but they did not years ago when King Leopold was investing his spare money in the Congo, and the terrible atrocities in connection with the rubber industry were being committed.'[49]

When the federal government finally enacted conscription, many workers went into hiding, and military police, aided by special constables, scoured the woods for them. Among these draft evaders was Ginger Goodwin, blacklisted for his part in the Vancouver Island coal miners' strike of 1912-14, and subsequently Socialist Party candidate in Ymir riding, which included Trail. As financial secretary of the Trail local of the International Union of Mine, Mill and Smelter Workers, he was the union's leading protagonist dealing with Consolidated Mining and Smelting Company. He was also in the running for the post of deputy minister in the new British Columbia Department of Labour, his union's nomination endorsed by the VTLC. In short, Ginger Goodwin was a labour contender to reckon with. Originally declared unfit for military service, he was later reclassified and moved to Class A, even though he was probably suffering from tuberculosis. At the end of July 1918, special constable Dan Campbell discovered Goodwin on the shore of Comox Lake on Vancouver Island, and shot and killed him with a soft-nosed bullet of the sort used for hunting big game. Campbell was charged with murder, but was later exonerated by a special inquiry at which he pleaded self-defence. Goodwin, like other draft evaders, was known to possess a rifle for shooting small game for food. The court preliminary investigation heard police testimony that a rifle was indeed discovered in the dead man's hand, but this evidence was called into question by the fact that Campbell had been alone with the body for some minutes before his superior officer arrived on the scene. Labour bluntly accused Campbell of carrying out 'shoot to kill' orders. 'What we want to know,' demanded Bill Pritchard at a special meeting of the VTLC, 'is if the military authorities, in the roundup of evaders, will shoot a man on sight for his labor activities.'[50]

Led by the Metal Workers, the VTLC sent out a call for a twenty-four-hour general strike to protest the shooting. At noon on 2 August, Vancouver union men stopped work in memory of Ginger Goodwin, and the city gradually ground to a halt. Perceived as an unpatriotic gesture when the Empire was still fighting the Hun and was allegedly threatened by the Bolsheviks, this action galvanized businessmen and other anti-socialist citizens. They organized a demonstration of returned soldiers, providing them with cars, and late that afternoon a hot-headed crowd of some three hundred veterans descended on the Labor Temple, broke down the door, and shattered windows. Helena was in the office with VTLC secretary Victor Midgely at the time. Soldiers seized him and forced him out a second-storey window onto a coping. When he managed to climb back inside, they would have pushed him out again if stenographer Frances Foxcroft had not rushed to the window and stood in front of it, defying them to attack a woman. They wrestled with her, but she stood her ground and Midgely was saved.[51]

Recounting the episode many years later, Helena confesses to being 'pretty nervous' because she had in her purse three hundred dollars in union dues from the laundry workers, whom she had just organized. She does not mention the attack on Victor or Frances's brave defence of him.[52] In retrospect, she may have wished that she too had gallantly rushed into the fray. Instead, she had reacted prudently, politically, and in the event had not been assaulted, though the half-crazed soldiers, wildly striking out in all directions, throwing record books and papers to the floor and out the window, and already provoked by one defiant woman, might very well have ripped her purse out of her hand. The laundry workers' union dues were saved and Victor too, though he was beaten up and forced to kiss the flag, and Frances was badly bruised. The violence continued the next day, when soldiers again attacked a labour headquarters, this time the Longshoremen's Hall. Charging up a long flight of stairs, they were met by longshoremen who beat them back using chair legs as staves.

When Helena brought the laundry workers out on strike early in September, Vancouver workers were in a fighting mood. The Laundrymen's Association gave the laundry workers an ultimatum: leave the union or lose your jobs. In defiance, girls and women at seven laundries stopped work and went on the picket line. Some were being paid as little as $7.25 per week, with no overtime pay for more than 48 hours. Already, in the few weeks of its existence, the union had won a 48-hour week and time and a half for overtime. Now they were demanding $12 for a 44-hour week. At first the owners refused to discuss the wage scale submitted by the union, but eventually offered $10.50, which the workers refused, measuring it against the $13.20 minimum wage settlement achieved in Washington. A few days later the owners agreed to the union's wage scale, but refused to submit to the demand for a closed-shop, that is, the restriction of employment to union members only. The laundry owners were adamant, not least Alderman Thomas Kirk, a major shareholder in one of the large laundries.[53] The union held firm. The deputy minister of labour, as mediator, brought the laundry owners' new offer to the union. He reported to the meeting that the owners thought that 'Miss Gutteridge was the cause of all the trouble, that the girls would not have known that eight, nine and ten dollars a week was insufficient to live upon had she not have [sic] told them, and that she, Miss Gutteridge, was responsible for the demand of a closed shop.' Challenged to correct this view, the meeting erupted in wild cheering and clapping, and voted unanimously to refuse the offer. The women felt their power. They could take on Alderman Kirk and all the other owners. They would stand firm and get a decent wage and a closed shop too. 'The owners are on their knees now,' gloated Helena.[54]

They had reason to be confident. Eighty-five per cent of the laundry workers had joined the union and solidly supported the strike. The whole labour movement was behind them. Money for the strike fund came in from unions all over the province. VTLC president Ernest Winch and secretary Victor Midgely joined the strike committee. The Steam and Operating Engineers, whose members were crucial to the operation of the laundries, were ready to support a general strike in aid of their union comrades. 'The laundry workers have decided to fight to the last ditch,' wrote Helena, 'and have shown that they are worthy of the support and assistance of organized labour. The Labor movement cannot allow it to become a failure.'[55]

The first benefit whist drive and dance for the strike fund was a roaring success. 'Every branch of organized labor turned out in great style and numbers. It did one's heart good to witness such a feeling of fellowship that existed in that hall.'[56] The crowd was so large that a second orchestra had to be called in to play for the overflow in a second room. Helena spoke to the crowd from both platforms and was cheered and applauded. Here was leadership. Here was solidarity forever.

Helena was strong, her women were strong, and the men were behind them. But in their demand for a closed shop they were all unrealistic. They could not know that, despite lip service on the part of governments to the idea of collective bargaining and the right to organize, British Columbia workers would have to fight for another twenty years for those privileges.

And even as they were dancing, the Spanish flu was decimating their ranks. 'It is with deep regret,' Helena reported, 'that the organization records the death of four of the union members from the prevailing epidemic. All were from IXL Laundry Bros. George Baker, Nick Pervie, and Sisters Roxbury and Josie Liens were laid to rest in Mountain View Cemetery.'[57] A week later, longshoreman union leader Gordon Kelly died of the flu. The long funeral procession walked behind the band of the Musicians' Union playing the *Marseillaise* as a slow march. The city imposed a ban on meetings; consequently the VTLC could not collect strike funds in the usual way. Helena did not lose heart. 'Victory is in sight,' she urged, even as the death of her comrades was announced.[58]

The laundry workers, too, were still enthusiastic and full of fight, even though winter was coming on. They built wooden sheds for picket shelters. They sent a special picket to St. John's church to remind Alderman Kirk, when he emerged from prayers, of his Christian responsibilities towards them. The ban on meetings was soon lifted, allowing them to resume fundraising. As the strike entered its fourth month, however, the financial burden became too much for them and for their fellow unionists. They had raised nearly fifteen thousand dollars in all, but part of that money had to be used for the legal defence of one of their members, W. Geoffroy, convicted of assaulting a strikebreaker. Violence had erupted on the picket line. First, Alice Morrow, wife of the proprietor of the Star Laundry Company and, as a member of the Pioneer Political Equality League, one of Helena's suffrage colleagues, hit a striking driver over the head. The union did not lay charges. Then the laundry proprietors claimed Geoffroy had assaulted one of their workers who had crossed the picket line. The union thought the circumstances suspicious, for the woman strikebreaker did not report the incident for five days, and only at the urging of her employer did she lay charges against Geoffroy. He protested his innocence. His fellow union members believed him, claimed he had been framed, gave him legal support, and, when he was convicted and sent to jail, appealed his case. His defence was a costly business and weighed heavily on the union. The labour movement was sympathetic but could not continue indefinitely to supply the kind of financial support the laundry workers needed.

In the meantime, the Minimum Wage Board was preparing to hold its first conference. 'Hot Time at Labor Temple Meeting,' announced the

British Columbia Federationist, reporting the response of a vociferous crowd gathered to hear MLA Mary Ellen Smith and Attorney General Farris explain the new bill and its method of implementation. When Helena got up to speak, she roused the crowd still further:

> Miss Helena Gutteridge referred to [the] legislation as 'the grand child [*sic*] of public opinion' and hoped there were going to be several more grandchildren soon. (Laughter) No government could go ahead of public opinion (A man's voice – 'You've got to get a club to 'em'; and more laughter.) The Department of Labor, she said, was not what its name implied (Hear, hear); it was a department of 'capital and labor.'[59]

A few days later, in the first week of December, the board made its first award, establishing regulations for the mercantile industry. At the conference that brought forward the recommendations for the award, two of the three representatives from the disinterested public were anti-feminist Father O'Boyle and feminist Susie Clark. Employees faced employers across the table, and one Hudson's Bay Company department store employee found her boss sitting opposite her. The questionnaires submitted by store employees had shown their average cost of living to be a modest $16.81 a week, an estimate based on very scanty evidence, however, for only a very few women had responded. With earnings of $10 or $11 a week, they did not earn enough to cover expenses. A few experienced saleswomen earned as much as $25 a week, but a notions clerk was paid as little as $3 a week, cash girls, $6. The employers did not question the cost of living claimed by their store employees, even when pressed by Father O'Boyle to do so, but they refused to offer a wage that would meet it. Finally, an agreement was drawn up for a wage of $12.75 a week for women over eighteen, though one tough-minded employee refused to sign. Helena was not satisfied with the settlement, and said so. Women who had been receiving starvation wages would certainly benefit, she admitted, but many had dependents to support and should receive a breadwinner's wage. Moreover, the qualifying age should have been set lower, because employers would likely replace female clerks over the age of eighteen with younger ones not bound by the new regulations.[60]

Helen MacGill gave a more realistic assessment of the Minimum Wage Board's first award. Recalling the bargaining session between employer and employee, she wrote:

> The employees came hoping for $18.00 a week, but thinking that $16.00 might do. The employers that $5.00 was fair and $6.00 was liberal. Reconciling these two points of view and drawing them into reasonable

agreement was like trying to buy a diamond necklace in the fifteen-cent store. Long and prolonged discussion took place with the two opposing sides walking around in circles. The baffled but hopeful public representatives offering suggestions whenever they saw an opening, but were embarrassed in trying to get the lamb and the lion to lie down together with the lamb outside ... When after several straw votes all but one conferee agreed upon $12.75 for a forty-eight hour week, everyone heaved a sigh of relief.

Canada's first Minimum Wage order nearly dead aborning was launched! It was $2.25 less than some employees thought it should be, but $7.75 more than a number of employers deemed necessary ...

Long a champion of women's rights, Helen MacGill viewed the response of the employers with a shrewd humour that revealed her sympathies:

The best of the employers accepted it gracefully, they knew it was necessary; they hoped it might be good, but they took the chairman's assertion that it would not hurt, in the spirit that the patient takes the similar comforting but doubtful assurance of the dentist or the doctor. There were others who received the announcement with surprised resentment. They felt any action on the part of the employees was equal to the turning of an ungrateful worm.[61]

The laundry workers kept walking the picket line. Meanwhile, just before Christmas, the board decided on a minimum wage for laundry workers of $13.50 for a 48-hour week, or 28.12 cents an hour, an amount fairly close to their calculated cost of living of $14.85.[62] This wage was higher than the original strike demand of $12 for a 44-hour week, or 27.8 cents an hour, and also higher than the 26.56 cents an hour awarded the store clerks, who were not as aggressive as the striking laundry workers.

The laundry workers were still holding out for a closed shop, but at the end of December decided to call off the strike. They had failed in their attempt to unionize the whole industry. Eighty women and twenty men were now left without jobs, Geoffroy had been sentenced to an eighteen-month prison term for assault, and the union had to carry the burden of continued legal support for him as well as strike pay for their jobless members until they found work.[63] The union had made some gains. Some laundries had signed an agreement accepting a closed shop. More important was the fact that their militancy had won them a minimum wage higher than the union had originally demanded when they first went on strike.

These awards were hedged with special conditions that still allowed employers considerable leeway for hiring cheap female labour if they wished. Section 11 of the Minimum Wage Act made special provision for the wages and working conditions of girls under eighteen, in accordance with which the board established graduated wage scales over a two-year period, the top wage always below the legal minimum. The scale set for laundry workers under eighteen began at $8 for the first four months, with two 50-cent increments during the rest of the first year, increasing to $1 increments in the second year. The Act also made special provision for inexperienced women employees over eighteen, or apprentices, for whom the board could issue a special licence authorizing their employment at less than the legal minimum. Thus the employer could make thrifty use of the labour of mature women; however, the number of such special-licence employees had to be limited to one-seventh of the total number of workers. The board established a scale for apprentice laundry workers that began at $9 and increased by quarterly increments for a year, after which the minimum wage of $13.50 took effect.[64]

Helena and her laundry workers challenged these special provisions, demanding, and finally obtaining, a hearing with the board. They protested the two-year training period, inquiring with heavy irony if the board really thought a girl required two years to learn how to shake out sheets and pillow slips and to mix starch and starch collars. They protested the $8 minimum for girls under eighteen and, ignoring the explicit provisions for young girls and apprentices in section 11 of the Act, claimed that the board was empowered to deal only with the wages of females in certain occupations, trades, and industries. The age of said females, the union insisted, was not in question, as the Minimum Wage Act Amendment of 1919 made clear by substituting the word 'female' for 'women' in section 5. The argument had merit, but failed to accommodate section 11, which referred to 'girls under eighteen years of age.'

The board insisted that by an interpretation of the whole Act, it was empowered to fix a minimum wage only for females over the age of eighteen. The union representative leaped at this: if the whole Act were to be construed together, then the phrase 'adequate to supply the necessary cost of living' would surely apply to girls under eighteen as well. The *British Columbia Federationist* report of this interchange bore down hard on Helen MacGill, who maintained that such girls were not apprentices because they were 'contracted out,' and then defended their low wage:

> Mrs. Campbell [a union representative] pointedly asked Mrs. McGill [*sic*] whether eight dollars was sufficient to keep a girl and finally elicited the

answer that it was not, but, of course, 'they would have parents to help them.' The case of the girl without parents was put to Mrs. McGill and no answer could be obtained. The Minimum Wage Board have thus made it a legislative enactment of British Columbia that parents, as well as their daughters, must contribute to the profits of the boss by helping to support their girls working for a wage not 'adequate to supply the necessary cost of living.'[65]

Helen MacGill could not force the employers' representatives to agree to pay subsistence wages according to the letter of the law; rather, she had to negotiate with them, unlike Helena, who was free to sledge-hammer them with demands. Moreover, Mrs. MacGill pressed the case for women workers in cogent and incisive terms that surely influenced the board's decisions in a way that a less able and less sympathetic person would never have done, for she had a sound understanding of the economic and sociological obstacles confronting working women:

The low economic standing of women is not on a pin-money or waiting-for-marriage, or no-dependants basis. It is founded on custom, prejudice, the women's timidity and lack of confidence, their poor bargaining ability, their difficulty, in moving freely from place to place, their habit of not valuing their work, and their lack of opportunity and initiative to learn better work.[66]

The employees at the conferences could count on her to preside in a way that encouraged them to present their best case. Helen MacGill's daughter Elsie wrote:

She was a diplomat in the chair showing gentle concern for the personal feelings of conferees by finding time for them to make the speeches they had spent days in perfecting. She handled argument with finesse, was quick to catch the sense of the meeting, state it simply and push on with business. In stormy sessions she was a past master at the chairman's art of keeping control by firm application of the parliamentary rules that govern the conduct of public meetings.[67]

In essence, Helen MacGill agreed with Helena on the principle of the minimum wage and on the need for shorter working hours. She had read widely on the subject and visited the Industrial Welfare Commissions in Washington, Oregon, and California to obtain information and ideas on procedures. In her reports, models of research and scholarship, she put forward clearly the theoretical support for the new labour legislation that she was helping to administer, citing André Gide, Sidney

Webb, and Samuel Gompers, among others. Helena would have agreed with her conclusion:

> The theory, then, of the minimum wage is that no person or class has a right to make money at the expense of the health or well-being of any other person or class, and the community has a right to be protected from economic conditions which cannot exist without detriment to all.[68]

Despite her best efforts, Helen MacGill could not achieve full implementation of the Act: the actual decisions of the board were at variance with theory. The laundry workers and Helena concluded in their rigorous way that the board was manipulated by business interests to maintain the supply of cheap labour, and that Helen MacGill had been party to that betrayal.[69]

The Canadian Manufacturers' Association did indeed begin immediately to nibble away at the Minimum Wage Bill. The original bill had specified that no more than one-tenth of the employees in any plant could be special-licence employees. That number was increased to one-seventh the following year. In 1921 the legal number of special-licence employees and girls under eighteen was raised to 35 per cent – more than one-third. The CMA congratulated itself on its 'persistent efforts' to change the regulations and took the credit for getting this amendment passed.[70]

The CMA was not successful, however, in 1922 when it proposed that the composition of the board be changed to include two representatives of employers and two of employees. The Women's Industrial Union and Minimum Wage League, which was still in existence, rallied the support of the University Women's Club to protest this move, and they in turn organized seven other women's clubs to make representations to the attorney general and members of the legislature. The women won that round: the CMA did not obtain direct representation on the board. In 1923 the board again refused to amend the Act when it rejected the request of a number of employers for a lower minimum wage in manufacturing.[71]

As a result of Helena's efforts, the struggle to make ends meet was made a little easier for hundreds of women in British Columbia. The working day became a little shorter and not so physically draining. The lowest paid store employees and laundry workers were now being paid nearly twice as much as before the legislation was passed. Factory workers earning as little as $1.50 for a full work week of perhaps 46 hours were now earning nine times as much for fewer hours. In human terms – bread on the table for single mothers and boots on the feet of their children – such gains were significant, even though they affected a relatively small proportion of the female work force. The average weekly wage increased substantially too. According to statistical data gathered by the Minimum Wage Board, store employees were earning an average of 15 per cent more in 1919, and laundry workers 23 per cent more than in 1918, for fewer hours of labour. Some store managers were still keeping clerks selling on the floor for 77 hours and paying only the $12.75 wage legally required for 48 hours. But such infractions were not the rule; for the most part, women were now working fewer hours for more pay.[72]

However, legislation did not provide, as hoped, a wage 'adequate to supply the necessary cost of living.' Working women were still poor, actually living below subsistence level. Because they were used to being poor, most women had modest expectations as to how much was 'necessary,' as the laundry workers demonstrated in their response to the questionnaires sent out by the board. Their estimated cost of living was only $14.85 per week. By comparison, the Dominion Civil Service Commission in 1919 estimated a weekly minimum budget of $17 for a single person with no dependents.[73] Moreover, over the years the minimum wage tended to become viewed as an acceptable, and sometimes even as a maximum, wage, the cost of living callously ignored. On the whole, however, the Act of 1918 was a step forward for working women because they learned that their work had value and that they were important enough to sit across the table from their employers and bargain for wages. The contest was unequal: they were no match for department store managers and laundry proprietors; they were certainly no match for the CMA. But managers and proprietors and even the CMA now had to defend their policy towards women workers, something they had never had to do before.

Helena could not have played her part so well without the help of the Local Councils of Women, the New Era League, and other women's organizations. Two women in particular, Mary Ellen Smith and Helen MacGill, gave firm leadership, and with Helena made a powerful triumvirate: the persuasive politician, the intellectual clubwoman and legal expert in social reform, and the militant trade unionist.[74]

Meanwhile, the VTLC was being transformed in a way that would dramatically change Helena's life. Former impossiblists were now talking revolution by mass worker protest. By 1918 socialist radicals were a force in the VTLC, and under Ernest Winch, Victor Midgely, Jack Kavanagh, and Bill Pritchard were moving it towards industrial unionism and the tactic of the general strike. Helena in 1917 was the VTLC women's organizer and also a United Garment Workers delegate at VTLC meetings.[75] She had recently left the Tailors' and Tailoresses' Union for she was no longer working as a tailor but as a machine operator in the garment industry, probably as a result of lack of employment in the tailoring trade. In 1918 she was elected president of the United Garment Workers Union, affil-iated with the Trades and Labor Congress (TLC).[76] She did not simply sit back and let the radicals take over the union movement, as she herself indicated. In an interview, probably with Dorothy Steeves gathering mate-rial for her 1960 book on Ernest Winch, Helena told how on one occasion she stole a march on the radicals. Planning soon to implement their grand vision of an industrial union, they thought to organize the loggers within the American Federation of Labor, knowing that the loggers would be a powerful support once the One Big Union (OBU) was estab-lished. Victor Midgely was to organize them, 'but VRM was sick with flu,' explained Helena. The interviewer, combining third-person narrative and verbatim transcription, continues: 'And so H.G. and Birt Showler did the initial organizing. H.G. took around the bill [poster] to downtown [skid row] joints for an organisation meeting and next day there was a big meet-ing and they signed up 500 loggers. Next day Ernie [Winch] and Vic dis-covered about the meeting and they took over, got another meeting and more members.'[77] Winch later resigned as president of the VTLC to become secretary of the new union, which under the aegis of the OBU changed its name to the Lumber Workers' Industrial Unit (LWIU).[78]

At the Western Labor Conference in Calgary in March 1919, the British Columbia radicals joined with their prairie counterparts in proposing to secede from the Trades and Labor Congress of craft union-ists and instead bring all workers into a single organization – the One Big Union. Thus organized, they believed, the workers would in soli-darity force capitalism to yield power to them, the power that they held to be rightfully theirs as the producers of the country's wealth.[79]

In May, three months later, Winnipeg workers stopped work in a gen-eral strike that brought the city to a halt. The strike was not engineered by the OBU, which was not even formally organized until the strike was well underway, but the federal government was convinced that the OBU was responsible for it and was, moreover, a Bolshevik organization plot-ting to establish a syndicalist foothold of industrial soviets in western Canada. The strike caused repercussions in Vancouver. On 3 June VTLC unions, on the strength of a small majority in favour of a strike, walked out in support of their Winnipeg comrades and stayed out for a whole month. The police raided the offices of the *British Columbia Federa-tionist* in the Labor Temple and the homes of OBU socialists in the VTLC, seizing records and correspondence. They raided the home of Ernest and Linda Winch at 4:30 in the morning 'and took particular care to look under and inside the mattresses' for incriminating evidence. Winch was not arrested, but Bill Pritchard, on his way home from Winnipeg, where he had been at the founding meeting of the OBU and had indeed attended a meeting of the Winnipeg strike committee, was apprehended in Calgary and sent to Stony Mountain penitentiary in Manitoba along with other strike leaders.[80]

Helena did not take part in the Vancouver strike because she was opposed to industrial unionism and, as she said, 'Half of the unions didn't vote at all, others didn't give it a 50 per cent majority.' She 'walked out' in disgust over the decision to strike, but not before confronting Bill Pritchard:

> They set up a strike office in the Labor Temple with guards on the door. WAP [Bill Pritchard] told H.G. there would be blood flowing and the L.[Labor] Temple would be blown up. H.G. laughed in his face. H.G. was the correspondent for the Ottawa Labor Gazette and she wired every day that everything was peaceful and there was no trouble. WAP accused her of sending information to the government. They had a meeting in the arena every night. Everyone hoped the strike would be called off, but nothing happened, it was summer and good weather and they were having a nice holiday, so the strike lasted six weeks.[81]

'They were having a nice holiday.' Caustic, scornful words from Helena, remembering forty years later this betrayal of craft unionism and the disruption it had made in the labour movement, in her life. She was only a machine operator now, but she was still at heart a 'jour' and honoured the dignity of craft workers and the special knowledge and skill that set them apart from other workers.

In July a representative from the Trades and Labor Congress came to a VTLC meeting, demanded the council seals, and lifted the charter, thus formally ousting the renegade OBU faction. Only nine unions voted to stay with craft unionism. This remnant reorganized in August under a new name, the Vancouver Trades and Labor Council (International), and affiliated with the Trades and Labor Congress. As acting secretary, Helena had a key role in setting up the new council.[82]

In the midst of all this upheaval, Helena prepared to go to Ottawa to pursue even further her fight for the minimum wage, one of three delegates representing the working women of Canada at the National Industrial Conference in Ottawa on 17 September 1919.[83] She was not the unanimous choice of Vancouver women, however. A former executive member of the Minimum Wage League, Teresa Hartney, who had given evidence for the laundry workers at the Minimum Wage Board conference the year before, wrote to the VTLC 'representing working women of Vancouver' protesting Helena's appointment.[84] Evidently Helena had been the source of some dissension among the women she was marshalling to fight for higher wages, but that is as much as we know.

The conference grew out of a proposal by the Royal Commission on Industrial Relations of 1919, which noted that its recommendations on the minimum wage, hours of work, the right to organize, and collective bargaining were not under federal jurisdiction. The commission therefore proposed a meeting of business and labour to try for a consensus among provinces on these matters. At the Ottawa conference, employer and employee faced each other across the floor of the Senate Chamber, on one side the CPR and CNR, the Shipping Federation of Canada, Imperial Oil, Dominion Textile, and the Canadian Bankers' Association; on the other, miners and garment workers, bartenders and waiters, carpenters, steelworkers, and printers. Seventy-five union delegates affiliated with the TLC and representing workers from Cape Breton to Vancouver Island confronted their employers, represented in equal number. Helena faced her employer, garment manufacturer J.B. Thomson, who was on the minimum wage committee with her.[85] Ministers of labour were in attendance, with several premiers; and a so-called 'Third Group' comprising, among others, visiting dignitaries from England and the United States, and the former deputy minister of labour, William Lyon Mackenzie King, with his Rockefeller Plan for industrial conciliation in his pocket.[86]

After the opening preliminaries, during which both sides uttered inspirational banalities about brotherhood and cooperation, the participants soon revealed the profound disparities separating capital and labour, and the essential antagonism between the two sides. Helena was a leading protagonist for labour in two key items on the agenda: hours of work and the minimum wage. The only one of the four women delegates to speak in the plenary sessions, she was hard-hitting and provocative. Again and again, other speakers referred to her statements, for she was a labour advocate who had to be answered.

The conference heard how, in the United States, Henry Ford had implemented an 8-hour day for his auto workers with gratifying results for production. Similar results were reported from Britain, France, Germany, and other European countries where the 8-hour day had been generally adopted. A number of enlightened employers at the conference were in favour of instituting shorter working hours, but some very articulate hardliners balked at such a proposal, maintaining against all evidence that it was not possible to produce as much in 8 hours as in 9 or 10. Melville P. White, representing Canadian General Electric, became Helena's chief opponent on this question, placing the obligation for postwar recovery on the workers: they would have to increase production. He cited the Health Committee of the British Ministry of Munitions, which had concluded that 56 hours per week was the optimum for men engaged in heavy labour and 64 hours for men and youths in light labour, 'such as tending semi-automatic machines.'[87]

When Melville White sat down, Helena rose to speak. She wasted no time on amiable pleasantries but immediately answered his arguments, putting forward labour's claims forcefully and without a trace of diffidence. The eight-hour day was not labour's goal, by any means. It was only a compromise between what was best for the worker and what the average employer would demand. As to production, the workers were well aware of their responsibility, for they were the ones who had in large measure produced the weapons, done the actual fighting, and been maimed and killed in the war. 'There is no wealth except it be produced by the application of labour to the natural resources of any country in the world,' she declared, and concluded that hours of work had to be legislated to protect the worker from the accumulated fatigue that destroyed efficiency. She too had read the report of the British Ministry of Munitions, but had noted in it something that Melville White had not: that the falling-off in production among women workers had been ascribed to overwork. 'Coming as I do from what we consider the more progressive West,' she went on, 'I am astonished that there should even be any discussion on the enactment of legislation for an 8-hour day.' And then, carrying condescension to the point of insult:

> In this older portion of Canada you have become accustomed to older customs and older traditions, and it is a little more difficult to overcome old customs and old traditions than it is to institute customs in a newer country. Therefore we must overcome that difficulty before advocating a more ideal working day from the workers' point of view, and with a view to meeting with the co-operation of employers of labour.[88]

She would have sat down at this point, having used her allotted ten minutes, but some delegates called, 'Go ahead,' and so she returned to the attack. It was scarcely appropriate for Mr. White to cite production figures for 1917 as applicable to 1919, she charged, now that soldiers had become workers again and were producing food instead of munitions.[89]

'Miss Gutteridge somewhat lost her poise when applauded heavily by her fellow delegates on the employees' side of the chamber,' reported the *Province*, a Vancouver newspaper.[90] The VTLC sent her a telegram of congratulation. On the employers' side, Helena's sharp rebuttal was received with surprised interest. The presence of four woman delegates was a novelty in itself, but for an articulate woman to challenge the representative of a leading Canadian manufacturer was positively delectable. Not that these businessmen were disposed to take seriously a woman's utterances on economic matters of national importance.

They could gallantly doff their rhetorical hats in the presence of a woman like Helena; they could say, and did, that they admired her, but their prejudice against such women did not change: they still adhered to the old stereotype that the judgments of women were too emotional.

And, in fact, when the conference moved on to the question of the minimum wage, the first speaker for the employers appealed to this 'hardy perennial.' In his opening address, A. Munro Grier, president of the Canadian Electrical Association, attempted to put in proper male perspective 'the lady representative from Vancouver who spoke with a passion which one looks for upon the part of woman who devotes herself so keenly to those things which are near at hand, whether her own children, her own brother, or anything that is beloved.'[91] Men, he said, were more detached and forward-looking. However, he was in favour of a minimum wage for women and children, though not for men, because such legislation would interfere with the 'law' of competition and lead to a lower standard of living for the worker as the minimum became the maximum an employer would pay.

Chosen by the employees to lead the debate on the minimum wage, Helena began by dismissing the employers' general acceptance of the minimum wage as a 'death-bed repentance,' remarking that most of the provinces now had such legislation; Ontario, Nova Scotia, and New Brunswick were the only ones holding out. She then disturbed the atmosphere of kid-glove civility established by Mr. Grier by citing an instance of the gross exploitation of women workers. He expected passion from a woman? She'd give him passion. And a few rough facts too.

She had on arrival in Ottawa immediately gone out to do some research into women's wages in that city and had learned of a garment worker doing piece work for $3.37 a week, including two nights overtime. 'Right here in the city of Ottawa! An absolute fact, and it can be proven,' Helena exclaimed. For the operation the woman was performing on this garment, she was earning 4 cents a dozen, so that in order to earn $12 she would have to perform that particular operation 3,600 times. A fair wage would have been 16¼ cents a dozen – four times as much. Moreover, the employer was not even in competition with other manufacturers, for they were all receiving a standard price for this item. A minimum wage would protect manufacturers from that kind of unfair competition. 'That would be good business,' she observed, 'apart from the sentimental aspect, which most persons consider to be the view taken by women.' This last a stiletto thrust at Grier for his pronouncement on the 'passion' of women. She continued to level him by adopting a rather patronizing tone: 'Mr. Grier seemed to be labouring under the impression that we are asking for the establishment of a maximum wage. We are not doing anything of the kind ...'[92]

Helena was a good debater. She knew how to turn the arguments of her opponents to advantage. The employers, of course, were arguing that the high cost of wages would make their operations unprofitable. Helena did not harangue capitalists for piling up profits; rather, she acknowledged the profit motive as a fact of life and in answer quoted one of their own, a certain mill owner, who, she had heard, in justification of his huge profits, claimed 'that they were not operating those mills for the glory of God.'[93] Quite so, agreed Helena, inserting the thin edge of the wedge, and that being true of all business enterprises, when they calculated their operating costs, they should, she advised, budget for a living wage. Even if they simply regarded labour as a commodity, to get the most output from their human machines they should keep the labourers in good condition. Even an unskilled machine could be made efficient. This was an adroit argument, leading the employers from the agreeable idea of profit-making to a consideration of the source of profit in human labour and the Marxist idea of the subsistence wage.

On the morality of the living wage, Helena cited Prime Minister Robert Borden himself. She read from his opening address, in which he declared that workers ought not to be called on to sacrifice their health and well-being for the sake of industrial development. She did not believe that Canadian industries were in so fragile a financial state that they could not pay a living wage. Dominion Textile certainly was not: it had racked up a profit of 312 per cent throughout the war. If any industries were in desperate straits, well, they should go out of business rather than continue to exist by overburdening and ultimately destroying the worker.

She might have ended with the customary inspirational words about cooperation, brotherhood, and goodwill, but, being Helena, she instead fired a parting shot at point-blank range. All such talk was stuff and nonsense as far as she was concerned, unless employers lived up to the spirit of minimum wage agreements and gave their workers a fair shake. She told how, at the Minimum Wage Board hearings in British Columbia, the employers in the manufacturing industry had first pared down the women workers' proposed cost of living, going over each item on the budget, cutting down wherever they possibly could, and finally agreeing on a minimum wage of $14 for a forty-four-hour week. She was present at these deliberations, for they concerned, among others, her own trade of tailoring. When it came to paying the wage, the employers found a loophole in the Factories Act that allowed them to deduct $1.25 for the four hours not worked on Saturday afternoon. 'If that is the spirit of cooperation that is going to be shown between the employing class and the workers, it does not make us very hopeful,' she concluded. The conference would perhaps help to remove such 'anomalies.' A gracious note to end on, but she could not resist one final word, angry, sardonic, and conciliatory as a cold, wet dishrag thrown in the face of an opponent. 'It is a farce, though a grim one, to say that $14 is the living wage and then to pay only $12.75 after the work has been actually done.'[94]

Grier was not prepared to concede. In his final statement, he granted that he too was moved by tales of hardship, but had 'never been very greatly impressed with arguments based upon the particular and applied to the general,' an obvious put-down of Helena's single instance of exploitation in the Ottawa garment industry.[95] His remark demonstrated the essential disagreement between the two sides. For, as Melville White had earlier explained, the workers insisted on a social solution to the conflict between capital and labour, whereas the employers, while recognizing the reality of social problems, knew that economic problems had to be dealt with first. By economic he meant gross national product, investment of capital, interest rates, and profits. He did not consider $3.37 a week a fact of economic importance but, like Grier, part of a hard-luck story, a particular from which you could not make any general application.[96] Helena maintained that economic strategies were needed to solve social problems and that the Ottawa garment worker could be helped by legislation guaranteeing her a living wage.

In plenary session at the end of the conference, Helena reported unanimity in her committee on one issue – the passage of minimum wage legislation for women and children in those provinces where it had not yet been enacted. No agreement was reached on a minimum wage for men in unskilled labour. The employers wanted more investigation, another Royal Commission. Helena's committee also urged an investigation into the wages of female schoolteachers. The committee member seconding her motion was Montreal industrialist F.G. Daniels. He engagingly identified himself as 'executive head of that infamous corporation that was attacked' for having 'walked away with the slight profit of 312 per cent.' He told the conference that employers generally now approved the principle of the minimum wage for women and children.[97]

Evidently it was no longer politic for employers to oppose openly such legislation. Country after country had by now entered wage reform into the statute books, and the rights of labour spelled out in the Versailles Peace Treaty recognized that compensation in the form of better wages and working conditions was due to the returning soldier. Employers could still manipulate the minimum wage law discreetly, through quiet lobbying and resistance, which indeed the Canadian Manufacturers' Association did with some success in the next few years.

The committees on hours of work and labour organization did not achieve consensus: the employers did not accept the recommendation for an eight-hour day and asked for another commission to investigate hours of work. They conceded the right of employees to organize, but not the obligation of employers to recognize their unions.[98] Against collective bargaining, from British Columbia to the Maritimes, they set up an impregnable bulwark. Little wonder that Helena and her valiant Lilliputian army of laundry workers had been forced to retreat, when faced with entrenched power of such force and magnitude.

After the conference, Helena travelled to Hamilton to join other members of the British Columbia delegation at the annual meeting of the Trades and Labor Congress. Here the OBU speakers were firmly quashed, and a resolution from a western executive member proposing a soviet form of government was denounced and rejected. Helena ran for office but was defeated. Western representatives of all stripes, even loyal craft unionists, were excluded from the executive.[99] Before she left for home, she went to Sault Ste. Marie to campaign against Premier Sir William Howard Hearst in the Ontario election. Her three weeks in the East had brought her briefly into the national spotlight, giving her a chance to parley with influential Canadian industrialists on the same footing as Tom Moore, P.M. Draper, and other TLC leaders. She had conducted herself with enormous energy and élan. Not only was she high on politics, but she was also contemplating a whole new way of life: she was about to be married.

CHAPTER SEVEN

Back to the Land

The moon seen from the moon
is a different thing.
       – Margaret Atwood, 'Foretelling the Future'

Helena did not turn up for work on 11 October 1919, soon after her return to Vancouver. Instead, she and Oliver Fearn had gone 'across the line' to Bellingham and were married at the courthouse. Ollie had just returned from overseas, where he had served with the Canadian Engineers. He was a likeable young man, six feet tall, with dark brown hair and hazel eyes, quite handsome. He had just turned twenty-six; she was forty. She had long been a friend of the Douglas-Fearn family. He was a member of the United Sheet Metal Workers' International Association, and doubtless their union activities had given them many opportunities to meet and talk and get to know each other. The marriage came as a complete surprise to her friends and colleagues, who learned about it only after Ollie and Helena returned from their honeymoon at Mount Lehman, the little community in the Fraser Valley where Ida Douglas-Fearn, Ollie's mother and Helena's friend, now retired, had a little poultry farm. Helena was then living in North Vancouver, and Ollie moved in with her. She took his name, and henceforth was recorded in the VTLC minutes as Mrs. Fearn.[1]

Ollie had not volunteered for military service; he had been drafted under the Military Service Act of 1917. No Ginger Goodwin, he had not fled to the woods but had duly reported to the military depot to be enlisted in the Canadian Engineers just before Christmas 1917. He had five months of training in Canada and England before being posted to France in June 1918 with the Fourth Battalion, Canadian Engineers, with the rank of sapper. He joined his unit on 6 July and had four months of active service before his honourable discharge on 3 June 1919. He went back to his old job as tinsmith for Johnson Lee Sheet Metal Works on Pender Street, where he had first apprenticed.[2]

Helena and Ollie took the North Vancouver ferry across the inlet to their work in downtown Vancouver. Because of heavy unemployment in the tailoring trade, she had become a garment worker, employed around 1918 by James Thomson and Sons, makers of Twin Bute overalls and mackinaw plaid shirts, advertised as 'some of the swellest winter-and-rough-weather Work Shirts you ever wore.' As an operator of the heavy, noisy power sewing machines, she stitched sleeves and collars and cuffs for the man she would soon be facing across the conference table in Ottawa. The firm had signed an agreement with the United Garment Workers of America's local 160, and Thomson was regarded by unionists as a 'fair' employer. Soon after her return from the East, Helena went to work for Fred Perry and Frank Dolk, whose tailor shop was then on Dunsmuir Street, next door to the Labor Temple. Since she still belonged to the United Garment Workers and was in fact president of local 160, she must have been working as a garment 'finisher,' at least part of the time.[3]

Fred Perry, a brusque Scotsman, lover of classical music and alpine flowers, was an articulate socialist whose great pleasure was to have a little group of like-minded friends drop in at the shop to reconstruct society in heated discussion over a bottle of red wine. He was happiest in puttees and hiking boots, for he was a keen mountain climber, an early member of the BC Mountaineering Club. He also contributed papers to the Vancouver Art and Historical Society. During the week, however, he sat cross-legged on his tailor's table, basting navy-blue serge uniforms for streetcar men, police officers, and firemen. Navy-blue serge was not the most attractive material Helena had ever worked with, but at least this mountaineering socialist tailor was an interesting and congenial employer. Frank Dolk, a quiet little man, sat at the machine sewing the suits together. Frank and his wife, Molly, were Americans, 'good-hearted people.'[4]

Jim Barker remembers them affectionately from his childhood, when he used to visit the shop with his parents, who were good friends of 'Uncle Fred' and the Dolks. Jim recalled that there was something about Frank's face that made him think of General Eisenhower. Molly was 'massive' – not just big, but massive. She had a strident voice and was 'motherly in an enveloping sort of way,' and though not related to her any more than to Fred Perry, the little boy called her Aunt Molly. She was an 'outspoken feminist,' and Jim Barker gratefully remembers her part in the campaign for mothers' pensions because his widowed mother, Martha Jane Barker, was one of the first to benefit from the new legislation. Molly Dolk worked with Helena in the VTLC, especially in the campaign for mothers' pensions.[5]

In January 1920 Helena was elected general secretary of the VTLC (International), which was rapidly gaining strength: by the end of the year the nine loyal unions had been joined by sixteen more. It was a disheartening time for the labour movement. The postwar depression hit workers hard: the cost of living soared even as unemployment increased. The BC Federation of Labor, within which craft unionists had demonstrated solidarity time and time again since its founding in 1911, was disbanded as irrelevant in 1920. Even the Labor Temple, labour's home since 1898, now had to be relinquished, for a divided trade union movement could not support it financially. When the VTLC moved out of the Labor Temple in the fall of 1920, Helena had to vacate room 219, her office and second home during most of her Vancouver years.[6] The new office was at 319 Pender Street.

For Helena, the defection of the socialist radicals was a heavy loss, as some of them were friends as well as colleagues. If she felt discouraged, she did not allow her personal feelings to interfere with her work, and gave her best to the new VTLC, attending meetings faithfully and providing initiative and leadership. She continued to work for women's rights, lobbying with Susie Clark and Molly Dolk for mothers' pensions as well as protesting encroachments on the Minimum Wage Bill and seeking amendments to the Factory Act. All these matters she brought to the fore in VTLC meetings.

Meanwhile, Helena was preparing to retire. In England she had learned the tailor's craft and been initiated as an apprentice into its 'mysteries,' the special knowledge that was for craft workers alone, which they guarded against the intrusion of the uninitiated. She had even become one of the elite in her trade – a cutter. In Vancouver she found a declining industry and gradually became 'deskilled,' moving down the craft ladder from cutter to journeyman tailor to machine-operating garment worker. Tailoring, like shoemaking, was no longer a mystery. As one American tailor wrote, 'The invasion of the garment worker into our first and second class houses has spoiled our monopoly, and such secrets or mysteries as it once claimed to have, are now revealed to boys and girls in from two to six weeks training under a competent garment worker.' Sitting at her machine stitching heavy work garments, Helena quite likely felt the same sense of displacement.[7]

Fortunately, she did not depend on her garment worker's job for personal fulfilment. Since her arrival in Vancouver ten years earlier, she had led a highly political and public life. Her days had been filled with meetings and committee work, with speeches and demonstrations and delegations that she somehow scheduled around her tailoring job. Premier McBride knew of Helena Gutteridge; so did all the other premiers – Bowser, Brewster, Oliver. She had hectored them enough, sent letter after letter, telegrams, resolutions; confronted them in their council chambers with bold demands on behalf of an oppressed constituency. The women of the province knew her: middle class clubwomen with whom she had

many times allied herself, whom she had rallied and variously manipulated, challenged, and insulted; working class women whom she had
infused with heart and spirit, encouraging them to speak out and organize. Trade unionists knew her: she had become one of them and made
the VTLC one of her first loyalties.

As a trade unionist she had also experienced the rivalries within the
labour movement and the factionalism endemic to left-wing politics. She
decided to leave all that behind – enough of contentiousness. Now she
wanted peace and contentment. Like her father, she decided to leave the
city and go back to the land. Like him, she wanted to rediscover
Micheldever. She resigned from her position as general secretary of the
VTLC (International) in April 1921, and that summer moved with Ollie
to the little village of Mount Lehman in the Fraser Valley, only sixty-five
kilometres from Vancouver.

There Helena bought a three-acre farm. The triangular piece of land
was bounded on the south by the hypotenuse of the BC Electric Interurban Railway, on the north by Burgess Road. A large part of the property
was swamp. She purchased the farm with house and farm buildings in
her own name for eight hundred dollars. Where she got the money, we
do not know, and it is useless to speculate. Ollie's mother, Ida Douglas-
Fearn, had her poultry farm nearby, at the corner of Burgess and Mount
Lehman Roads.[8]

The Mount Lehman area was well settled by that time, even though
it was not yet fifty years since Isaac Lehman, carrying squirrel rifle and
axe, had staked out his clearing in the forest on the plateau above Matsqui Prairie.[9] Useful stands of timber still remained, providing logs and
poles, shingle bolts and lumber for logging companies and sawmills. At
the back of Helena's house on Burgess Road, there was a wooded area,
where in spring trilliums and salmonberry bloomed on the forest floor,
and in summer heavy white clusters of spirea and fragrant trailing hon-
eysuckle. Further west, where Burgess Road crossed Mount Lehman
Road, a little community had grown up, with general store and post
office, butcher shop and hardware store, and, further down the road, the
school, the Orangemen's Hall, and the Presbyterian Church, later the
United Church.[10]

Like many rural communities at that time, Mount Lehman lacked the
customary urban amenities. It did not have a water system: every family had to supply its own water, usually from a well with a pump and
carried water bucket by bucket into the house. Washday was a strenu-
ous business: the kitchen fire well stoked, the copper boiler filled with
water on the stove, and the clothes 'boiled' in it with shavings of strong
Fels Naphtha Soap; then scrub-board and galvanized iron washtubs with
hand-wringer screwed to the rim; the rinsing and wringing, the wash

water and rinse water thrice used as the wash progressed from white sheets and tablecloths to dirty socks and overalls. Nor did Mount Lehman have electricity: the BC Electric Company had not yet constructed power lines for many rural areas. Coal-oil lamps with wicks and Coleman gas lanterns with asbestos mantles were universal.

Helena and Ollie did not, however, live in impoverished cultural isolation. In Isaac Lehman's time, farmers had depended on the river boat for transportation, hauling their produce by wagon down to Fort Langley on the Fraser River. Later the interurban train between Vancouver and Chilliwack replaced the paddle-wheel steamboat, providing cheap and easy access to the commercial and cultural life of larger communities. Farmers shipped their ten-gallon galvanized iron milk cans on the interurban, together with their apples and pork and strawberries; and sawmill operators shipped their lumber and ties. A few people travelled by automobile; most went shopping and visiting in Vancouver and New Westminster by the interurban. Ollie had a Model T Ford but Helena was not dependent on it. She could travel equally well by interurban to a conference in Chilliwack or a lecture in New Westminster.

Their little three-room wooden house was not much more than a shack. At least that is how it is remembered by Hubert Farber, who as a young boy used to work for Helena. The outside was unpainted, as were the barn and all the other farm buildings. Without indoor plumbing, the house had no bathroom; the outside privy was at the end of the garden. Like most farm families at that time, they depended for heat on a wood stove in the kitchen and an airtight heater in the living room, central heating in farmhouses being a rarity. In summer the sun beat down cruelly on the little house, for it had no insulation. In winter, ice formed on the window panes. The kitchen was only a tiny lean-to added on next to the back porch. The wood-box beside the stove needed constant replenishing, summer and winter.

House and farm had their special beauties, which made up for the lack of amenities. The farm buildings were all back of the house, in line with Burgess Road: barn, garage, feed shed, packing shed, chicken houses. Between the barn and the garage, a tall dogwood tree bloomed lavishly in the spring in full view of the window beside the kitchen stove. The front of the house looked out on their own duck pond. By damming the little creek that ran along the west boundary, Helena and Ollie flooded the swamp and made a habitat for a colony of some one hundred domestic white ducks and several geese. They could sit on their front porch in summer and watch the ducks swim in the pond and contemplate, beyond the interurban tracks, the green expanse of Merryfield's farm. There was room for a garden and pigpen between the creek and the house, so they could grow their own food, produce some of their own meat. On the other side of the house, the well, bordered in summer by masses of orange nasturtiums, was flanked by two apple trees and a cherry tree. They had a cow called Bess, which Ollie milked when he was home. They had cats, cats all over the place, inside cats and barn cats. And an Airedale called Jim.

Helena was now Mrs. Fearn, poultry farmer. Originally, the farm had only one chicken coop, but Ollie built along the back fence a row of additional chicken houses, each one opening onto its own chicken run, with fences high enough to keep out the predatory wildcats that roamed the countryside. She had at least a thousand white leghorns, at most two thousand, and shipped as many as five or six crates of eggs a week. Kidd Brothers' egg truck came around three times a week, and in order to be ready for the pick-up, Helena organized her day around getting the eggs ready for shipment. The eggs had to be collected frequently during the day, and then processed one by one in the packing shed. First, each egg was cleaned with a little damp cloth and graded as to size on a small scale. Then it was 'candled' – held up to a light and inspected for blood spots, cracks, or other blemishes. Finally, if it passed inspection it was placed in the wooden egg crate, in the cardboard mould separating one layer of eggs from another. This routine demanded that Helena spend part of each day in the packing shed. In addition, she had to mix mash, a mixture of grains, for the chickens, fill their feed troughs, provide them with 'scratch,' and give them water. In the spring, when it was time to buy day-old chicks and pen them up in heated 'brooders,' she would be on twenty-four-hour duty for the first ten days, for, as every poultry farmer knows, the chicks will smother if not stirred up and made to move around every hour or so. After two weeks the chicks had to be sorted according to their sex, and the roosters were set aside to be raised for sale as fryers. And always there was the dirty task of cleaning the manure out of the chicken houses and keeping fresh straw in the nesting boxes. Raising chickens was heavy work, but Helena was a strong woman who could, Hubert Farber recalls, lift a hundred-pound sack of feed and walk off with it. At first she had Ollie to help with the work. Hubert's sister, Vermona Kirkland, has a storybook memory of Ollie digging in the garden, followed by a gaggle of ducklings who ate the worms as he dug.

The Farbers, on the adjoining farm to the west, were the Fearns' closest neighbours and Helena's very good friends. She used to drop by nearly every day on her way to the post office and McAskill's general store, for she had only to cross the creek and walk over the field to get there. Formerly a Wisconsin schoolteacher, now a sawmill operator, Emil Farber had just built a fine big house with oak panelling, fireplace, and ample bookshelves for his library. He and Helena had lively political sparring matches, she being a social democrat and he a radical socialist. Lillian Farber was her confidante; the two women talked to each other about their private lives, supported each other in time of trouble. The four Farber children were often at the Fearns' house. When Hubert and Vermona got the measles, Helena took little Audrey home with her in an unsuccessful attempt to protect her from catching them too. She was very fond of Audrey. There was much neighbourly exchange and intermingling between the two households, especially after Emil was killed in a sawmill accident and Lillian had to take in boarders to support the family.

Helena soon got to know the farm families south of the interurban tracks as well: Patrick and Agnes Moran, Fred and Ida Herron, the Bourys on Mount Lehman Road, Bill Merryfield and his ancient father, farming their piece of land since 1881. Helena found them all congenial, and their children soon discovered the Fearns' farm and the cherry tree and Helena's mandolin. She had a special friendship with Ida Herron, a warmhearted, hardworking woman who looked after the family farm herself. Fred Herron was a logger, home, like Ollie, only on weekends. Even with Ollie away all week, Helena did not lack companionship. And although she did not go to church, she was also friendly with the United Church minister, the Reverend Mr. Robert Moses, a former hard-rock miner, and his wife, and used to go driving with them.

At Mount Lehman Helena also enjoyed the pleasures of being part of a family. While working as head of the telephone exchange in Revelstoke after the war, her sister-in-law, Leslie Fearn, married Arthur Bennett, an American conscientious objector who had escaped the military draft in his country and taken refuge in Revelstoke. In 1924 the Bennetts moved to Nooksak River in the Mount Baker area of Washington, where Arthur was plant superintendent for Puget Sound Power and Light. Every month or six weeks, they would drive to Mount Lehman to see Leslie's mother, Ida, and on these occasions frequently visited Helena and Ollie. The two Bennett children, Alastair and Mettje, wandered freely back and forth between the two farms, which were only a quarter of a mile apart. Alastair Bennett later said that the family, including Grandmother Ida, called Helena 'Billy,' but he could not remember why. At his aunt and uncle's farm the children sailed boats in the pond, creating consternation among the ducks. They watched their Aunt Billy feed the chickens, and once she discovered them eating chicken mash, which did not harm them, though it earned them a proper scolding. Everyone complained about Jim, the Airedale, especially little Audrey, but Uncle Ollie always laughed and said, 'He's just getting stronger and stronger.' That was his little joke, his affectionate way of siding with a dog who smelled so powerfully from chasing skunks.

Helena's Mount Lehman reminds one of the two English country vil-
lages where the Gutteridges lived at different times: of Micheldever
where her father was born and of Petersfield where, for a time, he
retired. Little Thomas Gutteridge, Helena's nephew, scrumping for
apples from the neighbours' trees, frightened of the pig at the end of the
garden in a sense reappears in little Audrey, who didn't like old Jim lick-
ing her legs, and in the children who scrambled up the cherry trees and
ran about the chicken houses. Two idylls of country life, and they res-
onate for us as they surely did in Helena's memories of her father's country origins.

In rural retirement Helena was still active on behalf of women. In 1920
a branch of the Women's Institute had been formed in Mount Lehman.
In it Helena found a place where she could continue to apply her organizing abilities and express her concern for the education of women.
Women's Institutes originated in Ontario in 1897, and had become a recognized part of rural life in British Columbia. As counterparts to the
Farmers' Institutes, they came under the wing of the provincial Department of Agriculture, which gave them financial assistance. Their purpose was twofold: to educate women in the special skills needed by a
farm wife, such as preservation of food, management of money, efficient
and sanitary housekeeping, and wise child rearing; and to encourage
women to participate in community and government affairs as they
related to the home, farm, and school.[11]

Within a few months of her arrival in Mount Lehman, Helena was
already recognized as a member who could speak for the institute, the
obvious person to present a shower gift to another member. She was on
a committee charged with putting the local cemetery in order, and on
another in charge of publicity. She was chosen to give a paper at the
Lower Mainland conference of Women's Institutes in Chilliwack, and
in December 1922, still a relative newcomer, was elected president of the
Mount Lehman Women's Institute, succeeding Margaret Gamsby, a
Scot who was equally forthright and outspoken. With Helena on the
executive for 1922 were Margaret Gamsby and Ida Douglas-Fearn.
With these three strong-minded women in charge, the Mount Lehman
Women's Institute made its influence felt in local affairs.

Before long Mrs. Helena Fearn, socialist, and Mrs. Margaret Gamsby,
conservative, were at loggerheads over the conduct of institute affairs.
Although it was institute policy not to discuss anything of a political or
sectarian nature, Helena, even in retirement, adopted a very political
stance. Her influence was immediately apparent in the title of the
paper she originally planned for the Chilliwack conference: 'Woman's
Position in the World of Workers.' Some members must have objected
that the subject of women workers was too political and asked her to

change it to agriculture. Helena presumably gave way, for at the conference she gave a paper entitled 'Back to the Land and Why.' For Helena, however, everything was grist to the Marxist mill: a brief report of her talk reveals to the alert reader that she managed to talk about the world of the workers just the same and that she was enthusiastically received. She was 'an outstanding feature' of the conference – and little wonder: she apparently adapted ideas from her Marxist reading, notably the first pages of *The Communist Manifesto*, for her Women's Institute audience, but without using the language of Marxism. After all, the class struggle and the exploitation of the working class by the bourgeoisie would scarcely be perceived as relevant and appropriate by most of the women there. The title of her talk led them to expect an inspirational disquisition on the advantages of country living, but what they actually heard was a Marxist account of the evolution of capitalism from earliest agrarian times to the industrial present, stressing the inevitability of this historical process which in its working out would bring unemployment and poverty to the working class. 'No individual and no Government was to blame. Time only would work out a solution.' (Read 'What the bourgeoisie therefore produces, above all, are its own gravediggers.') Yet people could do at least one practical thing to help themselves: whether on a country acre or city lot, they could grow their own food.[12]

Social life at Mount Lehman was typical of most rural communities. The Women's Institute had its flower shows and garden parties. The Presbyterian Church not only held picnics and bean suppers but offered intellectual sustenance as well, in the form of the Reverend Mr. Thomas Oswald's 'popular and interesting lectures on Bunyan's *Pilgrim's Progress*, which draws a good crowd.'[13] There were Burns Night socials and whist drives and dances at the Orangemen's Hall.

Helena played the mandolin in one of the local orchestras that provided the music for these dances, Cars Lehman on fiddle and Herb Taylor on guitar. Sometimes they met at her house to practise. The mandolin, something of a rarity in local dance orchestras, was favoured for its strong beat, so Helena was a very welcome addition to the orchestra. Not having sheet music, the musicians played by ear, picking up the popular tunes of the day.

The Orangemen's Hall had a good floor and the whole community turned out for the Saturday night dance, including children, for parents did not hire babysitters in those days. The room was warm, heated by a big wood stove and, before the advent of electricity, dimly lit by coal-oil lamps in brackets on the wall. The benches along the walls were soon filled with sleepy children bundled up in blankets, watching the dancers waltzing, sliding, stomping by, casting long shadows in the lamplight, musicians receding on the stage and finally into a tunnel of sound. Halfway through the evening, refreshments were served from the little kitchen at the back of the hall, water for coffee and tea having been fetched in a milk can from the neighbour's spring. Women did not have to pay admission if they brought a cake.

The most intellectually stimulating social events at Mount Lehman were the meetings of the Mount Lehman Literary and Debating Society, which provided a lively community forum. The debaters included farmer and school trustee Richard Owen, active in the Fraser Valley Co-operative and the Fraser Valley Milk Producers' Association; loquacious Bill Merryfield, 'with an opinion on everything'; those two eloquent Scots, Donald and Malcolm McAskill, who owned the grocery store and hardware shop; mill owner and political radical Emil Farber, who named his youngest son Eugene Debs after the American socialist labour leader.

Almost as popular as the Saturday night dance, the monthly debate in the Orangemen's Hall was a family entertainment that the older children were early encouraged to attend. Sometimes the subject was banal ('Resolved, that city life is preferable to country life') or lighthearted and provocative ('Resolved, that a good-natured untidy woman is preferable to a cranky tidy woman'). Most often the philosophical and political issues of the day were examined in earnest: capitalism versus socialism; the question of disarmament; the idea of progress; and, at a time when universal medical care was still a socialist castle in the air, this provocative topic: 'Resolved, that hospitals and mortuaries should be owned and operated by the government and that all physicians and surgeons should be civil servants.'[14]

During the Fearns' first winter in Mount Lehman, the society staged a mock parliament over a period of some weeks. Danny Nicholson's Farmer-Labour Party was elected, with Emil Farber's opposition Socialists hurling questions at the new government. The Municipal Act and the Workmen's Compensation Act were amended in short order, as well as the Mothers' Pension Act, which was of special interest to Helena. Sometimes the debaters accepted a challenge in Abbotsford, Langley, or New Westminster; or a visiting team would come to Mount Lehman. After the concluding rebuttal and the judges' decision, the audience joined in the discussion over coffee and sandwiches and cake.[15] The Saturday night debate was, from all accounts, a first-rate social occasion, entertaining and stimulating. Fred Herron remembers the evening when he, a young whippersnapper of twenty years, argued that women should not sit on school boards. Helena took care of that obsolete view in a witty rebuttal, much to everyone's amusement. Fifty years later, Fred can still hear the laughter.

The neighbourhood children often visited at the Fearns', regarding Helena as a strict but benevolent auntie. She liked having them about, let them climb the cherry tree and eat cherries and sometimes took them with her into the chicken houses to help gather eggs. Her house was a meeting place for teenagers, Helena going about her work and popping in every so often to see what they were doing. They had parties in her living room; they contributed some of the food, but she baked cookies and cakes as well as the fruit cake that she kept wrapped in brown paper and stored in the oven. They played musical chairs with music from her wind-up gramophone, and of course that rite-of-passage kissing game, post office. And they danced, under her tutelage. *One, two, three; one, two, three* – that was the waltz; and hop, step-step; hop, step-step – the polka. They even found themselves attempting, quite creditably, the stately French minuet (and right and point and left and point and twirl your partner 'round), Helena strumming the tune on her mandolin. The mandolin was always in the living room, and any of the children were welcome to try to pick out a tune on it, with a little help and encouragement from her.

She encouraged the children to talk about their schoolwork. 'She should have been a schoolteacher,' reflects Hubert Farber. 'She had a way of bringing out things from you, your ideas, and then later on when we used to have these parties when we were getting older, she used to get into discussions about what was good and bad for boys and girls being together.' In other words, she took it on herself to give the teenagers a little elementary sex education. Her strong sense of social responsibility had by no means left her, only now it found expression, in part at least, in this kind of active parenting. She did not intrude as a busybody, however, and is remembered as a person whom parents and children alike could rely on for advice and help. As a girl, Stasia Moran Maguire once had a sty on her eyelid but refused to let her mother apply a hot compress, so her mother sent her to Helena. Stasia also recalls that Helena taught the children how to set a table for a party. 'But she never scolded us if we didn't do things to suit her. She talked very softly ... and told us the right way, but very gently.' On hot summer days Helena, a strong swimmer, took the children to Nicholson's Slough and taught them to swim. They would bring lunch, and Helena would usually have apples in her lunch basket. She was strict about making them wait an hour after lunch before going back in the water.

Rosita Herron Maw was especially attached to Helena, and sixty years later still speaks of her with warmth and affection, recalling the sing-songs at the Fearns' house, Helena strumming on her mandolin and singing with them the old favourites: 'When Irish Eyes are Smiling,' 'Red Wing,' 'Two Little Girls in Blue.' At these parties, Helena 'never let a situation get out of hand,' Rosita recalls. 'If there were any danger of it doing so, she would straighten it out right then and there. She was that kind of person. You wouldn't get away with anything with her, and you knew better than to try.'

Helena had a special concern for the girls. Rosita remembers that Helena arranged for the Fraser Valley Bookmobile to stop at Mount Lehman on Tuesday afternoons, when she borrowed books for them: *Little Women, Girl of the Limberlost, The Circular Staircase, Jane Eyre*. She taught them to play tennis and played with them. Rosita's most vivid memory reveals the full strength of Helena's maternal feelings. Rosita had cut her foot on a broken bottle. It was bleeding profusely. Her mother was not home. A playmate ran to fetch Helena, who took Ollie's Ford car and drove Rosita to the emergency room in Abbotsford, some eight kilometres away. Because her parents were not there to give consent, Rosita had to be stitched up without anaesthetic. Helena stayed with her, held her, comforted her, and even let her bite her (Helena's) arm when the pain became unbearable. 'She was that kind of person,' reflects Rosita. 'If somebody needed help, she was there.'

Hard physical work, friendship, community life, her own place in a small community – life in Mount Lehman was working out the way she had imagined. Except for Ollie. He was not happy with her, nor she with him. True, he had his job in Vancouver and so could contribute financially to the household. Like a good Mount Lehman husband, he came home on weekends and worked about the farm. He played soccer and was goalkeeper for the Highland Uniteds. When the team played in Bradner or Aldergrove or elsewhere in the area, the young people piled into his Ford and he drove them to the game. Actually, he was as close to them in age as he was to Helena.

The difference in age between Helena and Ollie was certainly cause for estrangement, but would not have been significant for a few years if they had at least been happy in bed. But they were not. Ollie soon turned to another woman, Rose Dennison, a widow with four young sons who had a farm in the Mount Lehman area and kept a store. In the interests of secrecy, he resorted to the usual deceptions. When Helena learned the truth, she was devastated. Playing cards at the neighbour's indeed! Yet Ollie would have said she was to blame: she had failed as a wife. No matter what she said, the law, the world was on his side. To add to her feelings of guilt and humiliation, she had actually believed Ollie's story, believed also, quite wrongly that the neighbour was in collusion with him. At least, Helena thought, she could do something about her own error, and by taking some of the blame regain some command over her life. In her scrupulous way, she wrote an apology to the neighbour. One day, outside McAskill's grocery store, she handed it to the woman, who read the letter with some surprise because she knew nothing about her supposed part in this domestic drama. She saw only a distraught, middle-aged woman inflicting more humiliation on herself, and listened while Helena told her that she was going to leave Mount Lehman because of Ollie's unfaithfulness. Reflecting on the incident years later, the neighbour was still moved to pity. 'It was plain to see that Mrs. Fearn was brokenhearted,' she said.[16]

Helena did not sue for divorce. However in November 1928, Ollie filed a petition for annulment of the marriage on the grounds that it had not been consummated. In December a court order appointed two physicians 'to examine and inspect the parts and organs of generation of James Purvis Olered Fearn [sic], the petitioner, and also of Helen Rise [sic] Gutteridge, the respondent.' If Ollie's allegation was true, and if he wanted to marry Rose without committing bigamy, he had no other recourse in law but to take this action, humiliating as it might be for Helena.[17]

To have the summons served by Tom Lehman, one of Mount Lehman's most respected citizens, compounded the humiliation. He would have known the contents, for he had to attach to it his affidavit to show that he had indeed served it. No one with any degree of self-worth would have obeyed such a summons, least of all Helena. In any case, she herself may by then have wanted out of the marriage. She did not respond to the petition; consequently, since in law uncontested testimony is taken for truth (for the law does not deal in absolute truth), on 21 December 1928 the marriage was pronounced 'absolutely null and void.'[18]

Those were days of anguish for Helena, who could not help thinking that everyone must be talking about her, pitying her. And indeed the children did overhear their parents: 'Oh, poor Mrs. Fearn, Ollie's run off with Mrs. Dennison.' The friendship of Lillian Farber and Ida Herron was a great support to Helena as she stoically went on with her life. With or without Ollie, the chickens still had to be fed and watered, the eggs cleaned and graded. She hired young Fred Herron to help with the farm work, and after him Hubert Farber. She found comfort in the company of the neighbourhood young people, having them at her house, teaching them, talking with them. They, for their part, did not desert her. 'We didn't know why he'd leave such a nice lady,' recalled Stasia Moran Maguire.

No comfort came from her mother-in-law. A rift had occurred between Helena and Ida now that they were no longer joined in suffrage combat. The two were essentially incompatible. Helena was working class, and Ida, aristocratic in outlook and humorously dubbing her own daughter's working class husband a 'peasant,' did not excuse Helena her humble origins. For such a woman, a common tailoress, to boldly take

advantage of friendship with the Fearn family and marry the youngest
son, nearly fifteen years her junior, was, in Ida's view, a betrayal. This,
at any rate, is how Helena's nephew accounted for Ida's 'disparaging'
attitude towards his Aunt Billy. Ida was quite unreasonable in her
class prejudice, for neither of her sons had as much education as Helena,
and Ollie as tinsmith and Douglas as logger-farmer were just as 'common.' The perceived failure of Billy Gutteridge as a wife only increased
the rift between the two women. As for Ollie, he was the black sheep of
the family, and he too was out of favour with his mother. He drank too
much, had a penchant for older women, and now had become the talk
of the neighbourhood.

Helena was not Ollie's kind of woman at all. She was altogether too
serious about the state of the world and, moreover, committed to
changing it. She read books and magazines; she gave lectures; she had
opinions and argued them in public. Ollie 'did not have the intellect that
she had,' but he was not one to object to a woman having her own intellectual and public life, else he would not have married her.[19] His own
mother had accustomed him to the feminist way of thinking and provided in word and deed an exemplar of the competent, independent
woman. Perhaps, however, he found Helena rather too challenging, as
indeed men often find such women, and as indeed his father, Samuel,
had found Ida to be.

The Freudian analyst of the 1920s would have found Helena a text-
book example of 'frigidity,' that is, a woman who with 'infantile obsti-
nacy' insists on her personal autonomy and, refusing to submit to male
domination, resists sexual intercourse.[20] But Freud must yield to the
experience of legions of men and women who have found the opposite
to be true: that feelings of strong personal identity can make one a joy-
ous sexual partner and that women who pursue selfhood, given reasonable living and working conditions, do so without detriment to
happy sexual experience, orgasmic or otherwise. No satellite woman,
Helena could reasonably have had every expectation of such a continuing experience. Moreover, judging from the way she gathered the
children of Mount Lehman around her – teaching them to dance and
swim, protecting little Audrey from the measles – she was an affectionate,
warmhearted person. She had strong nurturing feelings, but for whatever reason they did not translate into the conventional domestic sexuality that Ollie wanted, and she may have been baffled and
disappointed by her own response and by Ollie's response. Yet such
speculations about something so complex as the workings of the individual psyche are, to say the least, impertinent, and perhaps we should
just leave these two unhappy people in bed, pillows bunched up
around their ears, pretending to sleep.

But perhaps they had agreed to a companionate marriage: he psychologically bruised and raw from the ugly slaughter of war, she yearning for a home and family life, both seeking in a rural retreat *la vie en rose*. Perhaps Ollie had reneged on such an agreement, unable to measure up to Helena's high expectations for an unconventional sexual relationship. Some British feminists had embraced the social purity movement of the late nineteenth century in their attempts to exert control over male sexual practice, so strongly affirmed in the received wisdom that men's sexual needs were biologically determined and in all charity had to be met by the glad and generous services of women, whether they wished to proffer them or not. When Helena was a militant suffragist in London, the idea of a woman's sovereignty over her own body was a topic of general discussion among feminists, centring around the writings of such women as Elizabeth Wolstenholme Elmy, a member of the executive committee of the WSPU and much respected for her lifetime dedication to all aspects of the rights of women, whether in law or in government or in bed. For that matter, Helena might have read some of these ideas about sexuality in *The Champion*. Perhaps she had read Wolstenholme Elmy's *Phases of Love*, and put to Ollie its idea that sexual intercourse should be indulged in only for the purpose of reproduction. Otherwise, a man and woman should live together in a harmonious relationship that progressed towards 'psychic love.' Such an idea might still have appealed to Helena, recalling theosophical spheres of consciousness. Perhaps if or when Ollie insisted on his 'conjugal rights,' Helena cited more Wolstenholme Elmy, to the effect that a woman was not a man's slave and forcing a woman to have unwanted sex was, in fact, rape.[21]

Perhaps, perhaps, and then again, perhaps not. No evidence has been found to tell us what sexual expectations Helena herself had of women and men, whether in or out of marriage. She may very well have been one of those women of true virtue whom Charlotte Gilman envisioned as possessing 'that high physiological integrity which refuses to eat when it is not hungry – even to oblige,' but we do not know Helena's thoughts on sexuality or her innermost feelings about sex, love, or marriage.[22] She may have had a passionate sexual friendship with another woman, or even a passionate non-sexual one, but it is equally possible for her to have had either kind of relationship with one of the handsome young men in the VTLC. In none of her writings did she allude to the subject of sex in a theoretical way except as it touched on the social and economic status of women: on political rights, financial security, and working conditions. When reporting her own activities, she often employed the passive voice and seldom the first person, and she very rarely spoke of her personal life.

More possibilities: Annie Besant, one of Helena's former exemplars, had also urged continence on her followers: '"Theosophists should sound the note of self-restraint within marriage and the restriction of the marital relation to the perpetuation of the race".'[23] However, Helena had long ago left the Theosophical Society and its philosophical idealism for the materialist philosophy of Karl Marx. If any of Annie Besant's injunctions advising self-restraint in marriage still lingered deep in her psyche and influenced her relationship with Ollie, we will never know given the dearth of evidence. Christabel Pankhurst, whom Helena's mother-in-law had invoked as an exemplar, had seized on the idea that 'sexual vice' was the real threat to women's enfranchisement, and that the truly free and independent woman must cast off the chains of sexuality.[24] Again, neither Christabel Pankhurst nor her mother, Emmeline, could have been Helena's mentors any longer. Although in 1916 she wished others to acknowledge her claim to recognition by Emmeline Pankhurst, Helena had taken a different direction from the Pankhursts and the WSPU three years earlier, when she broke with the Pioneer Political Equality League and directed her efforts to the enfranchisement of working class women. Seeking labour's support, Helena made no mention in her campaign of Christabel's new arguments. Charlotte Gilman, whose pamphlet 'The New Mothers of a New World' Helena had distributed from her Labor Temple office, equated freedom for women with freedom for them to be the 'absolute arbiter' in sexual relationships, which happy condition would create in women the potential for ultimately producing a superior race of people.[25] Gilman's phrase, 'the women of the race' echoed in the rhetoric of British Columbia suffragists, and Helena herself had warned that a population of physically exhausted women could ultimately produce only 'a sickly degenerate race.' Almost certainly Helena was familiar with these new ideas about sex and motherhood. Yet when she urged readers of the Woman Suffrage Page to study Gilman's pamphlet, she did not take the opportunity to speak of the 'subject wifehood' that indulged male sexual appetite. Rather, she chose to emphasize the power of the vote to combat organized vice, leaving Ida Douglas-Fearn to utter in print a *cri de coeur* about brute male sexual exploitation in marriage.[26]

Helena left no personal journals, no diaries – unless they were destroyed with other personal papers after her death. Nor are we privy to Ollie's thoughts and feelings. All we have are the Supreme Court Cause Sheet listing the proceedings taken and the final court decision. The actual annulment hearing testimony has been destroyed. Ollie is dead. Helena is dead. We cannot ask them what happened to their marriage.

But even if we could, ought we to intrude on their lives with impertinent questions about so intimate a matter? This question must give a biographer pause, making her wonder if to reveal the confusion and emotional anguish of two people extricating themselves from a failed marriage is not a little too much like the voyeurism of a television camera on the nightly newscast, or, more indulgently, like coffee-break gossip. Yet perhaps such scrutiny is not voyeurism and the biographer may after all ethically indulge in gossip. Writing in *Parallel Lives* about five Victorian marriages, Phyllis Rose reflected that 'gossip may be the beginning of moral inquiry, the low end of the platonic ladder which leads to self-understanding. We are desperate for information about how other people live because we want to know how to live ourselves, yet we are taught to see this desire as an illegitimate form of prying.'[27] On the other hand, the emotional content of a life must surely be of legitimate concern to a biographer. With a subject like Helena, whose political work was her life, an exploration, however limited, of her personal joys and griefs, aspirations and disappointments can only engage our sympathy and add to our appreciation of her achievements.

In the early thirties, Ida, Helena, and Ollie all left Mount Lehman. Douglas Fearn remained on his farm in nearby Bradner. Ida settled in North Vancouver, where she gave music lessons and edited manuscripts for aspiring writers. Her rooms were scented with bowls of rose petals from her garden. Then she moved to Bellingham, where the Bennetts had rented a house for her. Leslie was concerned that her teenage children would not get a 'proper education' in the Nooksak River community. Not wanting Alastair to grow up to be a logger or a tinsmith or Mettje a telephone operator, she sent them to high school in Bellingham, where they lived with their grandmother during the school year. Ida continued to write poetry and articles, the clatter of her heavy typewriter filling the house at all hours of the day and night. Old age did not dull her mind or make her a less daunting protagonist. Living out her days in her daughter's house, she read the books on the banned list of the Catholic Church and then questioned her priest closely about books he had not read. Too frail at last to attend Sunday service, she had the priest call on her after church and grilled him on his sermon, he sitting at the foot of her bed, mildly submitting. She died in 1940 at the age of eighty-two.[28]

Ollie continued to work as a tinsmith, and later as a sheet metal worker. He married Rose Dennison and they lived on Victoria Drive in Vancouver, where she kept a grocery store. After her death in 1937, he carried on with the store, but he was no grocer and soon went back to his trade. He married again, had one daughter with his third wife, and adopted a son. In the 1950s he was a beer parlour waiter, drinking to excess. He ended his days as caretaker at Riley Park Community Centre in Vancouver and died in 1966 at the age of seventy-three.[29]

In 1932 Helena moved to Vancouver and found a home with Edith May Sneve, a widow, later Mrs. Duncan McDonald, who had a big two-storey wooden frame house at 2471 Triumph Street on the city's east side. The following year Helena sold the farm to Alberta miner Peter Nicholls for $950, with a down payment of $150. She immediately turned her interest in the property over to Mrs. Sneve. Then in 1934, she took back the title from Mrs. Sneve, as Nicholls had maintained throughout the right to purchase and had been making installment payments. It is not known whether these changes of ownership were carried out with cash payments or merely with token consideration.[30] In any case, Edith May Sneve proved a good friend to Helena by thus helping her become re-established in Vancouver during the difficult years of the Depression.

The property gave Helena a small income as well as capital to work with, and so in a practical sense contributed to her everyday life. Gradually, however, her eleven years in Mount Lehman became an island reef of memory, like Pavilion Road in Chelsea, the London ladies' clothing department, and the Pankhurst women; like the Carvell Hall Co-operative Settlement, the BC Woman's Suffrage League, the Vancouver Trades and Labor Council. Whatever the emotional cost of other memories, those of Mount Lehman were bought with painful self-knowledge and suffering. Although heartbroken when she left Mount Lehman, she never revealed her anguish. She did not talk about the farm or about Ollie and the Fearn family, but merely said that her marriage had been annulled, allowing Ollie to become a shadowy, nameless character in an episode of an interesting interlude in her past. She took what work she could find as a tailoress. At least, she is so listed in the *Vancouver Directory* for 1932-36. In her new home she brought out her Pankhurst photograph, always a cherished reminder of self-sacrifice and disciplined devotion to a cause, and rededicated herself to the political life. Aunt Billy with her chickens and ducks was gone forever, as was Mrs. Fearn, who played the mandolin and taught Mount Lehman teenagers to waltz and dance the polka.

CHAPTER EIGHT

Rededication: The Vision of the Co-operative Commonwealth

Men and Women! Give us mandate! This the pathway, clear-defined,
Leading us to fuller manhood, broader scope of heart and mind.
Seek the open trails of sunshine; quit the swamps of desolation!
Rout the cohorts of Reaction; ballot in the Federation!
    – Flare-Pistol Pete (Burnett A. Ward), 'Challenge of the CCF'

Helena returned to Vancouver during the very worst year of the Depression. In June 1932, persons registered as unemployed in British Columbia numbered 77,428, not including the hundreds that escaped the government count. Earlier in the year, Premier Simon Fraser Tolmie had abandoned his road construction work program for lack of federal funds. The road camps were shut down, throwing 20,000 men out of work and putting them on direct relief. In the hobo jungles all along the harbourfront, beneath Georgia Viaduct, behind the Canadian National Railway station, beside the city dump, men made crude shelters for themselves out of cardboard and wooden boxes and gunnysacking, scrounged for food, and cooked over little campfires. Outside Hamilton Hall, the provincial government relief office, the lines of the unemployed became longer and more restive, as more and more migrant workers, or 'transients,' flooded into Vancouver. They arrived on the freight trains, 'riding the rods' from eastern Canada and the prairies, only to find when they jumped off in Vancouver that there was no work here either. From time to time the dreary landscape of economic privation erupted in hunger marches and protest rallies. Labour's May Day parade that year was seen as a threat to law and order and a warship was dispatched to Vancouver from the Royal Canadian Navy base at Esquimalt. Less visible than the men in hobo jungles and relief office line-ups were the equally hungry, equally impoverished women whose ultimate choice might well have been between domestic service and prostitution.[1] For Vancouver, 1932 was a year of physical suffering and mental anguish.

Canada was among the countries hardest hit by the economic collapse of the thirties. Even so, throughout the country, a population pitiful in its need, humiliated by the ignominy of poverty, and angered by the injustice of it began to look for solutions. In the spring of 1932, these efforts began to coalesce into a new political dynamic. A number of left-wing Toronto and Montreal intellectuals and professional people formed the League for Social Reconstruction with the aim of trying to help remedy economic and social injustice through research and education. Farmers already organized in the United Farmers of Canada were looking for political solutions to the economic crisis and were receptive to overtures for common action from prairie labour parties. The Socialist Party of Canada, formerly British Columbia's Independent Labor Party, reluctantly conceded that there was room for social reform along with revolutionary Marxist theory. Sparked by the Ginger Group of radical MPs in Ottawa, including J.S. Woodsworth and Canada's first woman MP, Agnes McPhail, these organizations took the lead in founding a new national political movement with a socialist program – the Co-operative Commonwealth Federation (CCF). Formed in Calgary on 1 August 1932, the CCF was a political coalition of farmer, labour, and socialist groups.[2] In 1933 the party drew up its Regina Manifesto, setting forth its program for a socialist Canada, and chose Woodsworth as national president.

Helena immediately joined the movement and began to build her life around it. And so, despite the Depression, despite the physical suffering and mental anguish all around her, 1932 was a good year to return to Vancouver. This was also the year that brought together in Vancouver a number of vital and original women in whom political intellect and compassionate commitment to social reform were creatively and happily combined. Mildred Osterhout, a Vancouver schoolteacher, returned from a study trip abroad, where she had been doing social work among unemployed London dockworkers and their families. Mildred had studied at Bryn Mawr College in Pennsylvania, visited the new workers' housing estates in Vienna, gone on a student tour of the Soviet Union. She had also studied at the London School of Economics. She had walked and talked with Gandhi, then visiting London and staying at the settlement house where she was living. Now, her head full of Laski and the Webbs and her soul imbued with the spirit of Gandhi, Mildred was eager to change the world, beginning with the government of British Columbia.[3]

Sorbonne graduate Grace Woodsworth had abandoned teaching and French language studies for politics. She began her political career in the House of Commons as secretary for her father, J.S. Woodsworth, Independent Labor Party member for Winnipeg North Centre. In 1932 she made a good, strong socialist marriage with Angus MacInnis, MP for the working class riding of Vancouver East. With her marriage, she said, her 'real political life' began. In June 1932, when the parliamentary session ended, she took to the hustings with her husband and made forty-five speeches in forty-five days. They ended their cross-country tour in Vancouver in time for Angus to represent the Socialist Party at the founding of the CCF in Calgary.[4]

Lawyer Dorothy Gretchen Steeves, wife of First World War Canadian soldier R.P. Steeves, had left her native Amsterdam to return with him to small-town Vancouver. When the Depression struck, they became interested in politics, and in 1932 joined Mildred Osterhout and Grace MacInnis as founding members of the left-wing study group that became the Vancouver branch of the League for Social Reconstruction (LSR). Dorothy would win a North Vancouver seat for the CCF in the 1934 provincial by-election, joyously touring her riding to the skirl of bagpipes on that July evening. The victory was worth celebrating, for during her eleven years as a member of the legislature, she proved to be a brilliant protagonist for the CCF and did much to prepare the way for the social legislation that provincial and federal governments eventually passed.[5]

Frances Moren, graduate of a ladies' college in Bishop's Stortford, England, had learned something about working class poverty as a teacher in an English coal-mining town, and about the prairie farmer-labour movement in rural Alberta, where she taught briefly just after arriving from England. She was also much interested in the iconoclastic educational theories of English educationist A.S. Neill. Coming to Vancouver in 1924, she met Vancouver physician and humanitarian Lyle Telford, and co-edited his socialist newspaper, *The Challenge*. She joined the Socialist Party of Canada and became a well-known speaker. With Angus MacInnis's support, she was chosen in 1932 as one of the party's candidates in the anticipated provincial election of 1933. As it turned out, she did not run, but instead campaigned actively for the CCF. Torn between the claims of her public political life and those of her private life, she chose to abandon politics for her relationship with Lyle Telford, her lover and intellectual companion for the past ten years. Both Grace and Angus urged her to leave him and carry on with her political career. 'Come to Ottawa beside Miss MacPhail,' wrote Grace, 'In my imagination I often see you there.' And Angus, who had a few years earlier wanted to marry Frances, wrote, kindly but firmly, 'I do not see how I could now support you in your candidature, knowing as I do, that at any time the publicity given to your private affairs will make you useless, no, worse, a drawback to our cause.' However, the CCF provincial executive committee decided that 'the personal affairs of Dr. Telford are of no concern to the CCF.'[6]

In 1932 Frances was also working at the Vancouver birth control clinic that Dr. Telford established that spring, the second such clinic in Canada. Both Dorothy Steeves and Burnaby Juvenile Court Judge Laura Jamieson supported the program of the newly formed Birth

Control Association of Vancouver. Indeed, Mrs. Jamieson had been for twenty years a voice for social reform and the education of women, though she did not become publicly active in the CCF until 1938.[7]

By 1932 journalist Elizabeth Kerr had also arrived – politically and intellectually, that is. Hers had been a long journey, but she had been helped along the way by strong male attachments. Born in Glasgow, as a young girl she chafed against the constraints of a puritanical upbringing. Scotland, she later wrote, was 'that grim land ... where sex is indecent'; where 'to rise after 7:30 A.M. was to be utterly damned'; where reading was idleness and Satan 'roamed the earth finding evil for idle hands to do.' Fortunately, her youthful rebellion was tempered by her association with a student of Burns, one Duncan McNaught, 'the Maister,' who talked to her about the Bard and sang his songs. The Maister further allowed her to browse in his large private collection of Burns, whose poetry she read and loved and whose proud humanity she absorbed. In Canada she struck out on her own as a journalist and worked for newspapers in Vancouver, Calgary, and Montreal. She also contributed to Canadian magazines under the pseudonym 'Constance Errol.'

In 1914 she married one of Canada's leading journalists, Ontario-born James Blain Kerr, for many years senior editor of the *Vancouver Daily Province*, and settled down to raise a family. She became her husband's apt pupil, submitting her writing to him, reading the books he recommended. He was many years her senior, more conservative in his views. Eventually their father-daughter marriage broke down. When her cousin Grant MacNeil came to live with them in the late 1920s, she found in him yet another mentor – a socialist – one closer to her own age, and they fell in love. Betty Kerr walked out of her house and closed the door on husband and children to be with the man she loved. A short time later, she moved back home for a few years and in 1932 was somehow managing to hold together her complicated personal life – aging husband, children, newspaper work, socialist lover – and at the same time be an active member of the Socialist Party of Canada.[8]

Into this community of progressive women came Helena Gutteridge, bringing with her that long training in discipline and self-sacrifice in the suffragist movement in England and the rich political experience of her early career in Vancouver. These CCF women were a remarkable breed, for they managed their personal lives without necessarily submitting to the social strictures that still fettered women. Essentially family women, they were not 'bohemian' and they did not believe in free love, but they believed in themselves and found their own kind of liberation. They accepted the full implications of socialist thinking for equality of the sexes and acted on them, even when this meant flouting convention. Dedicating her life to socialism, Grace MacInnis chose not to have children. Mildred Osterhout could have dutifully accepted her role as the unmarried daughter looking after her widowed father, but not content to be an 'angel in the house,' she broke away for one liberating year that freed her for a fulfilling political life. Frances Moren disregarded the advice of friends that, for the sake of the movement, she break off her relationship with Dr. Telford, whose wife refused to divorce him. Instead she bore his child out of wedlock, suffered ostracism in the CCF, and refused to be ashamed. Not even the urging of good friends Grace and Angus MacInnis could change her mind, and her decision to withdraw from politics was regarded as a great loss to the movement.[9] Dorothy Steeves found support and companionship in her husband, but intellectual and political fulfillment with Colin Cameron, under whose influence she became more radical in her views.[10] Betty Kerr worked to support herself and her family through her writing, maintaining a relationship with Grant MacNeil that lasted until his death in 1976. They never married, but were regarded as a couple in the CCF even though they maintained separate homes a good part of the time.[11] Having devoted most of her adult life to the rights of women and the welfare of the working class, Helena was right at home among these women. And she herself had, at the age of forty, married a man nearly fifteen years younger, a daring violation of the proprieties.

Helena began her second political career by joining one of the CCF clubs springing up all across the country. They were not yet branches of the CCF itself, but rather adjuncts to the party created so that members of the League for Social Reconstruction could join without being branded socialist and so jeopardizing the educational work of the LSR.[12] The CCF clubs flourished, helped in British Columbia by the energetic Dr. Telford, who undertook to organize them throughout the province. 'The Nanaimo Missionaries,' Grace MacInnis and a then politically active Frances Moren, organized clubs on Vancouver Island. In 1933 the LSR became the Reconstruction Party and was admitted by the watchful Socialist Party of Canada into the Co-operative Commonwealth Federation, despite the objection of lawyer Wallis Lefeaux and other doctrinaire Marxists that 'the socialistic principles of the Reconstruction Party were in a very rudimentary state.'[13] In a continuing metamorphosis, the Reconstruction Party adopted the CCF clubs, then itself became absorbed by a new organization, the Associated CCF Clubs. Helena became an executive member-at-large for this group, and in this connection made contact with Dorothy Steeves and Mildred Osterhout. In 1935 a final merger eliminated the Socialist Party of Canada as a separate political entity and united it with the Associated CCF Clubs.[14]

In these first years the CCF generated an enormous amount of political and intellectual energy. It was served by not one, but three newspapers: *The Commonwealth,* the CCF official organ, though owned by its editor, Bill Pritchard, Helena's old comrade on the Vancouver Trades and Labor Council; the Socialist Party's doctrinally correct BC *Clarion,* edited by Harold Winch; and Dr. Telford's *The Challenge,* which followed a more eclectic political line. In the columns of the three newspapers, intellectual debate flourished among party members, ever vigilant against signs of backsliding liberalism. *Commonwealth* editor Bill Pritchard even dared to displace Marx in the name of Liebknecht, declaring that in the present world economic crisis the middle class, not the proletariat, would be the vanguard leading the world to socialism through constitutional change.[15] This kind of revisionist heresy from one who had been jailed because of radical Marxist utterances during the Winnipeg general strike provoked spirited opposition from doctrinaire socialists, among them Harold Winch, who objected vehemently to 'the quite obvious effort to wipe Marx in particular and Socialism in general out of the local political picture.'[16] Dr. Telford espoused the changing of the individual consciousness through education, quoting not Marx on the transition from quantitative to qualitative change, but literary critic John Middleton Murry on the transition from imagination to action by the delicate sensing of the 'fluttering tendril of change.'[17] Co-editor Frances Moren, more literary than her colleague, may have been responsible for that kind of unorthodox political thinking and writing. Even when the army of Austrian Chancellor Dolfuss attacked the socialist housing estates of Vienna, the Moren-Telford editorials counselled patience and seasoned reflection, and grieved that the socialists took up arms in self-defence. The more politically astute members of the CCF angrily came to the defence of the Austrian workers, one reader declaring that the whole article was 'redolent of Ramsay Macdonald's philosophy and would not disgrace him.'[18] Contradictions in ideology flourished within the CCF. Viewed dialectically, the new party was developing in a proper Marxist way.

Helena joined enthusiastically in subscription campaigns for *The Commonwealth*: '*The Commonwealth* is "Second to None," and sells on its own merits. I even hooked without any trouble an ex-president of the Liberal Association,' she crowed. Socialist news was different from ordinary news in the daily press. Aneurin Bevan, the fiery British Labour Party MP was to marry the equally fiery Labourite Jenny Lee; bold headlines announced Russia's new health plan and the Centenary of the Tolpuddle martyrs, who were transported to Australia in 1834 for union organization. Barry Mather, later a New Democratic Party (NDP) MP for New Westminster, in his 'Idle Roomer' column in *The Commonwealth* turned a quizzical and sometimes satirical eye on CCF personalities and on current events, as did cartoonist Fraser Wilson. More arresting was the full text, in August 1933, of the Regina Manifesto, setting forth the program of the CCF and ending with this historic socialist declaration: 'No C.C.F. Government will rest content until it has eradicated capitalism and put into operation the full program of socialized planning which will lead to the establishment in Canada of the Co-operative Commonwealth.'[19] Helena was right about her newspaper. In the thirties an eager readership welcomed its new perspective on the world.

Socialism was also propagated through radio. Dr. Telford had initiated radio broadcasts around 1930. When he joined forces with the CCF, he maintained control of 'Challenge Radio,' but other CCF leaders made full use of that program and also broadcast their own speakers. In addition, Mildred Osterhout broadcast a weekly program on CJOR, 'The Woman's Point of View,' sponsored by Ye Olde English Fish and Chips restaurant. Frances Moren managed Dr. Telford's program, contributed to the women's program, and served on the CCF radio committee. In 1933 the CCF broadcast to a very large audience four days a week on three Vancouver stations, CJOR, CKMO, and CRCV. Dr. Telford was especially popular. In some parts of Vancouver, walking down the street on a summer evening one could hear him from all sides, as all the radios were tuned to his program. In the Japanese quarter on Powell Street, a storekeeper who listened to Dr. Telford would attract a crowd of two or three hundred eager sidewalk listeners.

During the 1935 federal election campaign, Helena was on the air regularly. Radio stations had for some years been quite lenient about CCF speeches, but by the time Helena started broadcasting they were examining political content more rigorously. At CJOR, the station manager was sending all political scripts to his solicitors, something he had never done before. Radio talks were often a full half hour, for in those days no one knew that the attention span of the average listener was only about ninety seconds.[20]

In this stimulating political ambience Helena began to heal and grow, immersing herself in the party. She was a campaign worker in the fall 1933 provincial election, speaking to afternoon audiences in living rooms crammed to the doors with women eager to learn about the new political movement.[21] The CCF platform of social planning and its philosophy of cooperation and brotherhood found an enthusiastic constituency among working people hard hit by the Depression. Seven CCF candidates were elected across British Columbia, and formed the official opposition to the newly elected Liberal government of Premier Thomas Dufferin Pattullo.

1
Charles Henry Gutteridge, Helena's father, circa 1913, at Petersfield, England, with grandson Thomas

2
Sophia Gutteridge, Helena's mother

2

3
Chelsea Fire Station, London, built around 1880 on the site of Helena's birthplace, 216 Pavilion Rd., and number 214, Holy Trinity Parish Hall, another Gutteridge address.

4
Helena Gutteridge, Vancouver tailor, president Local 178, Journeymen Tailors' Union of America, 1914

5
Helena Gutteridge, right, with friend, possibly future sister-in-law, Leslie, circa 1915: 'Of course I was slimmer then and cut quite a figure.'

4

5

SUFFRAGISTS AND REFORMERS

6
Helena Gutteridge, founder of BC *Woman's Suffrage League, 1913, Minimum Wage League, 1917*

6

7
Lily Laverock, 1912, McGill honours graduate in philosophy, journalist, concert impresario, and Helena's long-time friend

7

8

8
Helen Gregory MacGill, LLD, journalist, BC's first woman judge; first woman to receive an honorary doctorate from the University of British Columbia, 1938

9
Elizabeth Ida Bramwell of Her Majesty's Nursing Staff, circa 1880, Perth, Scotland, wearing the Queen's uniform. Later Ida Douglas-Fearn, Helena's mother-in-law

9

10
Cartoon by Emily Carr in Western Woman's Weekly, *1918, two years after the referendum which won the provincial franchise for women*

11
Gravestone, Cumberland, Vancouver Island, recalling the summer of 1918 when the shooting of Ginger Goodwin precipitated BC's first general strike and the raid on Vancouver's Labor Temple

12
James Purvis Oliver (Ollie) Fearn, tinsmith, sheet metal worker, Helena's former husband (with second wife)

13
Helena Gutteridge Fearn's 'children,' Mount Lehman, BC, 1920s: bottom, Stasia Moran at Nicholson's Slough, and clockwise, Rosita Herron, Audrey and Hubert Farber and an older Audrey; centre, Fred Herron; not shown, Vermona Farber

CCF
COMRADES,
1930

14
Mildred Osterhout, later Fahrni (back right),
social worker, disciple of Gandhi (back left);
with co-workers at Kingsley Hall, London,
1931

15
Frances Moren, later Telford, 1928, teacher,
birth control advocate, Dr. Lyle Telford's colleague on The Challenge newspaper and
radio broadcasts

CCF COMRADES, 1930

16

16
Elizabeth Kerr, journalist, Helena's best friend, circa 1937: a 'lilting Scottish voice' and a passion for Robert Burns and socialism

17
CCF MLAS *Dorothy Steeves and Harold Winch, leader of the Opposition, circa 1940*

17

18

18
CCF *Summer Camp, Gabriola Island, circa*
1940. After porridge, bacon, and eggs, the
Regina Manifesto and the inevitability of the
new social order

19
Maximilian Paulik, early environmentalist,
founder of the BC *Forest Conservation*
League, consultant for CCF *Economic Plan-*
ning Commission, circa 1936

19

21

20

Helena Gutteridge, the first woman elected to Vancouver City Council, 24 March 1937: 'a faithful alderman'

21

Alderman Gutteridge taking the oath of office before Mayor George Miller, 30 March 1937

22

Good Grief! A woman on City Council! Cartoon by Fraser Wilson, 1988, faithfully copied from his original on page 1, Vancouver Sun, *27 March 1937*

22

24

23
Helena Gutteridge addressing the unemployed at Powell Street grounds, Vancouver, May 1938

24
May Day parade, Powell Street, 1930s: marching for work and wages

25
Helena Gutteridge, welfare manager, Japanese internment camp, Lemon Creek, BC, 1942–45

25

26

26
Welfare office staff, Lemon Creek: left to right, back, Fumiko Deshima and Wakiko Suyama with Masayo Suyama and Harry Yonekura

27
Hilda and Denny Kristiansen, just married, 1936. Owners of the 'CCF House,' 1220 Barclay Street, Vancouver, and Helena's 'family' during her retirement

27

If you belonged to the CCF, party activities occupied most of your leisure time. Your own local club engaged in a different activity almost every night of the week – public meetings, women's meetings, business meetings; whist drives, parties for young people, for birthdays, for Hallowe'en. Sunday Forums were popular, none more so than those held by the Stanley Park Club, originally a study group of the League for Social Reconstruction. In their Robson Street clubroom, under a sky-blue ceiling with silver stars – the work of two Ukrainian-Canadian club members – socialism in all its theoretical complexity was passionately scrutinized, debated, explained, and argued as true believer confronted revisionist heretic and old-guard socialist lectured political convert.[22]

In addition, the party education committee conducted study groups on Marxist economics and philosophy that met with an enthusiastic response. A summertime *Commonwealth* writer described one group which he thought, if anything, was too large:

> Twenty people sitting in the company rooms of anybody's home, both sexes, young to middle-aged, representing a typical cross-section of the CCF proletarian worker, proletarian unemployed to the petty bourgeoisie and the professional class. One is reading from 'What Marx Really Meant,' by G.D.H. Cole.
>
> Occasionally the reading is interrupted and a discussion ensues on the point involved. In any case, one chapter provides material enough for the evening's discussion.[23]

Newcomers read Edward Bellamy's utopian novel, *Looking Backward*, serialized in *The Commonwealth,* Upton Sinclair's *Letters to Judd,* and Fred Henderson's *ABC of Socialism.* When they had become familiar with the rudiments of Marxist dialectical materialism and had reflected on the idea expounded by party theoreticians that 'every organism when born contains within itself the seeds of its own destruction,' they moved on to George Bernard Shaw's *Intelligent Woman's Guide to Socialism* and G.D.H. Cole's *Intelligent Man's Guide Through World Chaos.*[24]

The CCF also carried on its education program at summer camps, coordinated for a number of years by Mildred Osterhout, convenor of the education committee. Along with a full menu of such staple socialist fare as historical materialism and Marxist economics offered by leading party intellectuals – teacher and poet A.M. Stephen, Angus and Grace MacInnis, lawyer Wallis Lefeaux, and national party president J.S. Woodsworth – a member could enjoy an outdoor holiday with swimming, campfire singing, and dramatics. Where else, after porridge, bacon and eggs, hot cakes, and coffee, could one sit under a tree and join in a discussion on state capitalism? Grace MacInnis, who led discussions on the Regina Manifesto, describes a study session from the Saltspring Island camp of 1934:

> A spacious tent. The patter of rain outside. The young people sprawled over the camp beds or stretched luxuriously on cedar spread on the ground. This is the lecture hall. And there is Frank Roberts addressing us from the improvised platform with its home-made blackboard. The panorama of history, with the increasing mastery of man over nature, unfolds itself as we listen. The inevitability of the new social order impresses itself on our minds.[25]

In this benevolent setting, the Regina Manifesto's call for the 'establishment in Canada of the Co-operative Commonwealth' was no abstract utterance. It was a practical political task.

Helena was not among these discussion leaders in the early years, though doubtless she attended the camps. She was valued, in any case, for her practical mind and knowledge of labour affairs, and in 1937 attended the camp on Gabriola Island to lecture and lead a discussion on trade unionism. At that camp Dr. Telford lectured on Freud and Marx, and MPS Angus MacInnis and J.S. Woodsworth came from Ottawa to talk about the state of the Canadian economy and about the rise of fascism. Dorothy Steeves spoke on socialized medicine and adult education, and Laura Jamieson on proletarian literature. Everyone helped with the chores – washing dishes, carrying water – J.S. Woodsworth setting an example by scrubbing the dining room floor. Around the campfire at night, the new CCF MLA for Comox, Colin Cameron, sang 'The Skye Boat Song,' Helena's friend Betty Kerr reported on her visit to the Soviet Union, and some literary members read the poems of Baudelaire in translation. There were sing-songs and comic skits, and Saskatchewan MP M.J. Coldwell was brought to trial for washing his shirt in the horse's drinking water. The camp was a family holiday, gathering everyone together in a happy association of believers.[26]

Drama was another tool in the service of socialist education and propaganda, a word that had not yet taken on pejorative connotations. The CCF Dramatic Club, organized by Dorothy Steeves, encouraged playwriting and mounted the efforts of young socialist playwrights like Don Smith and Denny Kristiansen.[27] Kristiansen was one of the founders of a workers' theatre group, the Progressive Arts Club, which brought honour and glory to Vancouver when in 1936 they carried home from the Dominion Drama Festival in Ottawa the award for the best play in English, Clifford Odet's drama of social protest, *Waiting for Lefty*. It was too powerful, however, for the Vancouver police, on the watch for subversive incitement to revolution. They stopped a Vancouver performance of the play and shut down the performance hall, the Ukrainian Temple, on charges of obscenity – in fact, one or two 'God damns' and too free a use of 'bastard.'[28]

A thirty-piece band further enlivened the socialist scene, and Helena was on the committee helping to manage its affairs. 'Think of it, comrades and friends,' enthused coppersmith and car repairman Arthur Turner, 'for our own functions, our picnics, our big meetings, and which can, with the Commonwealth Choir add to our already multiple activities, within and without our ranks.'[29] Bill Pritchard, whose great love, second only to socialism, was music, organized the choir and later the Cedar Cottage String Ensemble. The orchestra joined the choir in a Christmas program highlighted by 'Drums of Freedom,' sung by thirty-four CCF voices, and a Mozart serenade with eleven violins. Two years later, when the band began to falter from lack of money and flagging interest, it asked for a member of the provincial executive to attend its meetings. Helena was the obvious choice: she could speak to them out of her own experience of playing mandolin in a Mount Lehman dance band.[30]

Exuberant times for the CCF, for was it not a movement whose members were dedicated to the pursuit of the Good, a movement that would soon establish a new social order in Canada? In British Columbia the CCF believed they were well on the way to bringing about a radical change in government by constitutional means, and that they would be the ones to make that change, even as soon as the next election. In the meantime, urgent problems demanded solutions. People were going hungry, facing eviction because they could not pay their rent. Homeless men 'riding the rods' arrived every day in Vancouver from other parts of British Columbia and Canada, looking for work, for a meal, and for a place to sleep.

In June 1933 the Department of National Defence incorporated the British Columbia road camps, closed a year earlier, into their national relief camp program, designed by Major General A.G.L. McNaughton to prevent possible civil insurrection by unemployed men frustrated and ultimately rebellious over the futility and hopelessness of their lives. In April 1935 the men did rebel by walking out of the camps. They converged on Vancouver and created a crisis that could not be quelled even by Mayor Gerald Grattan McGeer's reading of the Riot Act. Prime Minister R.B. Bennett, turning a deaf ear to McGeer's and Pattullo's pleas for financial help, called the unemployed 'derelicts' and declared he had no intention of becoming a 'wet nurse' for them. One of these 'derelicts,' a twenty-six-year-old unemployed electrician, had been elected as CCF MLA for Vancouver East. With his swarthy good looks and passionate demeanour, Harold Winch was an eloquent advocate for the unemployed when he addressed the Liberal government in his maiden speech:

> We, the Socialist Members of the Opposition, are out, not to reform, alleviate or palliate the existing order of society, but to completely abolish it. But we realize that this cannot be done in a day; we know that that which must be done immediately is to answer the despairing cry of thousands of the people of BC, 'When do we eat?'[31]

The CCF understood that although it was important to press on towards the establishment of the Co-operative Commonwealth, the movement had to respond in a practical way to the cries for help from the unemployed and people on relief.

Helena really began her second political career by answering these cries. Indeed, she followed the full implications of unemployment to the root cause – in her view, the economic system – and assumed more and more responsibility for preparing the way for the Planned Society. She worked with Harold Winch and his father, Ernest, formerly an unemployed bricklayer somehow supporting his family on relief, now an indefatigable MLA for Burnaby. She worked with other political women: Susie Lane Clark, her old friend from suffragist days; MLA Dorothy Steeves, champion of the unemployed, marching with them on the street, even leading the procession; Sarah Colley, the 'CCF Mother' from New Westminster, who spoke so movingly about the transient unemployed as 'our boys'; Mildred Osterhout, high-profile director of the CCF education committee, whose broadcasts about the relief camps stirred compassion and resolve in her listeners; and Betty Kerr, Helena's best friend, who took up the neglected cause of unemployed women.

Helena was a frequent visitor at Betty's house. Their kitchen table conversations, judgmental and raucous, politically earnest but sometimes vulgar and irreverent, half understood and disregarded by Betty's children, were part of the background of the Kerr household. Both Helena and Betty were forceful speakers who could hold an audience, although neither presented a prepossessing appearance on the platform. According to the 1930s stereotype, both would have been considered old, Helena in her middle fifties and Betty ten years younger.

Helena had straight grey hair, bobbed quite short, topped by the inevitable navy-blue hat. She wore steel-rimmed glasses and her figure had filled out in a matronly way. She stood tall and carried herself well, commanding respect by her presence. Everything she said had substance and carried forward an idea. Her voice was rather flat and not particularly compelling. It had become Canadianized over the years, but still had some of its original English colouring.[32]

Betty had strikingly dark hair and eyes – one of them blind – though she was too short and plump to conform to conventional standards of beauty. But when she began to speak in her lilting Scottish voice, she became immediately attractive and readily won her audience and communicated her passion for socialism. Her face alight, she delivered a lucid, well-organized talk, punctuated with the occasional spontaneous snide remark, something the more judicious Helena never resorted to.[33]

The CCF provincial convention of 1934 tackled the problem of unemployment by setting up the CCF Unemployment Conference, so-called because it met frequently as a conference of delegates from the various CCF clubs and the CCF provincial council, not just to respond to events but also to take action on behalf of the unemployed. Its mandate from the convention was to 'establish ameliorative measures for the benefit of those suffering under the pressure of relief administration, until the time arrives when an adequate social system shall be established.' The 'ameliorative measures' consisted of organizing the unemployed, dealing with their grievances, and gaining concessions from the government. Helena and Betty were among the leading people in the conference. Grant MacNeil, Betty's companion and sometime housemate, was initially in charge of its organization. He had been for many years an aggressive fighter for the rights of Canadian war veterans, acting as their advocate and representative before government bodies. Articulate and well read, this stocky, red-haired Ontario Scot was said to deliver a speech in accents of 'sermon and pibroch rolled into one,' and more 'like the sound of a silver trumpet calling to a great spiritual conflict.' He was the ideal person to carry on an educational campaign to win the sympathy and support of the authorities and the general public. Meanwhile, the CCF MLAs cooperated with the conference through a Central Legislative Committee that brought the injustices and inadequacies of the relief system to the attention of the legislature and pressed for changes.[34]

By 1934 people no longer received their relief allowance in provisions – flour, sugar, beans, butter to be carried home in a gunnysack. Instead they received scrip, or vouchers, which they exchanged for goods and services. In Vancouver, the City Council's Relief Department issued grocery scrip every two weeks to the amount of $9.90 a month for the first adult, $3.85 for the second, and $3.75 for each additional dependent. Fifty cents to a dollar was allowed for light and $3.75 for fuel, depending on the time of year. The rent allowance ranged from $5 to $8. Thus a married couple received about $23 a month, a family with two children perhaps $33.50. Single women living at home received 22 cents a day or $6.60 a month for food, and a clothing allowance of $3. They found difficulty in leaving home to live on their own, because the shelter allowance was only 20 cents a day and the food allowance scarcely 25 cents. The plight of single homeless women was pitiful, all the more so because, unlike the relief camp workers, they were not organized. To keep them off the relief rolls, officials pressured them into domestic service jobs paying as little as $5 to $10 a month. If classified as transients, they did not qualify for relief, and there were no relief camps for them. However, in the interior of British Columbia jobs of a kind were found for some women. Concerned and angry social welfare workers reported that 'a network of protected bawdy houses' recruited unemployed Vancouver women ineligible for relief.[35]

At first Helena was the indispensable secretary who saw to the preparation of documents for executive secretary William Braithwaite and handled the correspondence and news releases. Susie Lane Clark was on the Advisory Committee and Betty Kerr headed the Women's Grievance Committee. The conference soon reported, in accents that could only have belonged to secretary Gutteridge, 'the closing of that rat hole recently known as the Institute. Your unemployment Council sealed its doom.'[36] The Single Men's Institute was the euphemistic name for a converted warehouse in downtown Vancouver where men physically unfit for the relief camps could sleep on straw mattresses without pillows or sheets – one hundred in one big room smelling of disinfectant – and have their food ladled out for them in the soup kitchen below.[37]

Economic distress was so serious that the CCF was willing to lay aside its customary perception of the Communist Party as a Venus flytrap only too ready to absorb mere parliamentary socialists in order to work with it to help the homeless, the indigent, and the unemployed. In a united front action, the CCF Unemployment Conference joined forces with the Communist Party's Provincial Workers' Alliance to draw up a brief for submission to the provincial government, a brief accompanied by an enormous citizens' petition. The resulting Joint Action Committee on Unemployment claimed to represent sixty-five organizations, but the prime movers were the CCF and the Communist Party.[38]

Meanwhile, the CCF membership had to be put into the picture, their feedback solicited and considered. Helena, Susie Clark, Betty Kerr, and Sarah Colley were among those sent out to the clubs to talk about the CCF Unemployment Conference and organize the petition campaign. The petition asked for a 50 per cent increase in direct relief, a food allowance of 45 cents a day for single persons, and a minimum of $1.75 per week for shelter with the privilege of choosing their own lodgings. It also asked that the government stop pressuring single women into accepting domestic service jobs instead of relief. It pleaded for free medical, dental, optical, and prenatal care for those too poor to pay for medical service. As many as thirty thousand people signed the petition. The accompanying brief urged the provincial government to take responsibility for administering relief, rather than leaving it to the municipalities, so that uniform regulations would apply and inequities between municipalities would be abolished. It made clear the moral implications for any humane government:

> These circumstances [living conditions] have arisen through no fault of the unemployed. It is not in the public interest that they should be compelled to accept a standard of living, vastly lower than that of their fellows, and so dangerously low as to imperil, not only the well being of themselves and their children, but the well-being of the entire community. The unemployed should not be treated as outcasts, nor should they be held in the bondage of hopelessness and perilous insecurity imposed upon them by the present conditions.[39]

The brief was duly sent to Premier Pattullo in Victoria, and on 7 December over a hundred people followed, sailing aboard the early morning CPR boat to Victoria, where eight of their number, including two schoolchildren, were to present the case to the premier and to the Minister of Labour George Pearson, and other members of the cabinet.

Duff Pattullo had been elected on the promise of 'work and wages,' and in order to impress on him their urgent financial need, the unemployed were allowed to speak for themselves, Grant, Betty, Susie, and Helena remaining in the background. Representative working class folk were to go forward to ask redress of certain abuses by those who held power over their lives, and to appeal to the government's benevolence. That morning in the Executive Council Chamber, delegation chairman Bob Lealess introduced his little group to the assembled cabinet: 'We think that the premier and cabinet should be as attentive and considerate as they possibly can because most of these people are first, on relief and second, they are not used to the formalities of such representative bodies as this, and are working men and women and children; consequently, they will do the best of their ability [sic] to present their case in a working class manner.'[40] Lealess's suggestion that they were humble, inarticulate people with no particular political experience to speak of was not strictly true: finding ordinary folk who could speak eloquently on their own behalf was not easy, and the committee moved to the fore several politically experienced people. Sarah Colley, a persuasive speaker and practised tactician, needed no special consideration. Nor did sawmill worker and committee chairman Bill Black, a veteran of Socialist Party wars, including the famous coup a year or two earlier at 666 Homer Street, when a rebel faction raided the SPC office and appropriated it for themselves. CCF secretary Mary McCormack had as a child attended political meetings in Ontario and stood on street corners selling Communist Party newspapers and handing out leaflets; the political history of her parents went back to that historic barn outside Guelph, Ontario, where the Canadian Communist Party had its underground beginnings.[41]

One by one the delegation approached the long table where their elected representatives were waiting to hear them. They had written their own submissions and spoke out of their own experience about hunger and poverty and looking for work and the ignominy of the relief system. Whatever their political experience, they were all ordinary working folk, after all. Bill Black spoke of being on relief for four years; of standing outside Hamilton Hall at midnight to be first in line in the morning to obtain a bundle of clothing from the city's Central Clothing Committee. Ex-serviceman J.H. Fitzer gave reasons for needing three meals a day and objected to being forced to share a bed with a stranger in a skid row hotel because of the meagre housing allowance for single men. Victoria housewife Ada Beaumont said that she had not replaced a bit of linen in fifteen years. Schoolgirl Yvonne Gillard said, 'We would like to go to the show sometimes, but mother cannot give us any money.' Mary McCormack pleaded for young women who had to delay marriage because of economic insecurity: 'Gentlemen, think for a moment. Do you think that we are devoid of all the instincts of a normal woman? There will be children whether illegitimate or not ... We are the mothers of tomorrow and unless we are properly nourished our children will be poor wretched creatures.' Sarah Colley, whose own infant son had died of pneumonia, asked for a prenatal allowance for pregnant women and for bottles and nipples for infants. 'It is for you to make this better,' she chided the premier in her soft Scottish voice. 'The very first thing this little mite needs is some warm clothing.'[42]

Though harassed by claims on a depleted provincial coffer, the government was not without compassion. Minister of Labour George Pearson assured the delegation that pregnant women on relief would receive additional assistance. The other demands were out of the question. Pattullo explained that relief was now costing the province $7,573,000 per year. To meet these new demands, the province would have to put out an additional $6 million, an impossible expenditure. He was applying pressure on the federal government, and eventually, he said, 'it will be forced to do things that have not yet been attempted.' In other words, establish a National Unemployment Board and initiate a 'nation-wide programme of useful public works and assistance to private industry.'[43]

Helena did not long remain the indispensable secretary and general factotum for the CCF Unemployment Conference. Not with her drive for leadership and relentless zeal, made more intense by her need to forget about her failed marriage. No longer having a family or neighbourhood life, she had to have somewhere to put her heart, and she put it into the movement. In 1935 she became a member of the conference executive, acting as secretary-treasurer with her own office secretary. She conferred and made decisions with chairman William Braithwaite, who had replaced Grant MacNeil, who was running as a candidate in the June federal election; and with vice chairman Roger Bray, butcher and expert sausage maker, arrested in 1919 for his part in the Winnipeg general strike, now employing his rhetorical skills as one-time Baptist lay preacher in the service of Marxist socialism.[44]

On 4 April 1935 relief camp workers began arriving in Vancouver, initiating a strike against the whole camp system that culminated in June in a cross-country trek to see the prime minister himself and to try to force from him a resolution of their hopeless situation. In downtown Vancouver mass meetings were held every afternoon on Cambie Street Grounds, where leaders reported to the assembled unemployed and offered directions for the next demonstration, the next appeal. From the time the strikers marched through downtown streets in early April until they boarded the CPR freight trains bound for Ottawa on 3 June, Vancouver was the scene of more public meetings, demonstrations, rallies, and parades than in any other two-month period in its history. The men, organized in the Relief Camp Workers Union, were billetted in divisions and they marched in divisions. On 28 April they marched to the Denman Street Arena, led by a contingent of CCF women carrying a Woodsworth banner. On 1 May they marched to Stanley Park and sang the *Internationale*. On Mother's Day they marched once more to Stanley Park behind a contingent of women, and fell out in orderly fashion to form a mother's heart. Discipline was strict and strong feelings of anger and resentment were contained, but when the men began to make little invasions into downtown department stores, the lid came off the pressure cooker. On 23 April a fracas between strikers and police broke out in the Hudson's Bay store. Mayor McGeer read the Riot Act. He was afraid of civil insurrection, and he made the telephone wires between Vancouver and Ottawa hum with urgent pleas for help that brought only adamant refusals from the federal government.[45]

The men were hungry and homeless. They stood on street corners and begged, holding out their tin cans, and then were arrested and jailed for violating a city by-law against 'tin-canning.' In one last act of civil disobedience, they occupied the Vancouver Public Library, vacating it only when promised eighteen hundred dollars for food. Public opinion was with 'the boys,' as the strikers were called. Their plight was truly pathetic.[46]

Meanwhile, transients continued to arrive in Vancouver on railway box cars from the East. Not all of them were men. Some women 'rode the rods' too. Nineteen-year-old Edith 'Judy' Rodgers, from Plymouth, England, on her own from the age of twelve, hopped a freight from a small Ontario town with two new friends from the Toronto Young Communist League. She had learned about Marx a few weeks earlier in shipboard conversations with a passenger who gave her a copy of the *Communist Manifesto* to put in her suitcase. With George Hill and Jeffrey Power she made her way across Canada on box car roofs or on flat cars or gondola coal cars in the blazing sun and pouring rain; or sometimes inside the box cars or, when they had to hide, crouched in narrow refrigerator compartments. They escaped being picked up by the railway 'bulls' or police until Red Deer, Alberta, where they spent the night in jail. Dressed as a young man, hair cut short, her disguise was not discovered until Nelson, BC, where a policeman scrutinized her soft, beardless cheeks and exclaimed, 'If you're not a girl, I'll eat my shirt!' And told them to get out of town, fast. Before they reached the coast, she became ill from the belching coal smoke, from hunger, fatigue and exposure. When at last they hopped off the freight in Vancouver, they were met by an organizer of the Single Unemployed Protective Association. 'Do you want to join our organization?' he asked. They all three answered 'Yes,' and, as Judy recalled many years later, 'This was my open door to Vancouver.' Judy and Jeff were married soon after.

The communist-led Single Unemployed Protective Association (wrestling matches for recreation, Young Pioneers singing 'Workers of the World Awaken' between bouts) was part of the Joint Action Committee on Unemployment in which the CCF Unemployment Conference participated for a time. Helena's part in the events of the spring of 1935 revolved around her position as secretary-treasurer of the CCF Unemployment Conference, which, like the SUPA, supported the relief camp strikers and took their part in confrontations with the authorities. Her annual report summarizes her political work that spring, which included helping to outfit 'the boys' for the On-to-Ottawa Trek:

From the time the strike of April 4th started, the Conference again worked with the rest of the CCF in arranging for funds to be collected, arranging for women to entertain the boys in their homes, assisting with tag days, in organization and carrying out of mass meetings etc., assisting in gathering supplies, clothing, etc. to start the boys off to Regina. And stand ready to again assist when needed.[47]

A Vancouver Police Department agent at the 19 April arena rally provides a glimpse of Helena at work, for he reported that members of the audience were asked to phone TRINITY 4328 if they could feed or house a striker. This was, the agent noted, the number of their CCF Unemployment Section [*sic*].[48] Helena would not have been surprised to know that she and her women colleagues were being spied on, for she had learned well the facts of political life as a trade unionist with the Vancouver Trades and Labor Council: she knew that CCF and communist organizations often came under police surveillance.

Helena's report gives no sense of the state of turmoil in Vancouver at this time. Characteristically matter-of-fact and businesslike, she made her report without emotional embellishment, even though only three weeks had elapsed since 1 July 1935, when the Trekkers joined in not-so-equal combat with the Regina police and the RCMP in what came to be known as the Regina Riot.

Yet the left-wing constituency did feel a great sense of urgency over the strike and its violent culmination; Helena no less than her comrades. Indeed, the turbulent events of the spring and summer of 1935 seemed to them to announce the beginning of the inevitable new social order that socialists had been working for, waiting for. 'There has been such a confusion of strikes and labor difficulties lately,' observes Mildred Osterhout in one of her April radio broadcasts for women, 'that I am sure you have been puzzled by the many uprisings of the working class.'[49] That she speaks of 'uprisings' was not unusual, for there had been a good deal of labour unrest in British Columbia in recent years. At Anyox in 1931, striking coal miners clashed with the police; in 1934, three thousand loggers halted operations for three months in a general strike throughout the industry that included a fifty-mile march of picketers to a camp employing scab labour. In April 1935, even as the relief camp workers were demonstrating on the streets of Vancouver, the striking Kootenay coal miners of Corbin were defending themselves against the assaulting police. In the June Shipping Federation lockout, police threw tear gas bombs and wielded clubs in an encounter with Vancouver longshoremen that became known as the Battle of Ballantyne Pier. To Vancouver socialists, these industrial conflicts were local versions of worker uprisings in Germany, Spain, and Austria.[50]

Tension had been building in Vancouver ever since the very first walk-out of the relief camp workers back in December. When Mildred Osterhout speaks of a sense of foreboding in the city, of a rapidly approaching crisis, she does not exaggerate. Certainly the authorities thought an insurrection was imminent. It was, after all, not yet twenty years since the Russian Revolution. And here in Vancouver, that very April, a crowd of eight thousand had given communist leader Tim Buck, newly released from prison, an enthusiastic welcome when he addressed them at the Denman Street Arena.[51]

When the men walked out of the camps on 4 April, Mildred Osterhout saw this 'uprising' as a prelude to the sweeping away of the unjust profit system: 'It is expected that a great mass of 5,000 will roll like a great wave from all parts of this province gathering strength as it converges on the center of Vancouver.' And then? She does not say. But, 'Join us,' she exhorts her listeners, 'in this endeavour to wipe out the relief camps and institute a new order of society with freedom and justice to all.'[52] By constitutional means, of course, for Mildred is no revolutionist, nor is Helena.

As the crisis deepened, Betty Kerr took over the task of organizing CCF women in the strikers' cause. Eventually Vancouver women had their own organization – the Mothers' Committee, later the Mothers' Council – that mobilized women from many Vancouver organizations to help provide food, clothing, and shelter for 'the boys.' CCF and communist women working together in their own united front provided the leadership.

In August Helena was still working for the Unemployment Conference on the immediate problems of the relief camp workers. Some two hundred had been blacklisted as agitators and denied reinstatement in the camps. They were begging on the streets, and two had been arrested and ordered to get out of town in twenty-four hours. The problem of single, unemployed, homeless men had not yielded either to 'ameliorative measures' or to militant protest.[53]

Helena and her colleagues in the CCF Unemployment Conference began to think that they would achieve more if they could initiate action on their own, and delegated Bill Braithwaite and Sarah Colley to appear before the provincial executive to request permission to launch their own protest meeting on behalf of the relief camp strikers. The provincial executive promptly squelched this proposal, which encroached on party authority, and told them to do their protesting through 'regular propaganda and campaign meetings.'[54]

Then, too, Helena and her colleagues began to perceive their efforts of the past year – the delegations and demonstrations, the emergency measures for blacklisted transients, provision of food and clothing for the unemployed – as being only stopgap rescue work. They wanted rather to grapple with basic economic issues. Bill Braithwaite had been organizing in rural British Columbia, setting up conferences in the Nanaimo-Alberni area and in Grand Forks. Matsqui, New Westminster, and Burnaby were ready to form their own conferences. Thus a new conception of the Unemployment Conference was emerging: all across the province local groups would not only respond to emergencies with protest marches and handouts of food and money, but would also attack the root causes of unemployment, somehow getting at the economic mechanism and cranking it up. The conference even wanted to change its name to the 'CCF Economic Council.' This initiative was promptly vetoed by the provincial executive, which reminded conference members that the provincial convention had given them their sailing orders and that they had to limit their activities accordingly. They could, however, bring their proposal to the 1935 provincial convention.[55]

The Unemployment Conference did just that. In their annual report to the convention, Bill Braithwaite and Helena Gutteridge proposed an expanded and transformed CCF Unemployment Conference:

> Some misunderstanding prevailed for a time with regard to the work of the Conference and it is just as well to here draw attention to the fact that not only are unemployed persons and relief organization the sole business of the Conference. The Conference covers a much wider field, and every phase of the problem of UNEMPLOYMENT, its cause, its abolition, industrial and agricultural problems, in relation to the present economic set-up and any phase of social lack due to such economic set-up. All these things are so inter-related that one section cannot be segregated from the rest. This, therefore, makes necessary an extension of operations of the Conference on a provincial basis.[56]

In any endeavour, Helena had a tendency to take over. Quite simply, she now wanted her organization to be central to the whole economic restructuring of the province, and the tone she adopted carried the assumption that she was right and that others would agree. The CCF Economic Council she proposed would 'co-ordinate labour organizations and form co-operative groups covering the whole field of agriculture and industry.'[57] The council chairman would be on the provincial executive.

The convention delegates took to the floor in heated debate, for to many the CCF Unemployment Conference, however worthy ifs motives, seemed to be proposing a major organizational change that would shift the party's whole mode of operation. The Saturday night session was a stormy one and ended without an agreement. Late Sunday afternoon, before the convention broke up, Roger Bray found a solution by suggesting that the existing Planning Commission do the work of the proposed Economic Council. This compromise was endorsed by the convention.[58]

In the fall, Helena left the Unemployment Conference to become secretary of the Planning Commission and so got what she really wanted, to be one of those actively preparing the way for a socialist government. But the Unemployment Conference continued to make waves. When it set up new locals, some clubs accused it of 'nullifying the work of the CCF Clubs.'[59] Others protested against their working on the joint committee with the communists. Consequently, the executive decided to recommend to the 1936 convention that the conference be disbanded and ruled that its work be halted until that time.[60]

After that convention, the CCF Unemployment Conference was replaced by the Industrial and Employment Conference, with locals in Vancouver, New Westminster, Victoria, and the Lower Mainland firmly under the control of a CCF Industrial and Employment Committee, with Roger Bray as chairman. The conferences continued to work vigorously, setting up strike action committees that organized twenty picket lines in the Burns Packing House strike. The Nanaimo conference wanted to enter municipal politics. Evidently the conferences still threatened to escape the bounds of party organization, but Helena, now head of the Planning Commission and a member of the provincial executive, was no longer an advocate for the conference. The provincial executive decided that such political activity was 'definitely unconstitutional,' and in a formal resolution admonished the Nanaimo conference to stay out of politics. Helena seconded the motion, for the view from the CCF centre was not the same as it was from the hinterland, where party organizations flourished with democratic abandon.[61]

Finally, at the 1937 provincial convention the party decided to abandon the CCF Industrial and Employment Conference too. Grant MacNeil made the recommendation, reported in the communist *People's Advocate*: 'A political party militated against the aims of economic organization and ... too many controversies arose.' The report further cited another CCF delegate's astute observation that 'the conferences are another expression of the united front and this question insists on bobbing up in spite of vetoes by the convention.'[62]

Here was the heart of the problem. In order to take really effective action, the CCF was often called on to unite with the communist workers, on strike committees or in delegations of the unemployed. But it was not always willing to do this. The 1937 convention rejected the united front by a large majority and supported the expulsion of that troublesome maverick, A.M. Stephen, who had defiantly allied himself with the communists in the League Against War and Fascism.[63] Helena supported the convention decision, demonstrating an unwavering loyalty to the party that strengthened her place in the CCF inner circle. She still gave out her occupation as 'tailor' or sometimes 'tailoress,' but her main work was with the CCF Planning Commission and her place of work was the party headquarters, newly moved to 539 Pender Street.

In the office of the CCF Unemployment Conference, her work had revolved around defensive action and temporary measures. In the Planning Commission office, the work was far different. Now Helena was one of those actually drawing up blueprints for a new society. Just two years earlier, in Regina in 1933, the founders of the Co-operative Commonwealth Federation had drawn up the party's National Manifesto, which contained this ringing declaration:

> We aim to replace the present capitalist system, with its inherent injustice and inhumanity, by a social order from which the domination and exploitation of one class by another will be eliminated, in which economic planning will supersede unregulated private enterprise and competition, and in which genuine democratic self government, based upon economic equality will be possible.[64]

The first plank in the manifesto dealt with planning and called for a National Planning Commission to be set up – a body of 'economists, engineers and statisticians assisted by an appropriate technical staff.'[65] The CCF fully expected that in British Columbia, where they already formed the official opposition in the legislature, they would win a majority in the next election and be called on to form the government. 'The revolution is just around the corner,' they said to one another. It was therefore a matter of some urgency for the British Columbia party to gather information about government finance and about all facets of industry – lumber, agriculture, mining, fishing, commerce – and on the basis of this research make concrete plans to present to the public at the next election.[66] The young Harold Winch brought a draft policy for a socialist government to a CCF conference with the League for Social Reconstruction in Ottawa, and received advice and guidance from LSR guru Frank Scott.[67]

Dr. Telford had started the research, and indeed had largely financed the early work of the Planning Commission with proceeds from his Challenge Radio Fund. Longtime socialist Matthew Glenday, an authority on concrete, took over as chairman of the commission in the fall of 1935. The provincial government's Economic Council under W.A. Carrothers of the University of British Columbia had also already undertaken a program of economic research and had issued reports. These provided basic economic data for the CCF Planning Commission. Glenday set up eight departments – Forestry, Finance, Labour, Public Release, Construction, Agriculture, Fisheries, and Policy and Tactics, the last chaired by Harold Winch. As a step towards creating a pool of technical expertise, he drew up a questionnaire that Helena sent to all the CCF clubs. Meanwhile, Glenday gathered material from diverse sources in preparation for drawing up a plan to establish a Co-operative Commonwealth government, and printed an appeal for suggestions in the CCF Bulletin: 'Any ideas as to the method of setting up a new social order will be welcomed, so please write us your suggestions.'[68] His appeal anticipated that of Keith Spicer's Citizen's Forum on Canada's Future in 1990-91, asking ordinary citizens for their ideas on the kind of Canada they wanted, and the six 1992 constitutional conferences that benefited from their participation.

The new social order the CCF had in mind was along the lines of the Labour government just elected to office in New Zealand. Its platform included guaranteed prices for farmers, statutory minimum wages, a national health insurance plan and pension system, unemployment insurance, employment development programs, and control of the central credit system – all of which were later legislated into the Canadian way of life by Liberal governments, including nationalization of the privately owned Bank of Canada in 1938 and Opportunities for Youth programs in later decades. Yet Matthew Glenday, reading at length from the New Zealand platform at the 1936 CCF provincial convention, described it as 'radical.' In fact it was, in those brutal times before governments took some responsibility for the welfare of their people. Possibly the most radical statement in the platform was the declaration that 'New Zealand's standard of living will be determined in New Zealand, by New Zealanders, in accord with New Zealand's resources.'[69]

'The ultimate goal is the complete socialization of industry,' declared Glenday when he first took over as head of the Planning Commission.[70] He was more radical than others in the CCF leadership. Returning from a study sojourn in the Scandinavian countries, Angus and Grace MacInnis reported with approval that railways, telephone service, and electrical power sites were indeed state-owned, as were some forest operations; but in Sweden the state operated mining enterprises in conjunction with private industry. For, wrote Grace MacInnis, 'Swedish socialists are not waiting for capitalism to destroy itself in one spectacular crash and then expecting to take over and administer the ruins. Even now they are quietly and steadily effecting the change to challenge private ownership ... And they are doing it without violence, without chaos. "Democracy" is coming to mean something very real in Sweden.'[71] Throughout Scandinavia, the trade union and cooperative movements, together with a strong social democratic movement, were successfully challenging the control of capitalist industry over the economy and implementing legislative measures with the power to enhance the lives of the people. In Vancouver socialists eagerly followed such developments: 'See the film "Norway Marches On," depicting the Norwegian Labor Movement's development and how the Socialist-Labor Government combatted the finance crisis,' urged an advertisement in *The Federationist*.[72]

The Planning Commission put the forest industry at the top of the list of those to be socialized, directing its attention for the time being largely to the harvesting of trees rather than their processing. The Commission believed that state-managed forests could absorb great numbers of unemployed and also bring in important revenues that would solve the economic problems of British Columbia. In order to formulate a plan of action, its Forestry Department needed technical expertise.

In answer to this need, along came Dr. Maximilian Paulik, a professional forester from Germany. A forestry engineer specializing in research chemistry, he had worked in Germany, Sweden, Poland, Yugoslavia, Russia, and Switzerland. He had left Germany with his wife, Irene, in 1925, and came to Alberta, where he worked briefly as a forester for William Aberhart's Social Credit government. Paulik's passion for trees soon brought him to British Columbia, where he was sure he would be able to make a real contribution to the science of forestry.[73]

In February 1935 he founded the BC Forest Conservation League, and as head of that organization presented a brief to the Pattullo government's Standing Committee on Forests, urging changes in logging methods and making other proposals for forest management. One such proposal was the designation of an area of forest that, under the management of an expert like himself, would provide a model for timber companies to follow.[74] To his extreme disappointment, the government rejected the offer of his services on grounds of financial hardship. Unspoken were the political considerations. As minister of lands in two former Liberal governments, Pattullo had pursued the idea of scientific forest management and his Forestry Branch had made timber-cruising inventories, employed radio communication and other new technologies, and gathered data on silviculture. However, the timber companies were opposed to any kind of government control over forests, even to so obvious a measure as a ban on smoking in the woods, and Pattullo yielded to the political pressure they applied.[75]

Meanwhile, the Paulik family was in straitened circumstances because, with the Nazis in power, they could not gain access to their German assets. Dr. Paulik again applied to the British Columbia government: 'I have been able to keep off relief and in an effort to remain so I am making this bid for some employment in your Forestry Department.'[76] Rejected once more, Paulik finally offered his services, without pay, to the CCF, and he became chairman of the Planning Commission's Forestry Department.[77] Going down to the CCF office became a daily routine for this big, jovial middle class German immigrant, whose enthusiasm for his work matched Helena's. She valued him for his technical knowledge:

experts like him, she said, could 'make plans that could be implemented as soon as the CCF becomes the government of BC.'[78] Paulik was not a socialist, however, and his wife, the daughter of the Baroness Van Hausen von Rosenberg, was from an aristocratic German-Russian family that had fled Russia in 1918. Trees were his passion, not politics.

In the thirties, logging companies leased timber limits from the provincial government and paid stumpage fees, as they do today. They practised clearcut logging, choosing only the best timber and leaving behind large areas of slash that created the conditions for devastating forest fires. Although the industry even then was beginning to regard forests as a renewable resource, it insisted that before new timber could be grown by artificial reforestation, the mature timber had to be cut down. This would be done through an accelerated program of cutting and planting, a method supported by the report of the Forestry Commission, the Sloan Report, ten years later. Unfortunately, tree planting is a costly business, and the timber companies were loath to put up the necessary money for reforestation. Paulik vigorously opposed this method of attempting to attain a sustained yield, and argued for a comprehensive plan of natural reforestation that would eliminate clearcut logging and introduce selective logging instead. Such a practice, he claimed, would leave desirable mature trees to seed new growth. The debate between these two opposing methods of forest management continues today.[79]

Paulik also believed that forests were a public resource that, if properly managed, could 'wipe out the effect of the entire depression.'[80] Seeking a solution to the problems of unemployment and poverty, the CCF found him a congenial ally. With his vast store of knowledge and experience at its command, the party formulated its forest policy. As a first step, the Planning Commission's Forestry Department, following Paulik's proposals, set up a CCF forestry training school and also acquired a forest plot for demonstration and teaching in Lynn Valley, on the north shore of Burrard Inlet. Now, at last, Paulik had his model demonstration forest. In July 1936, when Helena took over from Matthew Glenday as chair of the Planning Commission, she inherited Paulik and the forestry school. It enrolled boys over the age of eighteen, later sixteen – classes at night, three times a week; tuition at seventy-five cents a month, to be reduced to fifty cents if enrollment increased sufficiently. They would be trained to serve as 'forest guards, patrol men, fire fighters, forest protectors, superintendents of forest districts, reforestation foremen, tree-planting experts, game propagators, forest surveyors,' and in many other jobs as well. The school did not invite girls and women to enroll: in the thirties the idea of a woman forester would have been considered odd.[81]

Besides the training program, the Planning Commission attempted a publicity campaign to educate British Columbians on the need for state-managed forests and on their benefits to every citizen. Paulik supervised the preparation of a series of eight-by-eleven-inch handouts, providing the materials for brief, simple texts illustrated by cartoons, graphs, diagrams, and other drawings purporting to show how the forests, depleted by the mismanagement of private interests, could be restored to the people of the province through intensive management. Allegorical drawings simplified difficult concepts: a river in flood illustrating the 'FREE FLOWING OFF OF OUR FOREST WEALTH' with 'UNREGULATED PRODUCTION'; a dam with 'MARKET REGULATION' at the outflow representing 'PLANNED AND PERPETUAL ECONOMY' (this last is a concept that proved to be a survival mechanism for Canadian farmers of later decades trying to hold on to their subsidies and quotas).

The forests would be divided into administrative districts of some 50,000 to 60,000 acres under the direction of a 'State forest expert,' who would supervise five subdivisions of 10,000 to 12,000 acres, each under a forest ranger. Instead of being 'migratory workers' living in camps, the loggers would live in settlements with their families and enjoy all the amenities of community life. Allowing 150 acres of forest for each worker in the industry, the Planning Commission projected a population of 330,000 settlers in British Columbia's forests. The forestry handouts were intended to appeal to the self-interest of the average citizen (who was always male in those days): 'YOU ARE TOO POOR, MR. CITIZEN, TO ALLOW YOUR SHARE OF OUR TREMENDOUS FOREST WEALTH TO BE DRAINED AWAY. JOIN US IN THE FIGHT FOR A FOREST SCHEME IN WHICH BOTH YOU AND THE FOREST WILL RECEIVE ADEQUATE BENEFIT AND PROTECTION.' Text and illustrations were didactic, sometimes crude, often charming and half a century later, in the context of the failed Soviet Union, often touching in their innocent utopian vision. They breathe the 'earnest sincerity' that the Planning Commission hoped to find among its members and friends for carrying out its ambitious program. We do not know who the writer and artist were, but the ideas certainly came from Dr. Paulik, working closely, Harold Winch later recalled, with Colin Cameron.[82]

The CCF vision of a 'New Forest Order' was not completely utopian, however. Fifty years later, the idea of conserving our forest resources by careful management has been adopted by both industry and labour, though environmentalists of the 1990s urge preservation rather than economic use. The training project ran into difficulties, though. Although by July 1936 some 150 young men had enrolled in the school, the Planning Commission claimed to need '5,000 fully trained men ... at our disposition the moment we have gained control.' Despite huge unemployment, not many young men were interested. For those who were, the modest tuition fee proved to be prohibitive. Two forestry teachers resigned because of disagreements, and Paulik complained that the Planning Commission was not helpful, though he said he had always received cooperation from Helena. Regular classes were discontinued, and teaching was carried on by correspondence courses.[83]

Despite these reverses, the still-enthusiastic Helena reported that the work was 'going splendidly' and that she was still looking for several thousand men to be trained: what was needed was greater public awareness. If only people *knew* what was happening to their forests ... Why not make a newsreel? The CCF forestry department launched an 'appeal for funds to purchase a MOVING PICTURE MACHINE to compile records – a newsreel story of actual conditions in our forests. Donations gratefully received ...'[84] It was a brilliant idea for public education, anticipating today's video information programs, but unfortunately the newsreel project came to nothing. All Helena's best efforts and Paulik's expertise and dedication were not enough to get the forestry training school off the ground. Early in 1937 the school closed. In order to earn a living, Paulik resorted to importing fine porcelain and ornaments and sold real estate on the side. He did not give up on trees, however, and with his sons hiked up Grouse Mountain, where he filled their packsacks with seedlings to plant on their three-acre Richmond farm. Fifty years later, those trees were designated a heritage forest.[85]

Maximilian Paulik had been a godsend for Helena, but in the choice of Roger Bray as chairman of the Planning Commission's Labour Department, she was not so fortunate. Bray was a doctrinaire socialist with a command of socialist rhetoric but no knowledge of the art of government. An early draft of the Labour Code produced by his department was a hellfire-and-brimstone edict. Declaring 'the inherent and inalienable right of every human being to work in order to live,' it gave society the right to compel all physically fit adults 'to labour at socially necessary work.'[86] Regulations for every possible contingency in a person's work life were spelled out in elaborate detail, with the machinery for enforcing them – a Labour Valuation Committee, a Labour Exchange and Distribution Committee, a Committee of Technical Experts – in short, a vast and cumbersome bureaucratic machinery. The code would take effect within thirty days of the CCF taking office. It was, in its clumsy innocence, more touching than frightening.

Helena was dubious about this attempt to translate socialist theory into legislation. She sent a copy to MP Angus MacInnis in Ottawa, marking the document 'Incomplete' and 'Confidential.' MacInnis had a firm grasp on political realities, and while away in Ottawa he kept a close watch on the performance of his CCF colleagues in British Columbia. He did not reply to Helena immediately, but in correspondence with Wallis Lefeaux ruefully called the Planning Commission's Labour Code a 'gem,' an example of the misconceptions many CCF members had about the transition to a CCF government. He himself rejected the idea of instant socialism as an impossibility. The practical course for the CCF if elected was 'to proceed with the administration of capitalism,' all the while educating people in the faulty workings of the system and the need to change it.[87]

Lefeaux replied: 'One of the things that bothers me most is the lack of intelligent appreciation by a number of our so-called "leading lights" of what it would mean to take over the government of B.C.' He objected to 'practically all the work of this so-called Planning Commission,' and would leave the party if these 'optimistic anarchists' gained control of it.[88] In meetings of the provincial executive, Lefeaux was vociferous in his criticism of planners like Matthew Glenday. He was particularly explosive on the question of the forestry handouts, or 'graphs,' as they were called. Another member of the executive reported to MacInnis: 'Lefeaux [sic] got after the planners for sending out dope suggesting we would take over the lumbering industry and asked – Who says we will?'[89]

Wallis Lefeaux expressed his misgivings to the membership as a whole, insisting on the need to maintain democratic institutions and oppose totalitarian methods: 'We cannot afford to be elected to office with vast numbers led to think we shall immediately provide Work and Wages for all or revolutionize the entire economic and financial structure.'[90] Lefeaux was much respected in the CCF and his opinions carried a good deal of weight: the following year he was elected president of the CCF in British Columbia.

In his reply to Helena, Angus MacInnis voiced his criticism in a kindly and courteous way. He pointed out that the proposal to put the Labour Code into effect within thirty days of gaining office was tantamount to governing by decree, something that was in complete violation of the CCF National Manifesto, which declared that government should be by legislative enactment. He continued:

> Let us be quite clear on the point that if we are going to govern by decree, if we are going to put our edicts into effect by force, then we shall have to be prepared to meet force from our opponents. Our first concern then will be, not the building of our economic machinery, but the building of an army for struggle. In that process the productive machinery will deteriorate and instead of the masses having a better standard of living than they had under capitalism they will have a much worse one.[91]

He concluded with a sober admonition against the authoritarian approach to government of those who drafted this Labour Code. Keeping his hand on the wheel, he guided Helena and the CCF Economic Planning Commission by suggesting that they draft a program at the coming convention that would serve the political and economic development of the province and strengthen its relationship with the country as a whole. Helena had sent the draft of the Labour Code to MacInnis before she was elected chairman of the Planning Commission in July; therefore, she seems to have assumed responsibility for the work of the commission while she was still executive secretary. Confronted with the raw document produced by Roger Bray and his lawmakers, she sought feedback from a senior party member. She knew from working with Helen MacGill that the first step in drafting new legislation was to study what other jurisdictions had done, but with seven other departments to deal with besides Labour, she could not make the tutoring of Roger Bray a top priority.

After the 1936 convention, Helena was satisfied that the Commission now had a platform to build on: 'The adoption of a CCF Provincial Platform at the convention recently, has assisted the Planning Commission immensely,' she reported. 'The work of each committee is now definitely linked with and relates to specific portions of that platform.'[92] She was setting herself an enormous task: nothing less than the preparation of the main portfolios of provincial government: finance, housing, agriculture, fisheries, mining, distribution of oil and gasoline, education, and forestry. She appealed for people with technical and research skills to come forward and assist in 'the so essential planning for the new social order,' but, as she soon discovered, the CCF simply did not have at its disposal within the party the experts it needed for a complex intellectual and administrative task.[93] Well read and experienced in politics and administration, she herself could have served competently in the civil service or as a cabinet minister. Helena Gutteridge, Minister of Lands and Forests – she would have started British Columbia on the road to sustainable development.

Despite Helena's competence and ability, the Planning Commission was neither viewed seriously nor respected by some leading members of the party. Even as she strove to get on with her Planning Commission job, personal animosities, backbiting, and vituperation swirled around her. One member of the executive regarded the more radical socialists as a 'bunch of wreckers' who would have to be dealt with firmly:

> We have sat by, or used up our energies in doing all kinds of jobs, while the wrecking machine has been working. We have the Radio, 'the Planning Bee' working all hours for Telford. We have all the resources of the Organisation Committee, made up entirely of Winchites, all the Education Com-

mittee made up of Weaverites, which is another name for Winchites, working only as zealots will work. All with one object in mind, that is the procuring of the CCF for their own nefarious ends.[94]

Wallis Lefeaux was more judicious in his criticism. He observed to Angus MacInnis that 'gradually quite a number of our more intelligent members are beginning to see the foolishness of it all,' that is, of the idea of the immediate creation of a socialized state.[95] Was Helena one of these 'more intelligent members'? Her job was to create an embryonic civil service that would be capable of implementing the CCF concept of a socialized economy. In this she was simply carrying out the decision of the 1936 convention. The people she was working with on the Planning Commission – Harold Winch, Dr. Telford, Matthew Glenday – were equally dedicated to the immediate goal of establishing a socialist government in British Columbia. However, with Angus MacInnis as mentor, Helena was likely beginning to view the political evolution of British Columbia in a more realistic light.

As head of the Planning Commission and therefore a member of the CCF provincial executive, Helena was immediately embroiled in the political trauma of the 'Connell Affair.' The Reverend Robert Connell, former Anglican clergyman and CCF leader of the opposition in the legislature, was a Marxist scholar but no socialist firebrand. Before he became an MLA, he was known chiefly as the nature columnist for the Victoria *Times*. When he stood up in the legislature and gave that dogged old socialist Ernest Winch a public drubbing for his intemperate, revolutionary language, and as much as disowned his CCF colleague, the fat was in the fire. This clash of party personalities created a rift that Connell further widened when he opposed the 1936 convention resolution to socialize banking and credit, a measure that was not a provincial right under the BNA Act and therefore patently unconstitutional.[96] He voiced his opposition not during the convention but several weeks later, in the daily press. The policy disagreement brought to a head a deep-seated division in the party that had existed from the beginning between so-called 'revolutionary' Marxist socialists and a more lenient breed of right-wingers. Despite ideological differences, both factions worked for reform legislation, for, as Dorothy Steeves recalls, the 'stock revolutionary expressions' uttered so freely by left-wingers like Ernest Winch 'did not mean that they intended to set a torch to society.'[97] The party expelled Connell; he immediately formed his own, the Social Constructives, and took with him three other CCF MLAs, Jack Price, R.B. Swailes, and Ernest Bakewell, as well as Victor Midgely, one-time leader of the One Big Union, and Bill Pritchard, editor-owner of *The Commonwealth*, whose defection left the party without a newspaper. At the executive meeting that formally dealt with the rebels, Helena seconded the motion for expulsion.[98] In so doing, she declared herself one of those in the controlling group in the provincial CCF, aligning herself with the three remaining MLAs, Harold Winch, Ernest Winch, and Dorothy Steeves, all left-wingers. MP Angus MacInnis, who originally sympathized with the right-wing Connell, did not support him in the end.[99]

Helena also demonstrated her loyalty to the party on the question of working with communists in a united front. In response to a growing danger to world peace occasioned by Hitler's rise to power, a Canadian League Against War and Fascism had been formed. League president A.M. Stephen, one of the CCF's brilliant Marxist theoreticians, urged united action with the communists to make people aware of the fascist threat. By 1935 Canadian communists had done an about-face and adopted the United Front policy of the Third International, which advocated making common cause with left-wing and liberal parties and organizations. Thus the CCF, whom the communists had earlier labelled 'social fascists,' were now sought as allies. At their 1937 convention, however, the British Columbia CCF firmly rejected any kind of cooperation with them and expelled A.M. Stephen from the CCF. Dorothy Steeves and Mildred Osterhout were among the few who supported Stephen. Helena was not one of them. On this, as on all fundamental issues, she was loyal to the party, staying in the mainstream and accepting the declaration of the 1937 convention that 'the CCF itself is the people's front for Canada.'[100]

At the 1937 and 1938 CCF provincial conventions, Helena and Dorothy Steeves were both re-elected to the executive, and Betty Kerr joined them in 1938. On the ten-member executive there were now three women, a phenomenon that caused rumblings of concern among the men. CCF president Wallis Lefeaux was reported as saying that 'he would permit no woman to run him or any board that he sat on.'[101] This may have been merely male posturing. Or he may have thought the three women too preoccupied with reform and not sufficiently dedicated to revolutionary Marxism. But blunt-spoken Helena was evidently pleasant to work with. Interviewed in 1984, Harold Winch reflected, 'I was very fond of Helena Gutteridge, very fond of her.'

Helena saw the CCF as a part of an international political elite commanding her wholehearted devotion and service. She was, as Harold Winch said of himself, 'at the command of the movement.'[102] She wrote: 'The CCF is not a party in the conventional sense, but a part of a worldwide movement of forward-thinking men and women who can visualize a world in which co-operative effort will replace the present cut-throat competition, and in which security and plenty will replace poverty and insecurity.'[103]

And the new society is no mere vague dream. She can visualize it, for in her mind's eye she sees worker-operated industries eliminating relief handouts and employing the brains and physical energies of a productive work force. She sees subsidized housing replacing squalid tenements and cooperatives like her Carvell Hall Settlement for working women, this time supported by a friendly government. She sees community kitchens and laundries, rationalizing a woman's daily repetitive tasks.

At the 1938 national convention J.S. Woodsworth declared in an inspirational speech to the delegates: 'We must have something of the reckless abandon of youth, a sublime confidence in the future, a faith that, as the old hymn puts it "mocks at impossibilities and cries it shall be done".'[104] When she was elected to Vancouver City Council in 1937 at the age of fifty-eight, Helena was neither youthful nor reckless, nor would she have called her confidence in the future sublime. But faith in the movement she possessed undiminished. And she would indeed prove to be a public servant who mocked at impossibilities.

CHAPTER NINE

'A Faithful Alderman'

I shout LOVE in a land muttering slack damnation.
 – Milton Acorn, *I Shout Love*

On 30 March 1937 Helena Rose Gutteridge stood before Mayor George C. Miller and declared, 'I will faithfully perform the duties of my office, and will not allow any private interest to influence my conduct in public matters, so help me God.' She was now Alderman Gutteridge and she would require no conflict-of-interest guidelines. Helena's private interest was, as it always had been, public welfare, and she stoutly defended and promoted it during her two and a half years in office.

Barry Mather, by then a *Province* columnist, knew Helena well and attributed her election success to her 'mild persistence.' He would have agreed, however, that this was more than a personal success. The CCF, a strong political force, had given their candidate significant support; in addition, a constituency of loyal women had worked for her and were in large measure responsible for her victory.[1] Jubilant, today they pack the gallery to witness her swearing-in and savour the sweet moment. At last, a woman on City Council! Now they would make some progress! The New Era League is there in force – Mary Norton, Susie Lane Clark, of course – for two decades advocates of social justice, now stout supporters of the cause of the unemployed. Helena, the league secretary, wears their corsage of yellow roses and purple violets on her decent navy dress. As she walks to her desk, escorted by the sergeant-at-arms, she carries their gift of a basket of tulips and snapdragons, and they are sure that this is indeed the beginning of the new era that they have worked for since women won the provincial franchise in 1917. The crowd cheers and applauds.

To *Sun* reporter Doris Milligan, Helena seems 'smallish, middle-aged,' but she has 'clear, keen eyes that look at you cheerfully from behind spectacles.'[2] Alderman Fred Crone welcomes her on behalf of the other aldermen. She replies quite simply, 'Thank you very much. I'm pleased to be here.' Then, realistically, 'We may not always agree, but I hope that when we do disagree we will do it in such a way that we can meet again in a friendly manner.'³

This was not the first time she had encountered George Miller at City Hall. The year before, as part of a delegation representing the single unemployed, she had urged, or perhaps directed, City Council to find ways of further helping these men. Barry Mather reported the exchange that followed: 'Said the then alderman, George Miller, to this persistent lady [Helena Gutteridge]: "I suppose, madam, you could tell us how to run the city?" Replied the lady: "I have no doubt, sir, that we could".'⁴

That unwavering confidence in the rightness of her cause carried Helena past the initial hurdle of ill-concealed male disdain and resentment. Whatever their private thoughts at the swearing-in of a woman, Mayor Miller and the other aldermen soon discovered she was not going to tell them how to run the city after all. Instead, they found that Alderman Gutteridge gave herself wholeheartedly to her job, demanded no concessions to womanhood, but assumed in her matter-of-fact way that together they would run the city. She soon earned their respect.

Helena considered her election a victory for the CCF but also a victory for women, and on election night she thanked the women's organizations that had supported her. 'The time is near,' she said, 'when more women must take part in public affairs. It is absolutely essential that they do so to clean up social conditions.'⁵ Here again was the suffragist argument that women could make a special contribution to government because, as she said, they have 'a more sympathetic understanding of social problems, and civic governments are finding themselves more taken up with such matters.'⁶

This had been Helena's third try at running for alderman. She was first nominated by the CCF in the December 1936 civic election. As a member of the CCF Unemployment Conference, she had urged the entry of the party into civic politics, and in November 1935 it endorsed the idea of running civic candidates. The CCF civic program was based on the assumption that by applying its political philosophy of cooperation to the problems of city government, the achievement of the Co-operative Commonwealth would be advanced. The most important items in their aldermanic platform eventually found legislative fulfillment at some level of government in later decades, but in 1935 these were considered major innovations. The municipal franchise was still based on the idea of owning or renting property; the CCF demanded full adult suffrage. Social housing had yet to be accepted as a government responsibility; the CCF proposed a municipal low-cost housing program. A private corporation, the BC Electric, provided power and public transportation; the CCF proposed public ownership of public utilities. According to the Canadian constitution, the unemployed came under provincial jurisdiction; the CCF urged revision of the constitution to allow the federal government to take financial responsibility for the unemployed.[7]

But if the CCF obtained a majority on City Council, the School Board, and the Park Board, would it institute socialism? 'No – not at once,' explained *The Federationist* in 1937. The CCF would concentrate on public education, at the same time demonstrating through 'object lessons' the possibilities for social and economic development 'if we would turn our attention to the welfare of society as a whole instead of leaving each individual unit struggling to acquire competency without regard to other people's interests.'[8]

As a person of substantial platform experience and a campaigner of proven ability, Helena was an obvious choice to be the CCF's candidate in the 1936 election. Only owners of property valued at five hundred dollars or more were eligible to run for alderman, and candidates had to have their property registered in their name for a full six months before the deadline for submission of nomination papers. In order to satisfy the property qualifications for this and the 1937 and 1939 elections, Helena apparently made some financial arrangement with her friend Edith Sneve, employing capital from the Mount Lehman property to make her joint owner with Edith of the house at 2471 Triumph Street.[9] Helena did, however, finally turn the Mount Lehman farm over to Mrs. Sneve, who received title to the land in August 1937.[10] On her nomination papers Helena gave her occupation as housewife, an indication that she may not have found work as a tailor. She could have been living on payments for the Mount Lehman property and giving her full time to the movement; however, one report states that she was on relief. When she was elected to City Council, she drew an alderman's salary – $1,620 a year.[11]

Unfortunately, in the December 1936 election Helena was just two hours short of the required six months of property ownership, and so had to withdraw. Two CCF aldermen were elected, her former colleague Parm Pettipiece and A.M. Anderson, who could not take his seat because of a technicality. Helena ran again in the January by-election made necessary by his disqualification, but lost to Lewis Drummond McDonald, who was popular on the east side, where Helena also had her strength. She placed a respectable third, however.[12]

Two months later, she ran in yet another aldermanic by-election, this one occasioned by the death of Lewis McDonald. The CCF nominating meeting was energetically contested, five ballots being held before Helena finally eliminated the other contenders. On 24 March 1937 the people of Vancouver went to the polls for the third time in four months, and this time they elected Helena Gutteridge. She won with 5,017 votes, 358 more than her nearest opponent, trade unionist printer and former alderman Henry Lyman Corey, a Liberal. The *News-Herald* announced the news in a front-page banner headline: 'Miss Gutteridge Wins Election.' The *Province* and *Sun*, not in desperate need of boosting their sales, merely printed brief reports. But all three made her the subject of an editorial. The *Sun* bowed gracefully before Woman, with her 'instinctive sense of judgement and good sense that in man usually has to be acquired.' The other two newspapers admonished her to keep party politics out of civic affairs.[13]

The new City Hall was the creation of former Mayor McGeer, and Vancouver was still getting used to the new status conferred on the city by the imposing white sandstone tower designed by architect Frederick L. Townley. Beginning in 1886 with a makeshift tent, Vancouver City Council had met in a number of quarters over the years. Between 1929 and 1936, the Holden Building at 16 Hastings Street, next door to skid row hotels and near the waterfront, had served as City Hall, Woodward's Department Store, the police station, and Chinatown a few blocks away. The site finally chosen for the new building overlooked the city and North Shore mountains from the hill at Cambie Street and Twelfth Avenue, at the geographical centre of the city, but far removed, as befitted an acropolis, from the vulgar landscape and the gross and sordid commerce of everyday city life. Formally opened on 4 December 1936, the new City Hall gave Vancouver citizens a sense of importance when they entered the marble-lined vestibule to pay their property taxes, though many grumbled at such inordinate luxury: gold-leaf ceilings, the gold from British Columbia mines; solid cast-bronze lock plates on every door, engraved with Vancouver's coat-of-arms; elevator doors resplendent with symbolism – mountains and sea and forest, the western sun, and a seagull in flight. These were more than mere embellishments; they were claims to legitimate tradition that the ebullient Gerry McGeer boldly advanced on behalf of a reluctant city. When Helena came to her new place of work in the morning, the statue of Captain Vancouver at the entrance reminded her that even a city only fifty years old, and younger than she, had a history and could look to its own tutelary deity. Moreover, tradition could be borrowed: the gold and silver civic mace, symbol of the people's authority vested in the Council, was a replica of the mace of the city of London and the gift of the Lord Mayor himself when he came at the bidding of Gerry McGeer to participate in the city's golden jubilee celebrations.[14]

The response of the other two political parties to the growing strength of the CCF on City Council was to create their own organization, the Non-Partisan Association (NPA). The 1932 Kidd Commission, headed by British Columbia's top financiers and businessmen, recommended that non-partisan government replace government by political parties and urged the application of efficient business methods to the affairs of the province. Vancouver businessmen argued that the same principle should apply to civic government. The growing power of the CCF actually prompted the Liberal and Conservative parties to form a political coalition, the NPA, ostensibly non-partisan but in fact actively opposed to the CCF.[15]

In the December 1937 civic elections, only the second at-large election since the abolition of the ward system in 1935, the NPA won every seat but one on City Council. Helena held on to hers, but Alfred Hurry lost his, as did Parm Pettipiece, who, failing to be renominated by the CCF because he did not adhere to party policy, had run for the NPA instead, a rather strange alliance for a one-time member of the Socialist Party of Canada. The CCF made a good showing with 35 per cent of the total vote, but this did not translate into Council seats, for the NPA obtained 44 per cent, almost all of it from the city's west side.[16]

Uncompromisingly socialist and feminist, Helena was now helping to run the affairs of the city with eight male colleagues. They were all about the same age as she, with no particular pretensions to education or social status. One had been her antagonist in the Laundry Workers' strike of 1918 – former laundry proprietor, and alderman then too, Thomas Kirk, grown rather paunchy with the years but still vociferous and intent on eliminating government inefficiency and extravagance. Halford Wilson, son of an Anglican rector, was a bank clerk. John Bennett began work at age thirteen in a Lancashire cotton mill and was well read without the aid of much formal schooling. He never owned a car because he wanted to keep in touch with ordinary people. John Cornett, former reeve of South Vancouver, was a shoe retailer and grew chrysanthemums. Fred Crone had a cartage and storage company. 'Handsome Harry' DeGraves, an Australian, was a customs officer with the CPR. George Miller, one-time cigar factory foreman, travelling salesman, and office manager, had his own wholesale business. Almost all were experienced in civic politics. John Bennett, Vancouver's police commissioner in 1909, had been first elected to Council in 1924. After nearly twenty-five years as an alderman, he was presented with the Freedom of the City in 1947.

Helena's fellow aldermen were no more non-partisan than she. Kirk and Cornett had been Conservative MLAs in the Tolmie government of 1928-33, both stout supporters of the premier. Liberal Fred Crone, an Anglican, was elected to the legislature in 1937. Halford Wilson was Anglican, Conservative in politics. Henry Corey, a Christian Scientist, described himself as 'Non-partisan with Liberal leanings.'[17]

Council meetings usually proceeded with the courtesy and decorum imposed by Robert's Rules of Order and also by the unaccustomed dignity of the new council chamber, two storeys high, panelled with mahogany, the mayor's place on a dais with the aldermen's mahogany desks below, two semi-circles facing each other across the mace on its polished walnut table in the centre of the chamber. Barry Mather found the meetings in this chamber 'as stimulating as a Christian Science funeral.'[18] But from time to time a meeting would erupt in a lava of scalding words and a thunder of desk banging. *Sun* columnist Alan Morley describes one such meeting of the 1937 Council with the eye of a portrait artist: 'The first to spring to his feet is Thomas Kirk ... His rage is almost classic.' With 'Roman scorn ... he refutes passion with an avalanche of reiterated fact. He clinches each fact with a bang on his desk, as if he were nailing down the coffins of his fellow aldermen with his fist.' Next in Morley's portrait gallery is the 'kindly, bluff, roast beef-of-Old England bullish' John Bennett, transformed into a raging bull, head thrust forward, moustache fairly bristling as 'his words pour out in a thick mutter and rise to a challenging roar.' Fred Crone remains calm but makes clear his contempt for those who would run the city in such an unbusinesslike way. Parm Pettipiece, 'like a kindly, indulgent but upright father of a family,' infuriates the others by the reasonableness and irrefutable logic of his arguments. But fellow socialist Alfred Hurry 'insults the Council by making a brotherly squabble a matter of high principle,' 'sees plots in passing shadows.' When the family argument is over, he is the only one not accepted back into the fold, for the others still remember his suspicions and innuendoes. Helena, however, 'has caught the Council spirit ... She can be sharp, plaintive, outraged, shrewd, furious, sarcastic, insulting or menacing, all in turn and effectively, too, but she can forget it when the storm is over.' Halford Wilson, much the youngest, 'plaintively' defends himself against imputations of ulterior motives, for the rest of the councillors are too experienced to credit youthful enthusiasm. John Cornett, 'too old and wise ... to become embroiled,' remains silent, but 'if he disagrees, his mouth draws downward, his long nose gets longer and reddens at the tip.' Only when matters have come to a head does he utter some pungent remark, which generally brings discussion to a close.[19] Morley does not mention Mayor George Miller, biting off the end of a Havana, smoking one after another.

Helena was caustic and derisive in dealing with the young Halford Wilson, whose anti-woman and racist views aroused her vehement opposition. As a measure to combat unemployment, he proposed that employers not hire married women whose husbands had jobs; indeed, a letter to the Board of Trade and Service Clubs' Council had already been drafted at the request of City Council. At Helena's vigorous opposition it was put aside for further discussion, causing Wilson to remonstrate plaintively: 'It's a funny thing ... to ask the corporation counsel to draft a letter and then decide not to send it.' At the next Council discussion Helena won over all the aldermen except Wilson and DeGraves. 'Women have the greatest honor and responsibility in building happy homes,' Alderman Wilson earnestly asserted. 'It is somewhat degrading when a woman lowers herself to our standard and goes out to compete with men.'[20] Alderman Gutteridge easily disposed of this old anti-feminist chestnut:

> 'Let's let all this sentimental bosh go by and get down to facts,' she urged.
> 'Nobody ever objected to women scrubbing floors or bending over a washboard. This business of placing women on a pedestal is one of the oldest yarns I've heard. Men only object to women working when they start earning money.'[21]

With Halford Wilson, Helena even stooped to personal attack. He had been trying throughout 1939 to have Council adopt a measure to restrict trade licences granted to Orientals, and soon after the outbreak of war, in full patriotic flight, declared, 'The Empire is in enough trouble without further aggravation [from Oriental competition].' Helena, whose views on this racial question had changed over the years in line with the general move to increased solidarity of white and Asian workers, denounced Wilson's proposal as discriminatory and won the support of most of the aldermen. She commented sarcastically that she had heard that Alderman Wilson might soon be called for military service, and 'she wondered how council would ever get along without him.'[22]

The other aldermen, not excluding Halford Wilson, listened to Helena with respect, for she advanced her views persuasively and sometimes swayed them with her arguments. R. Rowe Holland, chairman of the Park Board, refused to listen, however; in fact, he would not let her speak. At one Park Board meeting, Helena, as regular Council representative, attempted to convey the views of a Council committee on the matter under discussion, only to be told by Holland that she had no right to take part in the debate. After an angry interchange, Helena shouted, 'Goodbye, I'm through!' She stormed out of the meeting, ignoring the urgent signals of her old friend, recently elected Park Commissioner Susie Lane Clark, to remain. Afterwards, angry and indignant, she complained to the press: 'He shouted me down every time I attempted to speak ... What's the use of me going to the meeting if I've got to sit there and listen?' Commissioner Holland merely regretted that Helena, whose faithful attendance had made her 'an institution with us,' had 'misconstrued the extent of her privileges,' adding that previous aldermen had never taken part in Parks Board discussions.[23]

Helena chaired the Building, Civic Planning and Parks Committee, and attended the seven other standing committees as well. She served on sundry special committees and represented City Council on the Town Planning Commission, the Vancouver Exhibition Association, and the board of the Alexandra Orphanage until its demise in 1938. As a member of the CCF executive, she was in the decision-making circle of the party, speaking for it from the public platform or presiding over meetings. During these years, home for her was as much the City Hall council chamber and the CCF office as it was her new home at 1195 East 54th Avenue. Her friend Edith Sneve had remarried, and when she moved with her machinist husband, Duncan MacDonald, from Triumph Street, Helena went with her and shared their house.[24]

Helena had a duty to her party to make every effort to carry out CCF policy at City Hall, wherever it applied. Certainly there was ample opportunity to do this in connection with such continuing problems as unemployment and the lack of decent low-cost housing. The CCF also urged a more democratic municipal franchise, based on term of residence, as in the provincial electoral law, and Helena argued for this change in Council. Under the Vancouver Incorporation Act, all male or female British subjects of the age of twenty-one had the right to vote if they were owners of property or tenants of real property in the city assessed at three hundred dollars or more. Lodgers and boarders were not considered tenants, therefore people living in housekeeping rooms could not vote. Nor could married women living in the family home but possessing no equity in it and owning no other property in their own right. Chinese, Hindus, Japanese, and 'Indians,' or Native peoples, were also excluded.[25] In September 1937, when Helena introduced in Council a proposal to extend the civic franchise to everyone with twelve months' residence who qualified under the Provincial Elections Act, the aldermen's response was 'a loud chorus of "No".'

> Discussion was limited to one question by Ald. John Bennett. 'Do you mean without property qualification?' he asked.
> Ald. Gutteridge – 'Yes.'
> Ald. Bennett – 'Ugh.'[26]

Alderman Gutteridge's motion for an enabling amendment to the City Charter was voted down. Two years later, when she again submitted this resolution and also one to remove property qualifications for civic election candidates, she was again defeated.[27] Even the Local Council of Women, which had helped elect her in 1937, was against extension of the franchise, explaining in its citizenship committee's 1941 report that 'young people with no property sense would vote for people with expensive tastes that might not be in the best interests of the community.' Helena remonstrated that full adult franchise would be 'in the best spirit of democracy.'[28]

Democracy would finally prevail over property in 1954, when the voters' list was opened to all tenants on the basis of residence. In 1966 twelve months' residence qualified tenants to run for office. Without property, however, they were still not allowed to vote on money by-laws. That final concession was made in 1972.[29]

Helena was not unduly preoccupied by the question of the municipal franchise except in the months preceding a civic election. More time-consuming were short-term practical problems unrelated to the socialist vision, like the complaint over the odours emanating from Ballard's Animal Food Factory. She and other members of a special committee visited the plant several times. They reported that they could not agree with complaints that the smell of cooking meat and biscuits was 'nauseating,' nor could they interfere with a legitimately established business operating in a sanitary way. More serious was the application of one Delip Singh to keep his cow in an eight-by-fourteen-foot lean-to against his garage in a residential neighbourhood. This was a delicate matter, for the cow had already been housed in the shed before the East Indian took possession. Delip Singh's lawyer charged discrimination, but the committee found that the barn itself was in violation of the Health By-law, and further declared that keeping a cow on this city street detracted from the residential character of the neighbourhood.[30]

In Vancouver at that time, gasoline and fuel oil storage tanks were located at random in the commercial and industrial district. As members of a special committee, Helena, Fred Crone, and Thomas Kirk inspected the storage tanks and were alarmed at the fire hazard posed by their indiscriminate location. In her report, Helena proposed acceptance of the Town Planning Commission's recommendation that wholesale storage of gasoline and fuel oil be restricted to three heavy industrial districts, with safety regulations for construction and maximum capacity.[31]

Of all the special committees, the one on housing most engaged Helena's energies. The need in Vancouver was urgent, for although the population had increased steadily since 1912, the number of houses built annually had decreased from nearly 3,000 in 1926 to only 190 in 1934. With the easing of economic conditions, housing construction had recovered slightly. Still only 600 new houses had been constructed in the first eleven months of 1937, and these did not provide any more affordable shelter for low-income workers, much less for the unemployed. Within months of taking office, Helena had to deal with Vancouver's housing problem and its inescapable dilemmas.[32]

First of all, she was asked to prepare a report on housing conditions in the West End, with special attention to basement suites, where tenants were often crammed into unwholesome, ill-ventilated spaces next to the furnace and washtubs. Under the original zoning by-law of 1930, such basement suites contravened health and building regulations. Even if they did not, even if they were pleasantly habitable, they could still be illegal. For in residential districts zoning was, and still is, based on the family unit. In a district zoned for one-family dwellings, each allowed only one housekeeping unit, a basement suite rented to non-family tenants would violate the by-law because the social composition of the house would then be altered from one-family to two-family. The number of storeys in a building was also central to zoning classifications: by definition a basement was counted as a storey when it was inhabited by 'someone other than a janitor.'[33] In two-family dwellings, the addition of such a suite would move the house into the multiple-dwelling classification.

Although Helena could do nothing to alter these social ground rules, she was at least able to make some basement suites legal. In her report, she recommended that one-third of the basement floor space in apartment buildings be allowed for suites, providing that they conformed to the building by-law. Zoning by-laws were consequently amended to make such suites legal. A member of the zoning board of appeal threw up his hands in despair over this measure and quit, objecting that in districts zoned for one-family dwellings the regulations were being strictly applied. This inconsistency arose out of the housing shortage. If the city tore down condemned buildings, if it did not allow basement suites and other makeshift living quarters, ordinary folk would be deprived of shelter, since substandard housing was all that they could afford.[34]

Helena was convinced that the way out of this dilemma lay in subsidized housing. The other members of Council were wary of any such scheme, as the city was bearing the financial brunt of a housing program for returned soldiers that the federal government had initiated to alleviate the housing shortage after the First World War. Under the Better Housing Scheme of 1919, federal loans had been made available to the provinces for the municipalities, who then had to guarantee the loans. Since the onset of the Depression, house owners were having difficulty making payments, and by 1938 over half of them had either failed in their payments or were in arrears.[35] The city then had to take over the mortgages, and this added financial burden did nothing to make Vancouver aldermen view government-assisted housing with favour.

Nevertheless the Council, yielding to pressure from Helena, approved the appointment of a special committee to make a survey of the housing situation in Vancouver and draw up a comprehensive housing plan for the city. Helena was chairman of the committee; the other two members were Frank Ebenezer Buck, chairman of the Town Planning Commission, and Albert Harrison, secretary of zoning matters at City Hall.[36]

The Town Planning Commission had been responsible for all the planning for Vancouver since 1926, when it was first established by a city by-law. A Town Planning Bill, drafted by the Vancouver branch of the Town Planning Institute of Canada, was introduced in the British Columbia legislature in 1922 by Mary Ellen Smith, although another three years passed before it became law. Even then it was not mandatory for municipalities. The only paid member on the Vancouver commission was its secretary and consultant engineer, J. Alexander Walker. A comprehensive plan for the city was its first task. For this it engaged the St. Louis engineering firm Harland Bartholomew and Associates, whose plan, completed in 1930, was never implemented. The section on zoning was adopted, however, and for the next forty years, Vancouver zoning by-laws were based on Bartholomew's model of the concentric city with a central commercial area surrounded by apartment and single-family dwelling zones.[37]

The Town Planning Commission itself was not influential in trying to solve Vancouver's housing problems, but the man who represented it on City Council's Housing Committee was a powerful influence, providing knowledge and expertise and matching Helena's missionary ardour with his quieter yet profound commitment. Born in Colchester, England, UBC professor Frank Buck started out as a journalist and came to Canada in 1902. Because of failing eyesight, he turned to horticulture, receiving degrees from McGill and Cornell Universities. For some years he was assistant Dominion horticulturist in charge of landscape architecture at the Central Experimental Farm in Ottawa, before coming to teach at the University of British Columbia in 1920. He was chairman of the Point Grey Town Planning Commission until Point Grey amalgamated with Vancouver in 1929, and he remained with the Vancouver commission until 1951, devoting twenty-five years to guiding the development of Vancouver. Helena first met Buck during the provincial election of 1933. She was on his campaign team when he ran, unsuccessfully, as a CCF candidate in Vancouver-Burrard. Later he won a term on the Vancouver School Board. A citizen must serve his city, he believed.[38]

The third member of the Housing Committee, Albert J. Harrison, was from Plymouth, England. As secretary of zoning, he was a stickler for the letter of the law, but he also wrote poetry, read English literature, and belonged to the Theosophical Society. Theosophists are declared egalitarians, but Albert Harrison, as president of the Hermes Lodge in

Vancouver, was known to balk at what he called 'petticoat rule.' For all that, he was gentlemanly and pleasant and wrote excellent reports. It is not known what he thought of serving on a committee chaired by Helena, but the subtext of the committee minutes reveals no personal animosity, and they did have a knowledge of theosophy in common.[39]

Helena's motion in Council to set up a special Housing Committee allowed her to seek help from 'public and semi-public bodies.' In this she had no difficulty. Housing had long been on the agenda of the Local Council of Women, the Vancouver Trades and Labor Council, and the Vancouver Council of Social Agencies. All these organizations sent representatives to the Housing Committee. The UBC Sociology Department was represented by Professor C.W. Topping, an LSR member familiar with the work of housing activists in eastern Canada. He assigned his students to the survey as a field work exercise. The Greater Vancouver and New Westminster Youth Council, conducting its own housing campaign, also asked to help with the survey, as did the left-wing Workers' Alliance.[40]

During the summer and fall of 1937, Dr. Topping's sociology students and members of the Youth Council went door-to-door along the downtown residential streets and waterfront, tabulating information for the Housing Committee's survey. They found that the slums of Vancouver, if not actually rivalling the slums of Victorian London, were shocking enough. Although there were indeed clean and tidy clusters of permanent waterfront houses in good condition along Burrard Inlet, for the most part from Bidwell Street to Boundary Road a population of some three hundred people lived in dilapidated houseboats or in houses built on pilings, most of them without a water supply and only half with electricity. Raw sewage washed over the tide flats directly from the waterfront dwellings. Even at the western end of Coal Harbour, where the dwellings were quite decent, the odour of sewage was pervasive. Another two hundred people lived in similar conditions along the north shore of False Creek. In downtown Vancouver, families with children were discovered living in a single room and sharing one toilet with as many as a dozen other people in a rooming house. Sanitary facilities were not much better in the West End, where the fine houses of Vancouver's elite had been converted to rooming houses with squalid little basement suites. In the downtown east side, at Main and Cordova, there were cabins inhabited by single men, usually old-age pensioners, and by a large population of Chinese. Here in the middle of the city outdoor toilets were still in use.[41]

The housing problem had its tragic dimensions, as Helena was well aware. Although Vancouver did not have a standard of housing by-law, city building inspectors could seek the aid of the Medical Health Officer to condemn a building as 'unfit for occupation as a dwelling place.' In the summer of 1938, just four blocks from Helena's house on Triumph Street on Vancouver's east side, three children died in a fire that swept a tenement condemned by the city. Two of the families who fled the fire found shelter in another condemned tenement nearby, already housing twenty families. A *Sun* editorial urged the city to take action:

> It [the second tenement], too, stands condemned and a notice bears witness to this in capital letters, 'NOT FIT FOR HUMAN HABITATION'. It is dated June 29, 1938.
>
> But under this notice is another, dated February 2, 1937, condemning the tenement and ordering its destruction within thirty days!
>
> Is the city waiting for another fatal fire before implementing the orders of its own department officials?[42]

Commenting on the fire, Helena pointed to other fire-trap tenements in the city. 'We cannot condemn these buildings,' she declared, 'because there are no other places for people to go ... We need a low rental housing scheme that will provide plenty of houses, to be let at whatever rental a low-wage earner can afford to pay.'[43] Evictions were part of everyday life in Vancouver: the sheriff came with his crew and carried the delinquent tenant's furniture and belongings out onto the sidewalk, or the city put the belongings of relief families into storage until they could find shelter. Where were such people to go, if not to some slum tenement or waterfront shack, perhaps already condemned by the building inspector? Often the city could not carry out its own demolition orders. Shelter for indigent women was a pathetic problem too; Helena's Housing Committee dealt with those cases individually.[44]

Helena knew that before slum conditions could be tackled, before a housing program could be developed, the city needed a standard of housing by-law, such as the one operating in Toronto, which set minimum standards of maintenance for all dwellings and required compulsory repair or demolition of rundown buildings. Under its charter, Vancouver did not have the power to adopt such a by-law. Helena therefore pressed City Council to seek the required amendment to the charter, and the provincial government passed this enabling legislation in the fall of 1938. A national building code did not yet exist, although at the urging of the recently formed National Planning Association, represented by George S. Mooney, the National Research Council had begun work on one. A member of the League for Social Reconstruction and of the CCF, Mooney was associate director of the Montreal Metropolitan Commission's Department of Planning and Research, and a dynamic force in the growing Canadian housing movement.[45]

Helena's Housing Committee was charged with the task of preparing a comprehensive housing plan for the city. Right at the outset Helena proposed government-subsidized social housing and Mayor Miller spoke for other members of City Council when he said that he had no objection to the city's 'playing fairy godmother to any suitable project' so long as it did not incur a financial burden for the city.[46]

Several years earlier, while Conservative Prime Minister R.B. Bennett was in office, the construction industry and the banks and mortgage companies had pressured his government to provide public funds for ailing private enterprise. With construction at a standstill and production of bricks and asphalt, sheet metal, and tile also coming to a halt, the National Construction Council told the Bennett government in plain Keynesian terms that 'the resources of the state should be utilized to stimulate industry by the provision of easier credit and cheaper money.'[47] Furthermore, state planning was necessary to keep a firm rein on a skittish market economy. The president of the Canadian Manufacturers' Association went so far as to say that planning, not laissez faire, would revive the economy. Mortgage and investment companies offered the government housing schemes for releasing government money into the housing industry via their own loan offices. They had money to let out, but did not want to finance housing that might create a surplus, for fear of adversely affecting the already disturbed real estate market. They were also opposed to any government housing programs that would make the government a financial competitor.[48]

Although no proponent of subsidized housing, the Bennett government set up a House of Commons Special Committee on Housing. Expert testimony soon convinced even the most conservative committee members that housing was an urgent problem and that, since private enterprise could not make a profit on low-rental housing, the government must take direct action to provide it. The committee's unanimous report concluded that the provision of adequate housing for Canadians was a social responsibility. Apprehensive that so explicit a statement would open the floodgates of state intervention, collectivity, and socialism, the committee prefaced this enlightened declaration by underlining the pre-eminence of individual initiative: 'Housing is primarily the direct responsibility of the individual co-operating with the local authority.'[49]

With an election pending, the Bennett government introduced housing legislation that, as historian J. David Hulchanski explains, was conceived and presented to the House not as a housing act but as a vehicle for studying the housing problem. Despite this disclaimer, legislation entitled the Dominion Housing Act (DHA) passed in June 1935, though it in no way implemented the committee's recommendations for a national housing policy. In a withering blast of derision across the floor of the House, CCF MP A.A. Heaps declared that the legislation had as little relationship to the report as a pig has to pig iron. Liberal members were equally critical, and even the committee's chairman, Conservative MP Arthur Gagnon, was disappointed in the bill. For the Act provided legislative machinery not for the building of affordable rental accommodation for the low-paid worker but for the building of houses for moderate-income people. Its aim was to encourage employment by stimulating the construction industry.[50]

The Bennett government assigned responsibility for the administration of the DHA to the Department of Finance, whose deputy minister, W.C. Clark, was an unrelenting advocate of reserving house construction for private enterprise. Under the terms of the Act, the government, through insurance or trust companies, would lend 20 per cent of the money for approved new houses at 3 per cent interest; the lending institution would put up 60 per cent, leaving an equity of only 20 per cent. The prospective homeowner would pay 5 per cent interest on the total amount borrowed. In British Columbia, businessmen carried out a vigorous campaign to inform people about these loans, but despite their efforts few took advantage of the federal program. Only 845 housing units were built in this province during the three-year period of the Act. Only a few mortgage companies took advantage of the provisions of the Act to lend out money for house building.[51]

In October 1935 the Liberals were returned to power in Ottawa, and in 1938 introduced their National Housing Act (NHA). It demonstrated that Mackenzie King was no more interested than Bennett in creating a national housing policy, as the preamble to the Act made clear: Overcrowding and unwholesome living conditions adversely affected the 'employability and efficiency of the urban population,' and even though meeting minimum standards of habitation was the responsibility of the provinces and municipalities, it was 'in the national interest that a limited experiment in low-rental housing should be undertaken now, creating needed employment and directing public attention to the importance of housing problems generally.'[52] The preamble made no declaration of the right of every citizen to decent shelter, nor did it declare that needed housing would be built; it did, however, assure Canadians that the government would indeed draw attention to the problem. Like Bennett, King remained at a safe distance from the country's housing problem. He did not set up a separate housing authority; instead, he left housing to continue under the aegis of the Department of Finance and Deputy Minister Clark. Low-rental housing if necessary, but not necessarily low-rent rental housing.

Part I of the National Housing Act preserved DHA legislation for assisting home construction for people of moderate income through government loans to lending institutions. Part II made other loans available to local housing authorities for low-rental housing, but the $3,000 houses thus projected were still beyond the financial means of those most in need of them, since the average worker earning only $550 or $600 a year could not afford to pay the necessary economic rent of $15 to $18 a month. The Act stipulated that the annual rental charged should not exceed one-fifth of the total annual family income. For most workers this amounted to a monthly rent between $10 and $12. Yet the Act provided for no subsidies to municipalities to make up the deficiency, but only loans that they would have to finance at a time when all governments were in serious financial straits.[53]

On these terms, the Liberal government made available $30 million in loans to local housing authorities for low-rental housing. A local housing authority could be a municipality, eligible for 90 per cent of the cost of construction or as much as $2,700 at 2 per cent, or it could be a limited-dividend housing corporation, eligible for 80 per cent of the cost of construction or as much as $2,400 at 1.75 per cent.

The government viewed the limited-dividend corporation with particular favour because such a corporation could combine the profit motive with philanthropy. As conceived by Deputy Minister Clark, limited-dividend companies would consist of 'private citizens who have a sufficient stake in the community and sufficient public spirit to induce them to give some time and energy to the constructive solution of a pressing community problem.' The corporation would be required to accept a maximum financial return of 5 per cent, finding compensation for this restriction of profits in 'satisfaction over a job well done and the thrill of leadership in a vital public service.'[54] This philanthropic approach to housing would not have been out of place in Victorian England, where landlords like the Earl of Cadogan responded to housing emergencies with appropriate gestures of noblesse oblige.

The amount of loan money allotted to Vancouver, $1,328,000, was enough to finance 250 houses. Even though this money would do nothing to house the lowest income group, Helena was pleased with this small response to the city's housing emergency. After preliminary negotiations with F.W. Nicolls, federal housing director, she reported to City Council that Vancouver could hope to get 'all of the gravy and none of the grief' out of its share of the federal housing money. In fact, she was so hopeful of more far-reaching legislation for social housing that she decided to apply pressure on slum landlords and announced a campaign to get rid of dilapidated and unwholesome dwellings. Building inspectors subsequently issued orders to landlords to renovate or have their buildings demolished under existing health and building by-laws. In the end, Helena's hopes were dashed. Vancouver, like other cities, got no gravy, but a full share of taxation grief.[55]

For the Liberal government was not seriously interested in getting people out of waterfront shacks and tenements. In fact, Mackenzie King even had qualms about lending money for housing to the provinces. A month before passage of the National Housing Act, he reassured himself in his diary that social housing could indeed be a means of relieving unemployment, but worried that the budget was 'following the example of priming the pump to a greater extent than I would like.'[56]

The 1930s was also the decade of J.S. Woodsworth and the Regina Manifesto, and the ground-breaking report *Social Planning for Canada* by the research committee of the League for Social Reconstruction. Among the authors of the report was Toronto landscape architect-social work professor Humphrey Carver, who wrote the section on national housing policy. He became one of the influential members of Central Mortgage and Housing, which after the Second World War designed the housing and community planning policies envisioning a new Canadian urban landscape oriented to the needs of its inhabitants. Looking back on his long career in housing and community planning, he reflected that in Canada, because of the rigours of climate and terrain, even politics ultimately yields to the 'compassionate motive.' In 1938, however, when he was a young community activist, compassion in government had not yet housed many Canadians. With George Mooney, Carver organized two national conferences on housing, in Ottawa in 1937 and in Toronto in 1939.[57] Helena knew of both Carver and Mooney through the Town Planning Commission and thus kept up with their activities.

The 1934 Bruce Report on housing conditions in Toronto had made housing reform a matter for government policy. Written by Dr. Harry Cassidy, another of the authors of *Social Planning for Canada,* and professor of architecture Eric Arthur, its recommendations provided a basis for housing reform in that city.[58] A group of enthusiasts, including Carver, established a Housing Centre in Toronto with the aim of stimulating public support for the proposals in the Bruce Report. On Toronto City Council, Adelaide Plumptre, Helena's Housing Committee counterpart, acted as liaison and representative for the Housing Centre. According to Carver, she would 'transfix an opponent through her pince-nez' and, much like Helena at a Council meeting, 'wither him with unanswerable words of truth.'[59] Helena was fortunate to be working on Vancouver's housing problems at a time when people like Humphrey Carver, George Mooney, and Adelaide Plumptre were creating a national dialogue on housing and mobilizing a national effort for housing programs.

The National Housing and Planning Association had been formed early in 1937 as a result of discussions at the annual meeting of the Union of Canadian Municipalities. Building code standards, low-cost housing, town-planning legislation, a housing education program – these were some of the objectives of the new association, which set out to organize branches in the larger Canadian cities.[60]

On this mission, secretary George Mooney travelled west to Vancouver in December 1937, met with Helena and her Housing Committee, and discussed national housing with them. Reporting this discussion to City Council, Helena put forward a resolution to be sent to the federal government, urging new housing legislation for low-income households that could not be helped by the Dominion Housing Act. Her colleagues on Council passed the resolution. At the Council table they commended her for her work in housing and put their approval on record.[61]

The visit of the charismatic George Mooney also sparked the formation of the Vancouver Housing Association. An old hand at organizing community groups, Helena was confident that such a group would serve her housing campaign as her Women's Employment League and Minimum Wage League had served her in the past. In the Vancouver Housing Association she would have a major ally. Founded within days of Mooney's visit, it constituted itself a branch of the National Housing and Planning Association. Helena was on the nominating committee, which brought in a slate of officers representing a wide range of constituencies. The chairman was Walter S. Owen, a conservative young lawyer who would one day be Lieutenant Governor of British Columbia; vice chairman the United Church's Associate Secretary of Evangelism and Social Service, the Reverend Mr. Hugh Dobson, an old social gospeller; secretary, John Jopson, from the Anglican Young People's Society; treasurer, P.R.U. (Peter) Stratton, an Oxford-educated accountant of independent means. Helena and Frank Buck welcomed the association as a means of tapping the sources of housing reform ferment in the East. More important, they planned to work with the association in reaching out, as Helena said, 'to public-spirited citizens who are anxious to assist, in a constructive way, with housing schemes.'[62]

A public-spirited citizen did come forward with help that more than fulfilled Helena's expectations. Peter Stratton had first become interested in housing reform in England, where he had participated in surveys of London's East End in the early thirties. A young British immigrant, he had worked in Vancouver for three years before being summoned back to England in 1933 to claim an inheritance. As a member of the Mansion House Council for several years, he worked as a volunteer researcher in Southwark, in the vicinity of the Elephant and Castle, accumulating, door by tenement door, gutter by gutter, a depressingly first-hand knowledge of the London slums. Little wonder that, despite the achievements of the Labour government in rehousing during the twenties, he wanted to escape England. He returned to Vancouver around 1936, and applied his experience to the Vancouver emergency. For over thirty years this gentle, unassuming man worked as a volunteer in housing and planning, with the Vancouver Housing Authority after the war, later with the Town Planning Commission and the Regional Planning Board. A man with a strong sense of social mission, after the Second World War he helped start the first family planning clinic in Vancouver and tried, without success, to have an apartment block for single girls built in downtown Vancouver. Peter Stratton also devoted many years to the Society for the Prevention of Cruelty to Animals. In fact Helena first met him in 1938, when her special committee granted him permission to erect a free animal clinic on a city lot. Humphrey Carver later paid tribute to this 'lean and ascetic figure ... ready to die like a Christian martyr for any of the humanitarian causes he espoused.'[63]

Acting for the Vancouver Housing Association in the fall of 1938, Stratton presented to the Housing Committee a proposal for a low-rent housing project of fifty houses to be erected by a non-profit housing society operating under Part II of the National Housing Act. He himself would donate four acres of the 5½-acre site near Trout Lake on Vancouver's east side. The city already owned the rest. The house plans were adapted from those issued by the United States Federal Housing Administration, and were modest enough. A two-bedroom house cost $1,269; the total cost, including land at an estimated $130 per unit, would amount to $1,500. The houses would be heated by sawdust burners; where there was no basement, by coal and wood heaters in the living room. Kitchens would be provided with a coal and wood stove, hot water reservoir attached, or with a gas range and coal-fired water heater. Planned before the postwar Age of Appliances, the amenities were simple and primitive. A ventilated cooler would be built into an outside wall of the kitchen for food storage; for laundry, 'either a tub in the basement, or a gas-fired copper on the English model located under a hinged draining board.' In winter, clothes could be hung to dry in the attic or in the basement. With operating costs for each unit calculated at $12.50 a month, including $15 a year for taxes, the estimated rent would be $16 a month. The houses would be grouped in such a way as to provide a playground for small children and at the same time to lower operating cost.[64]

Pacific Housing Corporation proposed a project for the same general area, beginning with a hundred units and allowing for another four hundred should expansion seem feasible. They would operate as a limited-dividend company and Toronto General Trust Corporation would provide financing. This project advanced as far as a meeting of the principals with Helena's Buildings, Civic Planning and Parks Committee.

All that was now necessary for the go-ahead was a report from the City Engineer on water and sewer facilities in the area and an amendment of the city charter, a mere formality. With some other aldermen, Helena visited the site. Standing on Renfrew Heights with its magnificent view of the North Shore mountains, she could envision a newly created community: the neat little houses, each with its own garden, the tree-lined streets, the playground echoing with the shouts of children at play.[65]

But Helena reckoned without the question of municipal tax exemption. According to the National Housing Act, municipalities would not be allowed to levy taxes on low-rental housing projects at a rate over 1 per cent of the cost of construction. This stipulation was to prove an insurmountable barrier because the aldermen said that such a tax clause was unfair to householders in the same area who had been paying regular taxes in the regular way through good times and bad. The aldermen also believed that the city could not, in any case, afford the loss in revenue entailed by the tax clause. Neither project was discussed further in committee. When City Council met early in January 1939, it voted against acceptance of Part II of the NHA because of the tax restriction. Mayor Telford favoured the NHA scheme, but all the aldermen except Helena were opposed. F.W. Nicolls came from Ottawa to meet with them. He was the one who had drafted the tax clause, convinced that lower social costs would more than compensate for loss of tax revenue. He was on solid ground: the case for economies resulting from slum clearance was by now well documented in surveys conducted in American and European cities. George Mooney had gathered the evidence and written eloquently on the subject, explaining that fireproof housing with proper sanitary facilities produced a wholesome environment that decreased the cost of fire protection, sanitary services, police protection, and other public services.[66]

Nicolls urged in vain that a distinction be made between economic and social housing. The Vancouver Housing Association produced figures to show that even with reduced taxation Stratton's project would comfortably pay for sewer, water, and road services.[67] The aldermen were adamant: they could not be convinced that low taxation would not put a burden on the taxpayer, and therefore continued to oppose the NHA plan.

The idea of social housing was still an unfamiliar concept in Canada. Part II of the National Housing Act, though cautious and limited, was still, as the Deputy Minister Clark reminded housing enthusiasts, 'a radical innovation in Canadian legislation.' In Britain, Sir Kingsley Wood, minister of health for the Conservative government, had announced that under the Housing Acts of 1930 and 1935, nearly a million people would be moved out of slums into decent dwellings by 1938, a good portion of this activity receiving government subsidy. In the United States

the Wagner-Steagall Act of 1937 provided for a federal housing authority that subsidized rents for existing social housing projects and financed
new ones under local housing authorities. In Scandinavia, the process
of socializing the whole housing stock was beginning, with the eventual
result that no stigma would be attached to living in state-subsidized
dwellings.[68]

In Canada governments kept themselves at arm's length from the
housing problem. In Vancouver, for example, the city's Social Service
Department distributed shelter allowance cheques to those on relief, but
the amount was too small – $5 to $8 per month – to enable the landlord
to cover taxes, let alone maintenance costs. Moreover, as the Housing
Committee discovered to their dismay, some families used their shelter
allowance to rent filthy waterfront shacks without water or electricity.
The committee wanted the address of the relief recipient written on the
rental cheque so that they could follow up such cases, but the social service administrator replied that this would impose an accounting problem, and besides the city regarded housing as 'the relief recipient's
problem.'[69]

Despite City Council's rejection of the NHA program, Helena did not
give up. At lunchtime meetings at the David Spencer Department Store
cafeteria, she, Frank Buck, and Albert Harrison devised strategies for carrying on the campaign. Once again they would mobilize community
support. Once again they would visit the waterfront shacks along Burrard Inlet and the basement suites in the West End and present yet
another report to Council. Then Helena would force the issue with
City Council.

Early in the new year, 1939, the three went back to the waterfront, visited the shacks, and again opened their hearts and minds to images of
poverty and squalor: a floating shack, a narrow plank leading to the
muddy shoreline, '2 dear little children ... sickly, pallid and underfed,
one playing with a pair of old boots, and the other lying sick in a box
crib.' Frank Buck's report on behalf of the Housing Committee was
angry, indignant, impassioned:

> When the tide is out they [the floating shacks] settle into mud, slime and
> filthy water. Water full of drifting waste and fouled with human excrement.
>   One area reeks with the stench of decaying things, another with the gases
> arising from the fountain-like discharge from a sewage outlet just beyond
> the shacks, a fountain of continuous pollution, and of eternal shame so long
> as it poisons the waters on which float the huts of human beings.

What Frank saw affected him powerfully. Afterwards, he had bad
dreams. He thought of the children: 'All day long when days are wet,

little ones are held in dark basement suites fit only for storage, as if they themselves were but storage materials and not potential citizens who tomorrow must play some part in our civilization.'[70] Helena was no less moved by the poverty and squalor she witnessed. 'Still no housing,' she fumed in *The Federationist*:

> Take a walk around the west end of the city, or the east end adjacent to town. Look at the outside first, unpainted, drab looking houses falling into disrepair. A wooden box hanging outside almost every window. What are they? Subsistence allowance refrigerators used by the relief families or families of low income inhabiting the house.[71]

She had just read Humphrey Carver's article 'Still No Housing' in the December 1938 issue of the *Canadian Forum*, and pleaded his idea of an annual government subsidy to the local housing authority to make up the portion of the rent that low-income families could not afford to pay. By this time, she had become quite bitter towards the Liberal government for not giving financial aid where it was so vitally needed. The loan plan was not a 'benevolent gesture on the part of the Federal Government,' she said, for it had amply protected itself in case of default of repayment.

City Council, however, could not be moved by either argument or investigative exposé. Hard economic facts had to be faced. Businessmen had suffered severe real estate losses because of the Depression and were more interested in property tax relief than in venturesome new projects with no guaranteed profit. A *Sun* editorial reflected the general feeling of property owners and real estate interests, contending that the Vancouver Housing Association should concentrate its efforts on 'rehabilitating some of those sections of the city which at one time were fine residential areas but have now run to seed.'[72]

In February 1939, a National Housing Conference organized by Humphrey Carver was held in Toronto. Delegates came from across Canada with their expertise in architecture and building and their impassioned ideologies in the service of better housing for Canadians. Neither Helena nor Frank was able to attend, but they asked Grace MacInnis, who was working for the CCF parliamentary group in Ottawa, to represent their Housing Committee, and sent her their strong recommendation that Vancouver City Council approve Part II of the National Housing Act. The committee had gained community support at a special meeting of the Building, Civic Planning and Parks Committee, where all the organizations present except one, the Associated Property Owners of Vancouver, expressed themselves in favour of low-rental housing projects.[73]

Grace MacInnis reported that the 1 per cent tax provision as applied to municipalities met with vigorous opposition, especially from the Ontario delegates, but that the western provinces wanted to try to obtain some housing under the provisions of the Act, hoping that their city councils could be prevailed on to accept the tax provision. The conference went on record as approving the terms of the Act.[74] Helena looked to the conference for influential support and for the momentum needed to swing the views of City Council around. Whether Vancouver's council chamber felt any vibrations from Toronto is doubtful, however.

By this time Helena knew that she was fighting a losing battle; nevertheless she kept on fighting. She helped organize the Vancouver Housing Association's educational campaign, hoping that it would influence City Council to change its mind, but she was weary and depressed by all the setbacks she had suffered. She attended a celebration for the opening of new quarters for the Lyceum Club, the special CCF club for women that she herself had founded. Dorothy Steeves thought she seemed 'grumpy.' Helena had reason to be: City Council was still rejecting low-rental housing under Part II of the National Housing Act.[75]

In June, Helena attempted yet again to make City Council change its mind. Surely, she reasoned, if community support were strong enough, they would listen. Once again she rallied Vancouver organizations: the Women's Guild of Shaughnessy Heights United Church, the Parent-Teacher Federation of Vancouver, the BC Old Age Pensioners' Benevolent Association, the Canadian Daughters' League, Chown Memorial Women's Association, the Civilian Pension Mothers' Association, the National Council of Jewish Women (Vancouver section), the Catholic Women's League of Canada, the Mount Pleasant Woman's Christian Temperance Union, the Federation of the Blind, the Vancouver Local Council of Women, the Canadian Young Theosophists, the Greater Vancouver Health League, the Building Trades Council, the BC Committee of the Home Improvement Plan and NHA. Before the Building, Civic Parks and Planning Committee, these organizations endorsed the NHA low-rental housing plan. Mrs. Roy Taylor and Susie Clark spoke, fighting now for human rights as they had in earlier decades fought for women's rights. Frank Buck urged the aldermen to exercise 'critical judgment,' spoke of 'kindness of action to *all*, patience and persistence.'[76] He spoke of sacrifice. At this June meeting, the only resolutions opposing the plan came from the Vancouver Federated Ratepayers' Association, the Vancouver Real Estate Exchange, and the Vancouver Associated Property Owners. Indeed, F.W. Nicolls reflected in a letter to the Housing Committee, that 'the agitation against the low rent housing project was being kept alive, principly [*sic*] by your real estate men.'[77]

In the end, City Council shelved all proposals for housing projects until a plebiscite could be taken on the question of the low-rental housing provisions of the National Housing Act. The decision moved a member of the Vancouver Board of Trade, C.J. White, to righteous comment: 'It's not the size of a house but the way it's kept that makes a slum. The human need in this city is largely a matter of inculcating the merits of using Capilano water and soap more frequently.'[78] No wonder Helena sometimes felt grumpy.

Peter Stratton, meanwhile, was preparing a comprehensive report for the Vancouver Housing Association as part of its educational campaign. For the past nine months, he had been doing the field work, sparing himself no pains. When he went into the Chinese quarter, he brought an interpreter along. 'Housing in Vancouver,' a report presented to the Housing Committee early in August 1939, is largely his work, testimony to the dedication of now-forgotten individuals who laid the groundwork for the legislation that would finally make social housing accepted as federal government policy. His report again contained searing documentation of human degradation: 'Man, woman and 6 children live in one room. 3 of the children sleep in a large clothes cupboard; the other 3 children sleep on the landing along with the cooking stove and the wood. The parents sleep in the room.' 'Family of 7 occupy two-room house. 6 persons sleep in one room. Boy sleeps in unventilated room in which toilet is located. Roof leaks – Very damp.'[79]

September 1939. War! Domestic concerns suddenly seemed less urgent. This was no time for a plebiscite on housing. Yet in November, Helena made one last attempt to save the low-rental housing plan. The March 1940 deadline for NHA loans was approaching. There was $1,328,000 for Vancouver, hanging like ripe cherries on an inaccessible branch. She urged City Council to request an amendment to the National Housing Act extending the deadline:

> The Housing Committee believes that while it would appear that the problem of adequate housing is crowded out of public interest by war efforts and war happenings, there is, none the less, a strong feeling that every avenue of expenditure for public improvement at home should be maintained at full capacity.
>
> It would be regrettable if the first effort of the Dominion Government towards the creation of adequate housing were allowed to lapse, through inaction on the part of municipalities. Canada has lagged far behind other countries in the matter of housing.[80]

Vancouver was not the only municipality that balked at the 1 per cent tax clause. Plans for housing projects in Montreal, Winnipeg, and

Regina were similarly halted. 31 March 1940 came and went, and not one penny of the federal government's $30 million of loan money had been touched.[81]

Helena continued to work on drafting a standard of housing by-law. Unfortunately, she was voted out of office in December 1939. Henry Corey took her place as chairman of the Building, Civic Planning and Parks Committee, and had the legal department draft the by-law. It called for dwellings, garages, outhouses, walks, and fences to be maintained in good repair, inside and out. Dwellings were required to be weatherproof and adequately heated, and to conform to building, plumbing, and electrical regulations. Inside walls had to be covered with material such as lath and plaster and maintained in good condition; floors, walls, and ceilings had to be dry, basements properly drained, and yards kept free of rubbish. And, reflecting Helena's concern for sanitation, every dwelling had to have a proper facility for food storage. The building inspector was empowered to notify the owner of necessary repairs to be carried out within sixty days, failing which the building would be demolished. The bylaw aimed at maintaining minimum standards, attempting only to remedy the worst defects. A Vancouver building inspector would have charged landlords with the same abuses as an Inspector of Nuisances in Victorian Chelsea. Henry Corey presented the draft by-law to City Council on 9 December 1940. It was immediately shelved.[82]

Meanwhile, Helena continued to work for low-rental housing, making it the main issue in her 1940 and 1941 election campaigns. Although she did not regain her seat on Council, she raised public awareness of the housing problem, especially in 1941, when the *News-Herald*, launching an attack on housing conditions in downtown Vancouver, printed her views. Reporters discovered the same poverty and degradation that Helena and Frank had witnessed: an old West End mansion crammed with tenants from attic to basement, everyone sharing one toilet; families eating and sleeping in one room, cooking on two-burner gas rings and electric hotplates. In downtown Vancouver, where the Queen Elizabeth Theatre and the Vancouver Vocational Institute now stand, rows of ramshackle dwellings stood among clean, bright warehouse offices. Throughout the warehouse district more than a dozen long sheds about twenty feet wide divided into ten or eleven 'cabins' provided quarters for single people on relief, or men and women living on their old-age pension of $20 a month. 'Luxury' quarters at $7 a month had electric light; standard quarters at $5 had kerosene lamps. Community toilets were located outside, as were water taps, sometimes with a covered sink. The cabins, heated by wood stoves, were fire hazards and were infested with fleas and bedbugs. The sheds were 'pretty damn old,' according to one occupant: 'Used to be used by the teamsters when the sugar refinery had horses.'[83]

'What happened to the Standard of Housing Bylaw ...?' Helena wanted to know. 'Has Ald. Corey forgotten it?'[84]

Alderman Corey, who was in favour of the by-law, replied that he had done his best to pass it through Council but had met too much opposition. Council members argued that existing health and building by-laws were sufficient to regulate housing maintenance, but they were loath to apply them for fear of reducing the housing stock even more. Interviewed by the *News-Herald* on housing conditions, Mayor Cornett had no comment. Alderman Miller was 'absolutely opposed to the city going into housing.' He believed in private initiative, 'but with the freezing of rents you cannot expect people to go into building from the investment point of view.' Alderman Worthington said, 'There is far too much agitation given to questions of this sort. It makes people unsettled and gives them a complex that they should have more and more.' Other aldermen recalled that the city was still paying mortgages for the federal government's housing plan of 1919. But in Alderman Halford Wilson, Helena found an unexpected ally: he was in favour of the standard of housing by-law and of the city adopting some kind of low-rent housing scheme.[85]

Now the housing crisis suddenly became urgent in a comprehensible way. Workers in shipyards, munitions plants, and other factories had to be housed or production for the war would suffer. A government corporation, Wartime Housing Ltd., was established, directly responsible to the minister of munitions and supply, to provide temporary housing for war workers. Soon new neighbourhoods of neat little cottages sprang up across Canada, built under Wartime Housing. In North Vancouver some 750 shipyard workers at Burrard Drydock Company and North Van Ship Repairs moved their families into new housing developments in various parts of the city and district. The houses were built without basements and heated by stoves, for it was intended that they would eventually be dismantled, but at least the grounds were planted with lawns and trees and shrubs. The school population exploded. Wartime Housing paid for half the cost of a new school and an addition to an existing one. In the municipality of Richmond, where Boeing Aircraft operated plants on Sea Island, Wartime Housing expropriated land for housing and again provided additional facilities – a fire-hall and a community centre. And so it was across Canada. In the five years beginning in 1941, Wartime Housing built more than 25,000 housing units. After the war, with its successor Central Mortgage and Housing (CMHC), it completed another 25,000 under special housing rental programs for veterans.[86]

Once the veterans were housed, Wartime Housing Ltd. was disbanded. Instead of using it as a mechanism for peacetime low-rental housing, the federal government, through its new agency CMHC, returned to a policy of financial assistance to private industry, encouraging home ownership. Prime Minister Louis St. Laurent was opposed to subsidized public housing, and succeeding governments did little to alter the reliance on market housing.[87]

In 1942, Frank Buck reflected on his experiences in the housing movement. He had 'no regrets and no apologies' for the 'nights of earnest study, weeks, months, years of attendance at all kinds of meetings,' but he felt deeply discouraged: 'My last report on Housing, like the autumn leaves on which I gaze at the moment drifted like one of those leaves into some dark nook where it will be swept into the limbo of discarded things.'[88]

Helena was also deeply disappointed that all her efforts to obtain low-rental housing had come to nothing. 'My proposals were just brushed aside,' she recalled years later.[89] She should not have felt discouraged: as Alderman Gutteridge she had focused the efforts of many local organizations for better housing and connected them with the national movement. She had spearheaded the attack on intransigence in government and, indefatigable proselytizer, brought the problem of housing into the public forum. With Frank Buck, Peter Stratton, and other members of the Vancouver Housing Association, she had laid the groundwork for the postwar housing movement in Vancouver.

Helena would not live to rejoice over the boom in social housing that began in 1969, a national development nurtured and cultivated by the dedicated advisory group of CMHC, Humphrey Carver among them. Dedicated to the philosophy of cooperation, she would also have rejoiced over the success of the cooperative housing movement, which would house people of moderate incomes with those on social assistance, professionals alongside working people, the disabled with the physically fit in communities that operated on democratic principles.

However, Helena did live to see at least the beginnings of public housing in Vancouver. In 1954 the 224-unit Little Mountain project between Main and Ontario Streets was opened, and in 1958 Orchard Park at Nanaimo Street and 41st Avenue opened with 169 units. These were conceived and directed by the Vancouver Housing Authority, the ultimate successor to the Vancouver Housing Association. Peter Stratton was still among the planners and initiators.[90] By this time Helena was in her seventies. Canada's attitudes towards housing had changed a good deal since the days of her Carvell Hall Settlement, and she had helped to change them.

Helena did not leave her post on Council with no recognition of her substantial contribution to the city. After her defeat in the 1939 civic election, a valedictory editorial in the *Province* was unreserved in praise of this 'faithful alderman,' declaring 'no council member has been more faithful or more zealous than she.' In generous acknowledgment of her unremitting fight for better housing, it concluded: 'Had the other members of the council evinced half her interest in this problem, Vancouver might, long since, have made some progress in satisfying the need for low-rent housing.'[91] The *Sun* paid similar tribute and added that she 'had been consistently in the van of every move for improvement of social conditions among the underprivileged.'[92]

Unfortunately, wartime politics intervened and destroyed her chances of being re-elected. But the war made new demands on her, as on all Canadians. Helena's war effort required her to store her household effects and leave the city to live and work in an isolated mountain valley for an indefinite period. The move came at a convenient juncture, for Edith MacDonald was again moving house, this time setting up a health-food restaurant – Helen's Tea Room – and living on the premises. She may have named it after Helena, but no memories have surfaced among old CCFers to prove that she had. Helena used to grumble about Edith's entrepreneurial ventures, pointing out in her singleminded and zealous way that the energy expended might have been better lent to political work. They remained friends, though after 1942 they were never again to share a house.

CHAPTER TEN

Helena at Lemon Creek

'There is a time for crying,' they said. 'But itsuka, someday, the time for laughter will come.'

– Joy Kogawa, *Itsuka*

The years on City Council were good ones for Helena, but the war changed everything – put the National Housing Act on hold, pressured the pacifist CCF to make compromises, and put strains on leadership and rank and file as they attempted to maintain a socialist stance in what seemed in those first months to be another imperialist war. In the House of Commons J.S. Woodsworth stood alone in opposition to the war, dissenting even from his own party. In the British Columbia legislature, CCF members stoutly maintained the party position: Canada should limit assistance in the war to providing economic aid. Due provision should be made for national defence, employing a volunteer militia, but there should be no conscription and Canada should send no forces overseas.

The Liberals and Conservatives hurled accusations of disloyalty against the CCF, to which CCF MLA Colin Cameron rejoined by denouncing as treason government treatment of unemployed youth. Harold Winch exhorted the government to clamp down on war profiteering and to impose an excess profits tax: 'Whose side are you on – the soldiers, the workers, the consumers, or the profiteers?'[1] German U-boats had recently torpedoed the British passenger ship *Athenia* and in the general closing of ranks against a common foe, anyone who stood apart was viewed with suspicion. When Dorothy Steeves, urging that the proper business of the legislature was human welfare, not war, took aim at British war policy, British imperialism, at the Empire itself, and accused Britain of being one of the wreckers of the League of Nations, there were cries of 'Shame, shame!' and the premier warned against treason. According to *The Federationist,* Conservative Herbert Anscomb declared that she should be whipped 'so that she could not sit down.'[2]

At the September provincial council meeting, Helena supported the CCF national policy on the war. However, she proposed a resolution expressing admiration for 'the courageous stand' of their leader in the House of Commons in holding firm to his pacifist principles. In this political climate of tension and distrust, she ran for re-election and was defeated by fewer than three hundred votes. Her CCF running mate, Alfred Hurry, was also defeated, so the CCF was no longer represented on City Council. Helena's personal defeat was blamed by some on her unfortunate remark at a Finance Committee meeting a year earlier, when plans for the visit of King George VI and Queen Elizabeth were being discussed. Helena objected to the idea of the city paying for the celebration. The *Sun* quoted Helena: 'We shouldn't be responsible for putting on a circus from which others benefit,' she declared. 'Let the people who benefit by the show pay for it.' Alderman DeGraves jumped to his feet. 'If you think entertaining the King and Queen is putting on a circus you've got another think coming,' he yelled.[3] In the ensuing furore, 'circus' became confirmed as Helena's word, though whether or not the *Sun* report was accurate we do not know. 'Circus Charge Cause of Row,' headlined the *Province*. In vain Helena protested that it was Alderman De Graves who had used the word 'circus.' In vain she protested that she was not disloyal: 'The King and Queen are very nice people and the idea of their travelling through Canada is a very nice one indeed,' she offered, propitiating, but she stuck to her guns.[4] 'The whole matter hinges on the financial situation ... not on the fitness of the visit,' she insisted. The CPR and CNR, jointly operating the just-completed Hotel Vancouver, would benefit enormously from the celebrations as tourists flocked to the city to witness the event. So would other hotel owners and merchants. Let them pay for the celebration; the city could endorse the visit without giving financial support.[5]

The incident was distressing for Helena, for she was a monarchist at heart and warmed to the humanity of the King and Queen. 'That is one of the chief reasons why the British throne stands as impregnable as it is,' she declared when the royal couple arrived the following May.[6] Helena was working for a new social order to replace the capitalist system, but she was confidently expecting this to happen without creating any cracks in the rock-solid British Empire. In one of her reports for the CCF Economic Planning Commission, she pointed 'with justifiable pride to the fact that in a perfectly constitutional manner, and within the British Empire, a Labor government is enacting the most progressive social legislation in the world.'[7]

On such matters Helena wore blinkers: it was immoral for the people to be given a 'circus' when they had no bread. She had been similarly rigid about proposals to spend $275 on the purchase of one of Captain Vancouver's letters and to send a civic representative to the Portland Annual Rose Show. At a time when Vancouver was preoccupied with the post office sit-down strike and its violent conclusion, she believed that the city's financial priority was to feed and shelter the unemployed. She 'almost snorted' at the proposal to have Christmas music played in Victory Square, 'declaring if there was a little more action and a little less sentiment "we might get somewhere in creating peace on earth".'[8] Standing up against the popular and appealing was not very politic, but then she always scorned expediency and never catered to the voters.

Helena's unpolitic position on the budget for the royal visit alienated some voters, but the main reason for her defeat was the unfavourable impression the CCF members in the legislature were making because of their policy on Canadian participation in the war. Dorothy Steeves's inflammatory speech in the legislature prompted the *Sun* to ask if the CCF was supporting democracy or tyranny in this war.[9] CCF journalist Betty Kerr reported that the climate had become distinctly chilly in the Local Council of Women meetings. At one meeting a few days after the outbreak of war, LCW members adopted a resolution affirming loyalty to the British Empire and urging the banning of anti-British propaganda. '"Let them come out in the open," shouted the mover of the motion ... glaring in the direction of the CCF, WIL [Women's International League for Peace and Freedom] and Women's New Era League.' Betty Kerr continues, 'The lady was not sure that some of us who are not violently in favour of our sons killing other women's sons, did not have a few bombs in our pockets right there.'[10] The atmosphere in the LCW had been far different in 1937, when Helena first ran for alderman. Then the LCW was friendly towards her and the CCF, supporting her wholeheartedly and reminding its members to vote for her. In wartime Vancouver, however, the women viewed her as someone not altogether to be trusted, and so she lost the widespread support of women's organizations.[11]

The Non-Partisan Association took advantage of this climate of suspicion to further alienate voters from the CCF. Two days before the election, its cleverly worded half-page advertisement appeared: 'Believing that party politics are subversive of good civic government ...,' it began; and concluded, 'Politics have no place in city government, and these citizens are united in this conviction.'[12] Then followed the list of citizens, including such leading members of the establishment as General Victor W. Odlum, Leon Ladner, Sherwood Lett, Stanley S. McKeen, A. deB. McPhillips, Colonel Victor Spencer, and W.H. Malkin, providing ample witness to the conservative partisanship of the NPA.

The NPA accused CCF candidates of taking orders directly from their party, and quoted the minutes of a CCF city convention to prove it: 'The regional committee of the CCF is empowered to supervise and direct all civic representatives as to the policy to be pursued in civic affairs.'[13] NPA candidate Jack Price, former CCF MLA, cited this statement at a public election meeting in the West End. He was one of those who had broken with the CCF in the Connell split of 1936. Now here he was, proving beyond any doubt his new allegiance by turning the obvious and innocent into damaging slurs and innuendos. At another election meeting, CCF candidates had to defend themselves against accusations that they had communist sympathies. At a third meeting, Alderman Corey, referring to the Connell split, said the better element of the CCF had defected at that time. Helena and Susie Clark, who was defending her Park Board seat, jumped to their feet at once to object to this slander. Unperturbed, Corey declared that CCF aldermen who had not followed the party line had been 'liquidated.' In fact, CCF policy was nothing more politically devious than low-rental housing and help for the unemployed. Against this kind of opposition, Helena could not hold her seat on Council, nor were any of the other CCF candidates elected. She placed sixth, but it was some comfort that Jack Price placed seventh.[14]

Helena tried to regain her seat in 1940 and again in 1941, without success. In 1941, besides the housing issue she campaigned for more sanitary disposal of garbage. Garbage used to be delivered to dumps within the city, one on the east side on False Creek flats and another at Broadway and Keith Drive. Killing the rats infesting the dumps was a favourite after-school sport for neighbourhood boys, who took aim with rocks and BB guns. Householders in the area surrounded their houses with rat traps, which the captured rats carried off if the traps were not spiked down. Helena and her running mate, Susie Clark, were photographed standing atop a thirty-foot-high dump. 'What a mess!' exclaimed Helena. This was good copy, and the *News-Herald* duly reported her words: 'An incinerator is the ultimate solution ... But first we must take steps to clean up rat infestation here and the breeding places and find a way to dispose of garbage so the rats can't breed.'[15] She spoke knowledgeably about the possibility of using incinerators and recycling the heat thus generated. City Council attacked the *News-Herald* as alarmist. 'Scare headlines,' said Alderman Worthington. 'Terrible propaganda for the city,' exclaimed Alderman Buscombe. 'No different than in any other city,' grumbled Alderman Jones.[16]

With four aldermen to be elected, Helena placed fifth, losing by a substantial margin to Jack Price, who was successful on his third try.[17] This was her last bid for civic office.

Released from her Council duties by her election defeat in December 1939, Helena once again gave all her time to the CCF, taking on the job of chairing the Organization Committee. Politics was her work, in or out of office. She had, of course, continued to serve on the provincial executive of the party while alderman. In the new year she had no time for regrets about her defeat at the polls. Mackenzie King had called an election for March 1940, and she was immediately swept up in the CCF election campaign. The Organization Committee had to plan the routing of election speakers throughout the province and decided that Helena herself should go on a speaking tour to support Bert Herridge, CCF candidate for West Kootenay riding, which the Conservatives had held since 1925.

Transportation was a problem, however. Although the CCF did have an old automobile for driving around British Columbia on organizational work, clearly one vehicle could not serve so large a territory during an election campaign. Organizer Ernest Winch solved this problem by basing Helena's itinerary on that of a travelling optometrist, who offered to take two CCF speakers as passengers on his circuit through the southern interior of British Columbia. His van was fitted up as an office, with an assistant, Miss Ingram, in charge, so there could not have been much room for Helena and her young colleague, Olive Greer, later Vailleau, who was to speak on behalf of CCF youth.[18]

Optometrist McLeod, with Miss Ingram and the CCF campaigners, started out at noon on 25 February. The old Yale highway was deep in snow, and they did not reach Hope, 155 kilometres away, until four o'clock. Leaving Hope and entering the Fraser Canyon, they drove that night along the narrow road at 25 kilometres an hour through a heavy snowstorm, scarcely able to see the edge of the canyon precipice, which in places dropped 250 metres to the river below. After Boston Bar, the road climbed steeply up Jackass Mountain, bringing them at half past ten to Lytton, at the junction of the Fraser and Thompson Rivers. Here they stayed the night, and in the morning drove 40 kilometres along the Thompson to Spences Bridge, where they began their crossing of the high Thompson Plateau in the Coast Mountains.

Their ultimate destination was the West Kootenays of southeastern British Columbia, where they would set up campaign headquarters in the smelter towns of Trail on the Canada-U.S. border and nearby Rossland, where a large number of the workers from the Consolidated Mining and Smelting Company lived. These towns were shut off from easy commerce with the southwestern part of the province by the Coast Mountains and, beyond them, the Monashee Range. The Hope-Princeton highway through the Coast Mountains had not yet been built, and the road through Alison Pass, which would give ready access to southeastern British Columbia, had not yet been blasted out. The road to the towns of the West Kootenays turned eastward at the border town of Osoyoos in the Okanagan Valley, east of the Coast Mountains,

and ran along the Canada-U.S. border and over the Monashees. The problem was to reach Osoyoos. The route lay north from Hope to Lytton and
Spences Bridge, then doubled back south southeasterly to Keremeos,
where, only 50 kilometres from the border, it turned north once more to
Penticton. Here it turned south again to reach Osoyoos at last. Between
Osoyoos and Rossland, the Monashees still had to be crossed, but at least
the route all lay in an easterly direction.

From Lytton on, wherever Mr. McLeod stopped to set up shop, CCF
supporters held a public meeting, usually with Helena as one of the
speakers, joined from time to time by a CCF candidate. Ernest Winch had
done well by his campaigners: they always found the local people
waiting, the beds turned down, the kettle boiling for tea. The local hall
was usually booked, but once a garage had to serve as a meeting place;
another time, a barbershop. Small meetings were arranged in friendly
living rooms. A collection was always taken, and Helena reminded her
audience that the CCF depended on the small donations of ordinary folk
like themselves to finance its campaign. Unlike the old-line parties, the
CCF did not receive any money from big business. Olive kept a diary of
the trip: 'Feb. 27, Tues. Left Merritt 8:30 A.M. and reached Princeton at
11:15. It was a rough trip, cold and snow. Helena and I addressed a splendid audience [about] 100 present. Collection was $9.05. Tea with James
Berryman. This was a nice town.' With a generous audience, she might
have added, for in those days, when bread was five cents a loaf, ten cents
per person was a good collection.

At Grand Forks, only some sixty-five kilometres from their destination, heavy snow made the road impassable. They had to detour into the
United States, south along the Kettle River, then north again along the
Columbia River. They crossed into Canada again near Trail, which
they reached on 2 March.

The hardy little band spent two weeks in the Trail-Rossland area. Mr.
McLeod tested eyes and prescribed glasses with the help of Miss
Ingram, while Helena and Olive addressed audiences, appealing to the
Italian miners and smelter workers who lived in the Gulch at Trail or to
the ranchers and farmers on the neighbouring bench lands. In the six
months since the beginning of the war with Germany, the true extent of
Hitler's megalomaniac ambitions were not yet understood by the countries who had taken up arms against him. Accordingly, Helena on the
CCF hustings qualified her support of the war. 'We have received no opinion from either the Chamberlain government in England nor the King
Government in Ottawa with regard to what the present war is being
fought for,' she told a capacity Rossland audience. The war was not the
only issue in this campaign, she went on. Canada had domestic problems to deal with that required the adopting of new social legislation.

The old-age pension should be increased and made available at age sixty-five instead of at seventy. Unemployment was still a major problem: an unemployment insurance act should be legislated. Civil liberties at home were in danger of being violated by possible implementation of the War Measures Act. And what of the veterans when they returned home? What provision was to be made for their health and welfare?[19]

After that crowded public meeting, Helena and Olive spoke to ten eager women in the nearby village of Warfield. On 6 March Olive wrote in her diary: 'We hiked from Warfield to Rossland and were given a ride by a policeman. Tea in K.P. [Knights of Pythias] Hall with over 66 people present. A very fine affair. Afterwards we went to a free dance put on by the Liberals. Gerry McGeer arrived at 11 P.M.'

After two weeks of this kind of campaigning, they left the Kootenays, returning to Grand Forks by way of the United States and then west through the Canadian border towns of Greenwood, Midway, Rock Creek, Bridesville, and Osoyoos, then north to Oliver. Leaving Olive to follow her own itinerary, Helena went on through the Okanagan with Mr. McLeod and Miss Ingram, and spoke at Penticton and then Vernon, where Olive arrived by bus from Kelowna. Helena met her at the bus stop and 'hustled me off to deWeile's for lunch.' At Kamloops the night before the election, Helena and Olive addressed a crowd of seven hundred, after which CCF provincial leader Harold Winch, black eyes flashing, brought the campaign to an enthusiastic close with impassioned rhetoric. Election day brought disappointment, however. Mackenzie King was returned to office with a large majority – over 50 per cent of the national vote. He had, after all, borrowed parts of the CCF platform on social legislation, including unemployment insurance. The CCF won only eight seats, and West Kootenay was not one of them: the Conservative incumbent, W.K. Esling, retained the seat he had held for twenty years. Bert Herridge obtained six thousand more votes than in 1935, but he did not win West Kootenay until 1945, when Esling stepped down.

Olive's diary concludes: 'March 28. The drive down the Fraser Canyon was breath-takingly beautiful and we enjoyed every minute of it. It was quite a contrast to the slow treacherous trip we had made on the way up. Home by 5 P.M.'

After the high of the election campaign, Helena returned to her everyday work on the provincial executive, but now she was no longer drawing an alderman's salary and had to look to the future: she could not live on her savings indefinitely. Then, too, the fall of France and Belgium and the evacuation of Allied troops from Dunkirk in the summer of 1940 made Canadians aware of the chilling threat of fascism to western democracy. Under the National Resources Mobilization Act of 1940, all Canadians were required to register and give an account of their education, training, and employment experience, and Helena indicated in her completed questionnaire, dated August 1940, not only that she wanted paid employment but also that she was now willing to contribute to Canada's war effort. Women were flocking by the thousands into war industries and into every other sector of the economy, and she wanted to be one of them, though perhaps not a Rosie the Riveter. She therefore considered her responses carefully.

She said that she was unemployed and had not worked at all in the last twelve months. This was not true: she had been an alderman drawing a salary of $135 a month in 1939, but evidently wishing to maintain her anonymity, perhaps not wanting to be identified as the contentious former Alderman Gutteridge, she merely spoke of experience in 'civic administration' and in 'labour organisation.' Then, too, for a public figure she was an unusually self-effacing person: she tended to use the passive voice in her writing and in news reports had always avoided the pronoun 'I.' On the National Registration form she gave her year of birth as 1881 instead of 1879 as on her birth certificate, making herself a more employable fifty-nine instead of sixty-one. For some mischievous reason, or perhaps simply because of its prestigious associations, she gave her mother's birthplace as Oxford instead of London. Besides, Oxford went well with Hampshire, her father's place of birth. The Gutteridges, you know, country people. One thinks also of how she changed her name from Nell to Helen to Helena. She announced two regular occupations – 'secretary' and 'farming' – and two other skills – 'organization' and 'sewing,' not tailoring. With her characteristic willingness to pitch in and help, she also said that she would accept special occupational training in 'anything needed.' 'Do your circumstances permit you to serve in the present national crisis, by changing your present occupation to some other for which you are qualified?' 'Yes,' answered Helena, and she could move away from home if necessary. As it turned out, she would indeed be called on to serve after Japan attacked Pearl Harbor in 1941.[20]

For the time being, however, Helena continued her political work. When she was appointed provincial organizer in the fall of 1940, the CCF clubs were in a slump, with membership totalling only twenty-five hundred across British Columbia. Some clubs, she reported, were 'mere skeletons,' District Councils were 'dead or dying.' A different form of organization was necessary. She divided the province into regions, each with a director appointed by the Organization Committee. Within each region, the provincial electoral constituencies were in charge of a district organizer. Each constituency in turn had its own divisions, with chairpersons appointed by a local district organizer. Thus small rural communities took direction from local people whose job it was to see that a CCF club took root and developed. Meanwhile, the Organization Committee in Vancouver, at the centre of the operation, kept tabs on the progress being made. One imagines Field Marshal Helena with a map of British Columbia on the wall of her office, pinpointing each new village or town where a CCF club marked a gain in political territory. Sometimes the population was so sparse that a CCF club could not be maintained. Helena therefore created a member-at-large category, allowing individuals the privileges of club membership.[21]

'It is tiresome work,' she acknowledged. But she rolled up her sleeves and applied herself to the prosaic organizational task, distributing application books, leaflets, and registration forms, and providing instructions and general assistance. She was on occasion a little too zealous. The secretary of the Saanich CCF Council certainly thought so. Helena went over his head in her efforts to organize his area. He took umbrage at this high-handed action and asked her to consult him in the future.[22]

Meanwhile national organizer Grant MacNeil had planned to travel through parts of British Columbia to sign up members-at-large, but foul weather and punishing roads were insurmountable obstacles. Instead he concentrated on breathing life into the faltering clubs. Harold Winch had visited West Kootenay towns on his way back from a Regina conference and encouraged the formation of a number of new clubs.

The results of the organizing campaign were gratifying. 'New life is again arising in the Movement, particularly outside Vancouver,' Helena assured the March 1941 convention. Vancouver, however, was still 'very stagnant.' The convention gave her a vote of thanks in appreciation of her work and 'for her stimulating organizational suggestions.'[23]

In the meantime, the party structure in British Columbia underwent its own reorganization, becoming more centralized. All the separate committees were subsumed under one umbrella, an elected Administration Committee of three, each of whom had the ultimate responsibility for half a dozen committees and committee chairmen. In 1941 Helena was one of that grand triumvirate, with Reginald Bullock and chairman Wallis Lefeaux. Helena took charge of Economic Relations, Speakers and Radio, Agriculture, Publicity, Municipal Affairs, and the Hostess Committee. She also ran as a candidate for Point Grey in the provincial election of 1941. One of the main CCF issues in that campaign was the old-age pension. The CCF demanded that the provincial government pressure Ottawa to increase the amount of the pension from $20 to $30 a month and to lower the qualifying age from seventy years to sixty-five. To eke out her own scanty income, Helena resorted to going door to door in the 1941 census. She also found work as a stenographer.[24]

On 7 December 1941 the war took an unexpected turn with Japan's

bombing of the American naval base at Pearl Harbor. This event shat-
tered the lives of a west coast ethnic group that unluckily was of the same
race as the attackers. Canada declared war on Japan; Hong Kong,
Malaysia, and the Philippines capitulated; and 'All BC Coast Attack Area,'
'Prince Rupert Bristles with Defense Units,' headlined the *Sun*. Premier
Pattullo himself announced the air raid signals. One Saturday night in
June 1942, a Japanese submarine was reported to have lobbed shells at
the wireless station at Estevan Point on the west coast of Vancouver
Island, creating little tremors of alarm. This was an isolated incident and
public alarm was unjustified: the Canadian military high command
judged actual invasion a virtual impossibility.[25]

In any case, Japan was the enemy, not the Japanese in Canada.
Although the Canadian military command had, even before Pearl Harbor, assured the federal government that the Japanese living in British
Columbia – the Langley strawberry farmers, the Steveston fishermen,
the Powell Street shopkeepers, the United Church and Anglican cler-
gymen – posed no threat to national security, an anti-Oriental element
long active in the province stirred public apprehension about the danger of fifth-column activity and warned of possible rioting if the
Japanese were not removed from the coast. The federal government did
nothing to dispel these fears. Indeed, some Liberal MPs, led by Vancouver
Centre's Ian Mackenzie, urged the federal government to take immediate
action. Alderman Halford Wilson (Helena's old adversary) and his
Pacific Coast Security League with the vociferous cries of hunter against
hunted also played on the fears of British Columbians. The federal
government did not reassure people that any fears of invasion were
unfounded.[26]

On 16 January 1942 the Canadian government, implementing the War
Measures Act, passed Order-in-Council PC 365 establishing 'protected
areas' from which enemy aliens could be excluded. Shortly afterwards,
one such area was declared – a hundred-mile-wide zone from the
Pacific coast to the Cascades. At first, in January, only Japanese nation-
als were removed, but soon the distinction between them and Canadian-
born Japanese was abandoned. On 24 February Order-in-Council PC 1486
was passed, authorizing the expulsion of all Japanese, whether Canadian citizens or not. The British Columbia Security Commission (BCSC)
was then formed to carry out the expulsion and to relocate this population of twenty-one thousand uprooted people.[27]

Although its policy had always favoured equal rights for all races and
religions, the CCF agreed with the decision to evacuate, 'for reasons of
defense' and for the safety of the Japanese themselves, who were
believed to be potential victims of an uncontrollable racist backlash. One
commentator suggests that the CCF was also driven by 'the exigencies

of practical politics.' It is hard to believe that the movement dedicated to bringing about a more just world could have been thus influenced, yet even J.S. Woodsworth, 'the Saint in Politics,' had been sometimes hard put to maintain his absolute position of fairness on the Oriental question. Dorothy Steeves and Colin Cameron, neither of them known for taking pragmatic positions, gave their approval. Harold Winch and Grant MacNeil were members of a Citizens' Defence Committee with representation from across Vancouver's political and economic spectrum. Both Winch and MacNeil agreed with the committee's appeal to the federal government for immediate and total removal of the Japanese population from the coast. (Although the majority of those expelled were Canadian citizens and are rightly called Japanese Canadians, in order not to exclude those who were not officially citizens, I use the term 'Japanese' to include both groups.)[28]

Grant MacNeil was appointed secretary of the British Columbia Security Commission. He thought that the Japanese had to be moved for their own protection, and according to one CCF spokesperson, accepted the position with the commission so that he could help make sure the Japanese were treated fairly.[29] According to Hilda Kristiansen, he was the one who offered Helena a position as welfare worker among the displaced Japanese. Helena was not on the provincial executive in 1942, not having been re-elected to the CCF Administration Committee, and so was not a party to the policy meetings on the question of the expulsion. We do not know her stand on this question, though she probably would not have taken the job had Grant MacNeil not urged humanitarian treatment.

The offer came at an opportune time because she was no longer at the very centre of CCF decision making. Not that she was at loose ends by any means. She had been appointed to head the party's Municipal Committee and as such still attended provincial council meetings. She was also helping to organize the Vancouver Women's School for Citizenship, drafting a constitution with Laura Jamieson. However, she had to earn her living as well, and as a welfare worker she would be able to do so in a more meaningful way than as a stenographer. She therefore welcomed the opportunity to be of humanitarian service to the victimized Japanese, with whom she sympathized. She could also be of service to Canada at war, for by now the magnitude of the fascist threat to the free world had brought the reluctant CCF on side.[30]

In the spring and summer of 1942, temporarily interned under execrable conditions in former livestock stalls on the Pacific National Exhibition grounds of Hastings Park, the Japanese began to be shipped by train to the interior of British Columbia, where the Security Commission had set up 'relocation centres' in and around five little ghost towns in

the Kootenays – New Denver, Slocan, Greenwood, Kaslo, and San-
don. A sixth camp, Tashme, was built a few kilometres from Hope on
a six-hundred-acre farm in a valley in the Cascade Mountains. Some fifteen hundred people who had the resources to be independent of the
Security Commission resettled elsewhere, also outside the protected
coastal area. Even though these relocation centres were not enclosed by
barbed wire, the Japanese understandably experienced them as internment camps: by the sweeping provisions of order-in-council, the Security Commission had full control of their lives, dispossessing them of
property, limiting their movements, subjecting them to inspection,
scrutinizing their bank accounts, and censoring their mail. And their very
isolation contributed to the feeling of being imprisoned.

By the end of October 1942, nearly twelve thousand Japanese, most
of them Canadian citizens, had been moved to the Kootenays. However,
only short-term provision had been made for housing them, abandoned hotels and shops offering rudimentary shelter in some of the
towns. Not until 1 July did the Security Commission announce that it
would build houses, thus permitting the men who had been sent to road
camps earlier to be reunited with their families. In the meantime, tents
were set up to accommodate several thousand evacuees in the Slocan
area, and these unfortunate victims of racial prejudice and war camped
in the outdoors.[31]

By autumn hundreds of houses had been built, row upon row hastily
put down in a farmer's field or abandoned orchard, without electricity
or indoor plumbing. They were rough, three-roomed cabins, six by ten
metres, built out of 'green' shiplap, with no interior finishing wall.
Two families were assigned to each cabin, sharing 140 square metres of
living space.[32]

The federal government gradually evolved a policy for dealing with
the needs of this displaced population. The plan was to create self-supporting communities where a man could earn a living for his family by
logging, cutting firewood, and working on the roads in nearby towns.
By the fall of 1942, however, five thousand uprooted people were more
or less camping in the Slocan area alone. With such an influx of people
with so few resources of their own, unemployment, poverty, and sickness inevitably became problems.[33] The BC Security Commission was fortunate in obtaining the services of two social workers of great
compassion and intelligence to supervise the welfare program. Highly
regarded today as a pioneer in the field of public social welfare, Amy
Leigh in 1942 accepted a leave of absence from her job as director of welfare for Vancouver to set up the welfare system for the camps. Her friend
Martha Moscrop, today remembered by social workers for initiating the
practice of in-service training, carried on as general supervisor, direct-

ing the welfare managers hired for each camp.[34] Vancouver Anglican Church workers Grace Tucker and Margaret Foster followed their Japanese parishioners to Slocan; Grace acted as welfare manager. A deaconess in the church, she had lived and studied in Japan for three years, learning the language and customs in order to better serve the Japanese in Canada. She was 'horrified' when the expulsion was announced: 'We never thought it would happen in Canada.'[35]

In May 1942 Helena resigned from the CCF Municipal Committee. She may have begun work among the interned Japanese in Vancouver as early as the summer of 1942. The evidence for this conjecture lies in a story about a teapot that Hilda Kristiansen said Helena set great store by because a Japanese friend or client had given it to her, presumably before she left for the Kootenays because she later sent to Vancouver for it. In August she attended her last CCF provincial council meeting, and in the fall left the coast for Slocan, where she reported to Grace Tucker. When the houses at Lemon Creek were ready, Helena was appointed welfare manager there and took full charge from the beginning of 1943, when Lemon Creek became a separate project with its own administration.[36]

The Lemon Creek Relocation Project was one of three interior housing settlements built for the Japanese near the town of Slocan, sixty kilometres north of Trail in the Selkirk Mountains. It was located about eleven kilometres south of Slocan, in a little valley between the Valhalla Range of the Selkirks on the west and the Slocan and Kokanee Ranges on the east. Forests of cedar and fir, jackpine and tamarack rise on either side to the tops of the mountain ridges. The creek has its source in the waters flowing out of Kokanee Glacier. The scenery in this mountain valley is magnificent, but one can readily believe that the sense of isolation might become oppressive for people from the West Coast, like the Japanese, or like Helena herself, who were accustomed to city life or easy commerce with it.[37] Today a paved highway penetrates the mountain fastnesses of the Slocan Valley, but in those days the main road connecting southeastern British Columbia with the West Coast stopped at Grand Forks and became a narrow, winding gravel road following the southern branch of the Canadian Pacific Railway through the forest to Nelson and Slocan. The main link with Vancouver was not the road but the railway, the Kettle Valley passenger line of nostalgic memory. The train left Vancouver in the morning and arrived in Slocan the next morning, an overnight trip of some twenty hours.

Half a century later, the traveller seeking the past in Slocan finds scarcely any sign of the Japanese presence during the war, and upon inquiry learns that two Japanese, perhaps three, are still living in the town. One of them is an old woman in a crumbling two-storey house behind a high barricade of stove wood, protection against the Kootenay winter. An ancient crone, she hobbles to the door to greet an inquiring researcher. She cannot speak much English, but thanks her visitor with a courtesy truly humbling. Townspeople remember the Japanese kindly, saying they got along well with them. A local historian recalls with affection the young Japanese Canadian girl who, as a nanny, became part of the family. A Scandinavian old woman grieves again for another such a girl, a dear friend who committed suicide, and the retelling brings tears to her eyes. Such tragedies, testimony to personal suffering, did occur, even though Slocan accepted these displaced people in a kindly way. The tourist information centre is housed in a building modelled precisely on the six-by-ten metre shacks that housed the Japanese, a commemorative marker charged with meaning, and the attendant knows the history of the original houses and is eager to tell it.[38]

The Lemon Creek Relocation Project was razed a long time ago. On the site in 1986 stood a modern post-and-beam holiday lodge with an Emily Carr print in the washroom, an Al Purdy poem in large script on the dining room wall, and a book on the art of bonsai on the bookshelf. The outside world has come to this valley. The proprietor of Lemon Creek Lodge, an articulate and discriminating man, offers a choice of Dijon or plain mustard on ham and, after a friendly lecture on the art of pouring wine, brings out an old newspaper photograph of the Lemon Creek Japanese Relocation Project. Yes, the lodge is located on the site of the housing project – right there at the back of the photo, and to the left on what was Kootenay Street. In fact, he can show you the remains of one of the little gardens. He takes his guest outside in the hot sun and shows, with a certain modest reverence, a patch of wild rose, soopalallie, and kinnikannik enclosed by a circle of large stones. He has added two pottery Japanese lanterns and a few small trees, including some bonsai evergreens: everything in character, nothing to desecrate the little shrine to the stoicism and dignity of this uprooted people. By a strange irony, as a child in the Manila that was ravaged by the Japanese and bombed by the Allies, he himself has experienced the irrational and violent dislocations of war.[39] His name is Keith Kessler.

When Helena arrived in Lemon Creek, she found a shack town laid out on a gravelly field, some 250 rough wooden dwellings row on row, separated by 'streets' named, in a hopeful, conciliatory gesture, after trees and flowers. The main street was Gilead. The Japanese population numbered some 1,800, nearly half of them children, and facilities and services were primitive. The mess tents had been closed down before families could feed themselves. Grace Tucker was summoned from Slocan to cope with the resulting emergency, and she recalls the night she spent writing welfare cheques for people who had no pots and pans to cook with.[40] Water was being trucked in; all the water for bathing, laundry, dishes, and cooking had to be heated on small stoves serving two families in each cabin, the green firewood burning fitfully and providing scarcely any heat. Eventually water was piped to taps on the streets, but there was never running water in the houses. Outside toilets had been dug – a total of 127 serving 534 families. The night was lit by candles or coal oil: no electricity and the Security Commission did not propose to supply any. Conditions did improve eventually. Straw palliasses were gradually replaced by mattresses. A very small emergency hospital, ten metres square, was built, and a first-aid man placed in charge. Three bathhouses were constructed on the Japanese model, a little larger than the hospital. The schools were wired for electricity.[41]

The elementary school was not completed until the spring of 1943. In the meantime, children attended classes in shifts, in some of the little three-room dwellings that served as schoolrooms. No provision at all was contemplated for the education of high school students. However, a parent-teacher's group 'bore the full cost of building a two-room high school,' and the Women's Missionary Society of the United Church staffed and financed both it and a kindergarten.[42] The Buddhist Mission established a temple: two houses joined together with a small porch at the entrance. The Japanese built themselves a log shack for their chess club. Local merchants established themselves in the vicinity and employed Japanese sales clerks.

Helena's first winter in Lemon Creek was the very worst the Slocan Valley had seen in years. The first snow came on Hallowe'en night, and heavy snowfalls soon stalled trucks carrying firewood. Temperatures dipped to minus six degrees Celsius. Water pipes froze. The unlined houses with spaces between the boards could not keep out the cold, which was so intense, even indoors, that it was impossible to sleep, even under great piles of blankets. By morning the frost would be halfway up the inside of the walls:

> Icicles dripped between the windows and nails inside the house were coated with frost. Unless we hit the door with a hammer to loosen the ice [said one Japanese householder], it would not open. The moisture dripped in every room. Among the shelves, inside the boxes and 'neath the bed. The puddles froze and melted as regularly as day and night. The bottom of the mattresses became green.[43]

Helena lived in the staff dormitory along with other members of the administrative staff and the RCMP constable. They had a pleasant lounge, comfortable beds, and good meals served in the farmhouse where Lemon Creek supervisor James Burns lived with his wife. Once Helena had gotten used to the rigours of the climate and the sound of coyotes howling at night, she did not suffer physical hardship, but the emotional climate was harsh. Donald Ewing, a Lemon Creek High School teacher, recalls that, being a conscientious objector, he had to be rather careful about what he said at the dinner table in the hearing of James Burns, for whom the presence of conscientious objectors in his camp was almost a 'personal affront.' Once, when Ewing expressed an opinion on Vancouver municipal politics, Burns allowed his pent-up resentment to escape, and in his Scottish accent 'stormed over his dinner that I was the last person who should express *any* opinions.'[44] As a condition of her appointment, Helena herself had agreed not to bring her socialist views to her job and not to discuss the CCF.

As welfare manager, she was exposed daily to the emotional trauma of a population of displaced people under constant surveillance and regulation. The RCMP had its office at the gates and kept tabs on every Japanese inhabitant. Remembering the three years of her childhood spent in the New Denver settlement, Shizuye Takashima wrote, 'I stare at the words 'R.C.M.P. Office' all in red. Their power seems to come through the very walls.' That power was conferred on quite ordinary men who were probably in their private lives kindly fathers or uncles. Donald Ewing says that the Mountie in charge of Lemon Creek was 'a mild-mannered sort who seemed almost embarrassed at the kind of regulations he had to enforce ... A letter to another Japanese in a camp just up the valley had to go to Toronto for censoring before being delivered.' All Japanese leaving by bus or any other means had to show their pass to the officer at the gate. Another Lemon Creek High School teacher, Joe Grant, recalls how he felt about these security measures: 'When someone told of seeing a Mountie shining a flashlight in the passengers' faces at night looking for Oriental features, I felt the first twinges of what it must be like to live in a police state.'[45]

The Mountie stationed briefly at Lemon Creek in 1943 and on regular duty in 1944 was Constable John William (Jack) Duggan, a tall, fresh-faced Irish-Canadian from Toronto in his early twenties, who played baseball with his charges without detriment to his surveillance duties, which, he says, did not require him to shine a flashlight in passengers' faces. The only time he really had to exert any kind of heavy authority was during 'the rice strike,' when some of the single men protested they were not getting a fair allocation of rice. Otherwise, he got along well with the Japanese, and fifty years later attended a Lemon Creek reunion to renew old friendships, which he still valued.[46]

The Japanese cooperated with the Mounties, for *enryo* (restraint) and *gaman* (forbearance) were ingrained attitudes. '*Shikata-ga-nai,*' they reiterated: it can't be helped.[47] Anger must be concealed. The Issei, born in

Japan, had passed on to their Canadian-born children, the Nisei, the respect for authority they themselves had learned in childhood, but neither group could conceal the unexpressed resentment they felt at being driven from their homes and reduced to poverty. They formed committees, demanded improved conditions, fulminated against Burns's 'ridiculous narrow mind' and 'dictator-like attitude,' and asked to have him replaced.[48] He, of course, servant of inflexible bureaucracy, was only carrying out instructions. One woman recalls how she appealed to him for a travel permit to allow her mother to return to Lethbridge, Alberta, to continue the medical treatments she had started there under the auspices of the Security Commission. Burns had to authorize this journey by obtaining a letter from the Lethbridge doctor in charge, but the letter did not come, and did not come. Finally the distraught daughter wrote directly to Lethbridge, and for such unregulated behaviour Burns harshly rebuked her. She stormed out of his office and slammed the door.[49]

Many younger children loved camp life, so different from the city, but the older ones absorbed the tensions in the camp and expressed their confusion and insecurity by being difficult in the classroom. Lemon Creek High School had 'some of the toughest boys of all the centres,' recalls Donald Ewing, 'and they got away with a lot before settling down to being good students.' The principal, Gertrude Hamilton, 'had a big heart and a stern manner,' but was no match for troublesome teenagers who wanted to know what was the use of a Japanese Canadian getting an education. They well knew the attitude of the provincial government, which had, after all, made no provision for their education after elementary school.[50] Some children were deeply unhappy. One boy simply disappeared and, never found, was presumed dead. A young girl also disappeared. Jack Duggan headed a massive search, combing the mountainside and both banks of the river for her. 'We had a bunch of men come down from New Denver and Slocan City ... Never did find her.' These tragic deaths shook the camp and plunged it into grief.[51]

Only three years earlier, the federal government had closed down the relief camps, the source of outright rebellion among unemployed youth. In the New Era League, the Vancouver Local Council of Women, and then on Vancouver City Council in the 1930s, Helena had many times taken up the problems of homeless migrants. Now she was again working on behalf of unwanted Canadians, dealing with their daily struggle to survive. As welfare manager, one of her most important tasks was to look after problems of economic hardship. Her years on City Council, and before that with the CCF Unemployment Conference, had given her valuable experience in dealing with the provincial and civic welfare systems. The welfare policy of the British Columbia Security

Commission was roughly similar. The Japanese were expected to be self-supporting as much as possible, however. The men and older boys could go out to the woods as loggers, they could saw and cut firewood for the camp, or work on construction and maintenance for 22½ to 40 cents an hour. Women could work as domestics in Slocan or as nurse's aides in the Slocan Community Hospital. With a five-day crash course in teaching supplemented by a few weeks of training in the summer, some young Japanese-Canadian high school graduates became the elementary school teachers. Twenty-two-year-old Miyo Goromaru, who had been ill with pleurisy and tuberculosis, began teaching Grades 7 and 8 without any training. Such 'inside' workers were paid $30 to $75 a month, except doctors and dentists, who were paid more.[52]

The Welfare Office was simply an upgraded regulation six-by-ten-metre dwelling adjacent to the Administration Building, with an open space between. Under a separate roof, Helena had some autonomy, which she exercised to the full. Her salary was fifteen hundred dollars a year, a generous stipend at a time when rural schoolteachers would consider themselves fortunate to be earning that much.[53] She had her own staff – two young women in the outer office with whom she soon developed a friendly rapport. Wakiko Suyama, later Kiyonaga, was twenty years old when her family was moved from Cumberland, Vancouver Island, where she had worked as a dairymaid and housekeeper. Her father, a coal miner turned logger, was sent to the road camp at Tashme. Wakiko's mother and the nine children (the eldest son lived in Japan) were among those who lived in tents in Slocan for several weeks until the houses at Lemon Creek were ready. Eventually Mr. Suyama was reunited with his family, but there were too many of them for one house; two of the brothers slept elsewhere. At first Wakiko was Grace Tucker's assistant in Slocan, where she learned her job; then she transferred to the new office at Lemon Creek to work for Helena, typing, filing, calculating maintenance allowances, writing cheques. Her pay was $50 a month, all of which she handed over to her parents. The family did not live well, but they managed somehow from one payday to the next.[54]

Twenty-five-year-old Fumiko Deshima, later Miyasaka, had been a bookkeeper and secretary for a Vancouver fruit and vegetable wholesaler at the time of the evacuation. There were eight in her family. At first she worked in the Hastings Park evacuation centre. When the time came for her to leave, she went with her ailing father to Lemon Creek to make up the required number for her sister's house: with only six occupants, it needed two more under Security Commission regulations. The wind whistled through the knotholes in the walls; the straw mattresses were soon damp and smelly. Fumiko's sister became ill, her father contracted pneumonia and died. Fumiko was fortunate to be employed in Helena's office, where she was especially useful as a caseworker. Helena judged her competent to visit families on her own. A young Nisei woman dropping in for a visit was much less intimidating than Helena herself arriving with an interpreter to inquire into family finances.[55]

In a population of some eighteen hundred, over 25 per cent needed maintenance, and Helena had to monitor the income of those who applied for it. They were eligible if they were completely destitute or if total earnings in the family or the amount of their savings were not adequate for their needs. In calculating eligibility for maintenance, she could exempt a third of a family's income as a 'reward for labour.' The food allowance was $12 a month for a single person, $23 for two, $29 for three, with $5 increments for each additional family member up to a total of eight. Families of more than eight received $3 for each additional member.[56]

In her little cubbyhole at the back of the office, wearing the inevitable small-brimmed navy-blue hat, Helena made out monthly reports in quadruplicate and compiled lists of persons on maintenance, emerging from time to time to deal with clients at the counter. She had gained a good deal of weight, and with her plump face and that comfortable merging of bosom and abdomen that comes with advancing years, looked reassuringly maternal. She wore her hair in a bun with bangs in front. Fumiko recalls that Helena had three dresses: plain navy, navy with white flowers, and a light-on-dark checked shirtwaist with short puffed sleeves.

Mothers came to ask for footwear for children or diapers for the baby. A family whose only support was a thirteen-year-old boy had no food in the house. Old people temporarily deprived of their old-age pension came to ask for glasses and false teeth. She had to investigate every case according to regulations set down by the Security Commission. Since Helena spoke no Japanese, either Fumiko or Wakiko accompanied her on family visits and interpreted for her. Following accepted social work practice for determining eligibility for maintenance, Martha Moscrop from her office in Vancouver sent out instructions: 'A study of the diet, budgeting and marketing of the maintenance families should be conducted over a period of time.'[57] This meant visiting the homes of poverty-stricken people to see what they had in their cupboards and what they were wearing for clothes, an errand that Helena found galling, to say the least.

Eventually, the massive weight of bureaucracy proved too heavy for her, accustomed as she was to being fully in charge, to dealing swiftly and directly with problems. Her relations with the administration office at Lemon Creek deteriorated, and ill feeling and impatience produced a confrontation when her office was moved into the newly renovated Administration Building, where she came under scrutiny and supervision. A visiting administrator reported: 'The Treasury complained of duplication of work between the Welfare Dept. and General office. This was corrected. Miss Gutteridge evidently feels that she is operating a separate office but no harm is now resulting. She is talking of resigning soon for personal reasons.'[58] It is safe to conjecture that, no longer able to operate freely as when she was in a separate building under her own roof, Helena became frustrated and dissatisfied – personal reason enough for wanting to leave.

The policy of the British Columbia Security Commission was essentially humane and fair-dealing, but, as might be expected in so large a government bureaucracy, was cumbersome in its operation, often sacrificing practicality to the exigencies of proper channels. Hospital referrals were a case in point. The BCSC hospital at Slocan requested James Burns to fill out Form G339-A in quadruplicate, which he, Helena, and the medical officer had to sign. Lemon Creek, however, had no doctor. It relied on its competent first-aid man, Tetsuo Kamitakahara, who was in charge of the Lemon Creek Emergency Hospital. Permission was therefore sought from the chief medical officer for Kamitakahara to sign the form. The answer came back from Colonel Lennox Arthur himself: No. They had plenty of time to summon the doctor from Slocan to decide whether the patient should be sent to hospital.[59]

Gladys Reynolds, an experienced nurse brought down from the hospital in New Denver to set up the BCSC hospital in Slocan, still bristles at the thought of the inexorable grinding of the bureaucratic wheels. Once she submitted a requisition for mustard. It came back with the query, 'What do you want it for?' 'For mustard plasters, of course!' she exploded. 'Well, be careful how you use it,' she was cautioned.[60] Forty years later, she was still angry. Angry that pregnant women approaching labour had lived in tents; that they had washed baby clothes out in the cold and, even when their houses were ready, had had to hang diapers and sleepers inside to dry. Angry that the RCMP had been everywhere, that the men in the Security Commission had 'treated the Japanese like prisoners.' Angry that everyone had had to bow to the Chief Commissioner. Grace Tucker at Slocan was just as angry when she recalled the hardships sustained by the evacuees through the rigid economies of the commission. Confronted with bureaucratic insensitivity, the Maintenance-Welfare Department of the Security Commission did its best to keep welfare matters under local control, trusting the welfare managers to apply regulations with common sense and due attention to extenuating circumstances.

Amy Leigh was particularly forthright in two cases of 'Indiscreet Spending' involving teenagers seduced by Simpson's Mail Order Catalogue. In Tashme road camp, a thirteen-year-old boy, #02199, House B 26, the sole support of a family of five, spent $7.95 of his semi-monthly paycheque of $18.07 on a pair of skates for himself from the mail order catalogue. In the same camp, a boy of eighteen, #13282, House B 32, also the working member of the family, was similarly reckless. Out of his $17.75 paycheque he spent $10.75 on an expensive windbreaker for his ten-year-old brother and $2.98 on a cheap one for himself. Their visiting caseworker supplied five pounds of rice from his own cupboard to feed the family until welfare manager Margaret Sage could arrange financial help for them. Amy Leigh had to justify her decision to help these two families in desperate need. Her memo, in quadruplicate, was sent right to the top, to Commissioner Austin C. Taylor and the chief accountant. She took a firm line, reminding the commissioner that families had not 'been specifically told that every cent of their children's earnings would be regarded as maintenance,' and demanding that such complex personal problems be dealt with locally by people in touch with the families concerned, and not by impersonal fiat at a distance of several hundred miles: 'It is my belief that the Treasury Officials should not attempt to make adjustments of any kind, where decisions regarding the eligibility for maintenance is [sic] concerned. This is the job of the Welfare Workers and must be handled by them.'[61] Austin Taylor himself is remembered for ways he found to get around regulations that hindered individual Japanese in the commission's employ from carrying out their jobs.

Given room to make decisions and act on them, Helena tangled with head office over maintenance matters. In the first months, if a woman came into the office to ask for warm winter clothing for the children or for baby diapers, Helena would write out a requisition and send it to Vancouver Central Clothing Committee, or perhaps give it to the woman to take to a local merchant. Soon, however, a memo was sent out from the chief commissioner to all welfare managers, complaining that too much clothing was being issued on their recommendation and charged to the project 'without the knowledge or approval of the Supervisors.' Henceforth, Helena would have to send every clothing order to James Burns for approval. In retrospect, the amount spent on clothing at Lemon Creek during Helena's second winter does not seem excessive. In July, August, and September 1943, when orders for winter clothes were placed, $1,405.79 was spent on clothing, including 66 pairs of boots and shoes. For a population of over eighteen hundred, this would come to 70 cents per person.[62] However, it was unreasonable not to pass clothing orders on to the supervisor for approval. So said wise old Amy Leigh in 1992, ninety-five years old and reflecting that proper channels made the world go round, after all, though of course if they got clogged you had to clear them.[63]

Letters came from head office. Wakiko remembers one in particular that was so strongly worded that Helena immediately composed a heated reply. By next morning she was able to be more judicious and toned down the wording somewhat before sending it off. Wakiko recalls that Helena did not express anger very often, though one could tell when she felt angry and frustrated by a certain look that came over her face.

In addition to handling maintenance problems, Helena also talked with the Japanese about their future, because the interior settlements were intended only as a temporary measure. The long-range policy of the Canadian government was to move the Japanese east of the Rockies or to send them back to Japan – 'voluntary repatriation,' or patriation in the case of Canadian-born Japanese. Ostensibly, they had a choice, but in fact they were under pressure to choose between difficult alternatives. The Department of Labour offered many inducements to persuade them to move east, and also applied to them National Selective Service regulations that required Canadian citizens to accept government direction to work in industries essential to the war effort. In February 1943 an order-in-council required the Japanese to move anywhere in Canada at the behest of the Department of Labour. At Lemon Creek, as in other camps, young persons reaching the age of eighteen were no longer eligible for employment by the Security Commission. There was at this time a labour shortage in Eastern Canada, but the Japanese in the camps were reluctant to move east and once again go through the trauma of resettlement. Some even tore up their National Selective Service cards and attempted to evade the RCMP.[64]

At Lemon Creek the Japanese came into the Welfare Office to talk things over with Helena. What should they do? Should they move east? Should they go to Japan? For the Nisei, born in Canada, the idea of moving to a foreign country was bewildering. Yet Eastern Canada was a continent away from their secluded mountain valley, and they were afraid to leave its security for unknown trials and challenges. Wakiko Suyama Kiyonaga recalls that Helena told them what Ontario was like, what they might expect to find there. She explained the conditions that applied to 'repatriation' and gave them what reassurance she could. In the meantime, Burns complained in his semi-monthly reports that the single men at Lemon Creek, encouraged by their parents, were refusing to take jobs in the East. According to most accounts, he was at heart a kindly man. Detailed to go back east to oversee the relocation of Lemon Creek residents, he was most concerned about his charges. A Slocan welfare worker remembers his worrying aloud: 'Oh, Miss Foster, I'm so worried about the bairns.'[65] However, on the question of eastern placement of young Japanese-Canadians, he was extremely severe:

> There is too much pampering and lack of compulsion in making these young men observe [National Selective Service] regulations. We should either deprive them of a high school education or strike their parents off the payroll of the camp in order to let their parents realize that they are subject to discipline and control.[66]

The government applied pressure to try to persuade the Japanese to accept relocation east of the Rockies. If they wanted to remain in Canada, they were told, they must prove their loyalty by accepting placement in the East. If they did not, finding employment might be difficult. The day of decision was 23 April 1945. That was when they had to declare themselves, and in the interior settlements, 81 per cent signed for repatriation. In Lemon Creek an even higher percentage did so, according to the impressions of one Nisei woman. Many, however, changed their minds before the final deadline five months later.[67]

If loyalty to the party is any indication, Helena's position on the ultimate fate of the Japanese was probably in line with CCF policy. The CCF convention in April 1943 had urged that the Japanese not be allowed to return to the West Coast because that area needed to be protected 'against the sudden return of an impoverished Japanese community under conditions provocative of disturbance.'[68] The convention further declared that they should be helped to find employment outside the protected area at prevailing rates of pay, and that their children should be given the same educational opportunities as other Canadian children. Helena is not on record as opposing the convention decision, if indeed she was able to attend the convention. After the war CCF MPs worked very hard to halt the repatriation orders and to provide restitution for confiscated property.[69]

Helena proved to be thoroughly competent in her job as welfare manager, though in her high-handed way she assumed more authority than the administration deemed appropriate for subordinate staff. Martha Moscrop nevertheless recommended that she get a pay raise of ten dollars a month after six months of service. Grace Tucker remembers Helena as a helpful colleague, judging that she got along very well with the Japanese in her care and that her achievement was all the more commendable because, unlike Grace, she came in as a complete stranger with no knowledge of the language. The welfare managers in the interior housing relocation centres held joint meetings from time to time to discuss common problems. Helena invited them all to Lemon Creek for one such meeting, arranging accommodation in the staff dormitory and making all the necessary arrangements. Grace remembers the occasion with pleasure. She shared Helena's room, with its comfortable bed and stacks of books. The weekend was beautifully sunny. The group sat outside after breakfast on Sunday morning and enjoyed watching the horses in the field.[70]

Helena is also remembered kindly by Japanese Canadians who lived at Lemon Creek. Fumiko Deshima Miyasaka says Helena was good to work for but opinionated and stubborn, and confesses to having many an argument with her. For all that, the atmosphere in the Welfare Office was pleasant. After a while the three women instituted a tea break, and, there being nothing to drink out of, Helena sent to Vancouver for six of her own china tea cups – white with a blue pattern and gold rim – and the teapot she had left behind. She was not a great socializer, Fumiko further recalls, but was not unfriendly. Fumiko cites the occasion when Helena took a visiting Chinese doctor to the *oforu* and bathed with her in the big rectangular community tub, along with other women soaking in the hot water and scrubbing one another's backs, the children splashing noisily.[71]

In Kapuskasing, Ontario, Helen Sakon, then a young mother, told a story from her Lemon Creek days:

> One day I went to the Welfare Office to register, as all of us had to do every month whose husbands were so-called enemy aliens, born in Japan.
>   Helena asked, 'When is the baby due?'
>   I replied, 'Probably today.'
>   Helena became very flustered and upset and shoved me out the door.
>   'Get on the ambulance and go to the hospital right now,' she ordered me.
>   The hospital was only seven miles away, at Slocan. But I did as she said. My daughter was born late that night.[72]

In Toronto, Miyo Goromaru, community college teacher and computer specialist, recalled that Helena bought a baseball bat for the children. In Hamilton, Ontario, Noji Murase, for whom Helena was 'the Lady with the Blue Hat,' recalled that she helped start a lending library and provided space for it in the Welfare Office, gestures in keeping with the old Helena who took such an interest in the young people at Mount Lehman.[73]

But Donald Ewing perceived another Helena. He had moved from the staff dormitory to live with colleague Joe Grant and wife Martha in their Lemon Creek house. Sometimes he would drop by for a chat with Helena in the staff lounge. They talked about various developments within the CCF; she regaled him with stories about Vancouver civic affairs, especially in relation to the CCF. He recalls her as a person who was 'coldly efficient, kind-hearted beneath a brusque exterior, but kept her clients at arms' length.'[74] The description is appropriate for the professional social worker who must maintain a certain distance between herself and her clients, but the young Donald may have been disappointed in not developing more rapport with a CCF comrade. In her midsixties and taxed by a stressful job, Helena for her part may not have had the energy to put more into the friendship. She was not an effusive person, and Donald may have looked to her for expressions of indignation and pity that were not forthcoming. Nor was she given to self-indulgent expression of emotion, but showed compassion in practical ways. Donald also remembers her as having 'a very masculine appearance' despite her conventional dress. Quite likely it was not her appearance but her authoritative bearing that struck the young man as masculine.

Jack Duggan remembered Helena as an educated, 'exceptionally well-spoken woman,' in appearance tall and 'heavy.' The word that came to mind was 'dowager' – in the sense of 'the Queen Mother.' Helena, he said, 'had a presence, make no mind,' and she 'brooked no nonsense.' 'You didn't take any liberties with her. You minded your p's and q's because no matter what position you were in [held], she was quite sharp-tongued when she chose to be.' Of course he was just 'a young whippersnapper,' but 'I'd like to think that my upbringing ... would have said elders were entitled to respect.'[75]

Helena resigned in the spring of 1945 and returned to the Coast. She gave the tea cups to Wakiko and Fumiko. 'But I would like to keep the teapot,' she said. By that time, the camp population had dwindled, a large number of the Japanese having been moved to other parts of Canada. Her two Japanese Canadian assistants opted to move east.

Fumiko joined two sisters already in Hamilton, Ontario, and applied for office work, following Helena's suggestion that she adopt an English first name to make the most of the fact that 'Deshima' did not sound typically Japanese. This little ruse did not work: employers were visibly nonplussed when she arrived for the interview, and Fumiko ended up doing domestic work and tailoring. She married James Yoshira Miyasaka when he returned from active service in India. When her daughter was sixteen, Fumiko went back to school to finish her Grade 12, worked as a factory hand, and finally found work commensurate with her abilities at McMaster University, beginning as clerk typist and rising to the position of Student Adviser in the Engineering Department. She is a devotee of Japanese dancing, and in retirement she and her husband like to waltz, tango, and two-step in their round-dancing group. They have one grandchild.

Wakiko married Kiheiji Kiyonaga and with their small child moved to Toronto, where Kiheiji found work as a spray painter for a manufacturing company. When her children were grown, Wakiko went to work for the Ontario Ministry of the Environment, rising to the position of senior secretary of the Policy Planning Branch. They have five grandchildren and live in a comfortable old brick house, where Kiheiji has discovered the secret of growing luxuriant African violets. Wakiko works as a volunteer with Japanese patients at a seniors' care facility.

Forty years after leaving Lemon Creek, Wakiko still serves tea in the white and blue china cups. 'When I think of Lemon Creek, I think of Helena Gutteridge,' she muses, and tells of Helena's generosity in lending money to a man who did not qualify for maintenance. Helena left Lemon Creek before he could repay the ten dollars. When he did repay it at the Welfare Office and Wakiko sent her the money, Helena wrote back, 'Keep it for your wedding present.'[76]

Helena's decision to leave Lemon Creek is understandable. Working as a civil servant was stressful enough, given the constraints imposed by government bureaucracy. Equally stressful was being daily witness to the mental anguish of her clients as they tried to decide between relocation or repatriation, while she herself was part of the establishment that was applying pressure on them to move away from their home province, British Columbia. As Fumiko observed, 'She'd had enough.' Yet Helena may well have remembered Lemon Creek with affection, for in a sense she caught there the echo of her Mount Lehman years, when she had been involved in the daily concerns of women and children and assumed the role of neighbourhood auntie. She kept the teapot to the end of her days, a token with a private meaning and a memento of her own efforts to seek redress for a people cruelly dispossessed by a Canada at war.

Epilogue

In 1944 Prime Minister William Lyon Mackenzie King stated in the House of Commons, 'It is a fact no person of Japanese race born in Canada has been charged with any act of sabotage or disloyalty during the years of war.'[77] In 1988, in response to the demands of Japanese Canadians, the government of Canada officially recognized the terrible wrong it had done them, and in a penitential gesture granted 'symbolic redress.'[78] The Kiyonagas and Miyasakas were among the thousands who qualified for financial restitution, one of the terms of the redress agreement. But, as Fumiko Miyasaka said, 'The money wasn't important. We appreciated the recognition that they had wronged us.'

CHAPTER ELEVEN

'The Holy Fire':
Still Burning

Born of the sun, they travelled a short while toward the sun
And left the vivid air signed with their honour.
                    – Stephen Spender, 'The Truly Great'

When Helena first returned to Vancouver from Lemon Creek, she rented a small house at 1408 West 8th Avenue, enjoying the luxury of space and freedom that it provided after three years in a dormitory. Then in 1947 she moved into Hilda and Denny Kristiansen's rooming house at 1220 Barclay Street, one of those big, three-storey houses that early in the century had graciously housed prosperous members of the West End business and social elite. She had one of the housekeeping rooms on the top floor. Rent was twelve dollars a month. It was a bright, pleasant room with a bay window overlooking the tops of the trees on Barclay Street, in the alcove, a table and gas plate for cooking. The sofa made up into a bed at night. She shared the bathroom down the hall with the other people on her floor.[1]

The Kristiansen house was in every way congenial to Helena, for it provided her with a CCF milieu, a safe harbour for her retirement years. Hilda and Denny were a young socialist couple who soon became part of her extended family, and for the rest of Helena's life their house and their family was her home. After two and a half years in an essentially hostile bureaucratic environment, Helena now had her own place, where socialism and feminism were in the air she breathed. Number 1220 Barclay was known as 'the CCF house.' Party members visiting from out of town found temporary lodging there. During conferences and conventions, CCF delegates and leading party members could be sure of a friendly welcome at Hilda and Denny's place.

Hilda Kristiansen had been a member of the CCF since she was a teenager in the party's youth movement, the Co-operative Commonwealth Youth Movement. She was the daughter of George and Augusta Moreland, British immigrants, conservative, middle class shopkeepers who had answered the call of Empire to colonize the West. They had become thoroughly radicalized by the hardships they endured as prairie settlers. Like many early Saskatchewan farm families, the More-lands' first home in Canada was dug out of the side of a hill and finished with sod, railway ties, and wooden slabs. George Moreland was a founding member of the Saskatchewan Grain Growers' Association, which with the Farmers' Union of Canada in 1926, formed the United Farmers of Canada. He was at the founding convention of the CCF in Calgary in 1932. Augusta Moreland was as active in the movement as her husband, and was one of Helena's CCF contemporaries.

Hilda had also been strongly influenced by one of her teachers, Frances Moren, who boarded with the Morelands when they were still living in Saskatchewan. With her agreeable, gentle ways and progressive philosophy of education, Frances inculcated a sense of individual responsibility in her pupils and encouraged self-expression. She was at that rural school for only a year, but she established strong rapport with the Morelands. Ten years later, in 1934, when Frances, then living in Vancouver with Lyle Telford, wrote asking Hilda to come and look after their baby, Hilda accepted. Her parents followed a few years later.

In 1936 Hilda married a young Danish immigrant, Thorvald (Denny) Kristiansen. That was the year of the blazing success of the Progressive Arts Club production of Clifford Odet's *Waiting for Lefty*, with Denny playing a leading role in this militant play about striking taxi drivers. Times were still hard, but Denny at least had a summer job as a steward on the CPR coastal steamships. In the winter the Kristiansens had to go on relief, but they rented a rooming house, paying their own rent out of rental income from their rooms. So began Hilda's career in the rooming house business, the occupation of many Vancouver women whose husbands worked and lived most of the year away from home in mining or logging camps or on passenger steamships and freighters. In 1940 Hilda and Denny bought the house at 1220 Barclay, and with the zeal of the dispossessed for repossessing order, security, and civility, they began the long, tedious task of renovation. The Kristiansens were loyal and active members of the CCF, Hilda as president of the CCF Provincial Council of Women and Denny on the CCF Civic Affairs Council. (Their son Lyle carries on the strong family political tradition as NDP Member of Parliament for Kootenay West from 1980-84 and since 1988.) During election campaigns, a large sign on the rooftop announced the name of the CCF candidate for that area.

Most of the permanent residents were also CCF people, including two of Helena's political comrades. After her husband died, Augusta Moreland came to live at 1220 Barclay, in the room next to Helena's. On the floor below lived Jane Bury, one-time member of the Socialist Party of Canada and literature convenor for the CCF as long as anyone could remember. Widowed during the First World War, she had raised a son and daughter on her small pension, and looked after an ailing mother as well. Her son, James Bury, had become a well-known labour leader.

Helena and Jane were old friends, having worked together in the movement for many years. Now in their old age, life had narrowed a good deal for both women, but they still had their work in the CCF and in their women's organizations. One night Jane would cook dinner for the two of them. The next night was Helena's turn. These women had learned survival.

Jane was short and plump. Her room spilled over with books and papers, photographs, cushions, knitting, houseplants; the good fragrance of home-baked cake and cookies lingered. Helena was tall and broader-bosomed. Her room was plain and utilitarian: no geraniums on the window sills here. Her books and papers were all tidy. Never any piles of dirty dishes. Breakfast finished, she would wash her cup and plate and put them away. Dinner was a simple matter – a fried chop, a potato, a salad, some fruit. On Jane's evenings, however, dinner was more elaborate: casseroles and puddings would appear on the table. Of course, preparing such meals was easier for Jane: she had a sink in her room, whereas Helena had to carry water from the bathroom. Even if she had had a sink, Helena would not have produced casseroles and puddings. She declared that Jane spent too much time cooking; Jane countered that she *liked* cooking. Their dinner conversation was lively and sometimes heated, sustained by their wide reading and experience and by the tensions resulting from a fundamental difference in personality, the one austere and disciplined, the other ample, more free and easy.

Helena continued her political work. She campaigned in both the federal and provincial elections of 1945. In the civic election of 1948 she rejoiced once again in a CCF victory: Laura Jamieson won a seat on City Council as Vancouver's second alderwoman. Darwin Charlton, a CCF field organizer, recalled Helena's dedication and style of work in a campaign. Describing a Vancouver Centre federal by-election in 1948, he said that Helena was always the first to arrive at election headquarters, the last to leave. Even though she was not the official campaign manager, her years of working at 'joe jobs' in the party, her wide acquaintance among the membership, and, most of all, her devotion to the CCF cause inspired campaign workers to work hard for their candidate. She, of course, went out canvassing with them.[2]

Helena was living on her savings, because she would not qualify for the old-age pension, available at age seventy, until 1949. The pension itself was not more than twenty dollars per month, graduated according to income and assets and payable only to persons passing a strict means test. In 1951 the federal government passed the Old Age Security Act, which provided a universal old-age pension without a means test at age seventy and raised the amount to forty dollars a month. Thus at the age of seventy-two, Helena's pension income increased substantially.[3]

In 1945, however, with only her small savings and no inkling that the federal government would rescue her from an impoverished old age, it behooved Helena to look to the future. To increase her income she took a job with Canadian Canners at their Aylmer plant in downtown Vancouver, and for two summers worked with younger women processing fruits and vegetables. Every day she worked a full shift, donning rubber apron and 'wet boots,' which slipped on over regular footwear, for sorting produce is messy work.

Standing in front of a conveyor belt all day is also fatiguing work, more so for a sixty-six-year-old woman. According to a first-hand account by a cannery worker in the technological seventies, sorting beans was still back-breaking manual labour. The workers stood in front of a conveyor belt on a wooden-grated platform, with water running underneath it and continually flooding the cement floor. Their job was to pick out any spotted or oversize beans and toss them on the floor before they reached the end of the belt, which was raised at an angle from the floor. The beans were carried upward towards the end of the belt, where they emptied into a large bin. The workers could stand erect if they worked at the top end, but then they had less time to grab the unwanted beans. If they stationed themselves closer to the bottom of the conveyor belt, they had more time to pick over the beans, but doing a better job earned them a sore back. They were not allowed to stop the conveyor in order to pick over the beans in a less hectic way. The cannery worker observed wryly, 'We were not mentally prepared to be physically abused.'[4] Unlike her 1970s counterpart, Helena, with her experience as an organizer for the Laundry Workers' Union, may have been mentally prepared for a sore back and tired legs, but this did not alleviate the fatigue and she arrived home at night exhausted. However, she considered the effort worthwhile. As she told Hilda Kristiansen, she was learning first-hand about the working conditions and wages of women cannery workers.

For Helena was still interested in the problems of women workers. Soon after returning from Lemon Creek she had become active in the CCF Provincial Council of Women, which made the welfare of working women one of their main concerns. At one Council meeting, Helena posed this problem on behalf of a Woodward's store employee: 'How can a working girl, earning $18.00 a week, after paying income tax, unemployment insurance, dental upkeep, and street carfares, clothe herself as her employer and the public demand?'[5] The question was rhetorical, and part of the solution, Helena still believed, lay in women becoming politically aware and fighting for their rights. Reporting a CCF women's council meeting, she announced with satisfaction that a number of active women's groups had been formed throughout the province 'in spite of diversions – two general elections and one civic election.'[6] The welfare of women was plainly still a priority for her. Now one of the elders, she also looked back and saw herself as an actor in the drama of women's liberation as she regaled a women's council meeting with recollections of the Pankhursts and the Women's Social and Political Union and her own part in the struggle for the vote. Moreover, her long experience in political and social reform had given her authority and stature in the community. As one leading British Columbia educator observed: 'In any group discussing an issue, whether in education, peace, health, social welfare, someone might say, "Well, let's ask Helena Gutteridge what she thinks." We thought of her as a resource.'[7]

In 1947 she became more active in the Women's International League for Peace and Freedom, founded in 1915 at the International Congress of Women at the Hague on the initiative of leading suffragists from Europe and the United States. Belgium and France were war zones, yet a thousand women from countries on both sides of the conflict, some of them even hazarding the beleaguered North Sea, travelled to the congress to protest against war and to act as envoys of peace. Among them was Toronto suffragist and pacifist Laura Hughes, niece of Minister of Militia Sam Hughes, who was more than a little disconcerted by her anti-conscription activities. The Hague congress set up the International Committee of Women for Permanent Peace, with American social philosopher Jane Addams as president.[8]

Leading Canadian women rejected official invitations to join the 1915 Hague congress, discovering that the call of Empire was stronger than their pacifist feelings. The National Council of Women of Canada declined to send a representative, though in her reply their convenor for the Committee on Peace and Arbitration, Emily Murphy, expressed her sympathy and 'heartiest approval of the Provisional Programme.'[9] The National Committee of Women for Patriotic Service, honorary president HRH the Duchess of Connaught, also civilly declined, and secretary Adelaide Plumptre wrote to Jane Addams that 'the time for peace has not yet arrived.'[10] The committee circulated 'An Open Letter Concerning Peace' opposing the congress: 'We have drawn the sword to defend the rights of the weak, the liberty of the many and the pledged honour of the Empire.' The open letter then appealed to women's sense of duty: 'And what is our share? ... To possess our souls in patience during war's hardships and uncertainties; to refrain from embarrassing our rulers by demands for a premature and illusory peace ...'[11]

On her return from the Hague congress, Laura Hughes met with women of the Toronto Suffrage Association and the Women's Social Democratic League to form a peace organization affiliated with the International Committee of Women for Permanent Peace. The climate was not propitious. When in the fall of 1915 the National Council of Women consented to give a hearing to Chrystal Macmillan, British representative at the congress and secretary, they allowed her only three minutes to speak on 'what women can do to prevent war.' The press accused her and Jane Addams of having 'fallen under the influence of the German plotters at the alleged [Hague] peace conference.' The Toronto Women's Patriotic League objected to Chrystal Macmillan having been allowed to speak at all. Nevertheless, Laura Hughes and her pacifist colleagues reported by mail to women across Canada, urging them to form peace groups. Helena later recalled that a Vancouver branch of the WILPF had been formed in 1917 and that she was among the founders on that historic occasion, which she particularly remembered as having taken place in the living room of her old friend Fanny Cowper. Helena and Laura Hughes knew of one another through their trade union activities, and we may speculate that Helena, a prominent member of the VTLC and a leading suffragist, was on Laura's mailing list. No other record of this early Vancouver peace organization has been found. The hostility that met Vancouver pacifists, anti-conscription speakers, and conscientious objectors and that culminated in the shooting of Ginger Goodwin could not have provided a climate conducive to the growth of a peace organization.[12]

The International Committee of Women for Permanent Peace called a second congress in Zurich in May 1919, where the national committees constituted themselves a new organization, the Women's International League for Peace and Freedom (WILPF). Women from sixteen countries – distinguished, vital, with keen political minds – applied themselves to the problems of postwar reconstruction, the victors with the vanquished. In a moving demonstration of friendship, Lida Gustava Heymann, German trade union organizer, embraced Jeanne Melin from the war-devastated Ardennes and declared: 'A German woman gives her hand to a French woman, and says in the name of the German delegation that we hope we women can build a bridge from Germany to France and from France to Germany, and that in the future we may be able to make good the wrongdoing of men.'[13] The congress subsequently repudiated the Treaty of Versailles and took a stand for universal disarmament, opposing the disarming of Germany alone.

Such vigorous initiatives were received with hostility in Canada. When in the fall of 1919 the WILPF held a public meeting to report on the Zurich congress, the Toronto *Evening Telegram* termed the congress 'infamous' and treated the WILPF with contempt: 'Though the meeting was extensively advertised, apparently the general public are not burning with curiosity to hear more. Only eleven people – seven women and four men gathered about the table.' A University of Toronto Classics professor, C.B. Sissons, recalls that, because of suspicion and tension on the campus during this time, the university cancelled the lectures that the 'venerable and venerated' Jane Addams was to have given for the Department of Social Sciences. To socialist Harriet Dunlop Prenter, secretary of the Canadian section of the WILPF, this incident revealed 'underhand work on the part of the dark forces of militarism.' 'We dare not risk bringing Mrs. Pethick Lawrence over here, though she is in the U.S.A.,' she wrote to Emily Balch, 'mainly because she is accompanied by an Austrian woman.'[14]

The WILPF was Helena's kind of organization, bold and utterly determined, its policies marked by reason and unblinking acceptance of reality. In 1920 the WILPF sent a fact-finding mission to Ireland and, finding that Sinn Fein was indeed the legitimate and popular choice of Catholic Ireland, supported Irish self-determination. They urged recognition of the new Soviet government, not as communist supporters but as compassionate humanitarians, believing that further violence against an already suffering and much-oppressed people was intolerable. In 1921, rather than join the anti-Bolshevik crusade of the western powers, it sent a representative to the International Relief Commission, where she was instrumental in obtaining the acceptance of two Russian delegates to the conference.[15]

A Vancouver branch of the Canadian Section of the WILPF was formed in 1921 by social democrats Laura Jamieson, Lucy Woodsworth, Kate Lane, and Dorothy Steeves, who said, according to one account, that she had been one of the Hague founding members. Helena left Vancouver in 1921 to live in Mount Lehman but, though she does not say so, still could have attended meetings. Peace work in the early twenties was difficult: WILPF executive member Margaret Perceval reported to the international secretary that the 'cold shadow of disapproval' hung over University of British Columbia professors who dared speak out against war. 'I must tell you,' she wrote, 'that we battle against fearful odds in this country, as we are a conservative people on the whole, and our patriotism mostly of the warlike and aggressive kind ... So that it is uphill work and really it is only those among the working classes who have knowledge of economics on the whole, who understand us.'[16]

Yet Laura Jamieson understood better the politics of peace. The Vancouver branch, she reported in 1922, had to avoid becoming 'a middle class organization with a middle class mind.' Becoming a working class organization would be easy, because some of their most 'ardent' members were labour people with radical views. 'So we aim to be middle class externally, while we strive with all our might *not* to be middle class internally, that is, to be far in advance of the general middle class in outlook, in information, and in leadership of ideas.'[17] She said she believed this to be the policy of the WILPF. Gradually the idea of working for peace became more acceptable in the twenties, and branches of the WILPF were formed across Canada. As national secretary of the Canadian section in the later twenties, Laura Jamieson worked with Violet McNaughton, women's editor of the Saskatchewan *Western Producer*, MP Agnes MacPhail, and others in an ongoing campaign to educate the Canadian public on the urgent need for world disarmament. Agnes MacPhail represented Canada at WILPF congresses and became the first woman to sit on the Disarmament Commission of the League of Nations. In 1929 the three women attended the WILPF Prague congress, returning to organize branches across Canada.[18]

The WILPF recognized that neither peace nor freedom was possible as long as economic and political repression were accepted instruments of policy among the powerful imperialist nations. In succeeding decades, wherever such repression occurred, it spoke out strongly for social and economic justice. As Jane Addams, first WILPF president, declared, 'peace and bread' were one cause. She won the Nobel Peace Prize in 1931, and her successor, Emily Greene Balch, linking 'peace and morality,' won it in 1946, each sharing the prize with another. The chairman of the 1946 Nobel committee spoke of 'the holy fire' that burned within such women as Emily Balch and Jane Addams.[19]

In 1931 Japan occupied Manchuria: the WILPF tried to influence the League of Nations to intercede, but it only stood by and watched the Japanese occupation spread south. In Germany and Austria, Hitler came to power in 1933; leading members of the WILPF were arrested, others fled to Switzerland. There, in the home of the League of Nations, they were branded as communists and their international secretary, who had visited Russia, was threatened with expulsion as an 'anti-militarist' and 'revolutionary propagandist.' As the world moved towards total war, the WILPF continued gamely to exert its energies against the advancing Nazi colossus, protesting the blockade of republican Spain, the bombing of Guernica, and the shameful betrayal of Czechoslovakia. By this time, some WILPF members, even staunch British Quakers, were beginning to conclude that pacifism in the face of Nazi barbarism was powerless and that military action might have to be taken.[20]

The frightening turn of political events in the 1930s moved the WILPF to reassess its aims and change its constitution to make social transformation a clear objective. Peace and freedom were still primary objectives, the main tasks being the campaign for disarmament and the development of a world organization for the peaceful settlement of disputes, but the organization's new statement of aims recognized that 'a real and lasting peace and true freedom cannot exist under the present system of exploitation, privilege and profit,' and declared the need for working through non-violent means towards 'a new system under which would be realized social, economic and political equality for all without distinction of sex, race or opinion.'[21] In Vancouver, the new emphasis on social justice was reflected in a 1937 resolution framed by the WILPF for the Vancouver Local Council of Women, of which it was an affiliate, requesting the provincial government to provide 'legislative guarantees' allowing workers to organize and engage in collective bargaining, and also to provide 'machinery for the just arbitration of industrial disputes.'[22] The 1937 resolution reveals the organizing hand of the CCF contingent: Helena Gutteridge, Dorothy Steeves, Susie Clark, and Laura Jamieson.

Even though the VLCW approved the 'legislative guarantees' for workers and supported measures to help the unemployed, the CCF women found working with the Local Council too constraining and formed their own umbrella group. Reporting to the WILPF international office, Laura Jamieson wrote that the Vancouver branch had joined with seventeen other societies to form the Federation of Progressive Women's Organizations. 'It will not operate in opposition to the Local Council of Women but to supplement it in matters where the very broad affiliations of the Local Council prevent it from passing measures of an advanced nature.'[23] Helena was on the committee that drew up the constitution of the new federation, which included a number of labour organizations and women's union auxiliaries, the Progressive Jewish Women, the very left-wing Mothers' Council, and the Nursery School Association, founded by Helena's good friend and housemate, Edith MacDonald.[24]

International peace was still the prime concern of the Vancouver WILPF, the strategy as enunciated by Laura Jamieson in the 1920s – to educate the middle class mind. In 1936 the Vancouver Peace Programme Committee, under the patronage of the Lieutenant Governor, the mayor of Vancouver, and the Anglican archbishop, held a series of events to celebrate the city's golden jubilee. The WILPF was one of many organizations working on this jubilee project, whose big public event was a rally on 9 August of ten thousand people from all walks of life at Malkin Bowl in Stanley Park. The working class, represented by a contingent of labour and socialist groups, had gathered earlier in the day at Cambie Street Grounds and marched in procession with their banners to join the thousands already assembled at Malkin Bowl. The WILPF organized the radio peace programs for the jubilee project, broadcast afternoons on CKMO in September and October. During the same period, it arranged its own regular Wednesday night peace broadcasts on the same radio station. 'We have found the heads of our radio stations much interested in Peace,' reported Laura Jamieson.[25]

In the 1930s the WILPF Canadian section had six branches: Toronto, Winnipeg, Regina, Calgary, Edmonton, and Vancouver. One of its activities was the annual peace ceremony at the Canada-U.S. border, at Niagara Falls, for example. In 1938 the Vancouver branch instituted its International Peace Arch Festival at Blaine, Washington. At that first meeting of fifty women from the Vancouver and Seattle leagues, Alderman Gutteridge was one of the main speakers. Even though she was extremely busy with her work on City Council, she still participated in WILPF activities. Interest in the WILPF increased in the months before war was finally declared. Dorothy Steeves reported on one occasion, 'Splendid meeting. Seventy women, house bulging, so that many had to sit on stairs.'[26]

The Vancouver branch worked independently, as did the other Canadian branches, for the Toronto national office was inoperative and had been for some years. 'I really have not done *anything* practically as National Secretary,' Anna Sissons confessed to international co-chair Gertrude Baer.[27] The Canadian branches did meet in Winnipeg in 1937, at a conference chaired by Lucy Woodsworth, and got as far as setting up a national section, but this formal arrangement failed to produce the expected unified action under the aegis of a Toronto headquarters. The failure is difficult to understand, given the apparent political compatibility of the women involved and especially the history of the woman chosen to be national secretary. Anna Normart Sissons, from a Philadelphia Quaker family, in 1913 married Charles Bruce Sissons, a cousin of J.S. Woodsworth. Like her husband, she was a Liberal. The Woodsworths and the Sissonses were close friends, but it was Anna, not Charles, who became an early member of the League for Social Reconstruction and, to her husband's embarrassment, a founding member of the Ontario CCF. Escaping the anti-communist discipline of party leader J.S. Woodsworth, she participated in the united front and headed the Women's Commission at the 1935 congress of the League Against War and Fascism, where Communist Party secretary Tim Buck and Sam Carr, both lately released from prison, shared the platform with leading CCFers Tommy Douglas and George Mooney. She herself chaired a discussion group that included communist Annie Buller. In 1937 the Toronto WILPF, led by Anna Sissons, urged the boycott of Japanese imports and the rescinding of the Quebec Padlock Law (Act Respecting Communistic Propaganda). It supported the Spanish Loyalists and Canadian 'Mac-Pap' volunteers in Spain through the Friends of the

Mackenzie-Papineau Battalion, measures that the Vancouver WILPF almost certainly approved.[28] CCF women in British Columbia also worked with communist women, even though provincial leaders were strongly anti-communist. Moreover, the Progressive Women's Federation, with which the Vancouver WILPF was affiliated, brought communist women under its umbrella. One can only conclude that soon after the Winnipeg meeting in 1937 and even before November 1939, when the Communist Party was outlawed by order-in-council, Anna Sissons and her WILPF friends, in line with CCF policy, abandoned the tactic of cooperation with the communists and became reluctant to associate themselves with the radical women of the Vancouver branch.[29]

As secretary of the Canadian section, Anna Sissons had to deal with Juvenile Court Judge Laura Jamieson; Violet McNaughton, founder of the Women's Grain Growers of Saskatchewan; and Beatrice Brigden, women's columnist for the *Manitoba Commonwealth* – tough-minded political women with strong working class sympathies. Moreover, leading members of the Vancouver branch Helena Gutteridge and Dorothy Steeves held political office, and Laura Jamieson would be elected MLA for Vancouver Centre in the spring of 1939. No longer as active in the political fray as she once was, Anna Sissons may have found these women politically reckless, even suspect. The Vancouver branch aggressively implemented the revised 1934 statement of aims of the Zurich congress, which made it their duty to work for social change and economic justice. Associated by their affiliation with the Progressive Women's Federation with such left-wing organizations as the Women's Auxiliary of the International Woodworkers of America, the Vancouver WILPF could not have earned much middle class credibility. Speaking for the WILPF in June 1938 after the police had evacuated the post office sit-down strikers, Laura Jamieson publicly aligned herself and the league with those who 'strongly deplored the action of the authorities.'[30] Alderman Gutteridge agreed with her that tear gas would not solve the problem of unemployment. The activities of the league became suspect, especially since the executive in 1938 were all CCF members. A few months after the outbreak of war, newly elected MLA Laura Jamieson, as president of the Vancouver WILPF, found herself hotly refuting charges that it was a communist-front organization. Such allegations were distressing to her and other CCF women for whom the united front had been a practical and honourable way of achieving socialist goals.[31]

As Germany continued its relentless march through Europe, meetings of the international organization became impossible and its activities were much curtailed. The Vancouver branch disbanded for the duration of the war, CCF women putting pacifism on hold to join in the battle against fascism – except Mildred Osterhout, now married to engineer

Walter Fahrni. Deeply committed to the Gandhian morality of non-vio-
lence, as a spokesperson for the Fellowship of Reconciliation, she publicly opposed the war in a lecture tour across Canada; sometime between
1940 and 1942. Then she joined Helena in the Kootenays as a teacher for
the Japanese Canadians in the New Denver evacuation camp.[32]

The Vancouver WILPF reorganized in 1947, President Mildred Fahrni
bringing together the faithful and indomitable band of CCF women
from the thirties. In the WILPF, Helena was once again working with old
friends from labour and socialist wars, including former MLAs Dorothy
Steeves and Laura Jamieson, now a member of Vancouver City Council. Jane Bury, Augusta Moreland, Mary Norton, and Evelyn LeSueur,
the last two from suffragist days, were again active members. Mildred
Fahrni soon left the group to accept a position with the Fellowship of
Reconciliation in Toronto, but the humorous and incisive Kate Lane, one
of the 1921 founding members, remained a member, as did Helena's old
friend and business partner Edith MacDonald. And Jean Cole, Edna
Gibb, Muriel Bladen, and a newcomer, Sheila Young, whose only politics was peace.

Sheila Young was an Englishwoman, the wife of a civil engineer, who
had belonged to the WILPF in England. She remained with the Vancouver organization through good times and bad, breathing new life into
it when it faltered. More than a proselytizer and lobbyist, she was
interested in substantive matters, such as working out new concepts of
peace and studying the economic and social consequences of disarmament. As president and then corresponding secretary of the Vancouver
WILPF, she composed the briefs, the letters of protest, the resolutions to
the federal government, and the reports to Geneva headquarters that
issued from Vancouver, all of them demonstrating a grasp of world
affairs and enormous intellectual energy. She earned the respect and
affection of Gertrude Baer and others in the international office, and after
the 1962 international congress was made a member of the WILPF's
newly formed International Consultative Committee on Peace
Research.[33]

On reorganizing in 1947, the Vancouver branch tackled postwar
national and international issues. With thousands of veterans returning
to civilian life, the housing shortage in Canada was more pressing
than ever. Helena again took up the problem, this time on behalf of the
WILPF, speaking on 'Housing – a Social Responsibility' at one of a series
of public meetings on vital questions of the day. The question of relo-
cating the Japanese who had been expelled from the coast in 1942, and
of assuring them their rights as Canadian citizens, was also of special
concern. Both Helena and Mildred Fahrni could bring to bear their own
experience and seasoned reflections. On the international scene, Canada

was shipping arms to Chiang Kai-shek. The Vancouver WILPF condemned this as a violation of the United Nations charter. Even more disturbing, the signing of the North Atlantic Pact in 1949 and the establishment of the North Atlantic Treaty Organization was inimical to everything the WILPF stood for. The Vancouver branch joined with the national sections unanimously opposing this new militarization, thus placing itself dangerously at variance with popular opinion in western Europe and North America.[34]

Soon came the realization in Canada, as in other countries, of the frightening potential of the atomic bomb for annihilating whole populations. Meeting in Stockholm in 1950, the World Peace Council launched the Stockholm Peace Appeal, an international campaign to abolish nuclear weapons. However, this campaign met with mistrust and hostility because the World Peace Council was suspected of being communist-led and the stockpiling of nuclear weapons was considered by the western bloc to be a necessary deterrent to possible Soviet aggression. The WILPF, mindful of oppressive political conditions in the eastern bloc, could not reconcile communist peace and freedom with western peace and freedom and officially declined to participate in the campaign, although many individual members and some national sections and branches did take part, including the Vancouver branch. Sheila Young recalls going door to door with the Ban-the-Bomb petition during this time when the 'red scare' made such work extremely difficult. We do not know if Helena did the same, but she may well have, considering her long experience in door-to-door canvassing. She certainly gave leadership on this issue, since she was resolutions chairman at the time.[35]

The work of the Vancouver branch was severely hindered by the tensions generated by the Cold War. McCarthyism was rampant not only in the United States but in Canada as well, and communists were hunted down by suspicious governments, discharged from their jobs, and often deprived of their livelihoods. These were the years of the Canadian Cold War spy trials set off in Ottawa by the 1946 revelations of a defecting Soviet cipher clerk, Igor Gouzenko. Epitomizing that hysterical decade for Canadians was, and still is, the tragic suicide in 1957 of Canadian diplomat Herbert Norman, who, despite security clearance from Prime Minister Pearson himself, continued to be hounded as a security risk by the United States Senate.[36]

The Vancouver branch of the WILPF found that freedom was in jeopardy even in its own city, and in 1949, during which time Helena was resolutions chairman, came to the defence of civil liberties in two cases:

Our Branch added its protest against refusal of the Benchers Law Society to admit a veteran, with four years war service, to the Bar. This young man had excellent credentials and academic standing. The reasons given were that he was a member of the Communist Party.

We also protested the action of our Civic Parks Board in refusing to give a contract to an outstanding eminent singer, because of his political affiliations.[37]

The young veteran was Gordon Martin. He refused to perjure himself and stood on his rights, but lost his appeal to the Supreme Court of British Columbia on the grounds that the Law Society required a member to be of good repute, and he, being a communist, by definition was not of good repute. Refused admission to the bar, he had to abandon his law career. To earn a living, he set himself up in a television repair business.[38] The singer was the Oxford-educated and multitalented Englishman John Goss, who had chosen to pursue his career in Vancouver and did much to develop the cultural life of the city. In 1949 he was one of the delegates to a Cultural and Scientific Conference for World Peace in New York who was arrested and expelled from the United States on charges of communist activities. On his return, he was to have taught at the BC Institute of Music and Drama, but the Vancouver Parks Board did not wish to be associated with a suspected communist and withdrew its sponsorship. When John Goss died four years later, a Vancouver music critic wrote that 'we in Vancouver were fortunate to have him in our midst for so many years.'[39]

The red menace also invaded the meetings of the Vancouver WILPF, where right- and left-wing views of the predominantly CCF leadership clashed, over Canada's policy towards NATO, for example. CCF national policy supported the alliance, although in the British Columbia section Dorothy Steeves led a determined fight against Canada's joining it, a position also taken by the Labour Progressive [Communist] Party. She was defeated, though narrowly: the CCF provincial executive voted in favour of NATO.[40] But the split within the CCF must have created dissension in the Vancouver WILPF, for presumably Dorothy Steeves spoke out against NATO at its meetings. A majority of members declared their opposition to NATO, deploring it as an 'uncalled for act of intimidation against the Soviet Union.'[41] When the Vancouver branch further urged the Canadian government to put the question of NATO to a national referendum, they were accused by a Member of Parliament of being communists, an allegation that it vigorously protested. The branch won an apology from him, but this encounter could not but alarm the membership and fuel the dissension between right and left factions.[42] 'The smearing is going on everywhere, not only in your own country,' Gertrude Baer wrote from Geneva. This was small comfort, however. 'We have had continuous sessions of this [internal strife] for over a year,'

Sheila Young reported. 'And it is *not* the LEFT that is causing trouble [her emphasis].'[43]

Anti-communist hysteria in the Vancouver WILPF came to a head over the question of postwar Czechoslovakia. The Soviet Union had put pressure on the Czechs to adopt communist institutions and join the east bloc. Some CCF members in the Vancouver branch proposed sending a resolution of protest directly to Czechoslovakia. Other members, including president Sheila Young, opposed the resolution, maintaining that it contravened WILPF regulations, which required all such resolutions to go through the international office in Geneva. Some CCF members then hurled accusations of communism at those opposed to their resolution, especially at Sheila Young, a supporter of the Canadian Peace Congress, suspect because it was led by former China missionary Dr. James Endicott, who advocated the peaceful coexistence of the Soviet Union and the West.[44] Sheila Young was a non-party person who reached out to everyone, no matter what their politics, declaring herself in favour of peaceful solutions to disputes and the abolition of atomic weapons. Mildred Fahrni described her as 'a committed pacifist, a member of the FOR [Fellowship of Reconciliation], a devoted Theosophist ...,' a person who did not judge people by their labels.[45] Undaunted by the anti-communist furore, she could not even approach the leader of the communist LPP to discuss peace strategies with him without worrying about guilt by association. She was an innocent who, if she knew the hard facts of realpolitik, chose to transcend them and work above them. A stickler for following regulations to the letter, she insisted on having the international executive rule on the charges laid against her. On behalf of the Vancouver members she wrote eloquently of the constraints imposed on people by violations of civil liberties:

> For ... where choice of right or wrong is the issue insofar as both individuals and collectivities are concerned, the tendency is to refrain from positive word and action, and consequent withdrawal from every form of progressive and articulate decision. Thus, to save one's reputation, and protect personal and family interest one must sacrifice the prerogative of free speech in a much-vaunted free world![46]

As a result of the political uproar, Laura Jamieson, along with some other CCF women, withdrew from the Vancouver WILPF. She had always been philosophically opposed to communism, always against any collaboration in a united front.[47] Losing her seat on City Council in 1950, she re-entered provincial politics and was elected to the legislature for the second time in 1952. Other longtime members, including Helena, stood firm. At a Toronto WILPF meeting addressed by Annalee Stewart

from international headquarters, a member asked the visiting Kate
Lane if Toronto had anything to fear from Vancouver. Kate Lane replied,
'No,' because Vancouver was 'functioning along the line advocated by
Mrs. Stewart.'[48]

Anna Sissons was still president of the Toronto WILPF and putative
national secretary of a non-existent Canadian section, still neither
willing nor able to create one. The reason this time was clear: 'We felt
in our Toronto WIL that perhaps you ought to know in Philadelphia that
the present VANCOUVER BRANCH [her emphasis] WIL seems to have
gone almost completely over to the Communist crowd. Some of our
very well known old members there have tried very hard to save it –
but have found it impossible – and therefore have found it necessary
to withdraw ...'[49]

In this political atmosphere the Vancouver women found it impossible
to establish a working relation with Toronto that would lead to the establishment of a national section. Anna Sissons gave no 'direction or guidance' and did not reply to the resolutions on international issues that
Sheila Young sent her. The friendly, non-threatening offices of Mildred
Fahrni were similarly rebuffed. Both women met with Mrs. Sissons in
October 1949, proposing a national conference to set up a Canada section; once again no success. American executive member Mildred Olmsted intervened, and received formal consent but not action. The
international office wrote, requesting a Canadian report for the Copenhagen congress in 1949; receiving no reply, it asked Sheila Young to prepare one 'if they maintain their silence.' The immovability of Anna
Sissons was a great hindrance to the Vancouver WILPF: since Toronto was
the official headquarters, Vancouver could not independently send
resolutions to Geneva. The Vancouver branch appealed to Geneva for
help, and the international executive, meeting before the Copenhagen
congress, adopted the recommendation that 'Vancouver be made the
National Headquarters of the Canadian Section.'[50]

Instead of honouring the proposal of the international office, the
Toronto branch sent Mabel Parkin as delegate to the 1953 congress, pre-
ceded by an emergency resolution that would have required a membership committee to pass on the political suitability of prospective
members. She was to make 'personal contact' and initiate 'an open discussion' on how to deal with 'members whose beliefs in the fundamental
principles on which the WILPF was founded had seemed to differ from
our own interpretation.' On technical grounds the resolution did not
qualify as 'emergency' and never reached the floor. Unequal to the
delicate task of establishing a modus vivendi with Vancouver delegate
Jane Angus, Mabel Parkin retreated with hurt feelings. At this impasse,
Gertrude Baer and others in the international office were plainly exas-

perated with the Toronto WILPF, although they tempered their letters with gentle pleading and firm direction. Meanwhile, in 1951, Vancouver declared its independence and began to deal directly with Geneva, effectively representing Canada.[51]

The 1953 Vancouver branch report to the WILPF international congress in Paris was passionate in its denunciation of McCarthyism, which had 'spread its tentacles of poison throughout the entire North American Continent,' generating among people 'a cowardly neurosis of fear.'[52] The report maintained the adherence of the Vancouver branch to the regulations and aims of the parent WILPF. In due course, the international executive met and completely absolved Sheila Young and the Vancouver members of all charges of communist activity. However, fears of being branded 'red' had reached such a pitch in Vancouver that one CCF member simply burned all the records of the Vancouver WILPF.[53]

And Helena?

'She was not a red-baiter,' said Sheila Young. 'She was interested in the welfare of the peoples of the Third World – basic rights of housing, water, food. Everybody admired her. She was blunt, forthright, very determined. Sometimes her face took on a stubborn look ... One word comes to mind that sums her up – justice. She wanted to see justice done.'[54] Wakiko Suyama at Lemon Creek had noted that look too on many occasions, a signal that Helena the welfare worker was summoning her energy to oppose bureaucratic intervention and demand justice.

Moreover, Helena's attitude towards communists was not inconsistent with CCF policy. J.S. Woodsworth was adamant in his refusal to cooperate with communists, regarding them as a real threat to the achievement of democratic socialism. In 1933 he had refused to join with the Canadian Labor Defense League, a communist front organization, in a campaign for the release of chairman Tim Buck and other members of the Communist Party executive from prison, yet he spoke out strongly in the House of Commons against their arrest. In subsequent years the CCF continued to be eloquent in defence of civil liberties while still rejecting the united front overtures of the Communist Party. In 1937 Helena, as a member of the CCF provincial executive, had joined the anticommunist majority to vote for the expulsion of A.M. Stephen. She agreed then with the CCF that the defence of freedom from the onslaught of war and fascism would best be served by socialist champions of freedom, the CCF, without the help of the communists. Then political loyalty was the main issue, not simple justice, for the CCF *was* justice. In 1949 she could defend Gordon Martin and John Goss in the name of justice without feeling disloyal to the CCF, even though such an action might mark her as being sympathetic to the acknowledged CCF enemy. She could look, after all, to the example of J.S. Woodsworth.[55]

In the inflamed political climate of the 1950s, the Vancouver WILPF could not maintain public credibility. President Jean Cole, replying to a male critic, observed that 'the mere mention of peace, co-operation and understanding in world terms, tends to either send people scurrying for shelter or bring out the tyrants and hypocrites who shout "Communists" or "eccentrics".'[56] Under such pressures, the Vancouver membership gradually dwindled, but Helena stayed with Sheila Young and the WILPF. In 1958, two years before Helena's death, the Vancouver branch secretary wrote to Geneva, 'We have just had a birthday party for one of our older members on her 80th birthday, Miss Helena Gutteridge.'[57]

By the mid-1950s Helena had receded a little from the scene of women's rights, yet she always maintained a proprietary interest, for she could not let go of the cause that she had made her own since the days of the suffragette struggles in London. From time to time, she and Susie Clark would attend a meeting of the CCF Provincial Council of Women. They would engage in the discussion, sometimes turning vociferously on each other in a display of heated involvement that left the other women exhausted.[58]

For recreation Helena went to concerts. Lily Laverock, still active as a concert impresario, was her companion, providing tickets to the symphony or ballet. Her favourite pastime, however, was going to the races. She had a lifetime pass, presented to her when as alderman she had served on the Vancouver Exhibition Board. During the racing season she budgeted a certain amount for betting on the horses, and would leave at four o'clock in the afternoon for the track. She was philosophical about her losses, which did not amount to much since she would not place many bets. Her main satisfaction, says Hilda Kristiansen, came from seeing those beautiful animals run.[59]

Helena never became an old woman graciously accepting the charitable invitations offered the elderly for a nice outing, a drive around Stanley Park, perhaps. Once, when a well-meaning friend asked her if she would like to join such a party, Helena refused, privately wondering why she had been invited, unless, as she confided to Hilda, it was to help with 'those old crocks.' Helena herself was at least five years older than the women in the party.

She never retired from the active mental life. She got up in the morning, made herself ready, ate breakfast wearing her navy-blue hat (no sitting at the table in her dressing gown), then left the house for the day, often going to the Vancouver Public Library to look up articles in journals. She thought it important to keep abreast of contemporary political events and social issues. In 1957 she was still an active member of the Town Planning Commission, chairing the occasional meeting. On Monday nights, she attended meetings of the Women's School for Citizenship. She kept in touch with old friends. In an interview at the age of seventy-eight, she said, 'I try always to follow the advice I give to other women: Take an interest in public affairs. Keep yourself informed and express your opinions. Above all, be active.'[60]

Looking back on her own active life, she continued, 'My greatest recollections are of the battles we fought, of the many changes in our world in the space of a few years.' She was thinking of the Minimum Wage Act for women, the Workmen's (now Workers') Compensation Act, the Mothers' Pension Act, and of all the women she had worked with to push and prod the provincial government into writing this reform legislation. She was thinking of the evolution of unions into powerful agents for workers' rights, won by years of organizing, years of struggle. Of the new social legislation that the CCF had fought for and eventually won: family allowances, unemployment insurance, the old-age pension, and, in Saskatchewan, universal hospital care, Premier Tommy Douglas's bold precursor to Canada's Medicare program. But, she said in that last interview, 'There's still a lot to be done!' She reminded women that 'they owe it to themselves to develop their abilities and to work for a better, peaceful world.'

Helena was still fanning the holy fire in women, and her own was still burning, though her health was failing. She began to suffer from bilious attacks that gradually became worse. At such times she rejected company, just wanting to be by herself. Ultimately, she learned that her illness was cancer of the pancreas.[61] However, she never made any display of discomfort or grief that might elicit sympathy. She stayed in her room and drank water, stoic and uncomplaining. Hilda never even knew when she was going to visit the doctor. One of the women she used to visit was a former Mount Lehman neighbour, Ethel Damen, then living in a nursing home in Point Grey. When Helena was saying goodbye one day, she told Ethel that she would not be coming to visit her again. She did not say she had cancer. Soon afterwards she was too ill to stay at home and went to the hospital. Jane and Hilda and Edith visited her there, but her stay was very short, almost as though even now she could order what remained of her life and avoid a long, protracted illness. And so, on 1 October 1960 without any fuss, without causing undue trouble for her friends, she died.

Lyle Telford died three days before. His memorial service at the Unitarian Church was attended by a crowd of 350 mourners, as befitted a man who had enjoyed a public and private life both of which had been rich and eventful, the private life openly acknowledged. In his eulogy, the Reverend Phillip Hewett spoke eloquently of Telford's social and political work, describing him as a 'torch bearer for the human race.' Helena had also been a public person, certainly a torch bearer, but her memorial service in the chapel of Mount Pleasant Funeral Home was simple and spare. The funeral arrangements provided no limousines, no outer case for the casket – and 'no flowers, by request.' The fact sheet in the records of Mount Pleasant Funeral Home poignantly underlines how completely Helena had made herself a public person, submerging her private life. Edith MacDonald provided the information, but even she, close friend that she was, could not supply certain basic facts. She knew Helena's birthday, for friends often celebrated that occasion, but not the correct year of birth or the correct age, eighty-one. Name of Father: 'Not known.' Maiden Name of Mother: 'Not known.' Birthplace: 'England.' Relatives: 'Many Friends.' In England, meanwhile, her nephew Thomas Gutteridge and niece Lilian Delchar did not know that she had died, did not even know that she had lived in Canada these many years, and she had long since lost touch with Leslie Fearn and her children, to whom she was Aunt Billy. The daily press paid respectful tribute, but the brief obituary notice that Edith inserted in the *Sun* was the truly moving and eloquent valedictory: 'She leaves many friends and associates to remember her life-long work for peace and justice.' That is certainly how Helena wanted to be remembered.[62]

Her ashes were scattered; no gravestone bears an epitaph in her memory, though she herself unwittingly had supplied one many years before. When she first arrived in Vancouver and set up the Evening Work Committee of the Political Equality League, she wrote to the *World*, urging women to support the suffrage newspaper that she was founding and to work in the suffrage campaign. Their reward, she said, would be the franchise. And, she added, they would be able to say with Robert Louis Stevenson, 'I know what pleasure is, for I have done good work.'

Those words are her epitaph.

Notes

CHAPTER ONE: CHELSEA CHILDHOOD

1 Lilian Delchar, interview by Irene Howard (IH), 10 May 1987.
2 Charles Henry Gutteridge birth certificate, General Register Office, London. Unless otherwise stated, the names of Gutteridge family members; their dates of birth, marriage, and/or death; their occupations; the cause of death; and their addresses are taken from certificates from this London office. Census for England and Wales, 1871.
3 Alfred Beaver, *Memorials of Old Chelsea* (London: Elliot Stock 1892), 344-45. I am indebted to Chelsea Library for sending me this material. 'Cadogan and Hans Place Estate,' Map of 1880, Chelsea Library. Reginald Blunt, *An Illustrated Handbook to the Parish of Chelsea* (London: Lamley 1900), Second Itinerary. 'Plate XIX, Chelsea in 1879,' *An Historical Atlas of Kensington and Chelsea*, comp. B. Curle and P. Mearn (London: Kensington and Chelsea Public Libraries 1971).
4 Peter Wright, with Paul Greengrass, *Spycatcher: The Candid Autobiography of a Senior Intelligence Officer* (Toronto: Stoddart Publishing 1988), 238-39.
5 Thea Holme, *Chelsea* (London: Hamish Hamilton 1972), 255-57.
6 Beaver, *Memorials of Old Chelsea*, 344-45; Patricia Pratt, *Historic Chelsea in Maps, 1700-1894* (London: The Royal Borough of Kensington and Chelsea Libraries and Arts Service, n.d.); Holme, *Chelsea*, 127; Thomas Faulkner, *A Description of Chelsea and Its Environs* (London: 1810), 433-38.
7 *Chelsea Vestry Reports* (CVR), 1869-70, cited in letter to IH from Chelsea Library, 22 Sept. 1983. Ibid., app. 24, 196-97.
8 Charles Booth, *Labour and Life of the People*, 2 vols. (London: Williams and Norgate 1891), 2:London, cont.; and *Appendix to Volume II*, ed. Charles Booth, 1891, 5.
9 *Chelsea Rate Books*, 1881 and 1886, as cited in Chelsea Library to IH, 22 Sept. 1983. Census of 1881. Register of Voters, 1885-87, cited in Chelsea

Library to IH, 5 Jan. 1984.

10 *CVR*, 1886-87, 24-25.

11 Ordinance Survey Map, 1884, Chelsea Library; Chelsea Library to IH, 4 July 1985. Booth, *Appendix*, 5. *Post Office London Street Directory* (*POLSD*), 1885; Chelsea Library to IH, 5 Jan. 1984.

12 *Chelsea, Pimlico and Belgravia Directory*, 1887; *POLSD*, 1887; *CVR*, 1886-87, 23-25. *The Builder*, 19 Jan. 1889, 50.

13 Booth, *Appendix*, 6; *POLSD*, 1894.

14 Census, Micheldever, 1851; Micheldever parish registers.

15 **1380:** Alfred B. Milner, *A History of Micheldever* (Paris: Herbert Clarke 1924), 240.

16 **Baring:** *The Victoria History of the Counties of England: Hampshire and the Isle of Wight* (London: Archibald, Constable 1908; reprinted 1973), vol. 3, 391. **'had a large cottage ... repair':** Milner, *History of Micheldever,* 240. **Wriothesleys:** *History of Hampshire*, 391 and Antonia Fraser, *The Weaker Vessel: [Woman's Lot in Seventeenth Century England]* (New York: Vintage Books 1985), 289. **'a cottage called ...':** *History of Hampshire*, 390. **Domesday:** William White, *History, Gazetteer and Directory of the County of Hampshire* (Sheffield: White 1878), 325. **King Alfred:** Milner, *History of Micheldever*, 8. **Romans:** Eric Rayner, 'Micheldever,' *Hampshire*, Apr. 1972, 45; Richard Whitfield, 'Micheldever,' *Hampshire*, May 1975, 44.

17 Harry Symes, interview by IH, Micheldever, 4 Apr. 1987.

18 Hilda Kristiansen (hereafter HK), interview by IH, 7 Apr. 1983. Thomas Gutteridge, interview by IH, 15 May 1983.

19 At an Ordinary Meeting of the Guardians of the Poor of Chelsea, Report, 11 Apr. 1894, 25. Christmas at the Workhouse is described in *West London Press*, 1 Jan. 1892; complaints against inmates refusing to pick oakum: Ibid., 8 Jan., Deborah Epstein Nord, *The Apprenticeship of Beatrice Webb* (Amherst: University of Massachusetts Press 1985), 181.

20 Holme, *Chelsea:* **'commodious house,'** 3; **Henry VIII**, 21; **Carlyle**, chs. 2 and 3; **Rossetti's peacock**, 173; **Whistler's mistress**, 202; **Wilde**, 215, 220.

21 'Annual Report of Medical Officer of Health' (hereafter MOH), 1879-80, *CVR*, app. 21, 111, and 116. The number of cases of smallpox has been tallied on the basis of a fiscal year from 1 Apr. to 31 Mar. MOH, *CVR*, 1885-86, app. 20, 136-39. **Coffin:** Charles Booth, *Life and Labour of the People in London*, First Series: Poverty, 3, *Blocks of Buildings, Schools and Immigration* (hereafter Booth, *Schools*) (London: Macmillan 1904), 224. Rhyme quoted by Anthony S. Wohl, *Endangered Lives: Public Health in Victorian Britain* (London: J.M. Dent and Sons 1983), 10.

22 T. Vigers and Co., Funeral Directors, Cash Book, 1869-1935, Victoria Library Archives, London. **Common grave:** Bailiff of the Royal Parks Office, Department of the Environment, London, to IH, 9 Nov. 1983.

23 Thomas Gutteridge and Lilian Delchar. He says that Lily took a job as a

'postie,' and was one of the first women employed to deliver mail. Deaths from tubercular meningitis were recorded for 37 children, aged five and under, in Chelsea in 1885: MOH, *CVR*, 1885-86, app. 20, 139.

24 MOH, *CVR*, 1878-79, app. 20, 99. **Carbolic acid:** Ibid., 1884, app. 22, 172.

25 A.W. Barclay, MD, Cantab., *Harveian Oration, Royal College of Physicians* (London: Harrison and Sons 1881), 38. See also *British Medical Journal*, 10 May 1884, 932-33.

26 MOH, *CVR*, 1879-80, app. 23, 147ff., and app. 26, 158-61.

27 *CVR*, 1885-86, app. 35, 'Royal Commission on the Housing of the Working Classes. Evidence Relating to Chelsea,' 221-26. *CVR*, 1879-80, app. 26, 'Proceedings Respecting "Oakham Street" and "Charles Place" under the "Artisans' and Labourers' Dwellings Act, 1868".' 158.

28 Anthony S. Wohl, 'Unfit for Human Habitation,' in H.J. Dyos and Michael Wolff, *The Victorian City: Images and Realities*, 2 vols. (London: Routledge and Kegan Paul 1973), 2:614-15. Wohl, 'Introduction,' in Andrew Mearns, *The Bitter Cry of Outcast London*, ed. Wohl (Leicester: University Press 1970 [first published 1883]), 32; Roy Jenkins, *Sir Charles Dilke: A Victorian Tragedy*, rev. (London: Collins 1965), 173; Nord, *Beatrice Webb*, 202ff.

From 1900, the London County Council built working class housing. 'By 1914 municipal housing in the provision of housing for the working classes had obviously made its mark, and the fear of political bodies playing the role of builder and landlord had weakened considerably': Wohl, 'The Housing of the Working Classes in London, 1815-1914,' in *The History of Working Class Housing: A Symposium*, ed. Stanley D. Chapman (Newton Abbot: David and Charles 1971), 42.

29 Asa Briggs, *Victorian Cities* (London: Odhams Press 1963), 326-27; Holme, *Chelsea*, 154.

30 *BC Fed.*, 27 July 1917.

31 London *World*, 18 June 1912, quoted in Robert Pearman, *The Cadogan Estate: The History of a Landed Family* (London: Haggerston Press 1986), 92.

32 Jenkins, *Sir Charles Dilke*, 114-17.

33 'Dilke, Emily ...,' *Dictionary of Labour Biography*, ed. Joyce M. Bellamy and John Saville (*DLB*) (London: Macmillan Press 1976), 3:64.

34 Quoted by Philip Collins, 'Dickens and London,' in Dyos and Wolff, *The Victorian City*, 2:549-50.

35 Holme, *Chelsea*, 136.

36 Ibid., 230-34.

37 Marjorie M. Barber, *A Short History of Holy Trinity Church Sloane Street, Chelsea* (n.d.), 9-10. The Church was dedicated on 13 May 1890. [Maude Douton], *A Book with Seven Seals* (New York: Ferrar and Rinehart 1932), 12.

38 *Holy Trinity Parish Magazine* (hereafter *HT*), 4(May 1888):35; 5(July 1889); 5(Dec. 1889), passim; 6(May 1890). Booth, *The Life and Labour of the People in London* (London: Macmillan 1902), ch. 1. **Minister's wife:** [Douton],

Seven Seals, 340.

39 Doris Milligan, 'Woman Alderman Says Housing Disgraceful,' Vancouver *Sun*, 31 Mar. 1937, 2.

40 'Once Arrested ...,' Vancouver *News-Herald*, 31 Mar. 1937, 8.

41 Booth, *Schools*, 205-8. For an account of the development of free elementary school education, see Brian Simon, *Education and the Labour Movement, 1870-1920* (London: Lawrence and Wishart 1965), 126-33.

42 Booth, *Schools*, 212, 216. Simon, *Education and the Labour Movement*, 137-42 and ch. 3, 'Class Divisions in Education – Public Schools and Elementary Schools.' *Chelsea News and Kensington Post*, 19 Apr. 1879, 1.

43 Booth, *Schools*, 216n. Log Book, Holy Trinity Girls' and Infants' School, 1906. I am indebted to Mr. J. Riley, Headmaster, Holy Trinity Church of England Junior and Infant Schools, for making the Log Book available to me.

44 *HT*, 4(Aug.-Sept. 1888). Henry Jephson, *The Sanitary Evolution of London* (London: T. Fisher Unwin 1907), 245.

45 *HT*, 5(May 1889), 41-42.

46 *HT*, 5(Aug.-Sept. 1889), 63; 4(Nov. 1888), 73; 5(Feb. 1889), 13. **Dilke:** Jenkins, *Sir Charles Dilke*, 380-96. Other sweated trades were the making of boots, mantles, cabinets, chains, and nails; also furrier and dock labour and upholstery: *Encyclopaedia Britannica*, 11th ed.

47 Quoted by Sir Charles W. Dilke in 'Memoir,' in Lady Dilke, *The Book of the Spiritual Life* (London: John Murray 1905), 112. See also *DLB*, 3:112.

48 *DLB*, 6:253-59, 3:65; Betty Askwith, *Lady Dilke: A Biography* (London: Chatto and Windus 1969), 184.

49 Quoted by Dilke, in 'Memoir,' 112.

50 'The Tailoring Trade,' in Charles Booth, *Life and Labour of the People in London*, First Series: Poverty, 4, *The Trades of East London Connected with Poverty* (London: Macmillan 1904 [first published 1889]), 37-68, esp. 46.

51 P.C. Hoffman, *They Also Serve: The Story of the Shop Worker* (London: Porcupine Press 1949), 33, 42-43.

52 See ch. 5.

53 Rosemary Dinnage, *Annie Besant* (Harmondsworth: Penguin 1986), esp. 62-67.

CHAPTER TWO: THE EMERGENCE OF HELENA

1 Barry Mather, 'Persistent Lady Who Strove and Arrived,' Vancouver *Province*, 24 Apr. 1937, 8.

2 Asa Briggs, *Victorian Things* (Chicago: University of Chicago Press 1989), 282-84; P.C. Hoffman, *They Also Serve: The Story of the Shopworker* (London: Porcupine Press 1949), 145-47.

3 This account of the life of a fashion workroom apprentice and of working conditions is from Hoffman, *They Also Serve*, 145-47, and from printed

material sent by Mrs. L.N. Poole, Archivist, John Lewis Partnership, Archives Dept., Stevenage, England; Mrs. L.N. Poole, 'Fashion Workrooms,' *The Gazette of the John Lewis Partnership,* 15 Oct. 1977; 'October, 1894,' *John Lewis Chronicle,* 4 Oct. 1947; '55 Years a Partner,' *John Lewis Chronicle,* 22 Oct. 1949. The last two are recollections of Miss D. Fisher, who began work in the John Lewis tailoring workrooms in 1894. No account of the Peter Jones workroom was to be found among the Peter Jones documents at Stevenage.

4 Hoffman, *They Also Serve,* ch. 4. Margaret Bondfield, *A Life's Work* (London: Hutchinson, n.d.), 62-72. See Margaret Bondfield, 'Conditions Under Which Shop Assistants Work,' *Economic Journal* 9(1899):277-86 for a comprehensive report of her investigations for the Women's Industrial Council.

5 Thea Holme, *Chelsea* (London: Hamish Hamilton 1972), 234-35; *The Builder,* 19 Jan. 1889, 50.

6 **Tonsley Hill:** Conrad Jamieson, Secretary, International Headquarters, Theosophical Society, Adyar, Madras, India, to IH, 21 Sept. 1988. I am indebted to Mr. Jamieson for searching Society records for me. *Empress of Ireland* ship's manifest 216583, 8 Sept. 1911, reel T-4781 (hereafter Ship's Manifest), Manuscript Division, NAC.

7 Clementina Black, 'London's Tailoresses,' *The Economic Journal: The Journal of the Royal Economic Society* 14(Dec. 1904):556-67.

8 Frances Hicks, 'Dressmakers and Tailoresses,' in *Workers on Their Industries,* ed. Frank W. Galton (London: Charles Scribner and Sons 1896), 23.

9 'Analysis of a Successful Cutter,' *The Tailor, Official Organ of the Tailors' Industrial Union of America,* May 1914. Beginning of the *Official Organ of the Tailors' Industrial Union of America,* Jan. 1914; reverts to *Official Organ of the Journeyman Tailors' Union of America,* 12 Jan. 1915.

10 Jamieson to IH, 21 Sept. 1988 and 25 Apr. 1989.

11 Rosemary Dinnage, *Annie Besant* (Harmondsworth: Penguin 1986), 85.

12 H.P. Blavatsky, *The Key to Theosophy: An Abridgement,* ed. Joy Mills (Madras: The Theosophical Publishing House 1972), 120-33, 134-50.

13 Ibid., 135.

14 Ibid., 143.

15 Interview by IH, 7 Apr. 1983.

16 Blavatsky, *The Key to Theosophy,* 145.

17 Mather, 'Persistent Lady.'

18 Fred L. Pick and G. Norman Knight, *The Pocket History of Freemasonry,* 7th ed., rev. Frederick Smyth (London: Frederick Muller 1983), 314; Florence M. Leveridge, *The Honourable Fraternity of Antient Masonry* [sic] (London, n.d.), 9-10. The first British lodge was officially named 'Le Droit Humain, No. 6: Human Duty,' in a switch from French 'right' to English 'duty': *The Co-Mason* (Jan. 1909):4.

19 Edith Ward, 'Foreshadowings,' *The Co-Mason* (Jan. 1909):7-9. See also Jan. and Feb. 1909, Jan. and Apr. 1910, and July 1911. I am indebted to J.M. Hamill, librarian and curator at the Freemasons' Hall, London, for making the Co-Masonry files available.

20 Dinnage, *Annie Besant*, 102.

21 Jamieson to IH, 3 Nov. 1988.

22 Sidney Webb, *London Education* (New York: Longmans, Green 1904), 142. For a full account of the Polytechnics, see pp. 135-74.

23 Archives of the Polytechnic of Central London. I am indebted to Gloria Chandos for her courteous assistance in allowing me the freedom of the archives.

24 Mather, 'Persistent Lady.'

25 Webb, *London Education*, 136.

26 Gertrude Tuckwell Papers, newspaper clippings, file 30, 1-9, Trades Union Congress Library, London.

27 M.W. Flinn, 'Introduction,' *Report on the Sanitary Condition of the Labouring Population of Great Britain, 1842*, from Edwin Chadwick's 1842 report, ed. M.W. Flinn (Edinburgh: University Press 1965), 58.

28 George Rosen, 'Disease, Disability and Death,' in H.J. Dyos and Michael Wolff, *The Victorian City: Images and Realities*, 2 vols. (London: Routledge and Kegan Paul 1973), 2:635-36.

29 Richard L. Schoenwald, 'Training Urban Man,' in Dyos and Wolff, *The Victorian City*, 2:677, 681.

30 *Hygeia, A City of Health* (1875), quoted in Anthony S. Wohl, *Endangered Lives: Public Health in Victorian Britain* (London: J.M. Dent and Sons 1983), 72.

31 Wohl, *Endangered Lives*, 72. In this account of the sanitary reform movement I have drawn generously on ch. 3, 'Tolerable Human Types,' 43-79.

32 Ibid., 68-69.

33 *CVR*, 1884-85, 31.

34 Wohl, *Endangered Lives*, 75.

35 Vancouver *News-Herald*, 22 Nov. 1941, 3.

36 The South Kensington Board of Education examination questions on Hygiene for 1907 are not available, but would have been similar to those on the Practical Hygiene for School Teachers examination of the Royal Sanitary Institute: *Journal of the Royal Sanitary Institute*, 21, part 1 (1900):246. For typical examination questions in sanitary science, see 19, part 3 (1898):488.

37 G.M.T. Large, Secretary, The Royal Society for the Promotion of Health, to IH, 5 Aug. 1983. I am indebted to Mr. Large for searching both the *Journal of the Sanitary Institute* and the special cumulative list, *Royal Sanitary Institute Index to Certificate Registers, 1877-1919, in Three Parts*, for Helena's name, as well as for checking with Bedford College for Women, which held a course in Practical Hygiene for Teachers in conjunction with the Sanitary Institute.

CHAPTER THREE: FIGHTING FOR THE CAUSE

1 *Votes for Women* (hereafter *VW*), 10 and 17 June and 15 July 1910. *The Suffrage Annual and Women's Who's Who* (London: Stanley Paul 1913), 188-89; Marie Brackenbury memoir, Museum of London, Suffragette Fellowship Collection, acc. no. 57.116/33, 34. Group C, vol. 2, 93-94. **Canadian background of Hilda Brackenbury:** Ibid., acc. no. 57.116/21, 78. E. Sylvia Pankhurst, *The Suffragette Movement: An Intimate Account of Persons and Ideals* (London: Virago Press 1977 [first published by Longman Group 1931]), 277.

2 *VW*, 10 June 1910, 602; 22 July 1910, 713. Pankhurst, *The Suffragette Movement*, 284.

3 Teresa Billington-Greig, 'Autobiographical Writing,' File 6, Fawcett Library, City of London Polytechnic, London.

4 Evelyn Sharp, *Rebel Women*, new ed. (London: United Suffragists [c. 1909]), 59-60, 63.

5 Andrew Rosen, *Rise Up, Women!: The Militant Campaign of the Women's Social and Political Union, 1903-1914* (London: Routledge and Kegan Paul 1974), 35-36, 46-47, 70-71, 76-77.

6 Christabel Pankhurst, *Unshackled*, 66-67, quoted in Jill Liddington and Jill Norris, *One Hand Tied Behind Us: The Rise of the Women's Suffrage Movement* (London: Virago Press 1978), 206.

7 Quoted by Les Garner, *Stepping Stones to Women's Liberty: Feminist Ideas in the Women's Suffrage Movement* (London: Heinemann Educational Books 1984), 46.

8 Teresa Billington-Greig, *The Militant Suffragette Movement: Emancipation in a Hurry* (London 1911), reprinted in Carol McPhee and Ann FitzGerald, eds., *The Non-Violent Militant: Selected Writings of Teresa Billington-Greig* (London: Routledge and Kegan Paul 1987), 179. For the autocratic evolution of the WSPU and the subsequent formation of the WFL see pp. 102-8 and 179-84. The breakaway group at first retained the name WSPU, then changed its name to the Women's Freedom League. Pankhurst, *The Suffragette Movement*, 265-66; see ch. 3, p. 45.

9 Vancouver *News-Herald*, 31 Mar. 1937, 8.

10 Pankhurst, *The Suffragette Movement*, 252-53, 277, 307. The government had threatened prosecution under the Tumultuous Petitions Act of Charles II.

11 Rosen, *Rise Up, Women!*, 107. Full accounts of the WSPU militant demonstrations are provided in Rosen and in Pankhurst, *The Suffragette Movement*.

12 David Morgan, *Suffragists and Liberals: The Politics of Woman Suffrage in England* (Oxford: Basil Blackwell 1975), 17, 33-34.

13 Ray Strachey, *Millicent Garrett Fawcett* (London: John Murray 1931), 252-53. Margaret Bondfield, *A Life's Work* (London: Hutchinson 1948), 84.

14 Teresa Billington-Greig, *Verbatim Report of Debate on Dec. 3, 1907: Sex Equality (Teresa Billington-Greig) versus Adult Suffrage (Margaret G. Bondfield)* (Manchester: Women's Freedom League 1908), 4-11.

15 Rosen, *Rise Up, Women!*, 34-35; Barbara Castle, *Sylvia and Christabel Pankhurst* (Harmondsworth: Penguin Books 1987), 84-85.

16 Castle, *Sylvia and Christabel Pankhurst*, 83.

17 Ibid., 82.

18 Vancouver *News-Herald*, 31 Mar. 1937, 8.

19 London *Times*, 20 June 1910, 10.

20 Ibid.

21 Pankhurst, *The Suffragette Movement*, 340; Rosen, *Rise Up, Women!*, 137.

22 *VW*, 22 July 1910, 704.

23 **Joachim, Leigh, Massy:** *VW*, 25 Nov. 1910, 122. **Wright:** SFC, acc. no. 57.70.1, Group C, vol. 1, 31-65 passim. **Duval:** *The Suffrage Annual*. **Duval family imprisoned:** Pankhurst, *The Suffragette Movement*, 340, 359. **Helena with Mary Leigh:** *VW*, 25 July 1910.

24 Pankhurst, *The Suffragette Movement*, 343.

25 Vancouver *News-Herald*, 31 Mar. 1937, 8.

26 Rosen, *Rise Up, Women!*, 99, 139-44. Pankhurst, *The Suffragette Movement*, 342-45, reports two men arrested. Helena's name does not appear in the list of arrests published in *VW*, 25 Nov. 1910, in relevant Metropolitan Police Files, PRO, Kew, England, or in the *Morning Advertiser* for dates of suffragist demonstrations with arrests, 13 Feb. 1908 to 26 Nov. 1910. According to the PRO, the police files contain 'no single comprehensive list of all the women arrested on that occasion' [18 Nov. 1910].

27 Quoted in Castle, *Sylvia and Christabel Pankhurst*, 89.

28 Rosen, *Rise Up, Women!*, 150-53.

29 Quoted in Pankhurst, *The Suffragette Movement*, 372.

30 Liddington and Norris, *One Hand Tied Behind Us*, 204-205.

31 Pankhurst, *The Suffragette Movement*, 417. See also pp. 402 and 516-19.

32 **Occupation on Ship's Manifest:** See ch. 2, p. 28.

33 Billington-Greig, *The Militant Suffrage Movement*, 138. See also Pankhurst, *The Suffragette Movement*, 411-14, 374-75, 383-84.

34 *The Champion*, Sept. 1912, 8; Mar. 1913. See also Catherine Lyle Cleverdon, *The Woman Suffrage Movement in Canada* (Toronto: University of Toronto Press (copyright) 1950), 114.

35 Vancouver *News-Herald*, 31 Mar. 1937, 8.

36 Ship's Manifest.

37 London *Times*, 8 Sept. 1911.

38 A.N. Homer, *The Imperial Highway* (London: Sir Joseph Causton and Son, n.d.), 9-15; Arthur E. Copping, *The Golden Land: True Story and Experiences of Settlers in Canada* (London: Hodder and Stoughton, n.d.), ch. 1; Bessie Pullen-Bury, *From Halifax to Vancouver* (London: Mills and Boon [1912]), 3-5.

39 Information about the ship's passengers is from the Ship's Manifest.

40 *Montreal Gazette*, 14 Sept. 1911, 12.

41 Names of stations and distances between them are given in Omer Lavallee, *Van Horne's Road: An Illustrated Account of the Construction and First Years of the Operation of the Canadian Pacific Transcontinental Railway* (Montreal: Railfare Enterprises 1974), 297.

42 W.T. Burall, *A Trip to the Far West of British Columbia: A 13,000 Miles Tour* (Wisback, England: W. Earl [1891]), 12.

43 [Canadian Pacific Railway Co.], *The New Highway to the Orient: Across the Mountains, Prairies and Rivers of Canada* (1893), 40.

CHAPTER FOUR: DEALING WITH TRICKY DICKY

1 Date of arrival calculated from number of days of rail journey per travel accounts.

2 Vancouver *Province*, 22 Sept. 1911.

3 B. Pullen-Bury, *From Halifax to Vancouver* (London: Mills and Boon [1912]), 338-41.

4 *The Tailor*, May 1913, Feb. 1914. Vancouver *Sun*, 17 Jan. 1914, 12. Cutters belonged to the International Custom Cutters' Association of America: *The Tailor*, Apr. 1914, 5.

5 Gillian Weiss, research file cards for '"As Women, As Citizens": Club Women in Vancouver, 1910-1928' (PhD thesis, University of British Columbia 1983); *Henderson's Greater Vancouver and New Westminster Directory (Van. Dir.)*, 1915.

6 Vancouver *World*, 1911: 5 Jan., 8; 6 May, 1, 5; 27 Sept., 3. Catherine Cleverdon, *The Woman Suffrage Movement in Canada* (Toronto: University of Toronto Press (copyright) 1950), 87.

7 VLCW Minute Book, 1920, UBCL, 165 (HG listed as paid for 1916 on page of individual members). Veronica Strong-Boag, *The Parliament of Women: The National Council of Women of Canada, 1893-1929* (Ottawa: National Museums of Canada 1976), 85; Cleverdon, *The Woman Suffrage Movement in Canada*, 12, 89; Wayne Roberts, 'Rocking the Cradle for the World: The New Woman and Maternal Feminism, Toronto, 1877-1914,' in *A Not Unreasonable Claim: Women and Reform in Canada, 1880s-1920s*, ed. Linda Kealey (Toronto: Women's Educational Press 1979), 22-23.

8 Cleverdon, *The Woman Suffrage Movement in Canada*, 5, 87-88; Linda Louise Hale, 'The British Columbia Woman Suffrage Movement, 1890-1917' (MA thesis, University of British Columbia 1977), 39-40.

9 *Womanhood Suffrage*, a speech to the Ontario legislature, 19 May 1893 (Canadian Pamphlet Collection, no. 1487, Parliamentary Library, Ottawa).

10 Quoted in Cleverdon, *The Woman Suffrage Movement in Canada*, 34.

11 Hale, 'Suffrage Movement,' 98-100. Cleverdon, *The Woman Suffrage Movement in Canada*, 28, 51, 86, 186-87.
12 Andrew McPhail, 'On Certain Aspects of Feminism,' *University Magazine*, 13(Feb. 1914):79-91.
13 Henri Bourassa, 'Le suffragisme feminin, son efficacité, sa legitimité,' *Le Devoir*, 24 Apr. 1913.
14 Nellie McClung, 'Hardy Perennials,' in *In Times Like These*, with an introduction by Veronica Strong-Boag (Toronto: University of Toronto Press 1917; reprinted 1972), 57-58.
15 Cleverdon, *The Woman Suffrage Movement in Canada*, 16, 29-31, 61, 47, 75-76, 89, 221-22.
16 Maria Gordon Grant, 'The Franchise,' *Report of the Woman's Christian Temperance Union* (1888):33. Biographical details about Maria Grant are from Gloria Whelen, 'Maria Grant, 1854-1937: The Life and Times of an Early Twentieth Century Christian,' in *In Her Own Right: Selected Essays on Women's History in BC*, ed. Barbara Latham and Cathy Kess (Victoria: Camosun College 1980), 125-46. See also Linda Hale, 'Appendix: Votes for Women: Profiles of Prominent British Columbia Suffragists and Social Reformers,' in Latham and Kess, *In Her Own Right*, 291.
17 Hale, 'Appendix,' 290, 300; Cleverdon, *The Woman Suffrage Movement in Canada*, 89; National Register of Archives, London, England, 20625, Emigration Societies, 'First Report of the Colonial Intelligence League,' 18 Apr. 1910 to 30 Apr. 1911. For the activities of the League in British Columbia, see its Minute Books and Annual Reports, Fawcett Library, City of London Polytechnic, London, England.
18 *The Champion*, Nov. 1912, 6.
19 Also referred to as 'books.' *The Champion*, Oct. 1912, 13. For an account of the philosophies of Frances Swiney and Lady Sybil Smith, see Sheila Jeffreys, *The Spinster and Her Enemies: Feminism and Sexuality, 1880-1930* (London: Pandora Press 1985), 35-39 and 51.
20 Mrs. Pethick Lawrence, 'Across the Atlantic,' in *Votes for Women* (Fall 1912). I am indebted to Sheila Stowell Kaplan for a transcription of this article.
21 Vancouver *World*, 5 Jan. 1911, 8. Research has failed to turn up Mrs. Brignall's given name or anything else about her.
22 Vancouver *World*, 17 Jan. 1911, 16; Cleverdon, *The Woman Suffrage Movement in Canada*, 89.
23 Vancouver *World*, 6 May 1911, 1, 5; *The Champion*, Jan. 1913. The resolution put at Dorothy Davis's meetings was as follows: 'That this Meeting realizes the urgent need that the Woman's Point of View should be directly represented in the control of Legislation and all affairs of the Nation, and deplores the injustice to herself and the loss to the State involved in her present political position; and preferring that British Columbia should lead the

other Provinces of Canada in all matters of Progressive Reform, rather than follow, it calls upon the Provincial Government to introduce and carry, during the coming Session, a Bill giving the Vote to Women on the same terms as it is or may be given to Men': Sir Richard McBride Papers (hereafter RMP), GR 441, vol. 49, file 97, BCARS. A similar resolution was put at Florence Hall's meetings.

24 **McConkey, Smith, Clark, Townley:** Hale, 'Appendix.' **Laverock:** 'Pen Portraits of Club Members,' *Triennial Booklet,* Vancouver Branch of the Canadian Women's Press Club, Add. Mss. #396, CVA. **Helen MacGill:** Elsie MacGill, *My Mother the Judge* (Toronto: Ryerson Press 1955), 42-54.

25 Vancouver *Province,* 20 Sept. 1911; 4 and 23 Sept. 1911, 18. Court of Appeal, 'Before Macdonald, C.J.A., Irving and Galliher, JJ.A,' *Western Weekly Reports,* 1:488-91.

26 Cleverdon, *The Woman Suffrage Movement in Canada,* 141-54. The five suffragists challenged Sec. 24 of the BNA Act: 'The Governor General shall from Time to Time, in the Queen's Name ... summon qualified Persons to the Senate; and subject to the Provisions of this Act, every Person so summoned shall become and be a Member of the Senate and a Senator': from the complete text of the Act in the *Encyclopaedia Canadiana,* 2(1970):9.

27 SBC, 1912, ch. 18.

28 'An Act to Provide for the Government of British Columbia,' *Public General Statutes,* 21 and 22 Vict., 1857-58.

29 'The Proclamation having the force of Law to declare that English Law is in force in British Columbia,' 19 Nov. 1858, cited in 'The English Law Ordinance, 1867,' *Laws of British Columbia,* rev. 1871, 214, which repealed the proclamation and made English law applicable on both the mainland and Vancouver Island. See also Helen Gregory MacGill, comp., *Daughters, Wives and Mothers in British Columbia and Some Laws Regarding Them,* 2d ed. (Vancouver: Moore Printing 1913), 9.

30 Sir William Blackstone, *Commentaries on the Laws of England in Four Books,* [ed.] William Draper Lewis (Philadelphia: Rees, Welsh 1902), 1, 427 (the 1753 University of Oxford Lectures).

31 MacGill, *Daughters, Wives and Mothers,* first published 1913. The following account of the legal position of women in BC is from the second edition (1913), especially pp. 13-25.

32 'Story of Women Suffrage in British Columbia,' Helen Gregory MacGill Papers, Add. Mss. 270, pp. 57-58, CVA.

33 Vancouver *World,* 18 Feb. 1911, 2.

34 **Wise:** Brian R.D. Smith, 'Sir Richard McBride,' *Conservative Concepts* 1(1959):26. Telephone interview with Mary Gallant, Nov. 1989.

35 Vancouver *Province,* 29 Aug. 1911, 6.

36 Margaret A. Ormsby, *British Columbia: A History* (London: Macmillan 1958; reprinted 1971), 362-63. RMP, GR 441, vol. 49, file 97.

272 Notes to pp. 60-66

37 Cleverdon, *The Woman Suffrage Movement in Canada*, 88; Dorothy Davis to Premier McBride, RMP, GR 441, vol. 49, file 97.
38 Vancouver *Province*, 15 Feb. 1913, 16; Victoria *Daily Times*, 17 Feb. 1913, 24. Maria Gordon Grant to The Right Hon. Premier of British Columbia, 14 Feb. 1913 and Janet C. Kemp to Sir Richard McBride, RMP, GR 441, vol. 49, file 97.
39 Victoria *Daily Times*, 20 Feb. 1913, 3.
40 Victoria *Daily Times*, 1 Mar. 1913, 8. **Place's bill:** *Journals of the Legislative Assembly of British Columbia*, 1913, 3 Geo. 5, pp. 55, 105, 115.
41 *The Champion*, 8 May 1912, 11; Apr. 1913, 5.
42 Gillian Weiss, '"The Brightest Women of Our Land": Vancouver Club-women, 1910-1928,' in *Not Just Pin Money: Selected Essays on the History of Women's Work in British Columbia*, ed. Barbara K. Latham and Roberta J. Pazdro (Victoria: Camosun College 1984), 204-5; Weiss, research note cards.
43 Vancouver *World*, 19 Mar. 1913, 1.
44 Pankhurst, *The Suffragette Movement*, 416.
45 Interviews by IH with Hubert Farber, 26 Apr. 1983, and Hilda Kristiansen, 7 Apr. 1983.
46 Vancouver *World*, 19 Mar. 1913, 1.
47 Vancouver *Sun*, 19 Mar. 1913, 18.
48 *The Champion*, Apr. 1913, 5.
49 Vancouver *Province*, 11 June 1913, 24.
50 Vancouver *Sun*, 18 May 1913, 8.
51 Hale, 'Appendix,' 296.
52 Vancouver *Daily News-Advertiser* (DNA), 18 May 1913, 10; 6 June 1913, 11.
53 Elizabeth Norcross, 'Mary Ellen Smith: The Right Woman in the Right Place at the Right Time,' in Latham and Pazdro, *Not Just Pin Money*, 357-58.
54 Hilda Kristiansen, interview by Clay Perry, 11 July 1980.
55 Reynoldston Research and Studies, Oral History Programmes (hereafter Reynoldston), Interview 41, 21 Feb. 1973, BCARS.
56 Pankhurst, *The Suffragette Movement*, 241, 356-58.
57 Reynoldston, Interview 41. The tape actually records a slip of the tongue: 'Mrs. Norton I wish those suffragists would keep out of my meeting ...' Since this does not make sense in the context, I have replaced 'suffragists' with 'socialists,' the word Mary Norton surely intended.
58 DNA, 10 July 1913, 11. Hale, 'Suffrage Movement,' 63-64.
59 Helen Gregory MacGill, 'Story of Woman Suffrage,' 57.
60 DNA, 19 July 1913.
61 VTLC Papers, Executive Minutes, 1913-20, 17 July 1913, UBCL
62 Cleverdon, *The Woman Suffrage Movement in Canada*, 90.
63 *The Tailor*, 4 Aug. 1914, [4].
64 Ibid., 21 Mar. 1916, 3.
65 *Western Clarion*, Feb. 1916, 8.
66 BC Fed., 6 June 1919, quoted in Dorothy Steeves, *The Compassionate Rebel:*

Ernest Winch and the Growth of Socialism in Western Canada (Vancouver: J.J. Douglas 1977), 52. **Lefeaux:** ibid. For an account of the philosophy of the SPC, see A. Ross McCormack, *Rebels, Reformers, and Revolutionaries: The Western Canadian Radical Movement, 1899-1919* (Toronto: University of Toronto Press 1977), 53-65; for impossiblism, 54; McVety, Pettipiece, 74. HG in SPC: 'Helena Gutteridge's Story, as told to Frances Gilstead,' Vancouver *Pacific Tribune*, 8 Mar. 1957, 11.

67 *Western Clarion*, Feb. 1916, 8. For the position of the SPC and SDP on woman suffrage, see Linda Kealey, 'Women in the Canadian Socialist Movement, 1904-1914,' in *Beyond the Vote: Canadian Women and Politics*, ed. Linda Kealey and Joan Sangster (Toronto: University of Toronto Press 1989), 174-78 and n. 10. VTLC leaders Victor Midgely and Bill Pritchard began with the SDP but switched later in the decade to the more revolutionary SPC, as did Ernest Winch: Steeves, *Compassionate Rebel*, 28-29.

68 Frederick Engels, *Socialism: Scientific and Utopian* (New York: International Publishers 1935). Karl Marx, *Critique of the Gotha Programme*, ed. C.P. Dutt, rev. trans. of the 1933 ed. (New York: International Publishers 1938), 10 in the 1986 printing.

69 *BC Fed.*, 3 Oct. 1913, 8.

70 Ibid.

71 **McBride:** Vancouver *Sun*, 20 Feb. 1913, 1. **Helena:** RMP, Correspondence, GR 441, vol. 49, BCARS.

72 RMP, Correspondence, GR 441, vol. 49; *BC Fed.*, 12 Dec. 1913.

73 *BC Fed.*, 12 Dec. 1913.

74 Harold Griffin, *British Columbia: The People's Story* (Vancouver: Tribune Publishing 1958), 55.

75 Vancouver *Province*, 15 Nov. 1913, 7.

76 Steeves, *Compassionate Rebel*, 20-21.

77 *BC Fed.*, 14 Nov. 1913, probably reprinted from the *Christian Commonwealth*. See also 'Will Woman Suffrage Save Economic Problem?' *Western Clarion*, 20 Dec. 1913, 4, a debate between 'Comrade Mrs. Stott' and Dorothy Davis of the PEL.

78 *BC Fed.*, 31 Oct. 1913.

79 Ibid.

80 Hale, 'Appendix'; 'Susan Lane Clark,' Newsclipping Files M1871, CVA.

81 *The West Ender*, 28 Apr. 1983, 6; **probation officer:** Weiss, research note cards. Two woman constables had been on the Vancouver Police Force since 1912, the first in Canada to be so employed.

82 Kealey, 'Women in the Canadian Socialist Movement,' 172; *BC Fed.*, 22 June 1917, 1; *Western Clarion*, 12 Dec. 1903.

83 *The Chronicle*, 10 Nov. 1911, 19, and 9 Dec. 1911. For a brief account of Lily Laverock's journalistic career, see Marjorie Lang and Linda Hale, 'Women of the *World* and Other Dailies: The Lives and Times of Vancouver News-

paperwomen in the First Quarter of the Twentieth Century,' BC *Studies* 85(Spring 1990):16.

84 *Triennial Booklet;* telephone interviews with Bertha Laverock, 15 Nov. 1984, and George Laverock, 26 Oct. 1988.

85 Richard and Winn Arnett, interview by IH, 11 Nov. 1985. Margaret Arnett to IH, 13 Jan. 1985 and 3 Apr. 1986; Margaret Arnett, interview by IH, Chelmsford, England, 16 Apr. 1987.

86 Vancouver *World,* 2 Mar. 1918, 7. Minute Book, 1920, VLCW gives Elizabeth Arnett's address as Winnett P.O., Main Street, Vancouver.

87 *Perthshire Courier,* 20 May and 3 June 1890. Birthdate of Elizabeth Ida Bramwell calculated from 1861 census, General Register Office, Scotland, and from the marriage certificate of Elizabeth Bramwell and Samuel Firn [*sic*], General Register Office, London. Al Bennett, Arlington, WA, to IH, 5 Apr. 1987, gives the birthdate as 1857.

88 Ida Douglas-Fearn, autobiographical memoir, from Al Bennett.

89 **Travelled to Germany:** see photograph CN485, 972.6, Langley Centennial Museum (LCM). **Catholicism:** see marriage certificate. **Brother:** *Perthshire Courier,* 20 May 1890; *Kelly's London Medical Directory,* 1897. See also J. Milne Bramwell, *Hypnotism: Its History, Practice and Theory* (London: A. Moring 1906), 37, 162-65.

90 A photograph of Queen Victoria Hospital, Southampton, 72-6-3 is in the Fearn collection, LCM.

91 Douglas-Fearn memoir; Al Bennett, interview by IH, Vancouver, Dec. 1987.

92 BC *Fed.,* 31 Oct. 1913.

93 British War Office (WO) 97 2788, Army Services; WO 16 1300, Muster Roll of Grenadier Guards. I am indebted to Roderick Barman for interpreting the War Office information and from it reconstructing the military career of Samuel Fearn.

94 Marriage certificate of Elizabeth Bramwell and Samuel Firn [*sic*], General Register Office, PRO, London, England.

95 Bennett letter.

96 Baptismal registers, St. Andrew's Cathedral, Victoria, BC.

97 Douglas-Fearn memoir.

98 Bennett letter; Douglas-Fearn memoir. Obstetrics Diploma, 72-6-1, Archival Register A984.147, LCM.

99 Leonard Philps, interview by IH, Bradner, BC, 1 Mar. 1983.

100 Bennett interview.

101 [Ida Douglas-Fearn], 'The Woman Soul,' copy of MS from Al Bennett.

102 *Van. Dir.,* 1912. DNA, 17 May 1913, 11; 6 June 1913, 11; Vancouver *Sun,* 2 Feb. 1914, 8.

103 S.J. Connelly, Archivist, Perth and Kinross District Council Library, Perth, Scotland, to IH, 9 Oct. 1987.

104 Bennett interview; *Nisbet's Medical Directory,* 1908.

105 Vancouver *Sun*, 11 June 1938, 1, 14.

106 Philps interview. *Van. Dir.*, 1912; United Sheet Metal Workers' International Association, Minutes, 28 May 1925, Add. Mss. 251, vol. 4, CVA. Bennett interview.

107 *BC Fed.*, 23 Jan. 1914.

108 *BC Fed.*, 26 Dec. 1913. **Amaternal woman:** see Ellen Key, *The Woman Movement*, trans. Mamah Bouton Borthwick, intr. Havelock Ellis (New York: G.P. Putnam's Sons 1912), 176-80.

109 'Once she had': [Ida Douglas-Fearn], 'The Woman Soul.'

110 **'Sacred':** *BC Fed.*, 30 Oct. 1914, 4. **'Coals,' 'sickly':** ibid., 16 Jan. 1914.

111 In *The Forerunner* 4, no. 6 (1912):145-49, especially p. 146.

112 *BC Fed.*, 17 Oct. 1913.

113 Gilman, 'New Mothers,' in *The Forerunner*, 146, 147.

114 **O'Boyle:** Vancouver *Province*, 2 June 1913, 22; **indignant:** Vancouver *Province*, 9 June 1913, 14.

115 All three quotations from Vancouver *World*, 16 June 1913, 14.

116 **Wylie:** Vancouver *Sun*, 5 Feb. 1913, 1. **Parker:** Vancouver *World*, 26 June 1913, 20.

117 Vancouver *Province*, 18 Nov. 1913, 21.

118 *BC Fed.*, 21 Nov. 1913.

119 *BC Fed.*, 30 Jan. 1914.

120 *BC Fed.*, 16 Jan. 1914.

121 Vancouver *World*, 16 June 1913, 14.

122 Olive Schreiner, *Woman and Labour* (London: Virago 1978 [first published, London: Unwin 1913]), 33, 146.

123 *The Champion*, 14 Jan. 1913, 4. For member societies see Bowser Papers, GR 441, vol. 171, file 293 passim, BCARS; and *Western Woman's Weekly*, 14 Feb. 1918, 7.

124 *BC Fed.*, 12 Dec. 1913, 1.

125 *BC Fed.*, 19 Dec. 1913.

CHAPTER FIVE: THE CAUSE VICTORIOUS

1 Transcript of evidence given by Helena Gutteridge before Royal Commission on Labour Conditions in British Columbia, GR 684, box 1, file 8, BCARS. Her evidence implies that the factory workrooms employed both men and women, in all but two places on piece work. For those two it is not clear whether she was reporting wages for women only or for both men and women; 'Report on Departmental Store Labour,' William Filtness, ibid., Box 4, file 15. *Labour Gazette*, Apr. 1913, 1105-7.

2 *Labour Gazette*, May 1914, 1288; June 1914, 1412; Aug. 1914, 189.

3 'Labour Gazette' file, RG 27, vol. 4, FAD, NAC.

4 Helena Gutteridge to the Hon. T.W. Crothers, Minister of Labour, 12 Nov.

1915, RG 27, vol. 4, FAD, NAC.

5 *BC Fed.*, 13 Feb. 1914, 8. *Labour Gazette,* Aug. 1913, 152.

6 **All quotes:** *BC Fed.*, 6 Feb. 1914, [25]. Vancouver *Sun,* 28 Jan. 1914, 5; 12 Dec. 1914, 8.

7 *BC Fed.*, 4 Sept. 1914, 2.

8 Ibid., 30 Oct. 1914, 4.

9 Ibid., 17 Dec. 1915, 4.

10 Ibid., 17 Dec. 1915, 4. For a discussion of 'female essentialism and radical feminism,' see Zillah R. Eisenstein, *Feminism and Sexual Equality: Crisis in Liberal America* (New York: Monthly Review Press 1984), 223-24.

11 *BC Fed.*, 11 June 1915, 3; 18 June 1915, 1.

12 Vancouver *World,* 1 June 1916; 15 June 1916, 11; Victoria *Daily Times,* 6 Apr. 1917, 12. Elsie Gregory MacGill, *My Mother the Judge* (Toronto: Ryerson Press 1955), 150.

13 Cleverdon, *The Woman Suffrage Movement in Canada,* 60, 62.

14 *BC Fed.*, 18 June 1915, 1; 11 June 1915, 3.

15 Gutteridge to Bowser, 14 Dec. 1915, William Bowser Papers, Correspondence Inwards (WBP), GR 441, vol. 171, file 293, BCARS.

16 Helen MacGill, acting secretary [USS], to Bowser, 15 Apr. 1916, WBP, GR 441, vol. 171, file 293.

17 Victoria *Daily Times,* 14 Apr. 1916.

18 Gutteridge to Bowser, 11 Apr. 1916, WBP, GR 441, vol. 171, file 293.

19 Cleverdon, *The Woman Suffrage Movement in Canada,* 96.

20 Vancouver *World,* 26 Apr. 1916, 10.

21 *Western Woman's Weekly,* 24 Jan. 1918, 1.

22 Vancouver *World,* 26 Apr. 1916, 10.

23 Ibid.

24 Vancouver *World,* 16 May 1916, 5.

25 Ibid.

26 Vancouver *World,* 17 May 1916, 3.

27 Ibid.

28 Vancouver *World,* 1 June 1916.

29 Cleverdon, *The Woman Suffrage Movement in Canada,* 63.

30 MacGill, *My Mother the Judge,* 151.

31 Vancouver *World,* 1 June 1916.

32 Vancouver *World,* 13 June 1916, 11.

33 Secretary's report, Vancouver *World,* 23 Sept. 1916, 15. The secretary refers to the BC Political Equality League as the Provincial Political Equality League and also as the PPEL. However, the Pioneer Political Equality League had been using the PPEL abbreviation for nearly four years.

34 Vancouver *World,* 16 May 1916, 12. Vancouver *Sun,* 1916: 8 June, 3; 9 June, 4; 19 June, 3; **Pankhurst quote:** Vancouver *Sun,* 10 June 1916, 3. **Jamieson quote:** ibid., 8.

35 Vancouver *World*, 2 June 1916, 7.

36 Vancouver *World*, 5 Oct. 1916, 5.

37 *BC Fed.*, 27 July 1917, 6. See ch. 6, p. 118.

38 Quoted in Pankhurst, *The Suffragette Movement*, 595, n. 1.

39 **Arnett:** Vancouver *World*, 3 Aug. 1916, 5. **Clark:** *Western Woman's Weekly*, 10 Jan. 1918, 5; Weiss, research notes. **Woodsworth:** Grace MacInnis, *J.S. Woodsworth, a Man to Remember* (Toronto: Macmillan of Canada 1953), 105-7, 127. **Steeves:** Steeves Papers, 'Autobiographical Notes,' Box 1, AMMC. **Jamieson:** Conversation with Stuart Jamieson, 9 Jan. 1992. For the differing attitudes and behaviour of peacetime pacifists and peace activists see Barbara Roberts, 'Women's Peace Activism in Canada,' in *Beyond the Vote: Canadian Women and Politics*, ed. Linda Kealey and Joan Sangster (Toronto: University of Toronto Press 1989), 276-77, 279.

40 Vancouver *Sun*, 15 June 1916, 3.

41 Vancouver *Globe*, 28 Nov. 1916, 8; 29 Nov. 1916, 4. Vancouver *World*, 13 June 1916, 3.

42 Secretary's report, Vancouver *World*, 23 Sept. 1916, 15. **Thumbnail biography of Mrs. Bryan:** DNA, 17 Sept. 1916, 10.

43 Names of male suffrage workers culled from reports of campaign meetings, Vancouver *World*, June-Sept. 1916.

44 Secretary's report, Vancouver *World*, 23 Sept. 1916, 15. **Biographical details for Perry and Smith:** Weiss, research note cards.

45 Vancouver *World*, 25 May 1916, 5; 31 May 1916, 5; 23 June 1916, 5, 7, 13, 17, 27 June and 4, 7, 12 July 1916, all references p. 5. The Mount Pleasant Suffrage League, in which Susie Clark was a leading figure, was in Ward V. Of eight city wards, the women only managed to organize in six.

46 Vancouver *World*, 19 Apr. 1916, 5; 26 Apr. 1916, 16.

47 Clark and Gutteridge to Bowser, n.d.; Bowser to Clark, 3 Aug. 1916, WBP, G441, vol. 171, file 293.

48 *BC Fed.*, 11 Aug. 1916, 2.

49 VTLC Minutes, 2 July 1914; 21 Jan. and 15 July 1915; 20 Jan. 1916. Unless otherwise stated, VTLC Minutes are for regular meetings.

50 *BC Fed.*, 11 Aug. 1916, 1.

51 Vancouver *World*, 8 Sept. 1916, 12. The *BC Fed.*, 8 Sept. 1916, 2, reports that she resigned as vice president, indicating that in the July semi-annual elections she had moved from general secretary to vice president.

52 Vancouver *World*, 23 and 24 Aug. 1916, 5.

53 Vancouver *World*, 13 June 1916, 11; 7 Sept. 1916, 16; 27 June 1916, 5; 9 Aug. 1916, 5.

54 *BC Fed.*, 3 July 1914, 2.

55 Ethel Wilson, *The Innocent Traveller* (Toronto: Macmillan of Canada 1960), 170. On the important place of the Chinese in the British Columbia economy, see Jean Barman, *The West Beyond the West: A History of British*

Columbia (Toronto: University of Toronto Press 1991), 133-36.

56 RMP, GR 441, vol. 49, file 97. See ch. 4, p. 60.

57 Vancouver *World*, 13 June 1916, 11.

58 On the relation of suffragists and other reform groups to the status quo, see Aileen S. Kraditor, 'American Radical Historians on Their Heritage,' *Past and Present*, no. 56 (Aug. 1972):148-49.

59 **Head tax:** *Canadian Encyclopedia*, 1st ed., see Chinese. **Riots:** Margaret A. Ormsby, *British Columbia: A History* (London: Macmillan of Canada 1958 [reprinted 1971]), 350-52; Alan Morley, *Vancouver: From Milltown to Metropolis* (Vancouver: Mitchell Press 1961), 122. **Komagata Maru:** Ormsby, *British Columbia*, 369-70.

60 Hans Bergman, *British Columbia och dess Svenska Innebyggare* (Victoria: privately published 1923), 165. I heard this story in 1969 in an interview with a woman who had been a child in that classroom.

61 Gillian Creese, 'Exclusion or Solidarity? Vancouver Workers Confront the "Oriental Problem",' *BC Studies* (Winter 1988-89):30-34. **McVety:** *Labour Gazette*, May 1913, 1272. **Nice:** see ch. 5, p. 82.

62 Quoted in Claudia Roth Pierpont, 'A Woman's Place,' *The New Yorker*, 27 Jan. 1992, 79. See also ibid., 83. (A biographical article on Olive Schreiner)

63 DNA, 2 Sept. 1916, 7.

64 Vancouver *World*, 2 Sept. 1916, 11.

65 Vancouver *World*, 11 Sept. 1916, 12.

66 Ibid., 25 Aug. 1916, 5.

67 DNA, 10 Sept. 1916, 23.

68 Ibid., 17 Sept. 1916, 18.

69 SBC, 1917, ch. 49. See also Audrey M. Adams, 'A Study of the Use of Plebiscites and Referendums by the Province of British Columbia' (MA thesis, University of British Columbia 1958).

70 DNA, 17 Sept. 1916, 18.

71 DNA, 13 Sept. 1916.

72 Percentages calculated on early returns in Vancouver *World*, 15 Sept. 1916, 3, and Victoria *Daily Times*, 15 Sept. 1916, 7. See Michael H. Cramer, 'Public and Political: Documents of the Woman Suffrage Campaign in British Columbia, 1871-1917: The View from Victoria,' in *In Her Own Right: Selected Essays on Women's History in BC*, ed. Barbara Latham and Cathy Kess (Victoria: Camosun College 1980), 95.

73 Cramer, 'Public and Political,' 95.

74 Victoria *Daily Times*, 27, 28, 30 Mar. and 4 Apr. 1917.

75 Cleverdon, *The Woman Suffrage Movement in Canada*, 100.

76 Victoria *Daily Times*, 6 Apr. 1917, 12; Cleverdon, *The Woman Suffrage Movement in Canada*, 100.

77 *Canadian Annual Review* (CAR), 1918, 730. Mary Ellen Smith got 10,213 votes, against 6,701 for the Conservatives.

78 *SC*, The Franchise Act, 1898, 61 Vic., ch. 14, sec. 5A. The exceptions were (1) Alberta and Saskatchewan, which, joining Confederation after passage of the Act, had a different federal franchise law that excluded women and Indians, and (2) the Yukon, where the same restrictions were in force. See also Vancouver *World*, 12 Oct. 1916, 9.

79 Cleverdon, *The Woman Suffrage Movement in Canada*, 120; *Canadian Encyclopedia*, 1st ed., under 'Borden, Sir Robert Laird,' by Robert Craig Brown.

80 *SC*, 7-8 Geo. V, War-time Elections Act, 1917, ch. 39, secs. 32, 33 on women; sec. 67 on aliens.

81 Cleverdon, *The Woman Suffrage Movement in Canada*, 124-29.

82 *HCD*, 1917, 5647.

83 Vancouver *Province*, 13 Sept. 1917, 14.

84 Ibid., 20 Sept. 1917, 6.

85 *BC Fed.*, 7 Sept. 1917, 1; 5 Oct. 1917, 4.

86 Quoted in Vancouver *Province*, 7 Sept. 1917, 11.

87 Cleverdon, *The Woman Suffrage Movement in Canada*, 131.

88 *HCD*, 1917, 5647.

89 Vancouver *Province*, 20 Sept. 1917, 3. Text of telegram, over signature of Mrs. C.E.M. Dickson: 'Regarding telegram from United Suffrage Societies of BC. This meeting consisted of eight Vancouver women who did not notify anyone outside of themselves of meeting. Patriotic women of Vancouver resent this being published as expressing their sentiments on the question.' See also her letter, Vancouver *Province*, 26 Sept. 1917, 8.

90 Vancouver *Province*, 29 Sept. 1917, 5.

91 *HCD*, 1918, I, 89.

92 *SC*, 1918, ch. 20. **Quebec MPS:** Cleverdon, *The Woman Suffrage Movement in Canada*, 133.

93 Thomas Hood, 'Song of the Shirt,' in *The Complete Poetical Works of Thomas Hood*, ed. Walter Jerrold (London: Henry Frowde 1906), 625.

94 *BC Fed.*, 27 July 1917, 1, 6.

95 Vancouver *World*, 9 June 1916, 5. Names of BCPEL members do not appear on the reported list of guests at the head table.

96 Vancouver *World*, 29 Sept. 1916, 5.

97 Ibid., 27 Oct. 1916, 5.

98 Ibid., 4 Nov. 1916, 5.

99 Ibid., 8 Nov. 1916, 5.

100 Ibid., 20 Dec. 1916, 5.

101 Gillian Weiss, '"As Women, As Citizens": Clubwomen in Vancouver, 1910-1928' (PhD thesis, University of British Columbia 1983), 81ff.

102 *SBC*, 1920, ch. 61.

103 Vancouver *Province*, 22 Mar. 1918, 6.

104 Vancouver *World*, 27 Nov. 1916, 5.

105 Vancouver *Province*, 22 May 1917, 8

106 Vancouver *World*, 18 Sept. 1917, 5. Weiss, research note cards.
107 Vancouver *Sun*, 14 Mar. 1920, 13.
108 *BC Fed.*, 30 Aug. 1918, 6.

CHAPTER SIX: HOURS AND WAGES

1 C. McDonald to editor, *The Tailor*, 8 Sept. 1914.
2 J.R. Wilkinson to editor, [Oct. 1911], RG 27, vol. 4, *Labour Gazette* file (here-after LG file), FAD, NAC. For an account of unemployment in Vancouver at this time, see Patricia Roy, 'Vancouver: "The Mecca of the Unemployed," 1907-1929,' in *Town and City: Aspects of Western Canadian Urban Development*, ed. Alan F.J. Artibise (Regina: Canadian Plains Research Centre 1981), 393-99. Allan Seager, 'Introduction,' in *Working Lives: Vancouver 1886-1986* (Vancouver: New Star Books 1985), 13. Robert McDonald, 'Working,' *Working Lives*, 26, 28.
3 McDonald, 'Working,' 28.
4 Gutteridge to editor, 11 July 1914, LG file. **Crèche:** *The Vancouver Annual*, 11, Pamphlet Collection, 1912-18, CVA, Van, Clark, and Stuart. Gutteridge reports in *Labour Gazette:* **teachers:** June 1915, 1411; **Woolworth's, Scotch women:** Aug. 1913, 152; **Chinese servants:** May 1914, 1288; **domestics:** May 1915, 1298. For a brief history of Vancouver's relief services, 1911-15, see Diane Matters, 'The Development of Public Welfare Institutions in Van-couver, 1910-1920' (BA graduating essay, University of Victoria 1973), 23.
5 VTLC Minutes, 21 May 1914. As general secretary, Helena likely received the same stipend as her predecessor, George Bartley.
6 *The Tailor*, Dec. 1913. **'Aristocratic':** ibid., 21 Dec. 1915, 3; *Van. Dir.*, 1920; *BC Fed.*, 30 Oct. 1914.
7 VTLC Minutes, 14 Apr. 1915.
8 Ibid., 5 and 19 Mar. 1914; *BC Fed.*, 12 Sept. 1913, 5; 22 Dec. 1916, 1; 17 Aug. 1917, 6; Vancouver *Sun*, 31 Jan. 1914, 11.
9 Charles Jacob Stowell, *The Journeymen Tailors' Union of America: A Study in Trade Union Policy*, University of Illinois Studies in the Social Sciences, vol. 7, no. 13 (Urbana: University of Illinois 1918), 27-43. C. McDonald to editor, *The Tailor*, Feb. 1914.
10 *The Tailor*, 9 Feb. 1915, 2.
11 J. Kavanagh, president of the VTLC, and R. Pettipiece to secretary, [JTUA], *The Tailor*, Nov. 1912 (monthly issues unpaginated).
12 *The Tailor*, Jan. 1913. See also 2 Mar. 1915, 3. For a running account of the amal-gamation negotiations see ibid., Aug., Nov., and Dec. 1913, May 1914; 15 Dec. 1914, 1; 5 Jan. 1915, 2; 9 Feb. 1915, 2 and 3; 11 May 1915; 7 July 1915, 1 and 4. For an account of tailors in Vancouver and Victoria, see James Robert Con-ley, 'Class Conflict and Collective Action in the Working Class of Vancouver, British Columbia, 1900-1919' (PhD dissertation, Carleton University 1986), 425-

30. For a full history of the JTUA, see Stowell, *Journeymen Tailors' Union.*

13 *The Tailor,* 8 Sept. 1914, [3]. Conley, 'Class Conflict and Collective Action,' 429-30. [Gutteridge report], *Labour Gazette,* Apr. 1913, 1079.

14 *BC Fed.,* 25 Sept. 1914, 1. Vancouver *Sun,* 15 Oct. 1914, 5.

15 *BC Fed.,* 9 Oct. 1914, 1.

16 Ibid.

17 McBride to Unsworth, 19 Dec. 1914, Premier, Official Letterbook, 9 Dec. 1914 to 1 Mar. 1915, 191, BCARS. *BC Fed.,* 16 Oct. 1914, 1. City Clerk to City Comptroller, 20 Oct. 1914, City Clerk's Series 1, Letterbook, 7 Oct. 1914 to 12 Apr. 1915, CVA (hereafter CC Letterbook).

18 Vancouver *Sun,* 28 Nov. 1914, 8. For the following account of Carvell Hall Co-operative, see *BC Fed.,* 23 Oct. 1914, 1; 30 Oct. 1914, 4; 20 Nov. 1914, 1; 27 Nov. 1914, 1; 11 Dec. 1914, 1; 18 Feb. 1915; Vancouver *Sun,* 1914, 26 Oct., 7; 30 Oct., 5; 2 Nov., 5; 3 Nov., 5; 10 Nov., 5; 12 Nov., 5; 23 Nov., 5; 4 Dec., 5; 8 Dec., 5; 12 Dec., 5 and 8; 21 Dec., 5; 28 Dec., 5; 'French Cabaret in Aid of Women's Employment League,' Pamphlet Collection, 1914-20, CVA.

19 *BC Fed.,* 25 Sept. 1914, 1.

20 Vancouver *Sun,* 14 Jan. 1915, 3; 25 Jan. 1915, 5.

21 The inscription reads 'Presented to Helena Gutteridge/by/W E League/Jan 1915.'

22 Gutteridge to editor, 15 Oct. 1914, and 'Statement re Unemployment and Releif [*sic*] in the City of Vancouver,' [1914], LG file; J.W. Wilkinson to editor, 24 Nov. 1914, ibid. *BC Fed.,* 27 Nov. 1914.

23 Vancouver *Province,* 19 Oct. 1914, 5. See also the reply of the *BC Fed.,* 23 Oct. 1914, 4.

24 *BC Fed.,* 19 Feb. 1915, 1.

25 Gutteridge to the Hon. T.W. Crothers, Minister of Labour, Ottawa, 12 Nov. 1915, LG file.

26 *BC Fed.,* 16 Oct. 1914, 1.

27 *BC Fed.,* 17 July 1914, 1.

28 Paul Phillips, *No Power Greater: A Century of Labour in BC* (Vancouver: BC Federation of Labour and Boag Foundation 1967), 42, note.

29 *BC Fed.,* 27 Nov. 1914, 1.

30 *BC Fed.,* 12 Mar. 1915, 1.

31 **Permanent foreigners; pure doctrine:** Gillian Creese, 'Exclusion or Solidarity? Vancouver Workers Confront the "Oriental Problem",' *BC Studies* 80(Winter 1988-89):33-34 and 37. Phillips, *No Power Greater,* 88-89.

32 VTLC Minutes, 15 Apr. 1915. City Clerk to City Comptroller, 20 Oct. 1914, CC Letterbook, CVA.

33 Canada, Department of Labour, *National Industrial Conference, Ottawa, September 15-20, 1919: Official Report of Proceedings and Discussions* (Ottawa: Department of Labour 1919), 108 (hereafter NIC Report). Creese, 'Exclusion or Solidarity,' 37.

34 Vancouver *World*, 1 Sept. 1916, 5.

35 Vancouver *World*, 5, 10, 14, 23 Aug. 1916, 5; 29 Nov. 1916, 9.

36 Victoria *Daily Times*, 1 Mar. 1917, 8.

37 *Western Woman's Weekly*, 10 Jan. 1918, 9.

38 *BC Fed.*, 26 Oct. 1917, 1.

39 MacGill, *My Mother the Judge*, 158.

40 Vancouver *World*, 2 Mar. 1918, 13. For the history of the minimum wage see Margaret E. McCallum, 'Keeping Women in Their Place: The Minimum Wage in Canada, 1910-25,' *Labour/Le Travail: Journal of Canadian Labour Studies* (Spring 1986):30-33; *NIC Report*, LII-LIII; Harold Underhill, 'Labour Legislation in British Columbia' (PhD thesis, University of California 1936), 136. For local support of the legislation, see *BC Fed.*, 22 June 1917, 1; University Women's Club, Minutes, 11 Mar. 1916, Add. Mss. 872, 1:1, CVA.

41 Vancouver *Province*, 15 Feb. 1918, 8; Vancouver *World*, 13 Mar. 1918, 5.

42 Vancouver *Province*, 2 Feb. 1918, 4.

43 Vancouver *Province*, 6 Mar. 1918, 1. None of the suffrage societies sent representatives, nor did the University Women's Club or the YWCA, although they were all on record as supporting the measure.

44 *SBC*, 1918, ch. 56.

45 British Columbia, Department of Labour, 'Report to the Minimum Wage Board of British Columbia,' in BC Sessional Papers, 1919, vol. 1, H61-H66, H72 (hereafter MWB 1919); 'Report of the Minimum Wage Board of British Columbia,' in BC Sessional Papers 1920, K81-K84 (hereafter MWB 1920).

46 MWB 1919, H75.

47 Vancouver *Sun*, 6 July 1918, 4; 26 July 1918, 3. **Talking:** Steeves, *Compassionate Rebel*, 47.

48 *BC Fed.*, 7 May 1917, 1. This paragraph is based on Phillips, *No Power Greater*, 71-74, esp. citing 'collective ownership'; *BC Fed.*, 8 Feb. 1918; Martin Robin, *Radical Politics and Canadian Labour, 1880-1930* (Kingston: Industrial Relations Centre, Queen's University 1968), 148-54; Steeves, *Compassionate Rebel*, 36-37.

49 *BC Fed.*, 27 July 1917, 6. See ch. 5, p. 89.

50 *BC Fed.*, 2 Aug. 1918, 1. For the story of Goodwin's labour activities and a detailed analysis of the investigation into his death, see Susan Mayse, *Ginger: The Life and Death of Albert Goodwin* (Madeira Park, BC: Harbour Publishing 1990), esp. chs. 8 and 12-14.

51 Steeves, *Compassionate Rebel*, 38-40; Phillips, *No Power Greater*, 72-74; *BC Fed.*, 4 Oct. 1918, 1.

52 'Helena Gutteridge,' report of an interview with HG [by Dorothy Steeves] on E.E. Winch, E.E. Winch Papers, 55A-16, AMMC (hereafter [Steeves], HG interview). From internal evidence I conclude that Dorothy Steeves interviewed Helena when researching Ernest Winch, and that this is her typescript summary.

53 *BC Fed.*, 6 Sept. 1918, 1; 13 Sept. 1918, 1; 4 Oct. 1918, 1. See 'Report of the Deputy Minister,' Department of Labour, BC Sessional Papers, 1919, H52, for a concise account of the strike negotiations.

54 *BC Fed.*, 11 Oct. 1918, 1; 25 Oct. 1918, 1.

55 *BC Fed.*, 11 Oct. 1918, 1. **Solid support:** 18 Oct. 1918, 1.

56 Ibid., 27 Sept. 1918, 1 and 5.

57 Ibid., 8 Nov. 1918, 1.

58 Ibid., 8 Nov. 1918, 1. **Kelly:** ibid., 15 Nov. 1918, 1. For the continuing story of the strike, see 29 Nov. 1918, 1; 20 Sept. 1918, 1; 13 Dec. 1918, 1.

59 Ibid., 29 Nov. 1918, 5.

60 Ibid., 6 Dec. 1918, 5. Vancouver *World*, 5 Dec. 1918, 2. Vancouver *Sun*, 6 Dec. 1918, 3. The *Sun* report erroneously cites Helena Gutteridge as business agent for the Women Retail Store Employees' Union. The retail clerks were organized under the Retail Clerks' International Protective Association, represented during the minimum wage public hearings by A.P. Glenn. Analysis of tabulated statements of wages of mercantile and laundry workers as given by employers, and the decisions of the Minimum Wage Board for these occupations are in MWB 1919, H61-H65.

61 'Canada Steps Out,' quoted in Underhill, 'Labour Legislation in British Columbia,' 141-42. It has not been possible to find this article or pamphlet.

62 MWB 1919, H62; *BC Fed.*, 20 Dec. 1918, 1.

63 Ibid., 3 Jan. 1919, 5; and 10 Jan. 1919, 8.

64 MWB 1919, H75. MWB 1920, K81.

65 *BC Fed.*, 20 June 1919, 2.

66 Quoted in Elsie MacGill, *My Mother the Judge*, 160.

67 Ibid., 160.

68 MWB 1919, H58.

69 *BC Fed.*, 20 June 1919, 8.

70 *Industrial Canada*, 1920, 183, quoted in Underhill, 'Labour Legislation in British Columbia,' 144. *SBC*, 1921, ch. 40, sec. 3.

71 Weiss, 'As Women, As Citizens,' 203; Underhill, 'Labour Legislation in British Columbia,' 144.

72 MWB 1920, K97-K98.

73 *Labour Gazette*, Aug. 1919, 862.

74 In Manitoba, where minimum wage legislation went into effect early in 1918, the awards were a good deal lower, even taking into consideration the higher cost of living in British Columbia. After the wage scale was moved upwards, the Manitoba awards ranged from a low of $11 to a high of $12.50: E. Parnell, member of Manitoba Minimum Wage Board: NIC *Report*, 111; cf. *Labour Gazette*, Dec. 1918, 1121. See also Linda Kealey, 'Women and Labour during World War I: Women Workers and the Minimum Wage in Manitoba,' in *First Days, Fighting Days: Women in Manitoba History*, ed. Mary Kinnear (Regina: Canadian Plains Research Centre 1987), 76-99.

75 VTLC Minutes, Executive Board, 4 Nov. 1918. VTLC Minutes 7 Aug. 1919.

76 **Garment Workers:** Canada, Department of Labour, *Annual Report on Labour*, 1918; ibid., 1919. Helena had left the JTUA to join the Tailors' and Tailoresses' Union: *BC Fed.*, 7 May 1917, 1.

77 [Steeves], HG interview.

78 See Steeves, *Compassionate Rebel*, 46-60, for Steeves's account of the radicals' organizing of the BC Loggers' Union, based on the Helena Gutteridge interview, and of the radicals' influence in the VTLC and the LWIU's part in the events of 1919.

79 A. Ross McCormack, *Reformers, Rebels and Revolutionaries: The Western Canadian Radical Movement, 1899-1919* (Toronto: University of Toronto Press 1977), 157-59.

80 McCormack, *Reformers, Rebels and Revolutionaries*, chs. 8 and 9; see also David Jay Bercuson, *Confrontation at Winnipeg: Labour, Industrial Relations, and the General Strike* (Montreal: McGill-Queen's University Press 1974), ch. 7. **The Vancouver strike vote was 3,305 in favour, 2,499 against:** Bercuson, 155-56. **Raids:** Steeves, *Compassionate Rebel*, 54-55.

81 [Steeves], HG interview.

82 *BC Fed.*, 1 Aug. 1919. Phillips, *No Power Greater*, 85.

83 NIC *Report*, 4. The other two representing women workers as a whole were Kathleen Derry, Boot and Shoe Workers' Union, Toronto, and Doris Meakin, International Brotherhood of Electrical Workers (Telephone Operators), Winnipeg. A fourth, Lena Cormier, was a delegate from the United Textile Workers, Moncton, NB. VTLC Minutes, 18 Sept. 1919, 17.

84 VTLC Minutes, 18 Sept. 1919.

85 *Van. Dir.* 1918 lists Helena Gutteridge as an operator for J. Thomson and Sons; among 'Employers' delegates' in the NIC list, 2, appears 'J.B. Thomson, James Thomson & Sons, Ltd., Vancouver.'

86 NIC *Report*, XV, 156-60. Before the war, King had been asked by the Rockefeller Foundation of New York to draw up plans for handling industrial disputes.

87 NIC *Report*, 60-73 passim.

88 Ibid., 67.

89 Ibid., 68.

90 Vancouver *Province*, 17 Sept. 1919, 5.

91 NIC *Report*, 104.

92 Ibid., 105. **Helena's speech on minimum wage:** ibid., 104-9.

93 Ibid., 106.

94 Ibid., 109.

95 Ibid., 114.

96 Ibid., 96.

97 Ibid., 186.

98 Ibid., 203-13, 220-27.

99 Toronto *Globe*, 27 Sept. 1919, 1.

CHAPTER SEVEN: BACK TO THE LAND

1 Certificate of Marriage, James Purvis Oliver Fearn and Helena Rose Gutteridge, Washington State Board of Health, Bureau of Vital Statistics, Whatcom County Auditor, Bellingham, WA. Unidentified newspaper clipping reporting the marriage, private possession. **North Vancouver address:** *Van. Dir.*, 1918: 1332 Chesterfield; 1920: 1342 Chesterfield. **Details of Oliver Fearn's military service:** documents from Personnel Records Centre, Government Records Branch, NAC, including 'Discharge Certificate,' 'Statement of Service in the Canadian Armed Forces,' 'Casualty Form – Active Service.' USMWIA, Minutes, 28 May 1925, Add. Mss. 251, vol. 4, CVA.

2 *Van. Dir.*, 1923.

3 BC *Fed.*, 29 Nov. 1918, 2. VTLC Minutes, 6 Sept. 1921. *Van. Dir.*, 1918 lists Helena as an operator for J. Thomson and Sons, and in 1920 as a tailoress for Perry and Dolk, 419 Dunsmuir Street; no listing for 1919. **Agreement:** VTLC Minutes, 6 Sept. 1921.

4 Jim Barker, conversation with IH, 25 Jan. 1992. Information about Fred Perry and the Dolks comes from interviews with Lillian Hill, 20 Oct. 1989, and Jim Barker, 30 Oct. 1989. **Perry obituary:** *The BC Mountaineer*, Dec. 1953.

5 The Mothers' Pension Act received royal assent in the BC legislature on 17 Apr. 1920: *SBC*, 1920, ch. 61.

6 VTLC Minutes, 15 Jan. 1920. Phillips, *No Power Greater*, 84-87.

7 *The Tailor*, 26 Oct. 1915, 3.

8 BC Land Title Office, New Westminster, Certificate of Indefeasible Title, no. 40617E, 1 June 1921. The Corporation of the District of Matsqui Assessment and Collector's Roll, 1926, provided the legal description: 'Pt. of S.E. quarter (SW) Sec. 12/Tshp 14. Map 282. 3.07 [acres].' The last mention of Helena in the VTLC Minutes is for 7 July 1921.

9 Matsqui-Sumas-Abbotsford Centennial Committee, *Where Trails Meet* (Matsqui-Sumas-Abbotsford Centennial Society, n.d.), 51.

10 Hubert Farber, interview by IH, 26 Apr. 1983. Mr. Farber supplied a detailed description of Helena's farm, the house, and buildings, and of the day-to-day running of the poultry farm. This chapter also draws on interviews with Dorothy Taylor, 16 Nov. 1982; Leonard Philps, 1 Mar. 1983; Florence Ryder, 7 Mar. 1983; Lucy and Ruth Owen, 1 and 7 Mar. 1983; Stasia Moran Maguire, 12 Jan. 1984; Fred Herron, Rosita Herron Maw, Mary Harvey, 13 Jan. 1984; Al Bennett, Dec. 1987. Telephone interviews: Vermona Farber Kirkland, 3 Jan. 1984; Beatrice Lehman, 10 Mar. 1983; Agnes McPhail, 10 Mar. 1983 (no relation to the MP); Dorothy Taylor, 2 Feb. 1990. The diaries of Richard Owen, 1905 to about 1945, provided much information about farming in the Mount Lehman area in the 1920s.

11 Carol J. Dennison, 'They Also Served: The British Columbia Women's Institutes in Two World Wars,' in *In Her Own Right: Selected Essays on Women's History in BC*, ed. Barbara Latham and Cathy Kess (Victoria: Camosun College 1980), 199-200.

12 *British Columbian,* 6 Sept. 1921, 7; 30 Sept. 1921, 5; 3 Oct. 1921, 3; 19 Dec. 1921, 2. The report on Helena's talk is in British Columbia Department of Agriculture, *The Agricultural Journal*, 6(Oct. 1921):230. **'Gravediggers':** Karl Marx and Friedrich Engels, *The Communist Manifesto*, ed. and annotated by Friedrich Engels, trans. by Samuel Moore, 1988 (Toronto: Progress Books n.d.), 21, first published 1848.

13 *British Columbian*, 11 Jan. 1921, 7.

14 *British Columbian* for 1921: 4, 19, 29 Jan.; 5 Feb.; 18 Mar.; 27 Sept.; 26 Oct.; Richard Owen, Diary, 13 June 1930.

15 *British Columbian*, 28 Nov. and 28 Dec. 1921; 14 Jan. 1922.

16 Dorothy Taylor, telephone interview, 2 Feb. 1990.

17 'In the Supreme Court of British Columbia in Divorce and Matrimonial Causes,' 1318/28, 8 Dec. 1928, Order Book, vol. 140, fol. 168; Supreme Court Cause Sheet 1319/28, BCARS.

   Even if Ollie and Helena agreed that their marriage was legally null and void and they decided to live apart, a declaration of the court would still have been necessary, then as now, to free them both and make them single again. A person in a similar marital predicament today might simply move out and live common law with the new partner. In the 1920s, such relationships were socially unacceptable, and Rose Dennison, with four young sons, could not have agreed to allow Ollie just to move in with her without injury to her own and her neighbours' sense of what was right and proper. I am grateful to Elspeth Gardner for legal information on this matter.

18 'In the Supreme Court of British Columbia in Divorce and Matrimonial Causes,' 1319/1928, 21 Dec. 1928, GR 1507, Order Book, vol. 72, fol. 26, BCARS.

19 Dorothy Taylor, interview, 16 Nov. 1982.

20 Wilhelm Stekel, 'Frigidity in Mothers,' in *The New Generation*, ed. V.F. Calverton and Samuel D. Schmalhausen (London: Allen and Unwin 1930), 12, cited by Sheila Jeffreys, *The Spinster and Her Enemies: Feminism and Sexuality, 1880-1930* (London: Pandora Press 1985), 182-83.

21 On the social purity movement and on the ideas of Elizabeth Wolstenholme Elmy and other early feminist sexual theorists, see Jeffreys, *The Spinster and Her Enemies*, chs. 1 and 2, esp. 'psychic love': 31-32. *Phases of Love*, 1893, was written under the pseudonym 'Ellis Ethelmer.' For an account of the writing partnership of Elizabeth Wolstenholme and Ben Elmy and of speculations about their marriage, see Pankhurst, *The Suffragette Movement*, 30-32.

22 See ch. 4, p. 75.

23 Annie Besant, *Theosophy and the Law of Population* (London: Freethought Pub-

lishing 1901), 6, quoted by Jeffreys, *The Spinster and Her Enemies*, 45.

24 Jeffreys, *The Spinster and Her Enemies*, 46.

25 Charlotte Gilman, 'New Mothers of a New World,' *The Forerunner* 4, no. 6 (1912):145, 148.

26 'Sickly,' *cri de coeur:* see ch. 4, pp. 73-74

27 Phyllis Rose, *Parallel Lives: Five Victorian Marriages* (New York: Vintage Books 1984), 9.

28 Bennett, interview.

29 *Van. Dir,,* 1933. Philps, interview; Department of Veterans' Affairs, Ottawa, Advice of death from Secretary, WVA District Authority, Vancouver, 17 Oct. 1966.

30 *Van. Dir.,* 1933. BC Land Title Office, Vancouver, Vendor's Assignment of Agreement for Sale, 104633-E, 19 July 1933 (The agreement for sale between Gutteridge and Nicholls was not found but is cited in the foregoing document, the transaction dated 11 July 1933); Indenture between Edith May Sneve and Helena Rose Gutteridge and Peter Nicholls, 107888, 3 May 1934; Certificate of Indefeasible Title, 107888-E, 11 July 1934.

CHAPTER EIGHT: REDEDICATION:
THE VISION OF THE CO-OPERATIVE COMMONWEALTH

1 'Province of British Columbia, History of Relief, October, 1930–December, 1937,' E.E. Winch Papers, 55A:24, AMMC. Marion Lane, 'Unemployment During the Depression: The Problem of the Single Unemployed Transient in British Columbia, 1930-1938' (Graduating essay, University of British Columbia 1966), 29-50.

2 Dorothy Steeves, *The Compassionate Rebel: Ernest Winch and the Growth of Socialism in Western Canada* (North Vancouver: J.J.Douglas 1960), 77.

3 Mildred Osterhout Fahrni, interview by IH, 3 May 1984.

4 Grace MacInnis, interview by Anne Scotton, 14 July 1977, UBCL.

5 Autobiographical Notes, Dorothy Steeves Papers, Box 1, UBCL; *The Commonwealth* (CW), 19 July 1934, 1. For a feminist analysis of the political careers of Dorothy Steeves, Grace MacInnis, Laura Jamieson, and Helena Gutteridge, see Susan Walsh, 'Equality, Emancipation and a More Just World: Leading Women in the British Columbia Co-operative Federation' (MA dissertation, Simon Fraser University 1983).

6 Hilda Kristiansen, 3 Aug. 1988, and Kathleen Telford Coffey, 3 Aug. 1988, interviews by IH. [Angus MacInnis] to Frances [Moren], 14 Nov. 1932; Grace [MacInnis] to Frances [Moren], 7 Nov. 1932; F[rances Moren] to Grace [MacInnis], 14 Nov. 1932, Grace MacInnis Papers, Box 4, 'Correspondence,' UBCL. **Telford**: Minutes, CCF Provincial Executive Committee (hereafter CCF Prov. Exec.), Summary for 1, 8, 13, and 15 Dec. 1934. Mary Scott to IH, 31 Oct. and 25 Nov. 1988.

7 Mary E. Bishop, 'The Early Birth Controllers of BC,' *BC Studies*, 61(Spring 1984):73-76, 81-83.
8 Register of Births, General Register Office, New Register House, Edinburgh; Papers of Elizabeth Kerr from Patrick Kerr; Sheana Kerr Livesay, 20 Nov. 1984, and Patrick Kerr, 18 Jan. 1984, interviews by IH; 'Pen Portraits of Club Members,' Add. Mss. 396, CVA. **James Blain Kerr:** Vancouver *Sun*, 22 Mar. 1944, 17; Vancouver *Province*, 22 Mar. 1944, 2. **Quotes:** Constance Errol (Elizabeth Kerr), 'The Women's Views,' *The Federationist*, 13 July 1939, 5. Ibid., 27 July 1937, 5. **Burns:** ibid., 27 Jan. 1938, 5. **As journalist:** *The Federationist*, 25 Feb. 1937, 8. *The Federationist* succeeded *The Commonwealth* in August 1936.
9 MacInnis-Moren letters, Grace MacInnis Papers.
10 Walsh, 'Equality, Emancipation,' 175-79, 203-4.
11 Patrick Kerr, Sheana Kerr Livesay, Hilda Kristiansen, interviews.
12 Michiel Horn, *The League for Social Reconstruction* (Toronto: University of Toronto Press 1980), 37-38.
13 Lefeaux to Angus MacInnis, 21 Apr. 1933, Box 54a:4, AMMC.
14 *CW*, 25 Oct. 1933, 12. 'Associated CCF Clubs (BC) Bulletin,' 15 Sept. 1933, Box 45:8, AMMC. *CW*, 6 Sept. 1934, 6. For an account of the evolution of the CCF at this time, see Steeves, *Compassionate Rebel*, 79-81, 96.
15 *CW*, 24 May 1934, 4.
16 *CW*, 20 Dec. 1934.
17 *The Challenge*, 5 Apr. 1933, 4.
18 *CW*, 1 Mar. 1934, 4; **quote:** *CW*, 8 Mar. 1934, 5.
19 *CW*, 5 Apr. 1934, 8 (the letter is signed 'H.G.'). **Manifesto:** *CW*, 9 Aug. 1933, 3.
20 *CW*, 1 Mar. 1934, 8; 8 Mar. 1934, 7; 28 Aug. 1935, 2. CCF Prov. Exec., 17 Sept. 1934, 128, Box 45:10, AMMC. Report by Dr. Telford to CCF Provincial Convention, July 1936, Box 45:12, AMMC. G.C. Chandler, mgr. radio station CJOR, to Mildred Osterhout, 29 May 1939, Mildred Fahrni Papers, UBCL. The 'Woman's Point of View' manuscripts are in this collection.
21 *CW*, 4 Oct. 1933, 8; 1 Nov. 1933, 7.
22 Ibid., 12 Nov. 1936; 29 Mar. 1935, 7; 25 Oct. 1934, 8.
23 *CW*, 26 July 1934, 3.
24 Ibid., 3 Jan. 1933, 3; 15 Nov. 1935, 8.
25 Ibid., 16 Aug. 1934, 1.
26 Ibid., 19 Aug. 1937, 3.
27 Ibid., 22 Mar. 1934, 6; 5 Apr. 1934, 5; 12 April 1934, 6; 28 June 1934, 6; 20 Sept. 1934; 18 Oct. 1934, 5; 13 Dec. 1934, 7.
28 Ibid., 22 Nov. 1935, 1 and 5; Vancouver *Province*, 5 Mar. 1976, 31.
29 Ibid., 8 Mar. 1934.
30 Ibid., 7 Feb. 1934, 2; 20 Dec. 1934, 6. CCF Prov. Exec., 13 Dec. 1936, Box 45:14, AMMC.
31 Harold E. Winch, *The Politics of a Derelict* (Vancouver: BC Clarion [1934]), Box

56a:5, AMMC. 'Wet nurse' and 'derelict' cited in 'Foreword,' Victor Howard, *'We Were the Salt of the Earth': The On-to-Ottawa Trek and the Regina Riot* (Regina: Canadian Plains Research Centre 1985), 8-11.

32 Ruth Bullock, interview by IH, 16 Feb. 1985. For perceptions of Canadian society regarding women and aging, see Veronica Strong-Boag, *The New Day Recalled: Lives of Girls and Women in English Canada* (London: Penguin 1988), ch. 6.

33 Bullock interview.

34 'Annual Report of the C.C.F. Unemployment Conference,' 24 July 1935, Box 55a:30, AMMC (hereafter 'Unemployment Conference'). **MacNeil:** quote from Helen Dickson column, *CW*, 10 Oct. 1935, 4; 12 July 1934, 5; Barry Mather, *Pertinent Portraits* (Vancouver: The Boag Foundation [1934]), 22-23.

35 Vancouver *Province* mag. sec., 16 Mar. 1935, 3. Government of British Columbia, 'Certificate of Registration and Application for Direct Relief,' issued to Mary McCormack, 1935, private possession. *CW*, 4 Jan. 1935; *The Federationist*, 31 Dec. 1936, 2. **Quote:** Grant MacNeil, 'I Cover the Breadline,' ibid., 26 Nov. 1936.

36 Ibid., 13 Sept. 1934, 2.

37 Ibid., 2 Aug. 1934, 1; 23 Aug. 1934, 1; Fred Moreland, telephone interview by IH, 25 Mar. 1985.

38 Mary McCormack Black, interview by IH, 21 Mar. 1985; 'Memorandum on Relief and Other Matters, presented by the British Columbia Joint Committee on Unemployment to the Honorable Premier and Cabinet Ministers of the Province of British Columbia,' 7 Dec. 1934, 1, in private possession. See also CVA City Clerk's Records, 16-C-2, file 9. The following account of the petition and brief is from this document (hereafter 'Memorandum'). **Communists absorbing CCF:** Walter Young, *Anatomy of a Party: The National CCF, 1932-1961* (Toronto: University of Toronto Press 1969), 263.

39 'Memorandum,' [2].

40 'Report of Delegation of Unemployed Sponsored by the British Columbia Joint Committee on Unemployment, Who Presented the Demands on behalf of the Unemployed of British Columbia, before the British Columbia Cabinet, December 7, 1934 at 10:30 A.M,' private possession, 1 (hereafter 'Report of Delegation of Unemployed').

41 Black, interview.

42 'Report of Delegation of Unemployed.'

43 Pattullo, 'Your Government and the Problem of Relief,' Vancouver *Sun*, 7 May 1935, 2.

44 'Unemployment Conference,' 24 July 1935, Box 55a:30, AMMC. **Bray:** Ruth Bullock, conversations, 1 May 1990, 9 Feb. 1992; Bercuson, *Confrontation at Winnipeg*, 143-44, 165-66.

45 For a full account of the relief camp workers' strike and the events leading up to the On-to-Ottawa trek, see Howard, *Salt*, chs. 3 and 4.

46 Howard, *Salt*, 74-77. The following account of a woman 'riding the rods' is from Judy Power, telephone interview by IH, 23 July 1992.

47 'Unemployment Conference,' 24 July 1935, Box 55a:30, AMMC.

48 Howard, *Salt*, 46.

49 Mildred Osterhout, 'The Woman's Point of View,' Typescript of radio broadcast (hereafter MO), 6 June 1935, Mildred Fahrni Papers, UBCL.

50 Paul Phillips, *No Power Greater: A Century of Labour in BC* (Vancouver: BC Federation of Labour and Boag Foundation 1967), 102-4. **Corbin:** *BC Workers' News*, 18 Apr. 1935.

51 Howard, *Salt*, 33.

52 MO, 4 April 1935.

53 CW, 23 Aug. 1935, 6. For a full account of the part played by CCF and communist women in the relief camp workers' strike, see Irene Howard, 'The Mothers' Council of Vancouver: Holding the Fort for the Unemployed, 1935-1938,' *BC Studies* 69/70(1986):249-87.

54 CCF Prov. Exec., 15 July 1935, 168, Box 45:10, AMMC.

55 CCF Prov. Exec., 15 July 1935, Box 45:10, AMMC.

56 'Unemployment Conference,' 24 July 1935, Box 55a:30, AMMC.

57 CW, 2 Aug. 1935, 2.

58 Ibid., 2 Aug. 1935, 2.

59 CCF Prov. Exec., 18 Apr. 1936, Box 45:14, AMMC.

60 Ibid., 21 Mar. and 18 Apr. 1936, Box 45:14, AMMC.

61 Ibid., 24 Oct. and 28 Nov. 1936, Box 45:14; 30 Jan. 1937, Box 46:1, AMMC; *The Federationist*, 25 Feb. 1937, 1.

62 *People's Advocate*, 9 July 1937, 2.

63 *The Federationist*, 8 July 1937, 4; Steeves, *Compassionate Rebel*, 114-16.

64 CW, 9 Aug. 1933, 1.

65 Ibid., 9 Aug. 1933, 1.

66 'CCF Economic Planning Commission, 1936 Convention Report,' Box 45:12, AMMC (hereafter Planning Commission Report, 1936).

67 Horn, *The League for Social Reconstruction*, 124-26.

68 CCF Bulletin, no. 1, 20 Nov. 1935. Planning Commission Report, 1936.

69 Planning Commission Report, 1936.

70 'Planning Commission Resolution and Preamble,' [CCF Provincial Convention, 1935], 3, Box 45:9, AMMC. See also 'How CCF Government Would Administer Industry,' *The Federationist*, 27 May 1937, 5.

71 *The Federationist*, 14 Jan. 1937, 8.

72 Ibid.

73 Irene Paulik, interview by IH, June 1988. Biographical details about the Pauliks are from this interview and from Will Paulik, telephone conversation, 24 June 1988. 'Forest Is First in Flood Control,' newsclipping, Vancouver *Sun* magazine supplement, 26 June 1948, Maximilian Paulik Papers, UBCL, unprocessed at time of writing.

74 H.G. Garrett, Registrar of Companies, to BC Forest Conservation League, 6 Feb. 1935. Newsclipping, [Vancouver *Sun*, 1935], Paulik Papers.

75 Robin Fisher, *Duff Pattullo of British Columbia* (Toronto: University of Toronto Press 1991), 148-57.

76 Paulik to Hon. A.W. Grey, Minister of Lands, 20 Dec. 1935, Paulik Papers.

77 M.M. Glenday to E.A. Cleveland, 24 June 1936, Paulik Papers.

78 CCF Provincial Council Minutes, 28 Nov. 1936, Box 45:12, AMMC.

79 For Paulik on reforestation, see Max Paulik, *Reforestation Policy of British Columbia: A Critical Analysis*, Researches into the Forest Economy of British Columbia, no. 3 (Vancouver: Foresta Publishers 1948). **Sloan Report:** ibid., 7, 12, and passim. I am indebted to Dr. David Hayley and Jeannette Leitch for discussing the CCF-Paulik forestry material with me.

80 Newsclipping, [Vancouver *Sun*, 1935], Paulik Papers.

81 **On CCF plans to socialize forest industry:** 'On the Road Toward a Better Forest Order,' a series of articles in *The Federationist*, beginning 17 Sept. 1936, esp. 15 Oct., 29 Oct., 12 Nov., 26 Nov. **Forestry school:** D. Berger, Secretary, To All CCF Clubs, May 1936, Provincial Convention Minutes, Box 45:12, AMMC (henceforth D. Berger). See also the set of illustrated publicity handouts (henceforth Forestry Handouts), RG 28-IV-1, vol. 85-1, CCF Papers, NAC. **Occupations:** Forestry Handouts, 'Forestry Training for Youth.'

82 See Forestry Handouts, esp. allegorical, no. 13; settlements, nos. 3, 8, 11; appeal, no. 5. **Earnest sincerity:** D. Berger.

83 CCF Prov. Exec., 18 July 1936, Box 45:14, AMMC.

84 *The Federationist*, 8 Oct. 1936, 3.

85 CCF Prov. Exec., 29 Aug. 1936, Box 45:12, AMMC; 5 Jan. 1937, Box 46:1, AMMC.

86 'Labour Code Department, CCF Economic Planning Commission,' Box 54a:7, AMMC.

87 MacInnis to Lefeaux, 29 Apr. 1936, Box 54a:7, AMMC.

88 Lefeaux to MacInnis, 4 May 1936, Box 54a:7, AMMC.

89 [Arthur] Turner to MacInnis, n.d., Box 54a:7, AMMC.

90 *BC Clarion*, June 1936, 2, Winch Scrapbook, Ernest Winch Papers, MSS 12, Burnaby Village Museum.

91 MacInnis to Gutteridge, 23 June 1936, Box 54a:7, AMMC.

92 *The Federationist*, 28 Aug. 1936, 3.

93 Ibid.

94 W.E. Turner to Friends, 22 Mar. 1936, Box 54a:7, AMMC.

95 Lefeaux to MacInnis, 4 May 1936, Box 54a:7, AMMC.

96 Horn, *The League for Social Reconstruction*, 124.

97 Steeves, *Compassionate Rebel*, 107.

98 CCF Prov. Exec., 8 Aug. 1936, Box 45:12, AMMC. For a detailed account of the Connell Affair, see Steeves, *Compassionate Rebel*, 107-10.

99 MacInnis to Midgely, 8 Apr. 1936, Box 54a:7, AMMC.

100 *The Federationist*, 8 July 1937, 6. CCF Prov. Exec., 16 Jan. 1937, Box 46:1, AMMC. For an account of the expulsion of A.M. Stephen, see Steeves, *Compassionate Rebel*, 114-16.
101 *The Federationist*, 7 July 1938, 5.
102 Harold Winch to E.E. Winch, Prov. Sec'ty, Socialist Party of Canada, 7 Apr. 1935, Ernest Winch Papers, MSS 12, Burnaby Village Museum.
103 *The Federationist*, 16 Sept. 1937, 4. On the CCF as a movement, see Young, *Anatomy of a Party*, 52-59.
104 Vancouver *Sun*, 30 July 1938, 32.

CHAPTER NINE: 'A FAITHFUL ALDERMAN'

1 Mamie Maloney, 'A Woman Views the News,' Vancouver *Sun*, 25 Mar. 1937, 4. Vancouver Local Council of Women (VLCW) Minutes, 12 Jan. 1937, UBCL.
2 Doris Milligan, 'Woman Alderman Says Housing "Disgraceful",' Vancouver *Sun*, 31 Mar. 1937, 2 (hereafter Milligan).
3 Vancouver *Sun*, 31 Mar. 1937, 5. For other details of the swearing-in, see Vancouver *News-Herald*, 31 Mar. 1937, 8; Vancouver *Province*, 31 Mar. 1937.
4 Barry Mather, 'Persistent Lady Who Strove and Arrived,' Vancouver *Province*, 24 Apr. 1937, 8.
5 Vancouver *Sun*, 25 Mar. 1937, 8.
6 Milligan.
7 *The Commonwealth* (CW), 8 Nov. 1935. *The Federationist*, 2 Dec. 1937, 6.
8 Ibid.
9 City Clerk's Series 4B, 'Record, Nominations and Elections,' 31-A-4, file 8 and 31-A-5, file 5, CVA.
10 Certificate of Indefeasible Title, no. 104633E.
11 Remuneration file, City Clerk's Office, Vancouver City Hall. **Relief:** Add. Mss. 54, microfiche 01925, CVA.
12 City Clerk's Series 4B, 31-A-4, file 8. *The Federationist*, 25 Mar. 1937, 1; Vancouver *Sun*, 13 and 14 Jan. 1937.
13 *The Federationist*, 18 Mar. 1937, 8. Vancouver *Sun*, 25 Mar. 1937, 1; quote on p. 4. Vancouver *Province*, 25 Mar. 1937, 4. Vancouver *News-Herald*, 26 Mar. 1937, 9.
14 Vancouver *Sun*, 20 Aug. 1936, 1. David Ricardo Williams, *Mayor Gerry: The Remarkable Gerald Grattan McGeer* (Vancouver: Douglas and McIntyre 1986), 195-98, 210-11.
15 Andrea B. Smith, 'The Origins of the NPA: A Study in Vancouver Politics, 1930-1940' (MA thesis, University of British Columbia 1976), 12-14, 35-36.
16 Calculation from election results, Vancouver *Sun*, 9 Dec. 1937, 1.
17 **Corey:** *Province*, 28 Aug. 1946, 5. **Kirk:** *Province*, 7 Dec. 1938, 18; 3 Oct. 1940, 8. **Wilson:** *West End Courier*, 28 Jan. 1976, 2. **Bennett:** *Province*, 20 Nov. 1958, 5. **Cornett:** *Province*, 12 Dec. 1940, 14. **Crone:** *Province*, 4 Apr. 1939, 16.

de Graves: *Province,* 10 Oct. 1967, 30. **Miller:** *Province,* 7 Dec. 1938, 18. See also Civic Federation of Vancouver, *Canada's Pacific Gateway,* Fourteenth Annual Yearbook, [1938], 8-10 (in Vancouver Public Library, Northwest Room).

18 *The Federationist,* 8 Feb. 1937, 4.

19 Vancouver *Sun,* 16 Dec. 1937, 6.

20 Vancouver *Sun,* 14 Feb. and 8 Mar. 1939.

21 Newspaper Clippings, 'Helena Gutteridge,' M3818 (hereafter M3818), 'Ald. Gutteridge Says Mayor, Others Drawing Double Pay,' 8 Mar. 1939, CVA.

22 *The Federationist,* 20 Apr. 1939, 2; **both quotes:** 28 Sept. 1939, 2.

23 M3818, 10 Dec. 1938.

24 *The Federationist,* 1 Apr. 1937, 7. *Van. Dir.,* 1938. The Certificate of Indefeasible Title regarding the final disposition of the Mount Lehman property in 1941 is in the name of Edith May MacDonald, wife of Duncan M. MacDonald, 1195 East 54th Avenue.

25 SBC. 'Vancouver Incorporation Act, 1921,' ch. 55, sec. 8.

26 M3818, 14 Sept. 1937.

27 *The Federationist,* 14 Sept. 1939, 2.

28 M3818, 8 Apr. 1941.

29 SBC, 1953, 'Vancouver Charter Act, 1953,' ch. 55, secs. 7, 8, 37. The spouse of an owner or tenant was given the vote in 1951: 'Vancouver Incorporation Act, 1921, Amendment Act, 1951,' ch. 107, sec. 8. Ethnic disqualifications were removed in 1948: SBC, ch. 113, sec. 2 and 1949, ch. 73, sec. 8. Tenant candidates: SBC, 1966, ch. 69, sec. 37(b).

30 City Clerk's Series 2, Special Committee Minutes (hereafter Spec. Cttee. Min.), 26D, vol. 69, 2 and 19 Sept. 1938, CVA.

31 City Clerk's Series 1, Correspondence Inward, 1888-1946, (hereafter CC Corr. In.) 17-A-1, vol. 215, Special Committee Files, (hereafter Spec. Cttee. Files) April to June 1937. City Clerk's Series 1, Spec. Cttee. Files, 27-D-2, 'Wholesale Storage of Gasoline and Fuel Oil,' 1937-38, Building, Civic Planning and Parks Cttee. Min., 9 Aug. 1938, CVA.

32 'City of Vancouver, Graph Showing the Yearly Growth of Population, the Registration of Births, Marriages & Deaths & the Number of Dwellings Erected,' reprinted from *BC Journal of Commerce,* Nov. 1937, in report of Special Committee on Housing, 15 Nov. 1937 (hereafter Housing Cttee. Report, Nov. 1937), Town Planning Commission Papers (TPC), Series 3, 61-C-6, 13:14, CVA.

33 '"Basement" shall mean a storey the floor of which is more than one foot, but less than five feet, below the average level of the adjoining ground. A basement shall not be counted as a storey in calculating the height of any building unless it is used for purposes permitted in a business district or as living quarters for someone other than a janitor': City of Vancouver Zoning By-Law 2074, passed 6 June 1930. Section 3 sets forth the ten zoning clas-

sifications, four of which are residential.

34 City Clerk's Series 2, Standing Committee Minutes, vol. 1-74, 7 June 1937, MCR-2. By-Law 2468, Vancouver City Council Minutes, 28 June 1937. An apartment house was defined as a building, excluding lodging houses and hotels, designed for three or more separate family units: By-Law 2074. Vancouver *Sun*, 28 July 1938, 1.

35 Catherine Jill Wade, '"Citizens in Action": Local Activism and National Housing Programs, Vancouver, 1919-1950' (PhD dissertation, Simon Fraser University 1991), 51-66. [Peter Stratton], 'Housing in Vancouver: A Survey of Housing Conditions in Vancouver,' 57, Frank Buck Papers (BP), UBCL.

36 Vancouver Housing Committee Minutes (hereafter Vanc. Housing Cttee. Min.), 28 June and 9 July 1937, BP, 12:9.

37 John Bottomley, 'Ideology, Planning and the Landscape: The Business Community, Urban Reform and the Establishment of Town Planning in Vancouver, British Columbia' (MA thesis, University of British Columbia 1971), ch. 5, esp. 225, 251-52, 265-73.

38 Vancouver *Province*, 26 Jan. 1951, 17; and 7 May 1953, 24.

39 Mrs. Gladys Cooper, telephone interview by IH; Vancouver *Province*, 4 Dec. 1956, 1.

40 City Clerk's Series 1, Spec. Cttee. Files, 27-C-6 'Survey of Housing Conditions,' 7 Oct. 1937 (hereafter Survey, 1937), CVA.

41 Housing Cttee. Report, Nov. 1937, passim.

42 Vancouver *Sun*, 8 July 1938, 8, 22. City of Vancouver Health By-Law 949, sec. 47.

43 Vancouver *Sun*, 3 June 1938, 1.

44 Wade, '"Citizens in Action",' 107. City Clerk's Series 2, Spec. Cttee. Min., 1939, vol. 69, pp. 313, 334, 343.

45 Gutteridge et al. [Housing Cttee.] to the Mayor and Council, 12 Feb. 1938, BP 12:8. Vancouver *Sun*, 16 June 1938, 26; City Clerk's Series 1, Spec. Cttee. Files, 1938, 'Charter Amendments.' An Act to Amend the Vancouver Incorporation Act, 1921: sec. 163 of ch. 5 was amended as subsection 105a as follows: 'For fixing standards of fitness for human habitation to which all dwellings shall conform; for requiring the owners of dwellings to make the same conform to any such standards; for prohibiting the use of such dwellings which do not conform to any such standards so fixed; for governing and regulating persons in the use and occupancy of dwellings and for appointing inspectors for the enforcement of the by-law.' George Mooney to J. Alexander Walker, 2 Nov. 1937, TPC, Series 3, 61-C-6, vol. 13:14. Wade, '"Citizens in Action",' 171.

46 M3818, 'Social Ownership of Homes in City Aim of Alderman,' 29 June 1937.

47 Alvin Finkel, *Business and Social Reform in the Thirties* (Toronto: James Lorimer 1979), 102. See also p. 104.

48 Major L.L. Anthes, reported in the *Financial Post*, 28 Apr. 1934, cited in Finkel,

Business and Social Reform.

49 Canada, House of Commons, Special Committee on Housing, Minutes of Proceedings and Evidence, Third Report, 1935, 20.

50 HCD, 24 June 1935, 3920, cited by John C. Bacher, 'Canadian Housing "Policy" in Perspective,' *Urban History Review* 15(June 1986):7. J. David Hulchanski, 'The 1935 Dominion Housing Act: Setting the Stage for a Permanent Federal Presence in Canada's Housing Sector,' *Urban History Review* 15(June 1986):23, 25, 28-29. The narrative history of the DHA presented here is based largely on Hulchanski's account and analysis.

51 SC, 1935, ch. 58. Vancouver *Sun*, 20 Jan. 1937, 1; 29 Jan. 1938, 22; Wade, '"Citizens in Action",' 152. 'Construction and Lending Activity under the 1935 Dominion Housing Act, 1935-1938,' PAC, RG 19, Department of Finance Records, vol. 709, 203-1A, 'NHA, Schedule C,' cited by Hulchanski, 'The 1935 Dominion Housing Act,' 33, 36.

52 SC, 'The National Housing Act,' 1 July 1938, ch. 49.

53 Hulchanski, 'The 1935 Dominion Housing Act,' 35. SC, 1938, ch. 49, Part II, sec. 15.

54 W.C. Clark, 'Loans for Low Rental Housing Projects under Part II of the National Housing Act,' an address delivered before the National Conference on Housing, Toronto, 20 Feb. 1939 (hereafter Clark), 5 and 12, BP 12:12. SC, 1938, ch. 49, Part II, sec. 13.

55 Vancouver *Sun*, 31 May 1938, 22; **quote:** 7 June 1938, 20; 9 June 1938, 1; 7 Feb. 1939, 20.

56 Mackenzie King Diary, 20 May 1938, NAC, quoted by Finkel, *Business and Social Reform*, 106.

57 Humphrey Carver, *The Compassionate Landscape* (Toronto: University of Toronto Press 1975), 54, 211.

58 Clark, "Loans for Low Rental Housing,' 2.

59 Carver, *The Compassionate Landscape*, 53.

60 J. Alexander Walker to Frank Buck, 3 Dec. 1937, BP 12:8.

61 Housing Cttee. to Mayor and Council, 6 Dec. 1937, BP 12:8. Vancouver *Sun*, 14 Dec. 1937, 8. **Commended:** *The Federationist*, 19 May 1938, 5; City Clerk to Housing Committee, 13 Sept. 1938, BP 12:8.

62 Housing Cttee. to Chairman and Members of Building, Civic Planning and Parks Cttee., 18 Aug. 1938, BP 12:8. VHA **officers:** J. Alexander Walker to George S. Mooney, 19 Jan. 1938, TPC, Series 3, 61-C-6, vol. 13:14. Wade, '"Citizens in Action",' 169.

63 Carver, *The Compassionate Landscape*, 161. Peter Stratton, interview by IH, 21 April 1988.

64 [Peter Stratton for Vancouver Housing Association], 'Project for the Erection of 50 Houses under Part II of the N.H.A.,' BP, 12:8.

65 Spec. Cttee. Files, 27-D-1, 'Housing Conditions,' 9 and 15 Nov. 1938.

66 Secretary, Housing Cttee., to George Mooney, 19 Jan. 1939, TPC, Series 3, 77-

B-5:6. Vancouver *Sun*, 20 Jan. 1939, 4. George Mooney, *Tax Exemption in Low-Rent Housing Projects*, cited in Clark, 'Loans for Low Rental Housing,' 15.

67 Vancouver *Sun*, 7 Feb. 1939, 2.

68 Clark, 'Loans for Low Rental Housing,' 2. Canada, Advisory Committee on Reconstruction, Subcommittee on Housing and Community Planning, *Final Report of the Subcommittee*, 24 March 1944 (Ottawa: King's Printer 1944), 42 and 67 (hereafter Curtis Report). Bacher, 'Canadian Housing "Policy" in Perspective,' 13.

69 Harrison to Bone, 21 Jan. 1939; Bone to Harrison, 26 Jan. 1939, TPC, Series 3, 77-B-5:6.

70 'Slums of the Water Front, Report on a Brief Survey of a Small Section of Vancouver's Water Front Slum Areas and Basement Suites in the West End, made by the Housing Committee of the City Council,' Jan. 1939, 1 and 2, BP 12:12.

71 *The Federationist*, 22 Dec. 1938, 6.

72 Vancouver *Sun*, 7 Jan. 1939, 4.

73 City Clerk's Series 2, Standing Committee Minutes, 1886-1948, Special Meeting of the Building, Civic Planning and Parks Committee, 14 Feb. 1939. MacInnis to Harrison, Feb. 1939, TPC, Series 3, 77-B-5:6.

74 Grace MacInnis, 'Report of National Conference on Housing,' TPC, Series 3, 77-B-5:6.

75 Vancouver *Sun*, 4 Feb. 1939, 1. Diary, 9 Feb. 1939, Steeves Papers, 6:1, UBCL.

76 Report of Housing Meeting, 16 June 1939, BP 12:11.

77 TPC, Series 3, 61-C-6, vol. 13:14; 77-B-5:6. Nicolls to Harrison, 12 June 1939, TPC, Series 3, 77-B-5:6.

78 *The Federationist*, 20 July 1939, 1.

79 Stratton, 'Housing in Vancouver,' 13ff., BP 12:6.

80 Chairman, Housing Committee to Building, Civic Planning and Parks Committee, 3 Nov. 1939, TPC, Series 3, 77-B-5:6.

81 Curtis Report, 28.

82 Annual Report of Building, Civic Planning and Parks Cttee., 31 Dec. 1940, BP 12:12; Henry Corey to City Council, 22 Jan. 1940, TPC, Series 3, 61-C-6, vol. 13:14. **Provisions of by-law:** Vancouver *News-Herald*, 12 Nov. 1941, 10.

83 Vancouver *News Herald*, 1941: 7 Nov., 15; 6 Nov., 3; 8 Nov., 8.

84 Vancouver *News-Herald*, 7 Nov. 1941, 5.

85 All quotations from Vancouver *News-Herald*, 12 Nov. 1941, 10.

86 [Catherine] Jill Wade, 'Wartime Housing Limited, 1941-1947: Canadian Housing Policy at the Crossroads,' *Urban History Review* 15(June 1986):41-42, 46, 47. In 1979, Central Mortgage and Housing became Canada Mortgage and Housing Corporation.

87 Wade, 'Wartime Housing,' 41-42; Carver, *The Compassionate Landscape*, 84; Bacher, 'Canadian Housing "Policy" in Perspective,' 15-16.

88 Vancouver Housing Committee Reports, 1942, BP 12:12.

89 'Helena Gutteridge's Story,' as told to Frances Gilstead, *Pacific Tribune*, 8 Mar. 1957, 12.

90 Vancouver *Sun*, 30 July 1966, 6. CVA, Vancouver Housing Authority Minutes, 18 Aug. 1953, Add. Mss. 671, 1:1. In October 1945, the Vancouver Housing Association amalgamated with the Housing Committee of the Vancouver Welfare Council to become the Vancouver Housing Committee: Call for General Meeting, 3 Oct. 1945, BP, 12:4.

91 Vancouver *Province*, 18 Dec. 1939, 4.

92 Vancouver *Sun*, 14 Dec. 1939, 4.

CHAPTER TEN: HELENA AT LEMON CREEK

1 Vancouver *News-Herald*, 4 Nov. 1939, 7. CCF **policy:** Dorothy Steeves, *The Compassionate Rebel: Ernest Winch and the Growth of Socialism in Western Canada* (Vancouver: J.J. Douglas 1977), 156.

2 *The Federationist*, 16 Nov. 1939, 6. See also Victoria *Daily Times*, 7 Nov. 1939, 16. Vancouver *Province*, 4 Nov. 1939, 1 and 2.

3 Vancouver *Sun*, 13 Oct. 1938, 1.

4 Newsclipping file, 'Gutteridge,' M3818, CVA (hereafter M3818), [*Province*], 13 Oct. 1938.

5 Vancouver *Sun*, 13 Oct. 1938, 1.

6 M3818, unidentified clipping beginning with remark by Mrs. H.L. Corey, 30 May 1939.

7 CCF Economic Planning Commission report, n.d., Paulik Papers.

8 Vancouver *Sun*, 12 July 1938, 3; 13 July 1938, 6; 23 July 1938, 2; 25 July 1938, 2. **Quote:** M3818, 7 Dec. 1938.

9 Vancouver *Sun*, 4 Nov. 1939.

10 Constance Errol [Betty Kerr], 'The Women's View,' *The Federationist*, 14 Sept. 1939, 5.

11 VLCW Minutes, 12 Jan. 1937, 4:16.

12 Vancouver *Sun*, 11 Dec. 1939, 3.

13 Vancouver *Sun*, 9 Dec. 1939, 19.

14 Vancouver *Sun*, 9 Dec. 1939, 19; Vancouver *Province*, 8 Dec. 1939, 14.

15 Vancouver *News-Herald*, 22 Nov. 1941, 3. **Rats:** Vancouver *News-Herald*, 19 Nov. 1941, 3. **Incinerators:** Vancouver *News-Herald*, 17 Nov. 1941.

16 **Aldermen quotes:** Vancouver *News-Herald*, 25 Nov. 1941, 5.

17 Vancouver *Province*, 11 Dec. 1941, 5.

18 Olive Vailleau to IH, 26 Feb. 1984. The following account of the speaking tour is based on Ms. Vailleau's transcription of excerpts from her own diary, 4-29 Mar. 1940.

19 Nelson *Daily News*, 4 Mar. 1940, 10.

20 'Transcript from the Dominion of Canada – National Registration,' Census

Pension Searches, Statistics Canada.

21 'Report of the Provincial Organizing Committee, Mar. 3, 1941,' Box 46:7, AMMC.

22 Sec'y Saanich CCF Council to Helena Gutteridge, 19 Jan. 1941, Box 60:8, AMMC.

23 Minutes, Eighth Annual Convention of CCF, BC section, Mar. 1941, Box 47:7, AMMC.

24 CCF Prov. Exec. Minutes, 26 Apr. 1941, Box 46:5; 17 Apr. 1942, Box 46:8, AMMC. **Census:** M3818, 'City's Housing Shortage Assailed,' 27 Mar. 1942. *Van. Dir.,* 1941.

25 Ken Adachi, *The Enemy That Never Was: A History of the Japanese Canadians,* intr. Timothy Findley, afterword by Roger Daniels (Toronto: McClelland & Stewart 1991), 208 and 401, n. 26.

26 Ann Gomer Sunahara, *The Politics of Racism: The Uprooting of Japanese Canadians During the Second World War* (Toronto: James Lorimer 1981), 16-17, 30-37. Brief submitted 21 Nov. 1984 to the government of Canada by the National Association of Japanese Canadians, *Democracy Betrayed: The Case for Redress,* 12-13 (hereafter NAJC Brief). Adachi, *The Enemy that Never Was,* 201-16. Muriel Kitagawa, 'Introduction,' in *This Is My Own: Letters to Wes & Other Writings on Japanese Canadians, 1941-1948,* ed. Roy Miki (Vancouver: Talonbooks 1985). See also Patricia Roy et al., *Mutual Hostages: Canadians and Japanese During the Second World War* (Toronto: University of Toronto Press 1990), ch. 4.

27 **Orders-in-Council:** Adachi, *The Enemy That Never Was,* 208-9, 216-17. Text of PC 1486: app. 4.

28 Minutes, Special CCF Prov. Exec. Meeting, 17 Mar. 1942, Box 46:8, AMMC; *The Federationist,* 19 Mar. 1942. Werner Cohn, 'The Persecution of Japanese Canadians and the Political Left in British Columbia,' BC *Studies* 68(Winter 1985-86):10-21 ('exigencies': p. 20). 'Reasons of defense': Grace and Angus MacInnis, *Oriental Canadians: Outcasts or Citizens?* (Vancouver: Federationist Publishing [1943]), 18. **Citizens' Defence Cttee.:** Roy et al., *Mutual Hostages,* 93-97. For J.S. Woodsworth's statement affirming 'equal rights to citizenship,' Feb. 1936, and the dilemma posed the CCF by the Oriental question, see Allen Mills, *Fool for Christ: The Political Thought of J.S. Woodsworth* (Toronto: University of Toronto Press 1991), 233-37.

29 David Lewis interview, quoted by Sunahara, *The Politics of Racism,* 54-56.

30 Minutes, Women's School for Citizenship, 26 Nov. [1941], Add. Mss. 466, CVA.

31 Roy et al., *Mutual Hostages,* 117-30. Kitagawa, *This Is My Own,* 103, 113-16. Adachi, *The Enemy That Never Was,* 248-60. See app. 8, Roy et al., for excerpts from Order-in-Council, PC 1665 establishing the powers of the BCSC, and Kitagawa, 'Introduction,' for texts of other orders-in-council regulating the movements of the Japanese.

32 Adachi, *The Enemy That Never Was*, 254; Roy *et al.*, *Mutual Hostages*, 121.

33 Ibid., 123.

34 Amy Leigh, interview by IH, 19 Feb. 1992. See also Sunahara, *The Politics of Racism*, 56.

35 Grace Tucker, interview by IH, 8 Apr. 1983.

36 CCF Prov. Exec. Minutes, 17 April 1942, Box 46:8, AMMC. Administration Committee Report, Box 46:8, AMMC. Grace Tucker, interview.

37 On this sense of isolation see Adachi, *The Enemy That Never Was*, 256 and Roy *et al.*, *Mutual Hostages*, 128-29.

38 For the attitude of Slocan people see Roy *et al.*, *Mutual Hostages*, 178.

39 Keith Kessler, interview by IH, 19 Aug. 1986.

40 Grace Tucker, interview. **Population:** Canada, Department of Labour, *Report on the Administration of Japanese Affairs in Canada*, 11. Cf. FAD, NAC, RG 27, vol. 640, File 23-2-2-1, 'Japanese Population in the Dominion of Canada as of July 30, 1944.'

41 J.S. Burns, Semi-Monthly Reports, vol. 26, files 1113 and 1120, RG 36/27, FAD, NAC.

42 Adachi, *The Enemy That Never Was*, 265. Full accounts of community life have been supplied by former Lemon Creek high school teachers in letters to IH: Donald Ewing, 10 Nov. and 14 Dec. 1983; Joseph Grant, 21 Nov. 1983; and Frank Showler, 16 Jan. 1984.

43 *New Canadian*, 3 Apr. 1943; also 30 Jan. 1943.

44 Ewing to IH, 10 Nov. 1983.

45 Shizuye Takashima, *A Child in Prison Camp* (Montreal: Tundra Books 1971), unpaginated, part 2. Ewing to IH, 10 Nov. 1983. Grant to IH, 21 Nov. 1983.

46 Jack Duggan, interview by IH, 3 July 1991.

47 Adachi, *The Enemy That Never Was*, 225.

48 T. Watanabe, Lemon Creek Japanese Cttee., to George Collins, 8 July and 21 July 1943, RG 36/27, vol. 26, file 1100, FAD, NAC.

49 Wakiko Suyama Kiyonaga, interview by IH, 5 June 1983.

50 Ewing to IH, 14 Dec. 1983.

51 Duggan, interview.

52 Adachi, *The Enemy That Never Was*, 259.

53 M.I. Brown to George Collins, 29 Apr. 1943, RG 37/26, vol. 1, file 1, 'Staff-BC-General, 1943,' FAD, NAC.

54 Kiyonaga, interview.

55 Fumiko Miyasaka, interview by IH, 31 May 1983.

56 'British Columbia Security Commission, Policy re Maintenance,' RG 36/27, vol. 10, file 305, 'Welfare 1942-43, 1946-47,' FAD, NAC.

57 'Bulletin for Staff Discussion,' 3 Feb. 1943, RG 36/27, vol. 10, file 305, 'Welfare 1942-43, 1946-47,' FAD, NAC.

58 [Administrator's Report, n.d.], 'Lemon Creek, Personnel,' RG 36/27, vol. 10, file 313, p. 3, FAD, NAC.

59 BCSC Hospital Unit, Slocan, to J.S. Burns, 25 June 1943; Naismith to BCSC Hospital, 5 July 1943; Colonel Lennox Arthur to Naismith, 10 July 1943; Naismith to Simmons, 15 July 1943, RG 36/27, vol. 26: file 1106, FAD, NAC.

60 Gladys Reynolds, interview by IH, 21 Aug. 1986.

61 Miss A. Leigh to Mr. A.C. Taylor, Mr. Eastwood, Mr. Hawkins, and Mr. Simmons, 7 Dec. 1942, 'Re: Indiscreet Spending,' RG 36/27, vol. 10, file 305, 'Welfare, 1942-43, 1946-47,' FAD, NAC.

62 **Quote:** Collins to Eastwood, 16 Mar. 1943, RG 36/27, vol. 10, file 305, 'Welfare, 1942-43, 1946-47,' FAD, NAC. 'Total Clothing for Three months: July, August & September, 1943,' RG 36/27, vol. 10, file 305, 'Welfare, 1942-43, 1946-47,' FAD, NAC.

63 Leigh, interview.

64 Adachi, *The Enemy That Never Was*, 261. For an account of the Department of Labour's dispersal program, see Roy *et al.*, *Mutual Hostages*, 139-50. The BC Security Commission was dissolved in February 1943 and its responsibilities transferred to the federal Department of Labour, without, however, changing personnel or letterhead.

65 Margaret Foster, interview by IH, 8 Apr. 1983.

66 J.S. Burns, Semi-Monthly Report, 16 Feb. 1944, RG 36/27, vol. 26, file 1113, FAD, NAC.

67 Adachi, *The Enemy That Never Was*, app. 10, p. 428 and pp. 300-1. The conflicts between government and evacuees with regard to repatriation orders are dealt with in Roy *et al.*, *Mutual Hostages*, ch. 6.

68 Grace and Angus MacInnis, *Oriental Canadians*, 18.

69 Adachi, *The Enemy That Never Was*, 305-6, 324.

70 Miss M. Moscrop to George Collins et al., RG 36/27, vol. 1, file 1, 'Staff-BC-General, 1943.' Tucker, interview.

71 A description of a visit to the *oforu* is given in Takashima, *A Child in Prison Camp*, part 5.

72 Helen Sakon to IH, 29 May 1983.

73 Miyo Goromaru, interview by IH, 31 May 1983. Noji Murase, interview by IH, 30 May 1983.

74 Ewing to IH, 10 Nov. 1983.

75 Duggan, interview.

76 Kiyonaga, interview.

77 HCD, 4 Aug. 1944, 5915, quoted in NAJC Brief, 6.

78 Adachi, *The Enemy That Never Was*, app. 14, 'Terms of Agreement between the Government of Canada and the National Association of Japanese Canadians.' Included in the terms were individual payment of $21,000 to those affected; the granting of 'Canadian citizenship to persons of Japanese ancestry still living who were expelled from Canada or had their citizenship revoked ... and to their living descendants'; the clearing of 'the names of persons of Japanese ancestry who were convicted of viola-

tions under the War Measures Act or the National Emergency Transitional Powers Act.' The text of the Government of Canada's acknowledgment of injustices suffered by Canadians of Japanese ancestry during the war is in Joy Kogawa, *Itsuka* (Toronto: Viking 1992), [289].

CHAPTER ELEVEN: 'THE HOLY FIRE'

1 Unless otherwise noted, details about Helena's personal life in this chapter are from Hilda Kristiansen, interview, 7 Apr. 1983.

2 Darwin Charlton to IH, 14 Oct. and 26 Nov. 1984.

3 *Canadian Encyclopedia*, 1st ed., under 'Old-Age Pension,' by Dennis Guest. The 1951 Act also provided a pension for the indigent between ages 65 and 69 who passed a means test.

4 Margerie Nelson to IH, 20 Nov. 1988. For an account of the overall operations of a food-processing plant, see Robert Griffin, 'Case after Case: Canning at Bestovall 1933-1963,' *British Columbia Historical News* 24(Winter 1990-91):3-8.

5 *CCF News*, 21 Jan. 1946, 7.

6 Ibid., 7 Mar. 1946.

7 Betsy McDonald in conversation with IH, 10 Sept. 1990.

8 Barbara Roberts, 'Women's Peace Activism in Canada,' in Linda Kealey and Joan Sangster, *Beyond the Vote: Canadian Women and Politics* (Toronto: University of Toronto Press 1989), 280. Gertrude Bussey and Margaret Tims, *Women's International League for Peace and Freedom, 1915-1965: A Record of Fifty Years' Work* (London: George Allen and Unwin 1965), ch. 1 and p. 25.

9 Murphy to 'My dear Madam,' 5 Apr. 1915, WILPF Papers, Western Historical Collections, Norlin Library, University of Colorado, Boulder, CO (henceforth WILPF Papers), microfilm reel 57 at UBCL.

10 Plumptre to Jane Addams, 14 Apr. 1915, WILPF Papers, reel 57.

11 Ibid.

12 **Hughes's peace organization:** Barbara Roberts, *'Why Do Women Do Nothing to End the War?':* *Canadian Feminist-Pacifists and the Great War,* The CRIAW Papers/Les Documents de l'ICREF, no. 13 (Ottawa: CRIAW/ICREF 1985), 2-6; Roberts, 'Peace Activism,' 280-81. **Macmillan:** *World,* 1915: 26 Oct., 4; 3 Nov., 4; 4 Nov., 6. See also Diana Chown, 'Introduction,' in Alice A. Chown, *The Stairway* (Toronto: University of Toronto Press 1988), xliii. **Vancouver branch:** "Helena Gutteridge's Story, as told to Frances Gilstead; Vancouver *Pacific Tribune,* 8 Mar. 1957, 12. **Hughes and HG:** *BC Fed,* 11 Feb. 1916.

13 Bussey and Tims, *Women's International League,* 30-32.

14 **Zurich:** newsclipping, Toronto *Evening Telegram* [fall 1919], WILPF Papers, reel 57. **Addams:** C.B. Sissons, *Nil Alienum: The Memoirs of C.B. Sissons* (Toronto: University of Toronto Press 1964), 157. Prenter to Balch, 17 May

1920 and 24 Sept. 1920, WILPF Papers, reel 57. The Austrian woman may have been Hague delegate Yella Hertzka, founder of the 'first women's agricultural college in Austria': Bussey and Tims, *Women's International League*, 30.

15 Bussey and Tims, *Women's International League*, 37-41.

16 Jamieson to Balch, 22 May 1921; Perceval to Balch, 4 June 1923, WILPF Papers, reel 57.

17 Jamieson to Balch, 12 Aug. 1922, WILPF Papers, reel 57.

18 **National Secretary:** Veronica Strong-Boag, 'Peace-Making Women: Canada 1919-1939,' in *Women and Peace: Theoretical, Historical and Practical Perspectives*, ed. Ruth Roach Pierson (London: Croom Helm 1987), 183-84. **McPhail:** Bussey and Tims, *Women's International League*, 49, 74, 82. **Prague:** Thomas Socknat, 'The Pacifist Background of the Early CCF,' in *'Building the Co-operative Commonwealth': Essays on the Democratic Socialist Tradition in Canada*, ed. J. William Brennan, Canadian Plains Proceedings 13 (Regina: Canadian Plains Research Centre, 1984), 58.

19 Bussey and Tims, *Women's International League*, 103 and 189. Jane Addams shared the prize with Columbia University President Dr. Nicholas Murray Butler, a founder of the Carnegie Endowment for International Peace; Emily Balch with John Mott, General Secretary of the World Student Christian Federation.

20 Bussey and Tims, *Women's International League*, chs. 1-12 passim.

21 Bussey and Tims, *Women's International League*, 122.

22 VLCW Minutes, 5 Apr. 1937, 4:17.

23 Jamieson to Headquarters, Geneva, 2 Apr. 1937, WILPF Papers, reel 58.

24 Vancouver *Sun*, 19 Mar. 1937, 10. Ramona Rose, '"Keepers of Morale": The Vancouver Local Council of Women, 1939-1945' (MA thesis, University of British Columbia 1990), 153; Vancouver *Sun*, 8 Oct. 1938, 13.

25 Vancouver *Province*, 16 July 1936, 5; 10 Aug. 1936, 6. Vancouver *News-Herald*, 23 July 1936, 2; 10 Aug. 1936, 6. Vancouver *Sun*, 10 Aug. 1936, 1. Notices for these broadcasts appeared in *The Federationist*, 11 Sept.-22 Oct. 1936, usually on p. 3. Jamieson to WILPF Headquarters, 3 Mar. 1937, WILPF Papers, reel 58.

26 *IXth International Congress of the Women's International League for Peace and Freedom at Luhacovice [Czechoslovakia], July 27-31, 1937* (n.p., n.d.), 146-47. **Peace Arch:** Vancouver *Sun*, 13 June 1938, 8. **Diary:** 31 Jan. 1939, Steeves Papers, UBCL.

27 Anna Sissons to Baer, 21 Nov. 1935, WILPF Papers, reel 58.

28 **Lucy Woodsworth:** Allen Mills, *Fool for Christ: The Political Thought of J.S. Woodsworth* (Toronto: University of Toronto Press 1991), 192. Anna Sissons's biography from Sissons, *Nil Alienum*, 46, 105, 112-14, 161, 189; LSR: Horn, *The League for Social Reconstruction*, 31. Program of Second National Congress Against War and Fascism, Dec. 6-8, 1935, WILPF Papers, reel 58. 'Annual

Report of Activities, Toronto WILPF, Oct. 1937-June 1938,' WILPF Papers, reel 58. The Padlock Act, 1937, was a Quebec law that closed down meeting places used for the dissemination of communist ideas: *Canadian Encyclopedia*, 1st ed., under 'Padlock Act,' by Eugene Forsey.

29 **Women's united front:** Irene Howard, 'The Mothers' Council of Vancouver: Holding the Fort for the Unemployed, 1935-1938,' *BC Studies* 69/70 (Spring/Summer 1986):282.

30 Vancouver *Sun*, 23 May 1938, 8.

31 Vancouver *Province*, 9 Dec. 1939, 35; and 16 Dec. 1939, 35. Laura Jamieson won Vancouver Centre in a by-election in the spring of 1939. On Beatrice Brigden, see Joan Sangster, 'Women and the New Era,' in *'Building the Cooperative Commonwealth,'* 86-87.

32 Mildred Fahrni, interviews by IH, 1984. See Irene Howard, 'Mildred Fahrni, the Making of a Pacifist,' *British Columbia Historical News*, vol. 19, no. 3 (1986):21-23. Precise year of lecture tour not yet established.

33 Sheila Young, interview by IH, 15 Nov. 1983; Bussey and Tims, *Women's International League*, 241. See WILPF Papers, reel 58, passim for Sheila Young's correspondence.

34 **Housing:** *XIth International Congress of the Women's International League for Peace and Freedom at Copenhagen August 15th - 19th, 1949* (n.p., n.d.), 100 (hereafter *XIth Int. Congr.*). For a brief summary of the special postwar concerns of the Canadian section of the WILPF, see Bussey and Tims, *Women's International League*, 187. **Arms protest:** Vancouver *News-Herald*, 25 Dec. 1947, 4; 7 Jan. 1948, 7. **NATO:** Bussey and Tims, *Women's International League*, 192. For statements of the Vancouver branch on Korea, admission of China to the UN, rearmament of Europe under NATO, see Sheila Young to Rt. Hon. L. San [*sic*] Laurent, 27 May 1952, WILPF Papers, reel 58.

35 **World Peace Council:** Bussey and Tims, *Women's International League*, 196. **Vancouver:** Sheila Young, interview by IH, 15 Nov. 1983. **Resolutions chairman, WILPF:** 'Vancouver Branch, Executive, 1950,' Edna Gibb Papers, UBCL. For members of the Vancouver executive, 1948-59, see WILPF Papers, reel 58.

36 *Canadian Encyclopedia*, 1st ed., under 'Gouzenko, Igor,' 'Rose, Fred,' 'Norman, E. Herbert.'

37 *XIth Int. Congr.*, 98. Helena was resolutions chairman of the Vancouver WILPF from 1949-51: Morgan to Bloch, 23 June 1949; Young to Secretary, WILPF, Geneva, 27 Sept. 1950, WILPF Papers, reel 58.

38 The Gordon Martin case is well-known in British Columbia. This account is from retired lawyer Elspeth Gardner, with whom Martin was articling at the time.

39 Vancouver *Sun*, 21 Feb. 1953. Vancouver *Province*, 7 Sept. 1940. Vancouver *Sun*, 12 Apr. 1949.

40 Young, *Anatomy of a Party*, 243; **Steeves:** Christina J. Nichol, 'In Pursuit of

the Voter: The British Columbia CCF, 1945-1950,' in *'Building the Co-operative Commonwealth,'* 131-32.

41 Young to Bloch, 26 Jan. 1949, WILPF Papers, reel 58.

42 *XIth Int. Congr.,* 100.

43 Baer to Young, 28 June 1950; Young to Baer, 29 Oct. 1950, WILPF Papers, reel 58.

44 Sheila Young, interview.

45 Fahrni to Olmsted, 27 June [1950], WILPF Papers, reel 58.

46 Vancouver Members per Sheila Young to Corresponding Secretary, International Executive, WILPF, 10 July 1952, Box 3:10, WILPF Papers, UBCL.

47 Stuart Jamieson, conversation with IH, 9 Jan. 1992.

48 Young to Olmsted, 23 Oct. 1949, WILPF Papers, reel 58.

49 Sissons to Rhoads, 17 Oct. 1949, WILPF Papers, reel 58.

50 Young to Baer, 23 Oct. 1949; Young to Olmsted, 28 June 1950; Fahrni to Olmsted, Bloch et al., 27 June [1950]; Bloch to Young, 11 May 1949. 'Emergency Brief from the WILPF, Vancouver Branch,' [9 June 1949]; 'Extrait du procès-verbal de la réunion du Comité Exécutif International, Copenhague, 10-13 et 20-21 août, 1949,' WILPF Papers, reel 58.

51 Sissons to Secretary, International Headquarters, 31 Jan. 1951; Parkin to Baer, Dec. 1953 (quotes); Stapledon to Sissons, 9 July 1953; [Baer], WILPF Permanent International Consultant, UN, to Parkin, 11 Nov. 1953; **Emergency Resolution:** Mabel L. Parkin, Chairman [Dec. 1953]; Sissons to Mohr, 12 June 1954; Mohr to Sissons, 21 June 1954, WILPF Papers, reel 58.

52 *XIIth International Congress of the Women's International League for Peace and Freedom, Paris, August 4th-8th, 1953,* 153.

53 **Burned:** Sheila Young, interview; corroborated by Mildred Fahrni.

54 Sheila Young, interview.

55 On Woodsworth and civil liberties, see Young, *Anatomy of a Party,* 240, 259. See also ch. 9, 'The CCF and the Communist Party,' especially 'enemies,' 278.

56 Vancouver *Sun,* 16 Aug. 1955, 4.

57 Kirkness to Tapper, 18 Apr. 1958. The *Sun,* 3 Oct. 1960, 7, states that Helena at the time of her death had been president of the WILPF for two years, but WILPF Papers, reel 58, do not bear this out.

58 Daisy Webster, interview by IH, 14 Oct. 1988.

59 Kristiansen, interview.

60 'Helena Gutteridge's Story,' Vancouver *Pacific Tribune,* 8 Mar. 1957, 12.

61 Fact Sheet 41/191; 10/788 from Mount Pleasant Funeral Chapel, 1960. The account of Helena's illness and death is from Kristiansen interview, 7 Apr. 1983.

62 **Telford:** Vancouver *Province,* 3 Oct. 1960, 11. **Many friends:** Vancouver *Sun,* 3 Oct. 1960, 28.

Selected Bibliography

Sources for specific information in the text are given in the notes for each chapter.

The following list of archival collections is of special interest, indicating the range of inquiry and the diversity of materials used, as well as acknowledging the assistance provided by archivists, librarians, and individuals.

ARCHIVAL COLLECTIONS

Canada

British Columbia Archives and Records Service (BCARS), Manuscripts and Government Records Division
>   Divorce Papers, H.R. and J.P.O. Fearn
>   William Bowser Papers (WBP)
>   Sir Richard McBride Papers (RMP)
>   Royal Commission on Labour, 1912-14
>   Visual Records Unit

British Columbia Land Offices
>   Land Assessment Offices, Clearbrook and Vancouver
>   Land Title Offices, New Westminster and Vancouver

Burnaby Village Museum and Archives
>   Ernest Winch Papers

City of Vancouver Archives (CVA)
>   Canadian Women's Press Club, Vancouver Branch Papers, Add. Mss.

    City Clerk's Records, Series 1-5
    Helen Gregory MacGill Papers, Add. Mss. 270
    Newsclipping Files, microfiche, M3818 (Gutteridge); M1871 (Clark)
    Photographic Collections
    Town Planning Commission Papers (TPC), Series 3: 61-C-6, vol. 13:14;
      77-B-5, vol. 6
    University Women's Club Papers, Add. Mss. 872
    Vancouver Housing Authority, Add. Mss. 671
    Wilson Family Papers, Add. Mss. 362
    Women's School for Citizenship Papers, Add. Mss. 466

Holy Rosary Cathedral, Vancouver, BC
    Parish Registers

Langley Centennial Museum
    Ida Douglas-Fearn Collection

Mount Pleasant Funeral Home
    Fact Sheets

National Archives of Canada (NAC)
    Federal Archives Division (FAD)
      BC Security Commission, vols. 1, 10, 26, 27 (RG 36/27)
      Labour, 1882-1981, Japanese Div., vols. 171, 648, 649 (RG 27)
      Labour Gazette (RG 27/4)
    Manuscript Division
      Co-operative Commonwealth Federation Papers
      MacGill, Elsie Gregory (MG 31 K7)
      Ship's Manifests, 1908-21, reel T-4781
    Personnel Records Centre, National Defence Records (RG 24)

Privately Held
    BC Mountaineering Club Papers
    William Black Papers
    Elizabeth Kerr Papers
    Hilda Kristiansen Papers
    Richard Owen Diaries
    Frances Telford Papers
    Olive Vailleau: Diary, 24 Feb. to 29 Mar. 1940

St. Andrew's Cathedral, Victoria, BC
    Baptismal Registers

Statistics Canada, Ottawa
    National Registration Records, 1940-46
University of British Columbia Library (UBCL)
    Angus MacInnis Memorial Collection (AMMC)
    Frank Buck Papers (BP)
    Mildred Fahrni Papers
    Edna Gibb Papers
    Hotel, Restaurant and Culinary Employees' and Bartenders' Union,
        Local 28, Papers
    Grace MacInnis Papers
    Maximilian Paulik Papers
    Dorothy Steeves Papers
    Vancouver Local Council of Women Papers (VLCW Papers)
    Vancouver Trades and Labor Council Papers (VTLC Papers)
    Women's League for Peace and Freedom Papers, microfilm (WILPF
        Papers)

University of Toronto Library, Thomas Fisher Rare Book Room
    Flora MacDonald Denison Papers

Vancouver Law Courts
    Probate Registry

Vancouver Public Library
    Historic Photographs Section
    Local History Collection

England

(Unless otherwise noted, all repositories are in London)

Battersea Library
    Local History Collection

The British Library
    Reference Division
        Maude Arncliffe-Sennett Papers, vols. 12-14
    Newspaper Library
        The Builder
        West London Press
        Votes for Women

Chelsea Library

Local History Collection

Fawcett Library, City of London Polytechnic
    Teresa Billington-Greig Papers
    British Women's Emigration Association Records
    Colonial Intelligence League Minutes
    Votes for Women

Freemasons' Hall
    Co-Masonry Files

Greater London Record Office and Library
    Holy Trinity Parish Magazine
    Local London Directories
    London County Council Staff Records
    Photographic Library

Hampshire Central Library, Portsmouth
    Local History Collection

Hampshire Record Office, Winchester
    Census Returns, 1841-81
    Micheldever Parish Registers

Holy Trinity Church of England Junior and Infant Schools
    School Registers and Log Books, 1906

John Lewis Partnership Archives, Stevenage
    Gazette of the John Lewis Partnership, 1977
    John Lewis Chronicle, 1947, 1949

Labour Party Library
    Women's Labour League, 'Leaflets, 1903-1918,' A12R

Museum of London, Suffragette Fellowship Collection
    Brackenbury Papers, Group C, vol. 2
    Ada Wright Papers, Group C, vols. 1 and 2
    Rosamond Massy Papers, Group C, vol. 1

Polytechnic of Central London Archives
    Examination Result Books, 1905-9
    The Polytechnic Magazine

Public Record Office, London and Kew
        Census Returns for England and Wales, 1841-81
        General Register Office, Births, Deaths, Marriages
        Metropolitan Police Records, MEPO 2/1410
        South Kensington Science and Art Department Records
        St. Andrew-Holborn Parish Registers, Guildhall Library
        War Office Records, WO16 and WO97
        Wills Calendars

Royal Commission on Historical Manuscripts
        National Register of Archives
                Emigration Societies, 20625
                Hyde Abbey: Winchester College Manorial Card Index

Royal Society for the Promotion of Health
        Royal Sanitary Institute Index to Certificate Registers

Victoria Library Archives
        T. Vigers and Co., Funeral Directors. Account Books

India

Theosophical Society, International Headquarters, Madras
        Membership Books

Scotland

New Registry House, Edinburgh
        Census Returns, 1851-81
        Wills Calendars
Perth and Kinross District Council Library
        Local History Collection

United States

State Historical Society of Wisconsin
        The Tailor
University of Colorado, Western Historical Collections
        WILPF Papers
Whatcom County Auditor, Bellingham, WA
        Marriage Certificate, Gutteridge and Fearn

INTERVIEWS, CONVERSATIONS, CORRESPONDENCE

With Irene Howard

Gutteridge Family History
    Lilian Delchar, Stan Gutteridge, Ned Gutteridge, Reg Gutteridge,
    Thomas E.C. Gutteridge, James Hunter, Harry Syme

Miscellaneous Topics
    Rose Aihoshi, Irene Apps, Margaret Arnett, Richard Arnett, James
    Barker, Al Bennett, June Black, Mary Black, Ruth Bullock, Kitty Car-
    son, Darwin Charlton, Kathleen Telford Coffey, Gladys Cooper, Jack
    Duggan, Donald Ewing, Mildred Fahrni, Hubert Farber, Margaret
    Foster, Mary Gallant, Joseph Grant, George Hamilton, Mary Harvey,
    Fred Herron, Frances Hicks, Lillian Hill, Helen Hurd, Stuart Jamieson,
    Jean Jamieson, Elizabeth Kealing, Gloria Kerr, Patrick Kerr, Vermona
    Farber Kirkland, Keith Kessler, Wakiko Kiyonaga, Hilda Kristiansen,
    Bertha Laverock, George Laverock, Beatrice Lehman, Amy Leigh,
    Sheena Livesay, Betsy McDonald, Agnes Gamsby McPhail, Stasia
    Maguire, Rosita Maw, Fumiko Miyasaka, Noji Murase, Frederick N.
    Nelson, Margerie Nelson, Mary Norton, Lucy Owen, Ruth Owen,
    Edgar Paulik, Irene Paulik, Will Paulik, Leonard Philps, Judy Power,
    Gladys Reynolds, Florence Ryder, Helen Sakon, Peter Stratton, Dorothy
    Taylor, Jean Thompson, Grace Tucker, Daisy Webster, Harold Winch,
    Jessie Winch, Sheila Young

Interviews by Others

Grace MacInnis, by Anne Scotton. UBCL

Mary Norton, no. 41, Reynolston Research and Studies. BCARS

Hilda Kristiansen, by Clay Perry

Index

craftworker deskilled, 127, 138; farm life, 139-41; and Mount Lehman children, 146-47; marriage, 136, 149-52; author's speculations on marriage, 149-52; works for unemployed, 164-72; and CCF Planning Commission, 173, 174-75, 178, 180, 182; elected alderman, 3, 185, 186; her special Housing Committee, 194-97, 198, 199, 203, 204, 206, 207, 209; in WILPF, 252, 256; attitudes and values, 15, 74, 83-84, 107, 127, 215; female friendships, 71-76, 148, 153, 164-65, 213, 240, 242, 257; political allegiances, 64, 66, 67, 155

Gutteridge, Sophia (née Richardson; Helena's mother), 4, 12, 13, 30, 32; parents of, 4; pregnancy and moving, 8

Gutteridge, Thomas Edward Charles (Helena's nephew), 11, 143; recalls grandparents, 12-13

Hall, Florence, 56, 59, 67, 91
Hamilton, Gertrude, 230
Hardie, Keir, 39, 41
Harrison, Albert J., 196-97, 206
Hartney, Teresa, 129
Hawthornthwaite, James H., 60, 117
Heaps, A.A., 200
Herridge, Bert, 218, 220
Herron family: Fred, 142; Ida, 142, 148; Fred Jr., 145, 148
Hewett, Philip, 258
Hill, George, 170
Holland, R. Rowe, 192
Holy Trinity Church of England Infants' School, 5, 21
Holy Trinity Parish Hall, 8, 23
Holy Trinity Upper Chelsea Girls' and Infants' School, 21
House of Commons Special Committee on Housing, 199
Housing, Canada, 187, 199, 202, 205-6. See also Dominion Housing Act; National Housing Act; Wartime Housing Ltd.
Housing, England and other countries, 7, 17-18, 205-6, 263 n.28
Housing, Vancouver, 194-96, 201-2, 206, 209, 211-12, 293 n.33, 294 n.34; and City Council, 199, 205, 207, 208, 209, 211; groups for and against low-rental housing, 197, 208; low-rental, 198, 199, 203, 204-5, 212, 213; slum conditions of, 197-98, 206-7, 209, 210-11; standard of housing by-law, 198, 210, 211, 294 n.45

Howe, Julia Ward, 54
Hughes, Laura, 244, 245
Hurry, Alfred, 190, 191, 215

Independent Labour Party (Great Britain), 39, 41, 42
Industrial unionism, 107, 117, 127, 128, 129
Industrial Workers of the World, 117
International Committee of Women for Permanent Peace, 244, 245
International Congress of Women (Hague), 244

Jamieson, Laura, 88, 89-90, 162; birth control advocate, 156-57; juvenile court judge, 156; MLA, 250; Vancouver City Council, 242, 251, 254; WILPF, 246-47, 248, 249, 254; Women's School for Citizenship, 224
Japanese and Japanese Canadians: as cannery workers, 82; and dispersal policy, 235-36; expulsion of from west coast, 223, 224-25; internment camps, 225-26, 229; Lemon Creek Relocation Project, 226-33; loyalty to Canada, 239; racist treatment of, 223; surveillance of, 225, 229; symbolic redress granted to, 239, 300-1 n.78. See also British Columbia Security Commission
Joint Action Committee on Unemployment, 166, 170
Jopson, John, 203
Journeymen Tailors' Union of America, 65, 105, 107; and eight-hour day, 106-7; and industrial unionism, 107; Local 178, 107

Kamitakahara, Tetsuo, 233
Kavanagh, Jack, 66, 67, 82, 127
Keller, Helen, 68
Kelly, Gordon (longshoremen's union leader), 121
Kerr, Elizabeth (Betty), 162, 164, 165, 167, 172, 184, 216; life of, 157, 158; and unemployed women, 166
Kerr, James Blain, 157
Kessler, Keith, 227
Key, Ellen, 73
Kidd Commission, 189-90
King, William Lyon Mackenzie, 130, 200, 202, 218, 220, 239
Kingsley, E.T., 66, 67, 117
Kirk, Thomas, 120, 121, 190, 191, 194
Kiyonaga: Kiheiji, 238, 239; Wakiko (née Suyama), 231, 235, 238-39, 256
Kristiansen, Hilda (née Moreland), 13, 21, 32, 224, 226, 243, 257, 258; life of,

PERMISSIONS

The quotation from 'Foretelling the Future' appears in Margaret Atwood, *Selected Poems 1966-84*, copyright Margaret Atwood 1990, Oxford University Press Canada. Used by permission.

The quotation from Milton Acorn is from *I Shout Love and Other Poems*, ed. James Deahl, Aya Press, 1987. Copyright 1987 by Mary Hooper for the Estate of Milton Acorn. Used by permission.

The quotation from Stephen Spender is from 'The Truly Great,' *Collected Poems 1928-1985*, Faber and Faber Ltd., 1985. Used by permission.

The quotation from *Itsuka* by Joy Kogawa, Viking Press, 1992, is used by permission of the author.

The quotation from Julian Barnes is from *Flaubert's Parrot*, Jonathan Cape, 1984. Used by permission.

Printed in Canada on acid-free paper ∞
Set in Palatino by Pickwick
Printed and bound in Canada by John Deyell Company, Ltd.,
    Lindsay, Ontario
Copy-editor: Frank Chow
Proofreader: Stacy Belden
Jacket design: Barbara Hodgson